King Vidor,
American

Frontispiece.   King Vidor, on a postcard made soon after his arrival in Holly-wood (circa 1915).

King Vidor, American

**Raymond Durgnat
& Scott Simmon**

University of California Press
Berkeley / Los Angeles / London

University of California Press
Berkeley and Los Angeles, California

University of California Press, Ltd.
London, England

© 1988 by The Regents of the University of California

Printed in the United States of America
1   2   3   4   5   6   7   8   9

Library of Congress Cataloging-in-Publication Data
Durgnat, Raymond.
  King Vidor, American.
  Bibliography: p.
  Filmography: p.
  Includes index.
  1. Vidor, King, 1895–1982—Criticism and
interpretation.   I. Simmon, Scott.   II. Title.
PN1998.A3V4826   1988   791.43′0233′0924   87-5994
ISBN 0-520-05798-8 (alk. paper)

Contents

Preface

King Vidor's *The Big Parade, The Crowd,* and *Hallelujah* have traditionally loomed large in histories of film art; his *Our Daily Bread* and *The Fountainhead* in histories of film politics; his *Duel in the Sun* in histories of film commerce. Many moviegoers find less-celebrated Vidor films among their most vivid memories—from *The Champ* to *Ruby Gentry*. Perhaps we may be forgiven for thinking that a full-length study of Vidor's work is astonishingly overdue—a situation for which we are not entirely blameless. A few words on our book's long genesis and its angle of approach:

In 1973 Richard Corliss, editor of *Film Comment,* took the bold step of devoting most of two consecutive issues to a fifty-thousand-word study of eighteen King Vidor films by one of the authors of the present work, Raymond Durgnat.[1] Restricted to Vidor's most readily available films, it was at once tentative, as a first reconnaissance; and digressionary, because it differed from many then-common assumptions: about how far movies are shaped by directorial self-expression, and how far by craftsmen working to a market consensus, by the studios, and by an ever-evolving public. In particular, it developed the work on structures of narrative form, meaning, and "ideology" in the last sections of Durgnat's *Films and Feelings.*[2] Awkward and "centrifugal" as it was, however, the essay was accorded a gratifyingly generous reception.

Its author's plans to return to it were thwarted partly by other pursuits and partly by irruptions in film theory. Academic film culture got knocked sideways by dogmas from radical politics; by paradigms hastily imported from, of all irrelevant fields, structural linguistics; by a semiotics clearly innocent of fifty years' work in semantics; and by a clutch of youthfully aggressive feminisms. If the resultant emphasis on meaning as the product of power relationships could be culturally very useful indeed, the penalty was a weirdly forced perspective, analogous to reading the history of democratic thought as if its principal aim were the continued enserfdom of the reader. Thus it's hardly surprising that certain feminist theorists (including those of the masculine gender) took a further, richly masochistic, step—resorting to Jacques Lacan, surely the most phallocentric figure in the history of those whom Freudians class as rogue psychoanalysts (and whose notions of male desire and manliness rule out any possible understanding of King Vidor).

Meanwhile, Durgnat's collaboration with Scott Simmon on some studies of the Western film led to Vidor's Westerns and back to Vidor.[3] Simmon drafted chapters on every other Vidor film extant in the United States and Britain, and revised the original text in the light of informal conversations with King Vidor and access to his papers. The new text made more transatlantic crossings than we'd care to count, with each of us adding on, hacking away, doodling polite and ornery marginalia. Though we've seldom been less than five thousand miles apart, there's no sentence that doesn't bear the marks of both of us. The end result is less a revision by two heads of a book by one than a largely new work. By a sort of amoebic reproduction, the original work has split into two halves, the "auteurist" half having grown into the present volume, the theoretical digressions being destined for a purer, more sustained form.

The theoretical traditions underpinning Durgnat's original text remain vigorous, having acquired the merit of avoiding the problems that led a so-called "structuralism" into the "post-structuralist" fetishization of ambiguity that emptied movies of authorial meaning altogether—whereas we believe, on the contrary, that much of art's interest for the reader lies in *reaching* the author's meaning. Ideally, the author's separate films form one body of work, with all its cross-correlations and cross-contradictions, on the basis of "internal evidence" within the films themselves, and not of "the name of the author." If Vidor hadn't existed, his films would make it necessary to invent him. To that extent, we incline to the traditional linkage of "life and works," with a pair of easy provisos: (1) that the life is germane only insofar as it somehow touches the works, so that (2) the works are devised less by the "whole man," neuroses and all, than by his encounters with cultural agendas—in this case, Hollywood's and America's.

The movie "author" is no more given to uninspected self-expression than the poet. More conspicuously (but not more radically) than artists in more "individualistic" media, he *edits* his own experience in view of what he shares with his target audience. His persona is not exactly a "false self" but a "spokesman," constructed lucidly, frankly, in the light of what his "unknown friends" in the audience will find of interest. In other words, self-expression involves the artist in first censoring most of himself out—just as the traditional actor must assume a mask, to filter out "noise" from what he really is, most of which is normally irrelevant to his themes. It's curious how quickly certain critical schools treat artistic texts as if they were naive effusions of the self. If from time to time we call Vidor "intuitive," it's in that rather technical sense in which a composer or a chess player performs his preconscious analyses on the basis of experience.

Though we *are* interested in distinguishing what's unique to Vidor's films from what American films share, we're equally interested in what artists share with one another; and both interests have urged us to compare Vidor's perspectives and his topics with works by fellow artists and craftsmen. Vidor's films are also his audience thinking its ongoing experience through, not merely its repetitive "myths," but its agenda of cultural problems. Had we but world enough and time, this book would move freely from Vidor's films to others, whether tracing a common genre, or cycle (a time-sliced slew of films), or mode (melodrama, comedy), or atmosphere (like *film noir,* in the sense of a mood shared across many genres). In practice, we've rested content to include just enough Hollywood patterns to establish Vidor's variations. An artist's themes can get lost among film lists and side issues, but the more common failure of auteurism is to imply, by omission, that one's subject is romantically original. However, an attraction of Vidor is the way he holds his own within two histories—of American social thought and of Hollywood filmmaking. In this respect, we're very traditional; the best auteurists, like Andrew Sarris, have delighted in explaining the similarities that establish a school or a culture, as well as the distinctions that establish the individual subject.

Movie auteurism has regularly sacrificed negative criticism to romantic enthusiasm, as if the critic's principal role were to further his client's title to a place on Parnassus. For such "enthusiasmism" some historical justification exists (film's low status on the cultural totem pole). Alas, the reaction came. The Brechtians persuaded the Marxists, who persuaded many film theorists, that the key function of criticism was "deconstruction," a wholesale skepticism—as if alienation from bourgeois art were a rare and prodigious feat, as if art and ideology somehow imprisoned the reader's judgment more firmly than straightjackets encased Houdini, and that long courses were required before your typical student could escape entrapment by discourse. To us, the problem has always seemed to lie not in criticizing a text but in reading it with such sympathy and rigor that one's criticisms apply *to* the text, not to some reductionist stereotype allegedly common to "bourgeois ideology."

After considerable hesitation, we decided to let this volume, short as it had to be, stress narrative and philosophy, rather than the mixtures of performance art and visual style that count for so much more in a film. It's partly a question of the gross inefficiencies of verbal language in relation to visual forms and their richness of meaning. Our experience increasingly teaches us that the detailed analysis of film in sequence can only be done in the presence of the film itself.* We hope, however, that sufficient traces of our approach to visual meaning remain (notably in discussing *Our Daily Bread* and *An American Romance*) to indicate how we derive meaning from visual form-as-style.

As Vidor's films never quite cluster into standard genres, we have followed Vidor's production in loose chronology, shifting around a title here and there, and relegating a few minor works to annotations in the filmography. The auteur of *this* critical text likes to think that the differences between its two heads have generated a new synthesis, and that its outsider/insider perspective on the United States has been fruitful. We hope others will develop the work done here, in many, even contrasting, directions. King Vidor's work is too rich and teasing for any one book to be "definitive" about it.

Raymond Durgnat   Scott Simmon
London   Washington, D.C.

---

*In this regard, we owe acknowledgments: Durgnat to students at the Royal College of Art (London), Dartmouth College (New Hampshire), and to Jarmo Valkola and students at the School of Art Education at the University of Jyväskylä in Finland and the Jyväskylä Arts Festival; Simmon to audiences at a Vidor retrospective in 1986 at the Library of Congress's Mary Pickford Theater, who took reasonable issue with many of his remarks and served as living testimony as to which Vidor films retain emotional force.

Acknowledgments

For encouragement and cooperation, we gratefully acknowledge:

Richard Corliss, editor of *Film Comment,* former Assistant Editor Brooks Riley, and the Film Society of Lincoln Center; Professor Maurice Rapf of Dartmouth College for an informal oral history vital to understanding the background of events within MGM; M. Walker Pearce, sociologist and friend, who helped one alien understand the mind of the South; Sidney D. Kirkpatrick, who proved a selfless guide through the Vidor biography and papers; and David Adams, King Vidor's grandson and business manager, so generous of access to those papers and to the still photographs reprinted here.

For making available film prints and other research material, our thanks go particularly to Charles Silver at the Museum of Modern Art, Charles Hopkins at the UCLA Film Archive, George Pratt and Kathleen MacRae at the George Eastman House, Ned Comstock at the University of Southern California, and George Feltenstein of Films Incorporated. Among Scott Simmon's colleagues in the Motion Picture, Broadcasting and Recorded Sound Division of the Library of Congress, special mention must be made of Patrick Loughney, without whose expertise—and equipment—the frame enlargements would have been poor things indeed.

For varieties of support, advice, criticism and hospitality, it's a pleasure to acknowledge Alan Gevinson, of the American Film Institute Catalog project; Karen Jaehne; Marshall Deutelbaum; G. G. Patterson; Barbara Savinar; John McAdam; Kevin Browlow; Claudia McNellis; David

Shepard; Leatrice Gilbert Fountain; and King Vidor's friend Katherine Palmer.

Finally, our gratitude to Peter Dreyer and Marilyn Schwartz at the University of California Press and to the steadfast faith of our editor, Ernest Callenbach.

A Note on the Illustrations

The photos from Vidor's films in this book are a mix of production stills (taken by a publicist on the set) and frame enlargements (from release prints). The trade-off, familiar in film studies, is between production-still sharpness and a necessarily hazier truth to the original image. Except as otherwise noted, the smaller (paired) photos are frame enlargements; the larger are production stills.

1

Introduction

Vidor times Four

A congressional medal struck after John Wayne's death has been jangling in our minds for some time. "John Wayne, American," it reads—as if being a gutsy winner were certifiably the essence of the United States. Our title recasts the medal to honor diversity. Sure, King Vidor's sweep honors the American dream, that sometimes ferocious religion, but it also ascends to its higher, more ambivalent, forms.

Critics during Hollywood's "classic" days were rightly severe about the spiritual rigidities of the studio system. But they often lost sight of veterans like Vidor, who never let Hollywood eclipse America. While the auteur theories of the 1960s corrected many injustices, they nonetheless cherished directorial consistency, not to say monotony, over diversity and intricacy, and found Vidor's very variety hard to handle. And wasn't there, also, a certain misogyny, or adolescent cult of toughness, in many auteurist selections (Hitchcock, Ford, Hawks, Walsh)? Generally, auteurists shared with genre theorists a preference for *either* hard-edge stoicism *or* soap-opera softness, a love of clear distinctions between men's and women's films (Hawks *or* Sirk, Ford *or* Cukor, Walsh *or* Minnelli). Until it became a "*politique,*" the auteurism of *Cahiers du Cinéma* was a fine, adventurous thing, alive to genre flexibilities, studio policies, the market, and the public. But it rapidly turned rigid. Whether through movie-buff affection for reliable craftsmen or through Marxist-structuralist notions of bourgeois ideology, too many auteurist studies treat some run-of-the-mill assemblage of Hollywood clichés as a "personal vision" or as a "structure" constituted by "the name of the author." More sweeping devaluations of art, as *witness*, would be hard to find. And they eclipse,

1

above all, the "chameleons." Jean Renoir was almost the only exception, thanks to André Bazin, whose every reflex was nonauteurist, nongenrist.

The narrow-angle lenses that film culture finds so congenial split Vidor into fragments. There's (1) the radical maverick of *Our Daily Bread* and *The Crowd*. There's (2) MGM's contract man, whose talent withers within its studio system. There's (3) the "humanist" of *The Big Parade* and *Hallelujah*. There's (4) the propagator of "hysteric" and "delirious" sexual struggles, leading off with *Duel in the Sun* and reaching a camp height in *The Fountainhead* and *Beyond the Forest*. Or then again: liberals had *their* Vidor, the socially conscious realist; French surrealists had *their* Vidor, the tempestuous subversive; middle-era *Cahiers*-ists had *theirs*, a muscular poet of elemental vigor. And we agree with them all—as far as they go.

Vidor's own philosophy has conspired here. From *The Jack-Knife Man* through *War and Peace*, he accepted widely divergent, even opposite, moral attitudes as spiritual integrity. He celebrated *that* as "relativism." His cinematic style can look no less inconsistent. Vidor #1, independently producing *Our Daily Bread*, refined "Russian" cutting, since he hadn't to fend off "the over-ambitious editor or producer." Vidor #2 devised what he called "flowing composition" that could only be used as shot, not cut up by some producer's editor.[1] "Contradictory" styles! But one logic, one mind, one man.

All these little Vidors cry out to be reassembled. The early, affirmative films link closely with his penultimate *films noirs:* as closely as aspiration with disillusion, confidence with tragic waste, thwarted energy with spectacular morbidity. It's tempting to reassemble the work in the way shared by the French right, ever quick to celebrate violent change, and by Marxist notions that bourgeois ideology is deconstructible by its concealed contradictions. By both logics, Vidor shrinks to an insular, schizophrenic mix of Will Rogers and Audie Murphy. And that *is* part of him: his small-town goodwill remembers how to clench a cocked fist. But much more important is the mix of instinct and judgment that brought Vidor to that key crossroads—between idealism and aggression, between immigrant and nativist, between rural and urban life—where America knowingly picks all its crucial quarrels with itself. To borrow Manny Farber's distinction, Vidor's art is termite art; but he's a volatile termite. To be sure, a too-quick look at his epics could suggest white elephant art.[2] Well, he hails from Texas. In certain art forms, genius has to be opportunistic. Begin by imagining Norman Mailer warbling Hank Williams . . . and vice versa.

Vidor's forays into independent production—before, during, and after Hollywood—exemplify his ideals. And yet certain studio assignments, such as *The Champ* and *Beyond the Forest*, now look much closer to his soul than contemporary critics, including Vidor himself, assumed. No doubt it was his hard luck to work the studio system when it was most rigidly an assembly line, and when the Hays Office ensured a narrow spiritual monopoly, a kind of screen theocracy. Many a promising director came to fit the studio cocoon so perfectly that freedom, when they found it, seemed to bewilder them. Vidor zigzagged between gambles with his own cash, wrestling against the formulae, and flowing with the river. His films are American at heart whether or not they have Hollywood gloss on top. Whatever advantages Hollywood's standardized culture had, its usurpation of the older, grass-rootsier, American cinema was a cultural disaster. Vidor's wily and diverse career makes a first history of the survival of that *other* American cinema—populist, rascally, and religious.

To start with, let's divide his career into six main periods:

Figure 1.   Vidor (center) and slateboard, in an unidentified Texas film (1914).

1. *Early Silents, 1913–1925.* Following the dissolution of his tiny independent company in Texas, Vidor moved to Hollywood, where he peddled a few scripts, directed shorts, and (in 1919) made his inspirationalist first feature, *The Turn in the Road*. Professionally, he advanced rapidly, directing for Ince, Goldwyn, Metro, and, with

its conglomeration in 1924, Metro-Goldwyn-Mayer. Most of this period's movies are only resourcefully executed samples of then-popular cycles. The earlier and independently financed features have worn best, or, shall we say, become more picturesque. The dominant model was D. W. Griffith, and the locale is rural, midwestern or southern, with social pressures presented as minimal. The individual triumphs over himself, the villains functioning largely as catalysts of interior "soul fights." Vidor's first inspiration was Christian Science, explicitly.

Figure 2.   Vidor and an alter ego, James Murray, star of The Crowd *(1928).*

2. *Late Silents, 1925–1928.* Now Vidor worked exclusively for MGM. *The Big Parade* was his towering popular success, *The Crowd* his critical success. Those productions, and *Show People,* do much to make this period MGM's most innovative. The keynote here is an optimistic view of the ordinary individual's spiritual survival, irrespective of worldly success, and of the adaptability of his "roots" to a new family, or squad, or street, or moral community.

Figure 3.   Overlooking re-creation of Lincoln, New Mexico, for Billy the Kid *(1930).*

3. *Early Sound, 1929–1935.* The period from *Hallelujah* through the "back-to-the-land" trilogy of *The Stranger's Return, Our Daily Bread,* and *The Wedding Night* is predominantly "populist," in *both* senses of that word—the strictly political sense of the turn-of-the-century radical agricultural movement and the looser film-history sense of a concern with the lower-middle classes. Populist hopes dominate even *Billy the Kid* and *The Champ,* but get disturbing qualifiers in *Street Scene, Cynara,* and *The Wedding Night.*

Figure 4.   On location for The Texas Rangers *(1936).*

4. *The Late Thirties and the War, 1935–1944.*   This period ended
with Vidor's permanent rupture with MGM (over their handling of
An American Romance). With the system's tightening grip everywhere evident, it was his least personal, artistically weakest, and
most spiritually confused. His emphasis switches to a low-key enthusiasm for *any* moral achievement within accepted social con-

texts. Rather than "average man" heroes who had learned hard lessons about their membership in the crowd, Vidor celebrates, not leaders exactly, but those willing to take on responsibilities for re-making society (notably in *The Texas Rangers, The Citadel, Northwest Passage,* and *An American Romance*).

Figure 5.   David Brian, Bette Davis, and Vidor, demonstrating a stranglehold, on the set of Beyond the Forest *(1949).*

5. *The Postwar Decade, 1945–1955.*   After the Selznick-Vidor fight over *Duel in the Sun,* Vidor worked for low-prestige studios (Warner Bros., Universal), for independent producers, and on his own. He relocated his artistic focus, and with a vengeance. The emphasis shifts to criticism of a corrupt social order and its widespread personal cynicism. *Film noir* bitterness set Vidor's ideas a challenge, but his attempt to counterfeit a strict *noir—Lightning Strikes Twice*—rings hollow. *The Fountainhead* resorts to that strange, but not so rare, position, misanthropic inspirationalism. *Beyond the Forest* and *Ruby Gentry* respond with a melodrama complex enough to overtake drama.

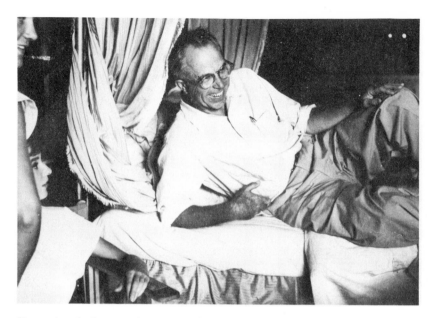

Figure 6.   Audrey Hepburn (partially obscured, on left) and Vidor (in "Natasha's" bed) on the set of War and Peace *(1956).*

6. *The International Films, 1956–1959.*   Vidor's last two epics (*War and Peace, Solomon and Sheba*) moved outside America, for their financing, their locations, their storylines, their themes, but are almost the apotheosis of "Hollywood" style. The productions were as troubled as their heroes, who can achieve only a qualified, mellow integrity.

This schema simplifies the "periods," but it'll do for now. No period excludes powerful impulses triumphant in the others. It's a spiritual education in itself to watch *Duel in the Sun* and *Ruby Gentry* and brood over how Christian Science could get around to this. King Vidor always responded to his times, while he followed—more or less stealthily and alongside commercial calculations—a personal evolution that was never a betrayal.

2

Hollywood versus America

"Vidor is far more an *epic poet,* given to large, almost abstract expressions of man's role in nature and society," writes Clive Denton, in one of the two short, interesting English-language studies of King Vidor.[1] Similarly the French: "On the name Vidor, cinema historians have once and for all stuck the label 'epic poet,'" notes Etienne Chaumeton, whose dissatisfaction we share.[2] In film criticism "epic poet" still suggests a certain simplicity of message that Vidor's films, however powerful, never quite accept, even on first viewing. Is "epic" lyricism, a narrow fidelity to strong experience, artistically more valid than a structure sufficiently tension-riddled to undermine intense, obvious moods? This auteurist question still hasn't been resolved.[3] Our operating aesthetic is that the most valuable works of art allow one *neither* just a pleasant wallow in one's favorite emotions *nor* just an intellectual diagram of some thematic circuitry.

One example: William Wellman's *The Public Enemy* is built on contradictory ideas about violence, about ethnic and family life, and seems to us more interesting—and more moving—than Howard Hawks's *Scarface,* whose perfection of atmosphere goes along with a single-minded put-down of a scapegoat in place of more diversified corruption. Both partisans of lyricism (those who prefer the Hawks to the Wellman) and aesthetic structuralists (whose connections with the political left might have been expected to breed a preference for structures involving strong contradictions) tend to assume that ideas and emotions, ideology and lyricism, are separate realms rather than closely integrated ones.

Vidor's own integration of those two poles is suggested by two of his reputations. On one hand, he was among Hollywood's resident intellectuals, who subtitled a 1964 independent film "An Introduction to Meta-physics." On the other, he was a neo-primitive prophet of sensuality and eroticism, ever ready to indulge his heroes' (or, more often, heroines') moral failings that arise from excesses of vitality. Still more schizo seems the gulf between the libidinous abandon of so many of Vidor's climaxes and the stream of gentle, almost pious, scruples of his autobiography.[4] Oddly assorted, too, his democratic "humanism" before World War II and his *noir*-era adaptation of Ayn Rand. And while Vidor's contention that he "always attempted to adhere to the 'earthier' themes" hints at a link between the land-reform theorizing of *Our Daily Bread* and the Lust in the Dust of *Duel in the Sun,* the complications that rapidly appear are not just *between* films but *within* them, at their very core.[5]

Our sense is that *both* reputations are deserved. One does Vidor equal injustice by approaching him either as a purely transcendental thinker or as merely a kind of epic lyricist of sensuality, devoid of ideas.

Vidor's deft manipulation of Hollywood entertainment patterns can disguise his bond to American thought. But, as he never tired of pointing out, his relationship to Hollywood was one thing, his relationship to his audience quite another. Some of the fun, we hope, in the following chapters comes from watching the ways in which Vidor's more personal themes have interacted with a sometimes profound, sometimes merely profes-sional or playful, response to a variety of genres, cycles, and themes, as well as to Hollywood's constantly evolving collective iconography. Holly-wood's set genres are like the stars and stripes—a hard-edged, stylized pattern that every American can stand up and salute. But the real Ameri-can flag should be a patchwork quilt of subcultures where every thread, stripe, blotch, and patch of bare canvas jostles all the others as in a Jackson Pollock—something pretty and rich, but so disorderly that it hints at an early death. Vidor's films don't fit the *critical* categories. They relate to *producers'* categories, such as "action film" versus "women's drama." But they rarely belong *within* them. Their characters are too mercurial, their space too open, their tone too restless; they never quite settle. We're left thinking about strains more than genres—the populist strain, the American regional strain, or the *noir* strain, crisscrossing within one story.

The Hollywood movie is collaborative. That's its weakness, that's its strength. Vidor's producers usually set initial limits and determined the final cuts. Yet Vidor's copies of the scripts reveal just how much he *wrote;* and he almost always sat beside his editors. Such facts of production sup-port our sense that his films are usually Vidor constructions, not just col-lective products branded with two or three characteristic "touches." To be sure, our focus on Vidor himself risks the usual reduction of collabo-rators to puppets—as if the only paradigm for creativity were Svengali.

Nor was *Cahiers* the only critical school to attribute a film's best ideas to whichever creator had so few that he kept repeating them. The problems dog our discussion of *Duel in the Sun,* Vidor's most troubled collaboration. His mid-thirties "back-to-the-land trilogy" proves instructive here. The three films share an identical motivating theme—city folk, faced with vanishing employment options, grab at a fresh agrarian start—filtered through a major studio (MGM's *The Stranger's Return*), an independent producer (Samuel Goldwyn's *The Wedding Night*), and King Vidor's own company (Viking's *Our Daily Bread*).

Collaborators, we ourselves have learned in the course of producing this book, must share certain affinities if their various qualities are to "take," even against their wills. The oddity of Hollywood, as hermetically sealed against certain American realities as it is, is its capacity for anticipatory, swift, and almost collective responses to moods and themes in the American air—to, one might well say, changing ideology. What first look like cases of auteurist obsession, or influence, or plagiarism, often turn out to be public property—themes and motifs that *are* a culture's iconography, beyond all possible copyrighting, legal or spiritual (for example, the affinities we note between *Duel in the Sun* and John Huston's *The Unforgiven*). Although "Hollywood" is definable as a homogeneous climate of opinion, it also unites different backgrounds, and the crisscrossings make collaborations as unpredictable as marriages. Certain pressures made Hollywood's agenda much narrower and more consensual than America's. The Production Code quite artificially curtailed shared themes and genres, slightly in 1924 and deeply in 1933. So did Hollywood's rightward bias, a more undercover affair, except, for example, in the movie campaign against Upton Sinclair in his bid for the California governorship, and the relatively easy success of blacklists.[6]

Consider the gangster genre. Much in Vidor made him a "natural" director of low-class violence on city streets. However, he never contributed to the genre, instead working all around it. Cagney as *The Public Enemy* (1931) may now seem a safely narrow focus for social criticism, more sop than substance. Yet much Hays Code ire was directed at *The Public Enemy*—ostensibly for its violence. Yet Vidor's *Billy the Kid* (1930) had just celebrated another serial killer, also Mom-fixated, without Hays Code objections. Presumably the gangster film's real offence was its contemporary city settings, which evoked contemporary social issues: slums, bootlegging, crooked and ineffectual cops. But if the gangster genre was one critical response to city poverty, Vidor's *Our Daily Bread* proposed another. Vidor's version of the Dead End Kids (the "innocent delinquents" in Wyler's *Dead End,* 1937) is in *The Champ* (1931). Its streetwise kid commits peccadilloes, not crimes, and quite enjoys his bad environment. We could posit some indirect suppression by the Production

Code, via its pressure on *everybody,* of a certain potential in Vidor's themes from the mid thirties through the war years. But, just as likely, Vidor censored himself. Until after World War II, and *noir,* when the underlying questions reemerge. When does energy become ferocity, or remorselessness amorality? When does one person's life force cannibalize another's? Vidor's *Ruby Gentry* (1952) ties those questions so fully into a socioeconomic structure that, as an American tragedy, it's arguably worth ten *Gilda*s, five *Maltese Falcon*s, two *Lady from Shanghai*s—as much as we love those films.

Most Hollywood movies are affirmative exercises in "received tensions." The spectator can select whichever meanings help him to enjoy a film, and overlook as merely circumstantial detail the issues that might offend him. This ambiguity is the result of an only too careful, only too clever, technique, inherited by Hollywood from show business generally (and indeed from political rhetoric itself), of seeking out and dwelling on factors common to as wide a range of opinions as possible, while omitting or skimming lightly over divisive or embarrassing options. Consider Vidor's most ferocious film, *Northwest Passage* (1940)—which can be read as a call to World War II intervention by interventionists, and as a call to strenuous self-reliance by isolationists. Just as ambiguous is his most radical film, *Our Daily Bread* (1934). Our discussions center on his ways of incorporating this underlying political ambiguity *without* impairing a politically salutary shock. For art can be "consciousness raising" (what a phrase!) even when it's "politically incorrect" (what a phrase!). The Hollywood challenge is to so blend opposing political attitudes that they cancel each other out ideologically while producing a double surprise dramatically. Ironically, the Hollywood practice is a lot more like the genuine ambivalence of art, and the deep structures of thought, than many courageously partisan political statements. That's another subject, and, just now, in the eighties, a sad one. Meanwhile, it's essential to weigh such genuine ambivalence against assumptions that entertainment films are never political (as to that, we agree with Peter Biskind's *Seeing Is Believing*)[7] and against militant tastes for the knockdown non-ambiguity of agitprop.

Clearly the whole question of what constitutes a film's "real" meaning is problematic. Is it the meaning that only *one* critic has been able to see, by the light of a uniquely accurate reading? Or that which most of its spectators saw, even if they were leaping to unjustified conclusions? Or some compromise between these positions? Even when we carefully distinguish an "intrinsic" (textual) reading from a "prevalent contemporary" reading, further complications must appear. How to acknowledge the plurality of cultures and views among spectators, but without reverting to a pseudo-objectivity that in practice denies all subjectivities but one? In the following essays, we've assumed that Vidor had learned, by experience and craft, to anticipate usual, or average, or in some sense normative, audience reactions pretty accurately—even though our words risk endowing with an impossible precision what spectators consciously experience as small surprises and displaced tonalities.

Questions of finesse and precision are central because so many of Vidor's films are unapologetic melodramas. This is not surprising in his early silents, made for an audience, a culture, so naive and so tolerant that it may now seem to be lost, lost, lost. It can take a kind of mental archeology to see those films as Vidor proposed and the era's ideology disposed. More troublesome yet is that even in Vidor's postwar *noir* epoch, from *Duel in the Sun* on, his films retained traits of "primitive" or, let's say, Griffithian melodrama. Thus their idiom was wildly out of sync with reviewers and English-language critics, who generally demanded a combination of underplayed, "tough" emotion and poetic realism, with the social compassion of neorealism the only recognized form of social consciousness. Critics reacted as if *The Big Sleep* (deadpan and lyrical) was just good, healthy all-American thrills, whereas *The Fountainhead* was out of Grand Guignol by Kraft-Ebbing. Indeed, the melodramatic mode of Vidor's best films throughout his career still presents difficulties to those who are inclined, or taught, to expect from art a fastidious mixture of earnestness, education, and what is sometimes called "humanism." Exacting critics may experience as lack of motivation or implausibility, what Hollywood, Vidor, the popular audience, and critics like ourselves experience as sharp shocks that exhilarate and ring true.

When confronted by melodramas with the violent and scandalous elements for which Vidor's are infamous, viewers may reject the kiss-kiss-bang-bang confrontation-climaxes (or, in the case of *Duel in the Sun*, the bang-bang-kiss-kiss) and fail to notice any subtler challenges. "Melodrama" normally revolves around either some violent physical action (as in Vidor's early silents) or some knockdown emotional equivalent ("passion" in some imprecise, global sense, as in *Stella Dallas*). There's nothing to prevent a film from being both a melodrama and a drama, which is where many of Vidor's fall. They expect their audiences to understand that conflicting emotions comprise a kind of dialectic (one excessive reaction provoking another) rather than a logical consistency—an understanding that tends to disappear as art comes under the aegis of academic rationalism.

Vidor's "strong dramas" had a curious, almost unique, way of straddling the division between "men's films" and "women's films." His unabashed way with emotion is nearer to D. W. Griffith and Charlie Chaplin than to his closer contemporaries William Wellman and Howard Hawks. John Ford, like Vidor, also comes between the two generations.

But if Ford is a "man's man," or the caricature of it, whether stiffly spanking women (*The Quiet Man, Donovan's Reef*) or stiffly saluting them, Vidor is more fluid, smiling, slick, vulnerable. If there's less suffering, there's more responsiveness; less slapstick, more adaptive humor. Of course, Vidor's studies of enthusiasm maturing haven't the compassion of Ford, who, as master of the male tearjerker, knows that even hard-as-nails working-class audiences will accept a lachrymose hero so long as his enduring toughness has been established, and especially when his grief is occasioned by some stout-hearted desire, like never retiring from the Seventh Cavalry. Ford settles for elegiac tradition, and a foursquare compassion for misfit victims of economic circumstance, while Vidor, always so close to Horatio Alger, thinks about strenuous self- and group-help. We detail this comparison with Ford in discussing *Our Daily Bread*.

Country and Western music is full of tearstained bars. Vidor's heroes cry, but not for long. Maybe his country and Western roots in Texas have something to do with his continuous willingness to bare male "weakness" and female volatility in family and love situations. If his films spanned the "women's" and "men's" categories, it's because he accepted, not matter-of-factly but quite lyrically, the strengths of women and the weaknesses of men. He's unafraid of their weakness, because (whereas tough deadpans from Hawks to Peckinpah are as drearily restrictive as the English stiff upper lip) grief and volatility are forms of strong life force.

Like Hawks and that generation, Vidor delights in knowing just how to hit, peak, and cut the emotional climaxes, to "bat it and go." In discussing the climax of *The Champ*, we suggest how a brusque style can be made to balance decisive feelings, in place of Hawks's only-too-consistent steely eyes. Or contrast their World War I films—Vidor's *The Big Parade* and Hawks's *Sergeant York*. Hawks's initially rustic, puritan, pacifist hero makes his private's progress to an Old Testament doctrine. He picks off dozens of evil Huns from the rear, as slick as shooting ducks, and finally enters the presence, if not exactly of God, at least of God's Own Country's president. But it's something in Hawks, rather than the requirements of wartime propaganda, that leaves his straightforward conversion story with a sense of deep problems slickly solved. Hasn't *The Big Parade*, for all its facile slapstick and a surface texture only intermittently more perfect, a profounder movement?

Given his frequent assignments to showcase such stars as Laurette Taylor, Lillian Gish, Marion Davies, Barbara Stanwyck, and Jennifer Jones, it's remarkable that Vidor contrived to avoid the "women's director" pigeonhole. (There is little parallel in any assignments for male stars.) However, that label secretly implies cozy interiors, domestic anxiety, a soft romance-novel focus—all of which could hardly be further removed from either Vidor's typically elemental milieus (notably, swamps and mountaintops) or the swaggering, potentially destructive heroines in his postwar films.

Vidor is a natural feminist, not an ideological one. That is to say, his women drive men crazy, and/or inspire them, and do what they want, without becoming superior beings. *Conquering the Woman* is one of his silent titles, and a frequent theme. Collaterally, Vidor's emphasis on energy leads to problems not so much of dominance, as of tense negotiations in response to virile fraternity. We'll have something to say in our notes on *Our Daily Bread* and *The Fountainhead* about the ways in which Vidor needs to be distinguished from the "male feminist." His idea of sexual roles is both traditional and none too rigid. Reciprocity constitutes its mainspring, not least in the mutual slap-downs that punctuate his work. And of the ways in which Vidor *should* be counted among the feminists, we'll say something in connection with *Stella Dallas* (its prominence in recent feminist analyses reinforces how the ostensibly confining "weepie" allows very wide angles on sexual politics). Pointedly independent professional women feature in several Vidor movies, including the early (and unfortunately no longer extant) *Poor Relations* and *The Real Adventure*.* No other Hollywood director of his era so often called on women collaborators—two-thirds of Vidor's films not written by him alone involved women screenwriters. To that extent, Vidor's women were written by women and watched by women.

An oddly persistent motif running through Vidor's work could be labeled "Momist" if that term didn't risk shortchanging the magic prescience of maternal figures—notably in *Proud Flesh, The Big Parade, Hallelujah, Billy the Kid, So Red the Rose, An American Romance, Duel in the Sun,* and *Ruby Gentry.* We'll defer detailed discussion of this, but one can't help but be struck by how often female strength and resolution revive the temporarily deadened life force of Vidor's heroes. While the box office might explain this "mother's angle" in the days of family audiences, something more personal looms through these idealized or sacrificing mothers, particularly next to stark views of marriage. One might take a tip from an F. Scott Fitzgerald story, "Crazy Sunday" (1932), which was based on the confidences of Vidor's second wife and star of several of his late silents, Eleanor Boardman. "The psychoanalyst told Miles that he had a mother complex. In his first marriage he transferred his mother complex to his wife, you see—and then his sex turned to me. But when we were married the thing repeated itself—he transferred his mother complex to me and all his libido turned toward this other woman."[8] Whatever the "gibberish level," suspected by Fitzgerald's hero, the expla-

---

*See the filmography for brief notes on these and other lost films not discussed in the text.

nation parallels David Thomson's conception of "women's pictures" as "maddened extensions of the Western cult of the Madonna," and as an ideal form for male filmmakers to "protect and project" emotional lives forbidden them—and doubly forbidden Vidor as a Hollywood intellectual.[9] (Vidor took a friendly revenge on Fitzgerald through the character details given the blocked novelist in *A Wedding Night*.) It's not that Vidor's films aren't just as true to Leslie Fiedler's American novelist psychopathy of strained marriages and idealized mother figures as is typical among Hollywood's "men's directors."[10] But Vidor arrives at that pattern by the opposite route, via tales of men who are hard pressed to match their women.

One could be forgiven for following the lead of the Directors Guild eulogy and dismissing Vidor as more "ladies' man" than feminist.[11] To put it gently, he was never the most enduring of partners. The evident flagging of his inspiration in the decade beginning in the mid thirties corresponds to a particularly frenzied era in his private life, including several well-publicized affairs, two marriage announcements, and a headline-making custody battle over his two daughters by Eleanor Boardman, complete with accusations of international kidnapping. By Vidor's own account, location shooting on *The Stranger's Return* proceeded while he was (a) having an affair with its star Miriam Hopkins and (b) commuting back to L.A. for six-evenings-a-week psychoanalysis. (Amazingly, the finished film is far better than routine, and King's reaction to the end of his affair with Hopkins—sawing the legs off their couch—has a batty flair worthy of his own melodramas.) Perhaps his strength *and* weakness, as a man and artist, came from the Westerner's restlessness he everywhere displayed—in genres, in studios, in his life.

When Vidor spoke with us in 1982 (a few months before his death at eighty-seven), he chose to bring up his mother's example as the guiding influence in his own lifelong fascination with Christian Science—a fascination that, frustratingly to him, stopped short of belief. The following pages repeatedly evoke the links between three American attitudes often treated as incompatible: the Puritan ethic, Emersonian transcendentalism, and a secular, enterprising dynamism. Much of Vidor's inspiration was generated by the tension between these three outlooks. Their common factor is man's role as the expansion of God's or nature's energies—and they even aggravate man's sins, as energy misled. Christian Science comes near to being the religion (made-in-U.S.A., and woman-made) that unifies such outlooks, even in defiance of that male concoction, "rigorous logic."[12]

Mary Baker Eddy's was a Massachusetts reaction, not unlike Emerson's, against evangelical revivalism and toward a natural pantheism. And yet Christian Science is best known for its rigid dismissal of scientific method, in place of which it puts an optimistic, not to say Panglossian, faith in the world and in mankind as God's direct reflection. Vidor prepared a biopic about Mrs. Eddy, *Bright Answer,* in which she calmly corrects the Sage of Concord in the midst of a somewhat unlikely social meeting: "Mr. Emerson, please forgive me, but you speak of sin as if it were a reality. . . . This seems to me to be the basis of our dilemma, trying to make evil an equal force."[13] In Hollywood, Vidor could hardly go so far as Mrs. Eddy in treating sin as "mortal illusion,"[14] but his way with villains and destructive heroes/heroines makes the sins of energy virtues by contrast with the absence of sin in a repressed, or dead, soul. If that idea is occasionally stressed by orthodox Christians like Georges Bernanos, it nonetheless runs counter to the normal Christian emphasis on restraint and immaculacy. In light of the contrast between Vidor's nearly pious autobiography and the complex morality of, say, *Hallelujah* or *Beyond the Forest,* one has to suspect that, like Blake's Milton, he's of the Devil's party without knowing it. And many Vidor films quietly repudiate orthodox or narrowly doctrinal Christianity (as in *The Sky Pilot, The Stranger's Return, Ruby Gentry, War and Peace,* and *Solomon and Sheba*).

Without denying the existence of the puritan strain to which French Catholic and *Cahiers* critics have rightly pointed, their general description of Vidor's films as "puritan" begs too many questions about varieties of puritanism—questions we address in connection with *Hallelujah.* If we more often label Vidor's thought as "transcendental," it's to incorporate the usual attributes of the New England movement—Thoreau's idealism about nature and rural communities, Emerson's individual intuition as a guide to the spiritual, Bronson Alcott's reformable democracy of self-reliant citizens. Still, it's also with the understanding that Vidor's was a strikingly nervous, restless transcendentalism, dissociated from the idealism of bodiless spirit, and related to the categorical imperatives of the life force itself. The wilderness in *Northwest Passage* isn't evil, as it was for the original Puritans; it's the challenge, the test, and in that sense, the *road* to God, that marks America's turn from puritanism to optimism.

Another of Vidor's unproduced projects, a quite faithful adaptation of Nathaniel Hawthorne's *The Marble Faun,* reminds us of their affinities. Hawthorne, too, was a melodramatic moralist, impatient with the ethereal hokus-pokus of a shallow transcendentalism, and mislabeled a Puritan perhaps because an American optimism made the very concept of sin touchy and reproachful. But for both artists, "sin" is usually redemptive. Vidor's script (first drafted, with Harry Behn, in 1954, and at one time titled *The Sinner*) centers on Hawthorne's Miriam and thus would have extended Vidor's postwar line of perhaps-justified murderesses—Pearl in *Duel in the Sun,* Rosa in *Beyond the Forest,* and Ruby in *Ruby Gentry.*

Vidor's transcendentalism was wide open to the pragmatism that looms so large in American culture. It affected his sense of what was reasonably possible, both for himself as a Hollywood artist and for his characters in their situations. Unlike puritanism, transcendentalism and pragmatism are undogmatic and adaptive creeds, particularly when combined with an individualism whereby each man must follow his own moral destiny. Each creed has its "herbivorous" and "carnivorous" forms, its reformist, responsible aspects and its laissez-faire ones, its moral uses and abuses. In their combination lies dynamism. For example, theories of evolution enable an apparently idealistic transcendentalism to accommodate the savageries of Social Darwinism, and thence to accept realpolitik and rat-race egotism. To put it another way, the Christian Science idealism of "Whatever is, is right" could mask the meaning of "Tough shit, but that's the way the cookie crumbles." The transcendentalist Margaret Fuller was mocked by Carlyle for saying she accepted the universe: "By God, she'd better!"

Would Vidor line up with Carlyle? Yes and no. At any rate, the unresolved tensions in the popular morality along whose wavelength he moves are dramatically expressed in his characters' incessant switching between resilience and sensitivity. His films pursue their tension-ridden course between social concern (rather than conscience) and optimism, between generosity and ruthlessness, between rugged self-reliance and brutal egoism. Not that the problems appear as brutally as they do in the films of Joseph Losey. But Vidor's profoundest films are those in which his transcendentalism knuckles down to grin and bear it, a Job who has to show a salesman's smile.

Since Vidor believes that each man must work through his own destiny where he is placed, he must give as many answers as there are places. Like Whitman, he "contains multitudes." But if he accepts popular assumptions, it is usually in an attempt to push things to some spiritual crisis. Ambivalent as the answers may be, this separates him from directors— like, say, Raoul Walsh and Howard Hawks—who, if genuine auteurs, are narrow, even monotonous in their repetitions. It puts him with people like Jean Renoir, who explore the contradictions of felt experience, never demonstrating cut-and-dried moralities.

The chapters that follow try to clarify some of the paradoxes—the central conflicts and small print—that comprise Vidor's love affair with America. It's easily assumed that troubled emotions are less discriminating than rational thought. Our assumption has been that troubled emotions are signals from intuitive thought—the kind that only seems vague because of the genuine difficulty of dramatizing it. Vidor's love affair with America was variously (or simultaneously) idyllic, recriminatory, indulgent, and imbued with a passion as subtle as philosophy.

3

1913 to 1925

"Into the Vale of Soul Making"

Whatever the freedoms of early Hollywood, it was not until *The Big Parade* (1925) that Vidor felt able to "break out."[1] Of the twenty feature films he directed in the six years before then, ten are known to survive—an unusually high percentage. Of those, most are of only historical or auteurist interest, although *The Jack-Knife Man*, *Wild Oranges*, and *The Sky Pilot* are more than that.

King Wallis Vidor, born February 8, 1894, was a third-generation Texan.[2] His paternal grandfather, Charles Vidor, had emigrated from Hungary during the Austrian reprisals against Kossuth's revolution and eventually settled in the port city of Galveston, where he worked as a cotton factor, becoming a naturalized U.S. citizen in 1868. King's father, Charles S. Vidor, was quite prosperous at the time of the birth of his son, the first of two children with his wife, Kate Wallis, and named in honor of her brother, King Wallis. The Wallis family were of venerable American stock, descendants of Davy Crockett's wife Elizabeth by her first marriage. (She was the mother of King's maternal grandmother.) Charles S. Vidor owned a hardwood forest in the Dominican Republic and sawmills in East Texas and Louisiana, and had introduced another mill to a small Texas community that took the name Vidor in 1910. But, soon after, his fortunes declined through an insurance business and oil speculation.

After grade school at the Peacock Military Academy in San Antonio, King Vidor's formal education continued at a private high school in Maryland. But at sixteen, he dropped out and entered the movie business as a ticket taker and occasional projectionist in a storefront nickelodeon

Figure 7. King Vidor as a child.

in Galveston. A 1913 hurricane provided the subject for his first film, shot with a friend's homemade camera. Some actualities, beginning with a troop parade in Houston, were sold to the Mutual Weekly newsreel. To judge from Vidor's own anecdotal account, his first stab at fictional film-making, a two-reel comedy, *In Tow,* was in all respects incompetent.

Matters improved when he was approached for collaboration by an-other Galvestonian, Edward Sedgwick, who, with his vaudeville family, had worked in some regional films. (Sedgwick also went on to a Holly-wood directorial career, but is now remembered mainly for shepherding Buster Keaton through his decline at MGM.) Together they formed the Hotex Motion Picture Company, the name conflated from their office in *Houston, Tex*as. Although their letterhead proclaimed Hotex "Producers of High Class Motion Pictures," their stock offerings stated an average cost of $350 to $500 for one- or two-reelers: "We have found that a loca-tion with maximum days of sunshine, such as that of Southern California and OUR OWN SOUTH, offers opportunity and the most profit from film production." Among the Hotex comedy-adventures, all directed by Sedg-wick and co-written with Vidor, were such unremarkable-sounding offer-ings as *The Heroes,* about the capture of a convict, and *Beautiful Love,* a "European" intrigue with a kidnapped countess, which must have taxed such company wardrobes as are on display in surviving stills (fig. 9). After failing with such entrepreneurial innovations as films free to the-aters to advertise Texas products—signed in promotional letters by "K. W. Vidor, Gen. Mgr., King Service Dept."—they sought national distri-bution. On the day of Vidor's marriage to Florence Arto, the couple set off for New York. A brief item in *Moving Picture World* (17 October 1914), probably the first mention of Vidor in a national publication, mangled his company name, but made things sound promising:

Hotel Will Release Through Sawyer

King W. Vidor, of the Hotel Film Manufacturing Company, Houston Texas, has been in New York City to arrange for a market for his company. He finally closed a contract with Sawyer, Inc., which firm will handle his company's pictures.

But only the following week, *Moving Picture World* announced that Sawyer's assets would be taken over by something called "The Colossus Feature Film Company." A slippery colossus, it took the prints and nega-tives and never returned a cent in royalties. As Vidor must have been dis-covering, the end was near for independent regional production. For the past year, he had been sending off scenarios to Hollywood and receiving only rejection slips. After picking up some money for an industrial docu-mentary about sugar refining in Houston, it was time to try the West Coast in person.

THE HOTEX
MOTION PICTURE
COMPANY

HOUSTON, TEXAS

PRODUCERS OF

MOTION PICTURES

KING W. VIDOR
PRESIDENT and GENERAL MANAGER

Figure 8.   Hotex brochure.

Figure 9.   Unidentified Hotex film (1914). Vidor is the cop on the left.

There, another of Vidor's old Texas flames, Corinne Griffith (herself just starting a major career in silents) found Florence Vidor a steady acting job at the Vitagraph studios, while Vidor took every picture-business odd job he could scare up, primarily at Vitagraph and nearby "Inceville"—prop boy, script clerk, bit actor. The titles of these are lost, as are most of the films themselves, no doubt. However, at least one survives, a harmless spy drama called *The Intrigue* (directed by Frank Lloyd; 1916), in which Florence, as the heroine's maid, opens doors inside the mansion (fig. 10a), while King, as a chauffeur, opens doors outside (fig. 10b). After months of script rejections, he sold his first, *When It Rains, It Pours* (1916), a comic romance about two lovers locked out on a wet night, to Vitagraph (for $30) because—so he claimed—they needed one that could be shot in the rain. Vidor's storyline for *Dan's Daring Drama* (a two-reeler directed by Al Santell; 1917?) seems to be a satire of his own frustration: one "Harmon Naigs, extra man at the Bunko Moving Picture Company" imagines a wild Arabian adventure, only to be booted out by a director more concerned with having props moved. "That's the trouble with these picture companies," complains Naigs, "They won't buy a good story when they see it." But soon enough, Vidor was hired as a writer in Universal's shorts department, where his efforts—to judge from synopses—seem to have been workmanlike.

His unlikely first opportunity to direct narrative films in Hollywood

a   b

Figure 10. The Intrigue *(1916). a: Florence Vidor and Lenore Ulrich; b: King Vidor, at far left.*

came from a certain Judge Willis Brown, a former Salt Lake City juvenile-court judge who had founded his own remedial "Boy's City" and had written nineteen scripts loosely based on his successes. Vidor made ten of these into two-reelers (all released between January and May 1918) before money problems interrupted the series. A reel from the first, *Bud's Recruit,* survives, and reveals a serviceably theatrical style, at its best with the child-hero (who subverts both his draft-age brother's shirking of the Great War and his society mother's "peace advocacy"). *Bud's Recruit* was the only episode not to include the judge himself, who at some point in each subsequent film is called on to resolve the crisis. As *Father Knows Best*–like as these sound, Vidor "deeply believed" in them, and the trade notices were, with few exceptions, excellent. A number of the episodes do have fascinating social content: *The Chocolate of the Gang,* about a black boy wrongly denied membership in an all-white club (with, significantly, "an excellent Chocolate and other colored performers, including Chocolate's mother",[3] not the whites in blackface still the rule for lead roles); *Thief or Angel,* involving a tenement girl arrested for stealing milk; and the final episode filmed by Vidor, *I'm a Man,* about a boy who proves his German-immigrant parents are more loyal to the United States than is a false Frenchman.

With financing from some of the same doctors and dentists who'd backed the Judge Brown series, Vidor was able to begin feature filmmaking. Nine physicians invested a thousand dollars each, incorporated as "Brentwood Films" (from the name of their country club), leased a building on Fountain Avenue as "Brentwood Studios," and left Vidor to make *The Turn in the Road.* It was an immediate success. He had only been able to afford to strike one print, but after an eight-week house-record-breaking run in Los Angeles, the film was purchased for national release by Robertson-Cole. Although not contractually bound, he stayed with the doctors throughout 1919, making *Better Times, The Other Half,* and *Poor Relations.*

Using advance money from the newly formed New York-based exhibitors' conglomerate First National (through whom he released his next three films—*The Family Honor* [1920], *The Jack-Knife Man* [1920], and *The Sky Pilot* [1921]), Vidor was able to build his own studio, dubbed "Vidor Village," on fifteen acres along Santa Monica Boulevard in Hollywood. Further reverses had necessitated his family moving from Texas to Arkansas, and Vidor now brought them out to Los Angeles, with his father to serve as "Vice President of King Vidor Productions." As with the old Hotex company, Vidor raised operating capital through public shares, some stockholders investing as little as ten dollars. But, again, independent production proved financially impossible, and within two years Vidor Village faced court-ordered confiscation of its movable property. The breaking point came with the troubled location shooting on *The Sky Pilot* (no snow when it was needed, and then blizzards when it came), exacerbated by Vidor's infatuation with his star, Colleen Moore. "King Vidor Productions" retained only enough money for a single demonstration scene from his next picture, *Love Never Dies* (1921)—although that scene, a spectacularly effective train crash created in miniature, was suffi-

Figure 11.   Vidor Village (1921).

cient to convince Thomas Ince to finance the remainder. (Vidor did regain control of his studio, but made no more films there and sold it in January 1923.)

As in their first months in Los Angeles, Florence Vidor was again their salvation. She had become a leading player at Paramount, and the couple now arranged a four-picture contract with Associated Exhibitors. King Vidor directed the first three: *The Real Adventure, Dusk to Dawn,* and *Conquering the Woman* (all 1922). But, with their marriage breaking up, he assigned direction of the fourth, *Alice Adams* (1923), to Rowland V. Lee.

At Metro, Vidor reached probably the lowpoint of his early career, transferring three stage plays to the screen: *Peg o' My Heart* (1922), Laurette Taylor's film debut; *Happiness* (1924), also with Taylor; and *The Woman of Bronze* (1923) for longtime star Clara Kimball Young. Intermixed were two films for the Goldwyn studios: *Three Wise Fools* (1923), starring his second wife to be, Eleanor Boardman, and *Wild Oranges* (1924), filmed in Florida at a time when such distant location shooting was becoming rare. When those studios merged in April 1924 under Louis B. Mayer's control as Metro-Goldwyn-Mayer, Vidor came along through his Goldwyn contract. *Wine of Youth, His Hour, Wife of the Centaur* (all 1924), and *Proud Flesh* (1925) were his four MGM assignments before he was allowed *The Big Parade.*

The Rudiments of
Vidor's Political Philosophy

"Try and secure a list of the members of the Christian Science churches and mail them a special invitation to see their beliefs demonstrated in a photoplay," exhibitors were instructed by *Motion Picture News* upon release of Vidor's second feature, *Better Times,* in 1919.[4] It's not easy to spirit oneself back to an era in American moviemaking that allowed the philosophic range implied by such advice. Vidor's first five features are lost, and many of his subsequent silents from the first half of the twenties are decidedly minor, but whatever else one can say of them, they seldom lack a religious idealism about the moral strength of the mind, or a "middle-American" faith in rural society. In the early features, an individualistic Christianity is mixed with an American version of the agrarian myth, persistent since Jefferson, of the healing open spaces. The resulting values are close to those of the Populist movement, which, strictly speaking, was an agrarian reform program of the 1890s although with ideals that permeated first the Democratic party and then the Republican Pro-

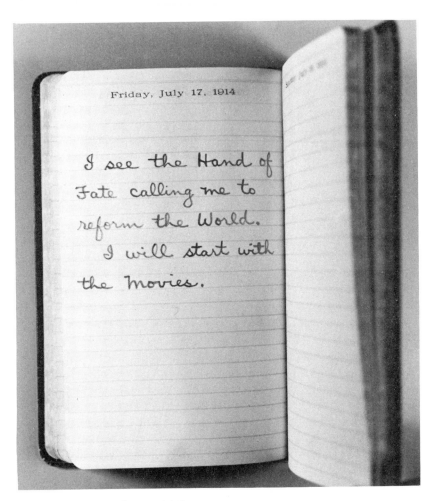

Friday, July 17, 1914

I see the Hand of Fate calling me to reform the World. I will start with the movies.

Figure 12.   King Vidor's 1914 diary.

gressives.* These attitudes of Vidor's were overlaid with others but never abandoned. And as difficult as it remains to see even his surviving early

---

*In film history, *populism* has the looser meaning of a focus on the lower classes, especially if seen "cross-sectionally" or as a "unity-in-diversity." We have differentiated by capitalizing the term for the largely rural, *political* movement, which reached its height with the William Jennings Bryan presidential campaign of 1896. Film's small-p populism tends to be friendly to ethnic diversity and outsiders, whereas the Populist movement was commonly hostile to the concerns of immigrants and even to city dwellers, central to film populism. Broadly speaking, Vidor's work grew from this early Populism into film populism, in ways noted later in this chapter and in connection with *The Crowd* and *Street Scene.*

silents, it's worth glancing at them here, if only for their naked political philosophies.

Of all Vidor's features, the loss of his first, *The Turn in the Road*, is most to be regretted. From all reports it was dramatically successful and heartfelt, something of a bare draft for the spiritual crisis in *The Crowd*. The storyline is quite frank:[5] Paul, overprotected son of a grasping capitalist who controls their isolated company steeltown, marries the more beautiful of the town minister's two daughters and lives happily, until his wife dies in childbirth. Already disillusioned with his father's materialism, he looks for solace from his father-in-law, who can only repeat the Calvinist sermons about "the will of God" that he has been delivering for thirty-five years. Anguished over the nature of a God who would permit such sorrow, Paul, now dubbed "the Searcher," flees to Chicago, where city temptations lead him lower and lower. Meanwhile, the minister's other daughter, June, also seeking to know "What is God?" finds a mentor in a "Mrs. Edmunds" (whose name may suggest Mrs. Eddy) who "calmly and confidently informs her that the answer is 'within you'" (as Vidor's original story put it). June raises Paul's abandoned son as a natural pantheist (dramatized through an improvised scene in which seven-year-old Ben Alexander demonstrated to the film crew his fearlessness of bees by letting them swarm over him). The boy softens his steel-baron grandfather, who has previously proved impervious to suggestions that he get "closer to nature," and so averts brewing violence over a wage strike. On a rainy night, the boy finds Paul, now a tramp, hiding in their barn, and brings him food—and the spiritual answers he's been seeking. When June discovers the two, she introduces them as father and son. Together the three begin a new family.

Similar elements infused *The Other Half* (1919), Vidor's third feature, which sounds like an entry in the class-conscious cycle of industrial melodramas that survives in such fascinating Thomas Ince productions as *Dangerous Hours* (1919) and William S. Hart's *The Whistle* (1921). A pair of war buddies turn civilian enemies when one accepts a job as a machinist in the other's company. The owner's refusal to make repairs results in an accident that blinds his former friend. And so it falls to their respective sweethearts—Florence Vidor and ZaSu Pitts—to restore harmony, the former writing newspaper exposés that lead the industrialist to "see" the error of his ways. Although doctors have despaired, the machinist simultaneously wills back his sight. About this picture's Christian Science, *Motion Picture News* commented, hopefully, "Even those opposed to it like doctors, etc., will be curious to know to what lengths this director will go."[6]

With *Better Times* Vidor lightened the tone into a rural comedy, without altering the philosophy. ZaSu Pitts helps her layabout father run a

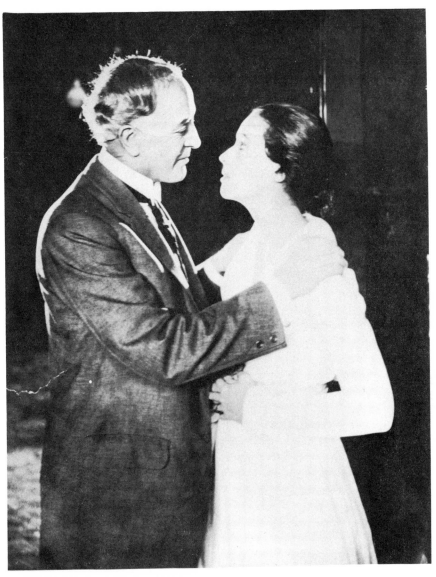

Figure 13. The Turn in the Road *(1919). Winter Hall (Reverend Barker) and Helen Jerome Eddy (June, his daughter).*

dilapidated health spa, and eventually earns the love of an ailing baseball star when she quotes him phrases from her Christian Science calendar and persuades him to ignore a doctor-prescribed abstaining diet. Several of Vidor's early unproduced scenarios follow such storylines: *Caviar and Cabbage; or, Love's Sanitarium* has another "pampered son of the idle rich" discover health only after his car breaks down on the way to a doctor's sanitarium. He's invited into a small community for some positive thinking supplemented with bowls "heaped high with steaming cabbage."

Such plotlines may well reflect Vidor's disillusion with doctors when, around the time he quit school, he developed a "nervous problem" none could diagnose—"dizzy spells, palpitations and the like."[7] The Denver specialist consulted by his parents employed experimental treatments; the swallowing of a rubber hose proving particularly traumatic. It's reasonable to suppose that the "doctors and dentists" financing Brentwood Films must have been Christian Science healers to have stood for such productions. But Vidor says not, and that he felt trepidation about how they would react to the films' "anti-materia medica."[8] They must have been impressed by success. Even Vidor's first feature away from Brentwood, *The Family Honor* (1920), ended its complicated "Southern" plotline with what reviewers took for Christian Science sentiments that "defy logic."[9]

Such overt Christian Science reflects a phase Vidor soon abandoned, both publicly and privately, and almost never discussed in later years, even when he flirted with it again in the sixties. But a sense of how persistent the individualist idealism behind it was is given by his most deeply felt unproduced post–World War II project, also titled *The Turn in the Road*, which he began in 1945, pushed strongly in 1954, and got as far as casting at Allied Artists in 1960. Its storyline bears little resemblance to his first feature, and its "searcher" is eventually embodied in a disillusioned Hollywood director. Still, bees again swarm harmlessly, this time over a mysteriously visionary girl, who also talks a temporarily blinded man back into sight. An alternate title relates the project to Vidor's first Hollywood optimism: *So Long Remembered*. Indeed.

All of these lost 1919 Brentwood films, as well as the features soon to follow, asked the same question, "Is Real Life Interesting?" which is the opening title of *True Heart Susie* (also 1919), the D. W. Griffith film they most resemble. "Real life" in both cases meant melodramas of midwestern and southern country life, with a Populist esteem for that world in contrast with inhumanities born of the city.

Fortunately, *The Jack-Knife Man* (1920) survives to suggest the visual pattern of Vidor's best early work. Without its survival, the homages paid Griffith by Vidor in interviews could seem merely the genuflecting of

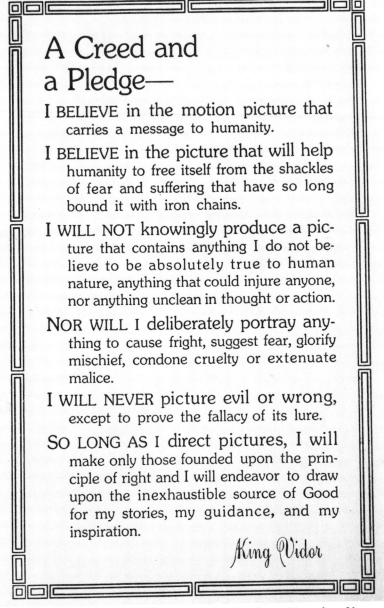

A Creed and a Pledge—

I BELIEVE in the motion picture that carries a message to humanity.

I BELIEVE in the picture that will help humanity to free itself from the shackles of fear and suffering that have so long bound it with iron chains.

I WILL NOT knowingly produce a picture that contains anything I do not believe to be absolutely true to human nature, anything that could injure anyone, nor anything unclean in thought or action.

NOR WILL I deliberately portray anything to cause fright, suggest fear, glorify mischief, condone cruelty or extenuate malice.

I WILL NEVER picture evil or wrong, except to prove the fallacy of its lure.

SO LONG AS I direct pictures, I will make only those founded upon the principle of right and I will endeavor to draw upon the inexhaustible source of Good for my stories, my guidance, and my inspiration.

King Vidor

Figure 14. From the Vidor Village investment brochure. More than fifty years later, Vidor commented: "I might have been stupid enough in my first few pictures to put out a creed that I wouldn't make pictures with violence or sex. . . . It was an advertisement, you know. . . . Right after it came out in the paper, I got arrested for playing poker in a sixty-cent game. The headlines were pretty awful. It didn't go with this idealistic statement" (DGA).

every director of his era. But whatever his oft-repeated admiration for *Intolerance* (whose sets dominated Hollywood when the Vidors arrived from Texas and in which he may have picked up a few days' work as an extra), we can't help agreeing with those who see Griffith's genius as more lyrical than epic, his ambitions notwithstanding.[10] Only chronologically was Griffith "the founding father of Hollywood"; as an artist he never accommodated its patterns. Although *The Jack-Knife Man* has a pace and spirit quite in sync with the Griffith of *True Heart Susie*, both directors were returning to the mode of Griffith's Biograph one-reelers of a decade before. Vidor's recollection that First National was displeased with the lyrical film he gave them, under budget, is supported even by favorable contemporary reviews, which found it "a pleasing reaction against" styles of the year.[11]

Griffith's shadow falls heavily on a bedraggled mother and child whose outlandish entrance into the methodical domesticity of a Mississippi river tramp, "Peter Lane," sets *The Jack-Knife Man* into action (fig. 15). Flinging open his houseboat door, she's silhouetted by lightning, then collapses down the steps in a soaking black mass at his feet. Griffith even works such an entrance, and the lingering death that follows, into the otherwise idyllic *True Heart Susie*. In tortured posture, "Liz" in the Vidor film duplicates Lillian Gish's exhausted faint through the doorway into the shelter of the Chinaman's shop in *Broken Blossoms*, released fifteen months earlier. Liz's wild, rain-soaked hair and delirious pleading of "I'll be good! Don't take him!" might additionally remind one of Gish's tainted mother fighting storms and river ice-floes in *Way Down East* (released three weeks after *The Jack-Knife Man*). However, straining for parallels with Gish's orphan of many storms isn't essential, as Vidor cast Claire McDowell, who also played leads for Griffith at Biograph, as his fighting mother. It's typical that Vidor would fasten on McDowell, who (unlike other early Griffith heroines, Mary Pickford, Mae Marsh, or the Gish sisters) was a tall and strikingly strong-looking woman in her Biograph days, with huge eyes and an angular jaw that telegraphed determination. One of Griffith's harshest—and strangest—films, *The Female of the Species* (1912), has her turn from strangling another woman at the cries of an abandoned infant. Some such tension between fierceness and maternal instincts supercharges her scenes in *The Jack-Knife Man* and makes her the perfect foil for the deliberation in Peter's every move. Even as he cradles Liz's head on his lap, her tangled black hair and desperately leaping eyes bring into his boat a new energy. Claire McDowell returns twice again for Vidor as a vital mother, memorably in *The Big Parade*.

After Liz's death, her young son stays on with Peter, who comes to be known as "the jack-knife man" because of the wooden animals he first carves to amuse the boy. Another tattered hobo, "Booge," steals the boat

Figure 15.   The Jack-Knife Man *(1920). Claire McDowell and Bobby Kelso.*

and boy, but the men unite against a common enemy—a river town's intrusive orphans' aid society. With its orphan inspiring a tramp, *The Jack-
Knife Man* links *The Turn in the Road* with Chaplin's *The Kid* (released
six months later; although in light of the eighteen-month production of
The Kid, the rampant speculation in Hollywood over Chaplin's "big" picture, and the fact that the Vidor and Chaplin films were both financed by
First National, some conscious connection is not impossible). The longshots of Peter walking from civilization to the horizon down dirt roads do
remind one now of Chaplin's favorite closing shots. Both films were no
doubt emotionally boosted by the decline in the U.S. population following World War I, the 1918 influenza epidemic, and the first real push for
birth control. The resulting higher status of children, and the increased
number of orphans, may also have had something to do with prolonging
the infantilism in Mary Pickford's persona.

One might cynically propose that the sentimental sympathy for the
lower classes in both Griffith and Chaplin pandered to the audiences they
began with, but something more fundamental made both artists cling to
such populist (in the film sense) sympathy long after audience demo-
graphics had shifted upward. Griffith's ideology, of course, was close to
that of an unreconstructed Southerner (resulting in those painful justifications in chapter 2 of every film history text). Nevertheless, Griffith is also

the first master of a pre-Hollywood "American" cinema of Populist (in the political sense) idealism, of social concerns dramatized through rural lyricism. While Vidor retains a certain southern provincialism, it is this larger tradition of small-scale rural dramas that inspired his first features. The panoramic closing shots of such Griffith one-reelers as *The Country Doctor* (1909) and *A Corner in Wheat* (1909) universalize the confined melodramas that precede them. With feature length, but small budgets, Vidor returned to this line. *The Jack-Knife Man*'s progress is interrupted by lyrical longshots of the loner gliding along the smooth river or struggling over rutted roads. "Vidor Village" was self-consciously guided by the midwestern spirit of "Booth Tarkington, Mark Twain and James Whitcomb Riley." [12]

Continuing in that milieu and spirit, if less successfully, is *Love Never Dies* (1921), a homespun North Carolina variant on Griffith's thrice-filmed "Enoch Arden" formula. A husband (Lloyd Hughes), mistaking his wife's abduction for desertion, flees town by train and reports his own death in its wreck as a way of denying everything about his rural hometown. As any Populist could have told him, this can lead to no good. After years spent in Chicago, with sterile financial success, his longing calls him back to "Ridgeville" to find a remarried wife and a son whose existence he has never suspected. Played straight, the storyline taxes even silent film's proclivity for characters who never get around to explaining things to each other. Leo McCarey's comedy version, *My Favorite Wife* (1940), makes more sense.

The film is structured by "John's" denials—of his mother, his rural trash sister, his wife's love, his hometown itself—until this man of little faith gets the ordeal he deserves by denying he's alive. On misunderstanding that his wife has chosen to leave him, he curls up in dejection on their bed and toys with and talks to her nightgown into the night (fig. 16a). A long take details his slow awakening in the same fetal passivity, which matches his wife's posture in her father's home (fig. 16b). Whatever the curiosity value of this humanization of melodrama, the sequence is just the sort that Karl Brown managed to more purpose in his rural melodrama *Stark Love* (1927) when he fashioned a context—rising floodwaters—to make us doubly anxious over his hero's fetal-posture despair in place of any active search for his love. No doubt an unfair anticipation of Vidor's *vital* tragic lovers to come (in *Hallelujah, Duel in the Sun*, and *Ruby Gentry* particularly) makes the mutual debility here even more annoying.

The hometown itself is given a distinct visual treatment upon John's return—less a matter of constricting nights in cluttered rooms than of open pastures and rushing rivers. The conflict between past and present husbands turns into a class conflict, fought with clothing, gestures, and

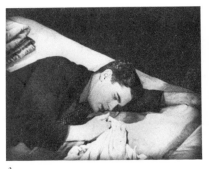 

a   b

Figure 16.   Love Never Dies *(1921). Lloyd Hughes and Madge Bellamy.*

manners. Right from the first shot of John's disgusted gaze into the street, he's too good for his "mother"—although audiences might accept that as a right conferred by ambition and his architectural talent (and, we discover, by her lie: she's not really his mother). Later, when John has prospered into immaculately pressed suits, the second husband, Joel, has degenerated to the rural trash level that John's sister's clothing had hinted of as a possible fate for John himself. Joel skulks around dressed like a Griffith tramp in tattered shirt, suspenders, and floppy hat, quite understandably distressed at the return of his wife's dead husband. John meets him with the essence of city civility, offering a firm handshake while expressing sorrow at mucking up his life. That kinda stuff doesn't cut it with Joel, who tries pathetically to muscle John out of town at gunpoint.

By this point, our sympathies are thoroughly confused. Eventually John throws off his city duds and turns man of action again, attempting (but failing, luckily for the resolution) to save Joel from a river suicide. Many of Vidor's favorite Populist motifs are here, but strangely mixed. Even *A Modern Prodigal* (1910), Griffith's odd "story in symbolism," combines motifs of city temptations, rural honesty, and river rescue in more involving ways. The genre, in its silent form, reached maturity with *Stark Love* and Frank Borzage's *Back Pay* (1922) and *The River* (1928).

The stage plays Vidor was assigned to bring to the screen after the collapse of his independent production company necessarily afforded fewer opportunities. Still, even within a severely restrictive assignment like *Peg o' My Heart* (1922), touches of his political philosophy shine through. The play had been a hugely successful vehicle for toast-of-Broadway Laurette Taylor. This was her first film, and her husband, also the play's author, J. Hartley Manners, took the role of producer, no doubt restraining Vidor from any thoroughgoing tampering with the well-known source, which had played something like ten thousand English-language performances by various companies within six years of its 1912 debut. It was hardly a smooth shoot—Vidor temporarily walked off the picture after the first day's chaos of location work with the stage-trained actress.

What was left him were choices of how to open up a one-set play and how to convey banter through pantomime. Both play and film chart the cultural comedy arising from the introduction (via bank failures and dying last wishes) of free-spirited, uneducated, Irish Peg into the stodgy British manor of her aunt, Mrs. Chichester. The play's trick, long in the tooth even by 1912, is to have British high society shown up by young Peg's moral honesty and sentimental love philosophy (which, naturally in the context, are indistinguishable). And, for good measure, she's the real moneyed heiress, condescending unbeknownst. It was exactly the sort of thing Mary Pickford had been regularly cleaning up with, most recently in *Little Lord Fauntleroy* (1921). Vidor's film was another box-office hit.

From the play's throwaway details, Vidor fleshes a sharp contrast. Introduced, after an early-Griffith pan across the landscape, is Peg's father (Russell Simpson), not as the blarneying jack-of-all-trades gone off to America implied in Peg's rosy recollections in the play, but as a revolutionary Fenian, rousing peasants for land reform from the back of his wagon (fig. 17a) and only feigning the irresponsible gypsy when colonial police gallop up. Thus, in the film, Peg's moral superiority is allowed to come less from "honest" sentimental love and more from being her father's daughter, following in his commitment to rural self-reliance.

The impression of the film version as a Populist revision is reinforced by the figure of "Jerry," the Chichesters' neighbor, who introduces himself to Peg as "a farmer." He is said to be a farmer in the play as well, but there it's as a whim in the jack-of-all-trades characterization parallel to Peg's father ("I can do a whole lot of things fairly well, and none of them

a   b

Figure 17.   Peg o' My Heart *(1922).*

well enough to brag about").[13] Vidor covers our suspicions of anyone cozy with the Chichesters through a new scene in Jerry's orchard (fig. 17b) and by making him an agrarian at ease with Latin botanical usage. When he's finally unmasked as "Sir Gerald," there's been (literal) groundwork for a synthesis lacking in the play between classes and countries, rural and society life, peasant and aristocracy. And when Sir Gerald comes from England to Ireland, asking amid the goats for Peg's hand, it's consistent as a peace treaty capper to politics-as-melodrama. Vidor, like Peg herself, managed here to hold onto a bit of himself within an alien world.

A second version of this storyline appears in Vidor's *Happiness* (1924), again based on a Hartley Manners play, and another vehicle for Laurette Taylor, with Brooklyn and uptown Manhattan standing in, respectively, for rural Ireland and England. Taylor's "Jenny" is another impoverished spitfire adopted by a bored socialite (Hedda Hopper) and given a dream future by marriage to yet another Renaissance man ("I'm an electrician, and a musician, and a poet, and an inventor, and a lot of other things"). The pattern was creaky in *Peg o' My Heart* and hardly bears repeating. But the parallels, and changes, do retain one interest: Vidor's *political* Populism, so tied to support of the country world, could grow into *film* populism, with its support of underdog vitality anywhere. His altered philosophy seems less arbitrary if one recalls how the Progressive movement tamed the reforms of the Populists into *urban* labor proposals. *Happiness* opens promisingly with what turns out to be the film's best sequence—a Thanksgiving Day dance on a Brooklyn side street, where a mix of nationalities and races compete casually, each dancing a few characteristic steps as Jenny, budding entrepreneur, passes through the crowd, collecting change in a tambourine. The sequence looks forward to *Street Scene* in both its facade staging and a certain stoopfront tension among the immigrant types. After a plotline of lost mothers and dying fathers that only Dickens could have pulled off, the coda puts Jenny, now settled into Coolidge-era business success, face-to-face with "herself"—another girl named Jenny, fresh off the Brooklyn streets, and as literally sniveling, but ambitious, as she once was. Vidor much later sheepishly admitted that the closing title ("And the endless chain of Jennys goes on in all big cities . . .") "sounds very much like me at the time."[14] But not until *The Crowd* does his populist generalizing, forcing New York's "little man" face-to-face with a clown who is "himself," find its coherent framework.

Vidor's fondness for disguised or blatant religious themes in these early silents was nothing like the subject of such wonder among reviewers as it would be today. The surprising range of allowable philosophies narrowed with each year of silent filmmaking, but the real rigidification began with the initial Hays Code—essentially set in place by 1924 through the trade organization "The Motion Picture Producers and Distributors of America," following a series of Hollywood scandals in 1922. Only Vidor's lost *Dusk to Dawn* (1922) prompted unanimous critical response that his way with the philosophic had gotten the better of him. It does seem to have been a highly curious item, crafted to use existing footage of a huge procession in India. Florence Vidor plays a dual role as an American and an Indian who, somehow, share the same soul. When the American sleeps, her soul shuttles off to India, but she experiences her other life in the form of dreams, or through some sort of "plasmic memory," to use the term of the Theosophists, who had done much to popularize Eastern notions of metempsychosis in America. Embarrassment over a bigamous soul is resolved when the Indian woman's husband the rajah dies and she throws herself on his pyre, thus freeing the American to marry her sweetheart. While Theosophical belief in faith healing parallels Christian Science, and Theosophical ideas about migrating souls have a common source with the transcendentalists' fascination with the "over-soul," perhaps Vidor didn't take these ideas too seriously. Even trade journals admitted that it was "unusually hard . . . to follow" and that, in any case, audiences wouldn't fall for the premise. "Pretty deep stuff, as it were."[15]

More successful with its religious theme is a surviving film, *The Sky Pilot* (1921). For a variety of reasons its raving sentiment and clichés don't strike the predominant notes, and it remains a compelling melodrama, with some startling stuntwork and unconventional characterizations that set the Western genre on its ear. As it incorporates elements of both Vidor's early individualist faith and fondness for rural self-help, we'll use it to close out this look at his early political philosophy.

When soft-jowled, clear-eyed John Bowers, in high-buttoned coat, bow tie, and umbrella, saunters into a "primitive, godless" small town, it looks like a stark clash. And when he's announced as a "sky pilot" (seaman's slang for preacher, but common in early Westerns), we anticipate a William S. Hart–style conflict between a minister's rigid, but fragile, puritanism and a rough cowpoke's flexible honor. An equally soft-faced preacher buggy-rides into a small town to open Hart's *Travelin' On* the same year, but with a shifty-eyed anxiety missing from Bowers's performance. The first surprise here is how the Pilot (as the cowboys call him) treats himself with the same lightness as Vidor's camera. He appreciates the joke of cowboys tip-toeing into the saloon-as-church in heaven-gazing, clasped-handed mock piety. From the first shot he's clearly not of the praise-the-lord-and-pass-the-ammunition Fighting Father Dunne school. Neither is he an evangelical "sin killer" of the type Vidor later scrutinizes in *Duel in the Sun* and *Ruby Gentry*.

a   b

Figure 18.   By the waters of Swan Creek I sat down and wept. a: John Bowers ("the Pilot"); b: with David Butler (Bill), in The Sky Pilot *(1921).*

His loaves-and-fishes sermon ends in chaos with a fistfight and the cowboys pelting him with stones to the edge of town ("Hard ridin' and soft religion don't mix, Mr. Parson"). His despair clashes with a glistening stream (fig. 18a). When Bill, the foreman, with whom he has fought, but who has admired his spunk, comes to ask forgiveness and offer work as a cowhand, there's a suggestive montage of images as the Pilot turns Bill's other cheek, to wash off the blood from their fight with river water, using the hanky that in the opening shots seemed one more emblem of his prissiness (fig. 18b). Already the film is well beyond what the "mythic" Western took from its literary model in Owen Wister's *The Virginian*, where a minister's puritan rantings about innate sin provoke the Virginian to trick him off the ranch.

There's a shifting of expectations in *The Sky Pilot:* its genre leads us to expect individualism triumphant; a minister leads us to expect puritanism embattled. But our hero turns out to possess a positive thinking vitality that coalesces a group into a community. His ministry has such blasphemous freedom that it's fitting when the cowboys secretly build him a church, with no cross in evidence and a horseshoe as pulpit icon. Transcendentalist ministry comes full circle when Bill gives his own loaves-and-fishes sermon. A rustling scheme had been discovered by Gwen (Colleen Moore), daughter of the "Old Timer," who is in reluctant league with the outlaws, but in her attempt to warn the cowhands, she has been thrown from her horse and left paralyzed—and thus useless in the physical West. Her desperate father pulls his Bible from the fireplace, where he'd tossed it after having grown angry with a God that would permit his wife's death, and pleads with the Pilot to pray over his daughter. But we never see him give any outward hint of prayer. He has that within which passes show. His ministry is closer to psychiatry—helping a cow-hand over the d.t.'s; explaining the nature of suffering to bedridden Gwen.

Befitting a Western, he must prove himself physically, but the genre's expected machismo is finessed. The Pilot's wit is a match for Bill's attempt to disrupt the first loaves-and-fishes sermon (well, yes, "that fella Jesus" could liquor us up if he'd a mind to—he did turn water into wine), but he must immediately turn fighting padre by besting Bill. This is the classic Western hero's union of moral right with organic excellence, except that there's something about a long, *almost* equal fight that punctures the mythic West. Exhaustion is pacifism's intrusion by way of realism, as in the epic fistfight between Gregory Peck (as the pacifist sea captain out West) and Charlton Heston in William Wyler's *The Big Country*. Bill has recourse to the guns unavailable to God's man, though that's acknowledged as a false victory in the riverside scene. Still, Vidor succumbs to the weaknesses of the genre in avoiding all the worthy questions that could have come up if the Pilot had, as the casting of Bowers leads us to expect, been knocked cold by the first punch. His heroism against facial type valorizes a dangerous-looking stunt that succeeds because it's so clearly performed by Bowers himself: Gwen is knocked unconscious by the fall from her horse and the Pilot straddles her body, shooing off the stampeding cattle. Vidor recalled that he first filmed the stunt with a dummy, but it looked unconvincing, whereupon Bowers volunteered.[16] His soft face becomes tied to a courage antithetic to the genre's "mythic" bravado.

From *Hallelujah* it's clear that Vidor was conscious of the temptations that seduce a merely vitalist ministry. *The Sky Pilot* is nowhere as fascinating as the 1929 film, but it touches on the temptations with visual subtlety. Again William S. Hart provides a useful contrast. The minister in *Hell's Hinges* (1916) is seduced by woman's ways and by his own repression. It's the opposite of *Hallelujah*'s temptation through vitality, and opposite also to the role of the woman in *The Sky Pilot*, who turns savior in pulling her parson from the water, without denying her sexuality. In the film's final moments, she recovers from paralysis in time to save him again, this time from the fire of his burning church. Colleen Moore had been in Westerns with Tom Mix, but she's used here with a knowing sophistication—straddling the Pilot as *he* lies unconscious and keeping a protective arm around him even after he's able to get on her horse. The intermittent sensuality of the film is doubly fascinating because of the genre's usual sexual sterility, and Vidor's mastery of the gestural stands out as it doesn't elsewhere. It's possible to imagine, from the example of the woman-shunning minister who dies in *his* burning church in Robert Altman's *McCabe and Mrs. Miller*, how a frontier minister could be beaten back by his community's sins into *heartless* pacifism.

a   b

Figure 19.   The Sky Pilot. *An active and passive Gwen (Colleen Moore).*

The round-robin of male/female heroism is a satisfying substitute for an invincible cowboy hero. Gwen is first seen galloping chariot-style on a horsedrawn wagon (fig. 19a). But soon she ties up her hair and exchanges wool chaps for a heavy plaid dress, emblems of separation from the active world. With this ladylike costume comes the loss of all the strength and skills she has displayed in saving the Pilot. She's easily carried back to her bedroom in impotent fury after overhearing the rustling plans (fig. 19b). Genteel female frills foretell literal paralysis. Her heroic recovery to save the Pilot from the church fire requires us to accept yet another of Vidor's miracle cures through willpower. Christian Science, no doubt, but the motif is hardly unknown elsewhere in silents, as with Mary Pickford's recovery from paralysis in the previous year's *Pollyanna*.

As if in compensation for his conclusion's farcical speed, Vidor holds the final shot of the just-married couple while a new anxiety creeps onto the Pilot's face (compare the final shot of *The Graduate*), as if he, too, has misplaced the events intervening between rescue and marriage. The moment has a lightness that distinguishes the best silent Westerns from the solemn sound-era Westerns that took to carrying the weight of a nation's history. The infusion of this rustic comedy-drama into *The Sky Pilot* undercuts the Western genre's solemn myth-making streak. Both genres were prevalent in the late teens and twenties, but film culture has rehabilitated only the poker-faced, more sentimental one. The cowboys in *The Sky Pilot* aren't gunslingers, but workers (mending fences is the Pilot's job) and pranksters (a side of the cowboy ignored until restored in the seventies via the redneck hero). In *The Phantom Bullet* (1926) Hoot Gibson resolves a classic vengeance situation (father murdered) by dressing in the foppish style of the Pilot until the murderer reveals himself. One can't conceive of John Wayne in that roundabout, comic-Hamlet degradation. Vidor's cowboys here are workers who relax through practical jokes

Figure 20.   Vidor and Colleen Moore, snowbound at the Truckee, California, location for The Sky Pilot.

(they pretend to be masked outlaws when they ride the Pilot to his new church). Despite the plotline and the Republican dream-vision of a stable labor force overlorded by a paternal businessman, it's an altogether more convincing West. As others have said, to understand the West as somehow a burlesque comes closer to pinning it down than to understand the West as somehow a myth.

The Sky Pilot comes far from its source in a severe morality novel of 1899 by the Canadian minister Charles William Gordon (who penned adventures as "Ralph Connor"). Vidor's individualist optimism supersedes Gordon's harsh Christian moralizing, just as it supersedes the strident *historical* optimism of the "mythic" Western. It might look typical of Hollywood that a happy end is substituted for the novel's tragic one, but such a switch is part of the faith in rural community self-help that drives the film—and that drove Vidor's early career.

Silent Film Cycles
and the Problem of Melodrama

There's a union of substance and style in Populist rhetoric itself that does something to account for the relative clarity of Vidor's earliest ideology. As historian Richard Hofstadter summarizes it: "Populist thought often carries one into a world in which the simple virtues and unmitigated villainies of a rural melodrama have been projected on a national or even an international scale."[17] Strangely enough, what is most alien now in Vidor's best work before he joined MGM is not its Populist underpinnings but that thought's expression through an extreme mode of melodrama.

Vidor maintained this mode long past his Populist years, and it is worth pausing before moving on to his major films to examine his early way with melodrama. *Wild Oranges* (1924) makes an engaging point of reference, with its look forward to the southern passions of *Hallelujah* and back to the southern lyricism of *The Jack-Knife Man*. Its minimalism seems to have given headaches to Goldwyn's ad writers: "Not One Massive Set! Not a Single Costume!" Its plotline is hardly more complex. A yachtsman, John, sailing the seas to forget his wife's death, anchors in a remote Georgia inlet. At dusk he spots a nude swimmer, Nellie. She rushes terrified to the decaying mansion in the woods where she lives with her emaciated, even more skittish grandfather and a cretinous bully, "Nicholas—half man, half child," who regularly drags her through the swamps to be snapped at by alligators until she responds to his kisses (fig. 21). John's anguish over leaping into this bizarre world is mirrored in Nicholas's murderous distress over his intrusion.

One way of making waking-life sense of such hokum is to confine it to

Figure 21. Wild Oranges *(1924).* Virginia Valli (Nellie) and Charles A. Post (Nicholas).

its two central characters: a von Sternbergian tough-but-passive man comes face to face with a Griffithian hands-fluttering belle through a Vidorian moment of sexual temptation (a nude woman swims through *Bird of Paradise* and *Duel in the Sun*, as well as through various scenes Vidor committed only to paper—*The Turn in the Road* remake and his draft for *The Wedding Night*). "Melodrama is the naturalism of dream life," in Eric Bentley's deft formulation,[18] and on some psychic level the three other characters *follow* from this moment of temptation. Nellie's grandfather, cowering behind bushes and shutters, seems an incarnation of her "curse of fear," bestowed by the "heredity" of the southern past, "the horror of the Civil War." John's first mate, Halvard, keeping things shipshape while anxious to sail away from this terrible becalmed bay, seems a superego projection of orderly sexual disengagement. Nicholas plays Caliban's "most ridiculous monster" to the marooned daughter and grandfather. The reason given for fearing him (a wanted-for-murder flyer) comes nowhere near matching what we see of the lunkish laborer, who twitches in an ecstasy of gap-toothed joy after Nellie's kisses. If Halvard is John's superego, his id is Nicholas, who is ruled by the sexual longing (mainly ankle fetish) that John represses.

For Nellie, the spit-and-polished yacht looks inhabited by "two nice old ladies," implying a touch of the American literary tradition of "odd couple" homosexual shipboard idylls à la Huck/Jim and Ishmael/Queequeg (fig. 22). ("Come Back to the Raft Ag'in, Huck Honey" was Leslie Fiedler's academically outrageous title for his 1948 look at the tradition.)[19] *The Jack-Knife Man*'s riverboat represents the same disengagement from the complicating world of dark women, but *Wild Oranges* is tougher on self-satisfied male attempts to drift from vital torment, and approaches the Faulknerian swampland passions to come in *Hallelujah* and *Ruby Gentry*. Women instigate melodramas of sexual panic for both silent-film drifters, but there is something more Victorian—or, OK, Griffith-like—about the panic induced in "the jack-knife man" after the desperately exhausted mother, sheltered in his boat, asks that he take off her soaking dress. The very idea sends him running aimlessly into the storm, flailing his arms, and finally cowering all night under a haystack. After that, the headlong outrageousness of *Wild Oranges* is a relief.

Intrusive hints of the world as we know it can be fatal to melodrama, and certainly would be to *Wild Oranges*. Its defense is to slash the world down to size—five players cut off from a social context. (Much later, Josef von Sternberg abandoned his cluttered sets to take the same option in *Anatahan;* it's no coincidence that another hothouse sexual obsession results.) The pillared mansion in *Wild Oranges* is only iconographically southern (fig. 23), and Civil War "horror" is evidenced by a single

Figure 22.   Wild Oranges. *Frank Mayo (John), Virginia Valli, and Ford Sterling (Halvard).*

title. Nellie, hemmed in by swamp and sea, has no neighbors. The mansion's interior has only the odd table here, bed there. The one outbuilding is furnished with the menagerie of a sparse nightmare (rats, cranes, bats). It's a bleak, bare aesthetic, quite unlike Victorian stage melodrama, with its often-changed sets stuffed with bric-a-brac. Its sparsity is also quite unlike the tie between realism and modernism—fascination with the world's impinging junk. Yet *Wild Oranges* is set in motion by a random piece of trash, the newspaper that blows in front of John's carriage, which frightens the horse, which causes the accident, which kills the wife, which starts the man on his long years at sea. The camera returns to the fatal newspaper at the close of this frenzied minute-long opening sequence. In a realist work, such a piece of trash might be part of an accumulation defining the opinions and ideology of its consumer (like the opening of Balzac's *Le Père Goriot*); in a modernist, it might suggest the interconnection of all the world's minutiae (like *Ulysses*'s "Elijah Is Coming" flyer). But the lingering final shot of *Wild Oranges*'s newspaper plugs into another, half-lost, ideology of the Heavy Hand of Fate (like the letter left lying in Hardy's *Tess of the D'Urbervilles*).

If, however grudgingly, one uses "melodrama" to mean a form, not a

Figure 23. Wild Oranges. *"The defeated South": Nellie's grandfather (Nigel De Brulier).*

failure, one can't complain of a lack of "reality" (that shifty word which, as Nabokov said, "wears its quotes like claws"). In melodrama, not only chance, but predictability, too, can shade over into fatalism (as in that most lurid of melodramas, *Oedipus the King*). One *can* complain if the melodrama is mechanical and unfelt, or if its parts never mesh. After Vidor's inspirational slump around 1940, it's his *re*-discovery of melodrama that surprises and disturbs drama's gray-flannel norms.

Alongside *noir*, his new social pessimism meshes with melodrama's darkness, its facility for projecting the unconscious into a world where, as Peter Brooks puts it in *The Melodramatic Imagination*, his study of the mode in nineteenth-century fiction, "nothing is spared because nothing is left unsaid." [20] Actually, *Beyond the Forest* and *Ruby Gentry* coincide with literary historians (notably Fiedler and Richard Chase) [21] waxing eloquent on melodrama's power to express American conflicts. But film critics, who lived in a world far removed from literature's, had just taken up neorealism, and felt betrayed on behalf of Vidor the thirties humanist.

Much later, the flip-flop revisionism of younger film critics short-changed melodrama by fanciful notions of what's socially critical (witness Fassbinder and others on, of all people, Douglas Sirk). All a far cry from the traditional nomenclature, where "drama" involved sophisticated psychological individualization, a certain plausibility and finesse, and was roughly "true to life," while in melodrama the conflicts were stark to the point of violence, enacted by stock types, with at best a stock surprise (the villain pets his cat), and with vehemence (like music) doing the work. Melodrama was the grosser, merely enjoyable, mechanism, incapable of state-of-the-art relevance. Insofar as movies rejoiced in vivid physicality, they tended to "action melodrama." In film culture, a shift in nomenclature has arisen that it would be pointless to resist, but that needs noting: "melodrama" is applied to what twenty years ago were called "dramas," in particular "woman's dramas." The reasons for the shift are multiple: (1) a preoccupation with genres (*film noir*, the Western, and so on) poorly represented in "English Lit." approaches to drama; (2) a lack of interest in the theater, the dramatic medium par excellence and thought to be filled with suspect bourgeois realism; (3) a feminist-era uneasiness over christening a genre after a gender ("woman's drama"), especially when that would stress the embarrassing possibility that women spectators were more accomplices in than victims of Hollywood ideology; and (4) an idea that melodrama, as the lower-class, more violent mechanism, might be the more subversive. Everybody's nomenclature is custom, not logic. The only problem is that *both* the old dismissal of "mere melodrama" and the new defenses of melodrama-as-social-criticism ignore the form's personal-individual interests and its potential transmutation into a poetic (for example, gothic novels or the Brontës).

In the American tradition, Vidor's tradition, melodrama has a perennial, if only recently respected, place. The tone (and, it must be said, the artistry) of *Wild Oranges* evoke that justly forgotten American gothic novelist Charles Brockden Brown (1771–1810), but even Melville and Hawthorne can be doughty melodramatizers. Their best-remembered characters come near incarnations of absolutes, clinging tragically to rationalism or puritan restraint, interacting in passion plays where psychology merely brings up the rear, never drives the plot. They're melodramas of morality.

For Vidor, passion itself *is* a morality. Monomania is not the only melodramatic structure. Quite as common is hysteria, with the flip-flop of ambivalence (*Duel in the Sun*) or the freak combinations of motives. His melodramas are often environmental too. They pivot on textures of extreme physical experience in elemental settings. Though they seldom have Jack London's stress on survival, or the homespun brass-tack aura of Mark Twain, they can weave between the two. They're more often atmospheric (or, as they say, "metaphoric"), like the weather in Tennessee Williams, a bit of nature infused into man. The arch example is the storm in *King Lear*, a melodrama so "hysteric" that drama meets myth, with not one subtle motivation from beginning to end.

In psychologically analytical films, or novels, the definition of exact motivation looms very large. This preoccupation has various roots, notably the puritan emphasis on "sincerity" and the Cartesian emphasis on clear ideas in consciousness as evidence of the indubitable. But the real puritan concern was moralism, not analysis, which probably explains why George Eliot, for example, moralizes so much, and Stendhal hardly at all. With Proust and the later Henry James, analytical techniques became so refined, and so *full*, that the narrator kept adding motives, and had difficulty in choosing between them. Paradoxically then, the "moral-analytical" approach—a concern with the *real* reason—became "synthetic" to accommodate a multiplicity of motives, which were often morally contradictory. "None of these hypotheses was absurd," Proust's ruminative narrator concludes more than once. Character became, again, an accretion of reasons, as vague as puritan "soul" was to begin with. Then Freud, a very great novelist indeed, substituted the "unconscious" for the soul, and a whole new set of irrational motivations came into play. Literature handed motivation and psychology over to the sciences. The *nouveau roman* is all about the impossibility of any thought ever accounting for anything, or anything ever accounting for thought. Samuel Beckett's great trilogy of novels laid bare the "bankruptcy" of Proustian/Jamesian motives by extending Cartesian logic to a point where *all* the narrator's hypotheses reek of absurdism.

Nonetheless, schoolmarm-type criticism long made psychological analysis the single norm outside any but the standardized genres. And thus, one way and another, criticism delegitimized melodrama. Yet even in works that, like, say, Hitchcock's, just about pass muster by psychologically analytical criteria, the statements of precise motives are merely one point in a pattern. They're really an "atmospheric," no more essential, and often less expressive, than the lyrical implications of the scenery. That's fine by the popular cinema, whose usual combination of terse dialogue and external visual action militates against the patient, sedentary exfoliation of obscure or complex motives. In our relatively lengthy essays on *Hallelujah, The Champ,* and *Duel in the Sun*, we trace out some ways in which an overall moral complexity—what Peter Brooks calls "the moral occult"[22]—can be *reinstated* in melodrama.*

---

* A closely related question concerns another high-culture assumption from which melodramatic films have suffered—that the moviegoer passively watches the action, asks no

Not that dislike of melodrama in film form comes merely from critical snobbery. For critics aren't always snobbish. They revolted against high-culture shibboleths to vindicate the Western and slapstick. Something more is involved. The *abstract* clash of melodrama gets undercut by photography itself. Melodrama's moral absolutes get buried beneath the dreck of the world. Much of the power of *The Scarlet Letter,* for instance, comes from Hawthorne's refusal to choose for us among the possibilities (whence sprang that rosebush in the prison doorway? was or wasn't there an *A* in Dimmesdale's flesh?). Hawthorne's novel looks so straightforward, and in words it is, but from Victor Seastrom to Wim Wenders, talented directors have found their inspiration sapped by its elusiveness. Even Huston's *Moby Dick* devolutes into a Klassic Komic because (1) *no* actor could incarnate the idea of Ahab, and (2) when film shows all, it forgoes Melville's tension between the concrete encyclopedics of whaling and abstract moral battles. Charles Affron's recognition of that essential conflict between photography and melodrama in *Cinema and Sentiment,* his superb study of patterns of high emotion in film, encourages a wider focus on tearjerking "sentiment." But that focus still skirts the problem of pure melodramas of dream logic and moral duality. *Wild Oranges*'s defense against what Affron calls the "particularizations of enactment and photography" is the extreme social isolation of its five characters.[23]

That said, another possibility keeps suggesting itself—perhaps *Wild Oranges* is only *half* a melodrama. Perhaps, like so many of Vidor's later features, it pits melodrama against drama, not to reach a compromise mode but as a sort of montage or dialectic between the melodramatic mode of portraying sexual fears and a nearly realistic one. In such a viewing, John frees Nellie from her (melodramatic) nightmare, just as she frees him from his (realistic) inertia. John gets some psychological complexity because he has almost as little to do as the grandfather—mainly sit on his yacht anguished (over fear of involvement) and guilty (over infidelity to his wife's memory). This isn't the sort of thing the silent *movie* does well, and Vidor must strain to bring it off, with John's false starts into action, his hands pulling back from a touch, even double-exposure

---

questions that aren't explicitly raised, and makes no criticism of what the heroes do. These always implausible notions are massively reinforced by structuralism and Eurocommunist theory (Althusser). However, "passivist" theories have never survived close scrutiny—we recommend Piaget's "constructivist" psychology; Edgar Morin's *Le Cinéma ou l'homme imaginaire* (Paris: Editions de Minuit, 1956) and *The Stars* (New York: Grove Press, 1960); and a superb pair of analyses by David Bordwell in *The Classical Hollywood Cinema* (New York: Columbia University Press, 1985), 37–41, and *Narration in the Fiction Film* (Madison: University of Wisconsin Press, 1985), 29–47.

phantoms of a languorous, caressing Nellie. Victor Fleming has even greater trouble dramatizing such Conradian moral doubt at sea, first in *Code of the Sea* (1924) and then in Conrad's own *Lord Jim* (1925). It's not impossible that *Wild Oranges* and those contemporary Fleming films were groping toward a way of dramatizing a widely recognized post–World War I issue, the loss of any clear-cut motivations for male action, let alone courage—an issue faced in *The Big Parade* (1925).

If John's anguish can evoke Joseph Conrad, Nellie, with her immediate, wild response to the world, is that favorite figure of melodrama (and indeed of poetic whimsy à la Jean Giraudoux), the fauve. Eric Bentley again: "The melodramatic vision is in one sense simply normal. It corresponds to an important aspect of reality. It is the spontaneous, uninhibited way of seeing things."[24] It is this melodrama-as-health that Nellie brings to John's torment. In her initial frustration, she compares him to a cast-iron dog she used to talk to, until it rusted away. She runs her hands lightly along his arms as they first talk, and what would be coquetry in others is her spontaneous way of taking in the world. She gives the yacht the same fluttery, tactile inspection. Emotional woman versus stoic man, perhaps, but the film expands outward, via melodrama's typically paranoid worldview, into scenic terms: her overgrown swampland versus his open sea. Her oceanic panic during a brief pleasure cruise is consistent with the contrast—until the deaths of Nicholas and her grandfather, when she can live with the ocean's "freedom."

Yet another reason for distinguishing *Wild Oranges* from some pure melodrama is Vidor's oft-repeated claim that he never used a villain in his films—a claim that is indeed almost accurate, as surprising as it is from a director so reliant on melodrama.[25] Not that his worldview is benevolent, what with passion's excesses abounding, only that, as with Renoir, "everybody has his reasons." If Vidor doesn't follow Mrs. Eddy in converting sin into "mortal illusion," he does pull back from scapegoat figures. In *Wild Oranges*, the hero/"villain" conflict generates no suspense; Nicholas is gigantic, clumsy, and slow-witted, a pre-Depression Lennie from *Of Mice and Men*. When he lunges with a knife drawn from under his butcher's apron, John gives him a swift kick back into the underbrush, where he uproots a vine and whips a tree. It's a Yankee/redneck battle of dress and posture, with John's natty yachtsman's whites remaining unsmudged (fig. 24). Nicholas meets every encounter with such Calibanlike emotionalism: he throws himself in the dirt after a run-in with Halvard and sobs on the stairs when Nellie escapes his advances. What evens up villain and hero are John's mid-film hesitations and retreat to the open sea—a pattern of weakened resolution typical of Vidor's other "Johns," in *Love Never Dies, The Crowd,* and *Our Daily Bread.*

Figure 24.   Wild Oranges. *Yankee versus redneck.*

One of the keen tricks back in *The Jack-Knife Man* was converting the sinister second tramp—a younger, more tattered, more heavily bearded character, who slinks into the picture with all the villainous trappings as he steals the houseboat and the boy—into a different type altogether, a quick-witted, insouciant leader of the floating male family. The traditional melodramatic version of this can be found in Griffith's *The Ingrate* (1908), where a starving backwoodsman is saved by another, but the former's insouciance turns ever more vicious until the benefactor finds himself with a beartrap on his leg, swimming across the river for his life.

The confusions we noted concerning the rural melodrama motifs in *Love Never Dies* extend also to Vidor's revisionism on the subject of villains. The second husband, Joel, may be something of a brute in denying his wife the middle-class leisure—sunny afternoons with gramophones and flowerbeds—that she enjoyed with her first husband, the reportedly dead John. As Joel dies on the sand after throwing himself over a waterfall, he chokes up last words as if he had a fiendish life to expiate. But the worst crime he can recount is having told their mutual wife the truth about John's false "mother." With all the lies and denials elsewhere, it's a strange deed to be treated as dastardly. Probably the nearest traditional melodramatic version of *Love Never Dies* is Henry King's *Tol'able David* (also 1921), with its real villainy when Ernest Torrence and his rural trash family appear from nowhere to cripple David's brother and kill his dog.

Both *Tol'able David* and *Wild Oranges* originated in stories by Joseph Hergesheimer. If Nicholas's redneck rage fits more smoothly into Vidor's film than that of the Torrence character into *Tol'able David,* if it seems less an arbitrary eruption, maybe that's because it's part of a more self-contained melodramatic world. Hergesheimer, now forgotten, is not completely negligible (in 1922 he easily beat out Eugene O'Neill as the most significant new writer in a critic's poll by *The Literary Digest*).[26] Another of his stories, "Juju," where the man simply shoots the woman who tempts him, suggests a version of *Wild Oranges* where sexual fears aren't projected onto expendable others. In the film, John dawdles so long that even slow Nicholas can carry out his threats to kill Nellie's grandfather should she ever try to escape. And yet, psychically, the death of this projection of the defeated Old South is basic to the happy end, where she confidently takes the helm.

Traditionally, film melodrama was allowed to redeem itself by sensitivity of style or mood or symbolism. The action might not depend on fine-tuned psychology, but the fine tuning was there in lyricism and a sense of place. For example, Orson Welles's *The Lady from Shanghai,* plotwise pure melodrama, turns "poetic" by virtue of its evocative settings (an aquarium, a mirror-maze). *Wild Oranges should* reek of tactile sensuousness, but Vidor remains a jackknife movements man and is unwilling to slow his mise-en-scène down to the swamp water speed of the Hergesheimer-styled "atmospheric" titles. This is quite unlike the European line in poetic melodrama, where much soulful brooding and dawdling guarantees the merits of such classics as Louis Delluc's *Fièvre* (1921) and Dmitri Kirsanoff's *Menilmontant* (1926). Probably, its principal American contemporaries were von Sternberg's films, infiltrated, like *Wild Oranges*'s, with something Poe-esque and with strangely paralyzed, drifting heroes, quite literally in *The Salvation Hunters.* The most astonishing synthesis of the elements of *Wild Oranges* came in F. W. Murnau's *Sunrise,* with its brute action, drenching atmosphere, and starkly melodramatic types. Vidor settles for a softer, self-contained, but psychically vital, atmosphere such as dreams are made on. Around the "Georgia" bayou, we might come upon *The Tempest*'s sea wrack, but never Savannah.

Vidor's move up to the new conglomerate Metro-Goldwyn-Mayer in 1924 brought a sudden halt to both his idiosyncratic philosophy and his

Figure 25.   Vidor barbering Wild Oranges' *heavy, "Buddy" Post.*

wilder melodramatics. Modern difficulties in assessing his four MGM films before *The Big Parade* come less from any alien substance or style than from their relationship to a forgotten—and generally forgettable— cycle of Jazz Age flaming-youth pictures. While the three surviving titles show a certain flair, they merit only a brief survey as a mark of the leap Vidor made out of the MGM rut with *The Big Parade.*

The "Jazz Youth" cycle owed plenty to an older theme, the tease morality in the marital infidelity cycle. That started off as heavily anguished transgressions of Victorian morality, as per *Three Weeks* and *The Cheat* (both 1915), but turned ever lighter and brighter through the twenties, until the 1930s screwball comedy pushed flirtation, teasing, and marriage from the realm of social issues altogether (probably because sex appeal now suffused everyday style). As for the "Jazz Youth" cycle itself, in its classic Clara Bow form, its demise sprang less from the Production Code tightening of late 1933* than from the lifting of Prohibition that year or the Depression itself—both of which made hot-shot bands of drunk rich

---

* "The sanctity of the institution of marriage and the home shall be upheld. . . . Adultery and illicit sex, sometimes necessary plot material, must not be explicitly treated or justified,

kids less fascinating—and from a general assimilation of freer styles, in the cities at least. Even mere dialogue brought an embarrassing new reality to the cycle, as in Clara Bow's painful effort to keep up the mad college-girl pace in her first talkie, Dorothy Arzner's *The Wild Party* (1929).

The five adolescents in *Wine of Youth* (1924)—Vidor's first to go out under the MGM logo and self-described as his "exploitation piece"[27]— careen down the road, escaping from "conventionality" to the "freedom" of a back-country "trial marriage," looking like an icon of the Roaring Twenties: "We're doing the glorious thing!" A recurring bit of business in the early reels has a flask-swigging party girl finally shoved unconscious into the shower. As she unfastens her clinging dress, careful framing lingers on naked limbs. And when, at last, she walks tipsily down the front walk, a loose sweater strand caught by a merrymaker strips her naked yet again. Exploitation all right, of a pale enough sort, and overridden by a reassuring morality: "youth" has always been this way; or, if it hasn't, there's a conscientious parent somewhere. Vidor's several escapees from city constriction faced a more stark rural world a decade later.

His Hour (1924), Vidor's second in this early MGM group, actually picks up elements of the coy, anguished spirit of *Three Weeks*. Both were based on Elinor Glyn novels, hot-cheeked romances old-fashioned by the twenties. There's little telling what Vidor intended to make of the European sexual decadence of *His Hour*, as the preview original was used by Louis B. Mayer at a meeting of MGM film directors as an ideal example of the varieties of passion *not* permitted in MGM product. As it exists, the film looks ill at ease with sensuality. A prim British woman is kept on an edge of sexual fear by a handsome Russian prince (John Gilbert, in the first of his five silents for Vidor). He kisses her neck at their first meeting and lingers his tongue along her hand when she feigns sleep. Finally he's worked himself into such a state that he steals her off to his snowbound hideout to have his way. Glyn's style reaches its climax when the young woman grabs the prince's gun and points it at her own head: "Touch me again and I'll shoot!" (or as Glyn put it with even more brio in her 1910 novel, "Well, better death than this hideous disgrace")[28] (fig. 26).

Typically, both in Vidor's versions and elsewhere in this mid-twenties cycle of sexual experimentation and marital triangles, the more outlandishly perverse or comic infidelities were palmed off onto Europe. The tamer American Jazz Youth films usually justified their exploitation by

---

or presented attractively. . . . Undressing scenes should be avoided, and never used save where essential to the plot" (*A Code to Govern the Making of Motion Pictures* [Washington, D.C.: Motion Picture Association of America, 1933]).

Figure 26. His Hour *(1924). "Touch me again and I'll shoot!" Aileen Pringle and John Gilbert.*

working their way back to the marriage issue. Thus the "trial marriage" for Mary (Eleanor Boardman) in *Wine of Youth* is prompted by her parents' bad example—long-suffering mother tied to habit-ridden businessman, who grouches over bills showing evidence of his children's profligate ways. As in Mal St. Clair's *Are Parents People?* (1925), the only apparently incompatible parents are brought round by the apparent immorality of their daughter. But *tone* here is everything. Vidor's dourer morality is closer to *The Mad Whirl* (1924), where the hard-driving and -drinking son takes his cue from parents who seek to be his "companions in fun." They surround themselves with lounge-lizards and flappers, but end thoroughly shamed by a moral saloonkeeper (who bides his time through Prohibition selling ginger ale). Vidor, or his editor, has fun with the clever physical comedy of the party sequences and with Mary's quick disillusionment with her campout "marriage," but the stark confrontations within her family make this the most title-clogged of Vidor's extant silents. If F. Scott Fitzgerald keeps popping to mind as the single artist to transmute pampered Jazz Age flaming youth into lasting art, then perhaps Lubitsch's continental comedies are cinema's *Tender Is the Night*, while films like *Wine of Youth* or *The Mad Whirl* remain its provincial *This Side of Paradise*. Irony was never Vidor's forte.

His *Proud Flesh* (1925), like Herbert Brenon's *Dancing Mothers* (1926) or *Children of Divorce* (1927) with Gary Cooper and Clara Bow, deftly bridged European marital hi-jinx motifs with Jazz Youth motifs by *originating* the dark problems in bright Europe, then shipping all the principals to America for the expiation of the sins of the dancing parents. If the implication lingered that in some foggy way Europe was yet again to blame for troubles America had to set right, that must have gone down well enough in the isolationist years of disgruntled veterans and restrictive immigration. *Proud Flesh*, as Vidor's last in this cycle, does touch on some wider interests in its clashing of ornate Old World styles and manners against American common sense. And its image near the climax of a he-man hero doubled over in tears, cuddled by his mother, looks odd indeed within the cycle. That interest and that image find their context only in Vidor's next film, *The Big Parade*.

Avoiding the Old World scapegoat, *Wine of Youth* discovers a more typical contrast for Vidor between Jazz Age speed and the pastoral escape. Ever the city folk, the five "honeymooners" are initially more frightened by a cow wandering into camp than by doubts about their experiment. (Five, since Mary, sensibly enough, has taken along two prospective husbands.) The urban/rural contrast here is worked out in full with *Married?* (1926), where New York flapper Constance Bennett can retain her western land inheritance only by a sight-unseen marriage to timber manager Owen Moore. Slinky, languid Bennett and her enervated companion, smoking and slouching on a couch, mock their "exciting life—dance, gamble, drink"—"Any yawn." *Her* sham log-cabin honeymoon produces the expected Western film moral of bringing the effete Easterner to her senses—and into genuine passion. Vidor's film, after some appallingly coy hints of desire in one of Mary's prospective husbands' glassy-eyed grabs at her nightgown, is stuck, bizarrely, with Mary opting for marriage after witnessing her parents' bitterness: "What's intelligence got to do with love?" Or with movie scripting, one is ready to shout from the side aisle.

Vidor's contention that "there were so many inhibitions and restrictions that it really took the guts out of the idea" [29] of a trial marriage bears the marks of after-the-fact special pleading, considering what other directors were able to finesse. But in 1924 Hollywood *was* beating a retreat from the triple scare of the Arbuckle case, the Wallace Reid overdose, and—Vidor's own longtime interest—the William Desmond Taylor murder. MGM cut *Greed* (1924) for more reasons than mere length, as is hinted by surviving stills of the ostensibly naked ZaSu Pitts writhing in

Figure 27. Proud Flesh *(1925). Plumbing, European- and American-style. Elea-nor Boardman (top, in white) and Pat O'Malley.*

her tawdry bed of gold. The force of the new 1924 Production Code combined with the taste of Louis B. Mayer, nobody's favorite mogul, and doubtless took a fatal toll on MGM's entries in this sexual hi-jinx cycle. For Vidor, almost its only source of interest must have been removed when the censoring of *His Hour* showed that other ways, or other studios, or other eras would have to be found before again pushing passion to the limits of melodrama.

4

1925 to 1928

"Silent and Amazed"

Vidor made six more films before the coming of sound, all for MGM, all but one of which survives.

The Big Parade (1925) established both Vidor and MGM itself. He brought it in at a modest $205,000, but production supervisor Irving Thalberg, seeing its possibilities, assigned George W. Hill to expand it with night battle scenes not involving cast members. Vidor painstakingly supervised the cutting (down to twelve reels, still four longer than any of his previous films) and always spoke highly of Thalberg's support, both here and with *The Crowd* (1928)—even more personal in conception, but with production costs twice those of *The Big Parade*.

After the shooting, but before the release of *The Big Parade*, Vidor negotiated a long-term contract with MGM, publicly reported at $2,500 a week, in return for which he gave up his 20 percent interest in the film, a financial mistake as it turned out. After a pre-release screening, Lillian Gish had written Thalberg a note of praise, and when she soon after also signed a major contract with MGM, she asked him for "the director and the entire cast" of *The Big Parade*.[1] Thus *La Bohème* (1926) became Vidor's next assignment. This was to have been followed by a project variously titled *The Glory Diggers* or *The Big Ditch*, about the construction of the Panama Canal, scripted, as was *The Big Parade*, by Laurence Stallings. But, after much advance publicity, pre-production was halted and Vidor was assigned to a period swashbuckler—now lost—*Bardelys the Magnificent* (1926), of which he was "a little ashamed."[2]

After *The Crowd*, Vidor accepted the "request to do a favor for Mr. Mayer" by directing Marion Davies for her mentor William Randolph

Hearst's Cosmopolitan Productions (which had been releasing through Goldwyn and was now incorporated into MGM). Vidor may have impressed Davies or Hearst when he helped Fatty Arbuckle (then working as "William B. Goodrich") with direction of *The Red Mill* (1926). His three comedies starring Davies—*The Patsy* (1928), *Show People* (1928), and (after *Hallelujah*) the sound film *Not So Dumb* (1930)—each carry the dual credits of "A Marion Davies Production" and "A King Vidor Production," suggesting a clash of egos or lawyers, but all involved spoke well of the experience. By MGM's figures, *The Patsy* cost about $250,000 and grossed $617,000, for a reported profit of $155,000. *Show People* was an even bigger success. *Not So Dumb* failed to break even.

In 1924 Vidor had been divorced from Florence Vidor. Whatever the circumstances of their breakup, a 1922 film, *Souls for Sale* (apparently something of a precursor to *Show People*) has curiosity value for starring his next wife, Eleanor Boardman, as a smalltown girl seeking a Hollywood career who encounters real-life celebrities, including King and Florence Vidor. King and Eleanor's September 1926 wedding at Marion Davies' Beverly Hills house has become infamous as the scene of the disas-

Figure 28.   The wedding of King Vidor and Eleanor Boardman. Among the guests (from left): Louis B. Mayer (on knees), Samuel Goldwyn, Elinor Glyn (over Goldwyn's shoulder), Irving Thalberg, John Gilbert (second row, between Thalberg and Vidor), and Marion Davies (next to Boardman).

trous "surprise" double wedding involving John Gilbert and Greta Garbo, whose failure to arrive led to Gilbert's fistfight with Louis B. Mayer.[3]

Having made three successive films set in France without having seen it, Vidor finally set sail in 1928, accompanied by Boardman and guides Scott and Zelda Fitzgerald. In Paris, Vidor met Hemingway and Joyce, and returned to America only after growing disturbed over items in *Variety* that Hollywood was converting "100 percent" to sound.

The Big Parade (1925)

The hoopla at America's entry into World War I in 1917 catches even James Apperson (John Gilbert), aimless son of a factory owner. After whirlwind training, hurry-up-and-wait army life asserts itself. But billeting in a French village has its compensations for manure-shoveling duties. Apperson comes to know Melisande (Renée Adorée), their love overcoming cultural and language barriers and finally his girl-back-home scruples just as his moving to the front tears them apart. Apperson marches wide-eyed, flanked by his army pals Slim and Bull, but they die in trench fighting, and Apperson himself is shot in the leg. In a church-turned-hospital, he learns of battles in Melisande's village, but his limping, panicky search proves worse than futile. The despondent, snappish, one-legged Apperson returns home to an embarrassed father and brother, to a sweetheart who feels for him only duty—and to a mother who quietly, strongly, sends him back to continue his search. In a wide French valley, the two lovers run to an embrace.

Vidor saw *The Big Parade* as the story of an average American, neither overly patriotic nor a pacifist, who goes to the war "for the ride and tries to make the most of each situation as it happens."[4] The film must settle on a specific background, and Apperson becomes one of Vidor's privileged heroes. An amiable, spoiled idler (whose temptation to languor is symbolized by the hot towel over his face in a barbershop), James has remained perhaps more empty, certainly less responsible, but also more spiritually *open* than his joylessly industrious brother. If he enlists, it is without commitment, rather bemusedly, his decision sparked by the brash marching music that sets his foot tapping, by the expectations of his uniform-dreaming girl, and by herd feelings ("The whole gang's going over!"). (Perhaps his closest movie nephew is Dean Martin in *The Young Lions* years later.)

Jim loses the girl whose frivolous beauty had seemed right for him to his brother. In return he finds not, like some of his English contemporaries, "the rough male kiss of blankets," but a more robust and humorous camaraderie. Slim is a riveter, Bull a bartender, and all the exhilarations of social leveling are paraphrased (with a disappointing imprecision) by the broadest slapstick brawling. In searching for a makeshift shower, Apperson ends up caught in a barrel, almost the corniest image from the rustic end of slapstick.

His "sentimental education" is extended by Melisande, who, as woman, as European, and as working peasant, is his social and spiritual antithesis. A title honors "The Women of France," who plow fields in their menfolk's absence and are well worthy of comparison with America's log-cabin matriarchs. When playboy Jim snatches a kiss, she knocks him down, then kisses his hurt and picks him up, her response to his liberty-taking having been Amazonian common sense rather than puritan disapproval. Earlier, this Diana catches the men naked and laughs amiably at their embarrassment. Her straightforward puzzlement at Apperson's seducer moves (fingers toying along her arm) is an apt, and at the time necessary, undercutting of Gilbert's *His Hour*/*Merry Widow* persona. Absent from the film are the ooh-la-la village girls unleashed on the screen the next year in Raoul Walsh's *What Price Glory*.

It was the success of Maxwell Anderson and Laurence Stallings' 1924 stage version of *What Price Glory* that had prompted Irving Thalberg to gamble on Vidor's subject—so long as Stallings himself was involved. From Vidor's notion of a passive hero, Stallings produced a five-page scenario in the form of a memo to Thalberg outlining the plotline, but with emphases consistently lighter than in the finished film (fig. 29). Vidor appropriated the harsher image of a veteran returning with one leg not from Stallings' scenario but from his person (he'd lost a leg at Belleau Wood). Vidor's most sweeping change was to bring back Jim's mother, who is parenthetically declared dead in the early versions.

In the finished film, one fears at first that she loves her bad boy a little too indulgently for his own good: she tempts him to become a ladies' man and a mother's boy. He rediscovers fraternity, not with his soon-forgotten biological brother, but in the true sense with the riveter and bartender. And through the French girl he rediscovers his "other" father. As her grandfather reads letters from the front, his patriotically sported saber proves so obtrusive that the young doughboy falls backward off his chair avoiding it. The joke in this Griffithian scene is on both the nations and the generations. It's also the comic side of civilian war romanticism, soon to be given the lie in the mudfilled trenches. The letters home are not so much read as translated into swashbucklerese. (War romanticism's other side comes via Apperson's hometown girl, who's "thrilled" when "we" go to war, and later sends letters envying him the beauty of the now-ruined French countryside.) Loosely, the film can be said to move from this rustic comedy (which has its place, alas, in most of Vidor's

```
Memo:
   Laurence Stallings to Irving Thalberg
   First draft - Original story.

                    THE  BIG  PARADE

        Conrad and Jim Apperson are sons of Delane Apperson of
   Charleston, South Carolina.  They live in a fine old house with
   a wall and a wooden gate, located near the Battery, Old Man
   Apperson carries on a coastwise shipping business which has been
   in the family 150 years,
        Conrad at 25 has had three years in the business.  Tall and
   dark, he is the model son, Generous, filled with guts, handsome,
   careful, mannerly, restrained, he is conscious of his family's
   place in Charleston, and has every intention of maintaining it.
        Jim at 21 has attended five colleges in succession, carrying
   nothing home with him but his suitcase.  Jim is big and blond,
   completely irresponsible.  Hasn't a grain of respect for family
   traditions, and practises few fleeting manners of the old South.
        Conrad thinks the world of Jim, since the younger boy appeals
   to his protective instinct.  Jim in turn thinks the sun rises and
   sets in Conrad's left ear.
        The Appersons, father and son (the mother is dead) think the
   world of Jim, but they are worried as to his future.  He doesn't
   wish to work, hates the idea of staid Charleston society, thinks
   that as long as he will inherit enough td live simply it would
   be silly to work at a business which did not interest him.
        Only one person in the world has been able to make Jim do
   things against his own will.  She is Justyn Devereaux, the girl
   next door.  Justyn is 19. straight as a mast. pretty as a red
```

Figure 29.   The opening of Laurence Stallings' outline for The Big Parade. *His version of the climactic trench battle includes Apperson amiably arguing with the German over the merits of their respective supply lines. "I'll call for mine," Apperson says, "We have more food and medical supplies." Stallings stressed the two-brother buddy-focus, and worked it through to an ironic end. Industrious brother Conrad motors through France with his wife, Jim's old sweetheart, to discover Jim and Melisande settled into a peasant cottage. Each brother pities the other.*

Populist silents), through "realism" (that relative term), to an earned pathos. And this sequence with the grandpa and his sword reflects one unifying structure: rustic comedy predicts the harsher issues. It's by his undone puttee that Melisande recognizes Apperson as the comic man from under the barrel—foretelling the one-legged soldier to come. Even lying in the shellholes, his pals' jokes are blackly prophetic. Slim, a flower on his stomach, asks, "Am I dead yet?" No, not quite yet. The broad comedy serves less as release from the intensity of battles (as often in Ford) than as its prefiguration.

The baptism of fire in Belleau Wood can, if one so wishes, be read as the consummation of the mother's boy's manhood. If war is hell, it is also purgatory, a nitty-gritty initiation by everything an enemy can throw at one. The film might seem to celebrate an archaically clear-faced American marching boldly forward, enjoying an improbably charmed existence, any discomfiture on his face signifying nothing truer than ham silent acting. (We've seen some recent audiences take the film that way.)

The scene has other meanings. The boy is too dazed to be terrified, and he's the unbloodied volunteer—one typical of many—driven on to a cause that isn't his own.

Two things keep him advancing, rather than running, the course of action individualism would prescribe. (Such meanly sober logic is Apperson's brother's.) Individualism here is about discovering and proving moral fiber. So the film concentrates less on the army machine, of which Apperson has agreed to become a part, than on his open, soft, anxious eyes, asserting the fears against which he advances. The powers driving him on are "transcendental" in the sense of some rugged life force. Vidor's emphasis on the physical (the brawls, the tobacco chewing, the contrast of hot towels and naked embarrassment) is also an emphasis on the nervous will.

Earlier, the untried troops marching along the roads in orderly columns have been attacked by "Flying Fritzie." They scatter (the right thing, not quite for the right reason). They re-form. Hesitantly, morale—as a morality—asserts itself, a prelude to the march in Belleau Wood itself. The two sequences are anagrams of each other. The airplane-and-open-road scene is done in longshot, and stresses the *mass*, its disruption and re-formation (fig. 30a). (It was suggested to Vidor by William Wellman, who'd witnessed such scenes, and shot in Texas by David Howard, working from notes on tempo and positioning signed by the thirty-year-old Vidor as "Pops.") The forest scene, done in closer view, is all verticals, men and trees, and a continuing advance played off against a continuous fear (fig. 30b). On the road, the wounded lie rocking in pain; in the forest, they just fall. The mostly static camera in the aerial attack gives way to a *sostenuto* tracking. The contrast of elements—of space, of light, of visual tempi—is already montage, in Eisenstein's sense of a contrast of

a   b

Figure 30.   a: The Big Parade's *first battles. b: Tom O'Brien (Bull), John Gilbert (Apperson), and Karl Dane (Slim).*

elements. It's what Griffith was the cinema's first great virtuoso of. Montage theory apart, it makes sense from the showman's angle. By way of prologue to the march through Belleau Wood, one needs an establishing incident, but sufficiently different not to sap the shock of that climax. Hence an episode was devised that contrasts *all* the elements of the climax except theme. It's the showman's practice in which Eisenstein first noticed the "montage of attractions."

Although *The Big Parade* (like its English counterpart, Anthony Asquith's *Tell England*) was often assumed to be "antiwar," Vidor's comments at the time of release suggest a related, but different, view: war's horrors are the precondition of war's heroism.* "Antiwar" covers a multitude of positions, and *The Big Parade* (whose title is ironic but not all that ironic) follows a common feeling then, that one can be antiwar, but one has to fight just wars or wars of liberation (like the American Revolution). All the same, the film sets its face against cheap heroics, for though the raw doughboys proved their mettle at Belleau Wood, it also wiped that cocky smile off the Yank face. And Vidor's balance can be tipped the other way—Keisuke Kinoshita's demonstrably *pro*-war *Army* (1944) includes an extraordinarily affecting final sequence, lifted wholesale from the middle of *The Big Parade*, as Kinuyo Tanaka (like Melisande searching for Apperson) desperately seeks her son among the anonymous rows of departing troops.

The surviving reel from Vidor's *Bud's Recruit* (1918) hints that *The Big Parade* resembles the seven-year Hollywood wait for post-Vietnam mea culpas less than a stepping back from wartime propagandizing entertainment to a philosophical neutrality. *Bud's Recruit* previews many of the home-and-hearth elements in the later feature: a spoiled son confronted with war fervor, a brother in every way his contrast, an overly doting mother whom he favors over his sweetheart. Vidor's joke in the short is to make the adolescent brother a paragon of wartime virtues (disciplining younger kids, pushing away his dinner on a "meatless day") while mocking the hefty mother for her "peace society" and the older brother for shirking. It hints at what *The Big Parade* might have been had Apperson had less will, his mother less strength, and if Vidor had stayed with Walsh-like bellicosity.

What's surprising and new in *The Big Parade* is its focus on ordinary doughboys in a war that, unlike World War II, was generally chronicled via officers (in twenties fiction notably in *A Farewell to Arms* and *Pa-*

---

* "In the Great War many were wondering why in an enlightened age we should have to battle. I do not wish to appear to be taking any stand about war. I certainly do not favor it, but I would not set up a preachment against it" ("World War Pictured through Veteran's Eyes," *New York Times*, 8 November 1925).

rade's End). That focus follows naturally from the notion Vidor gave Stallings: "I was playing with the idea that the man caused nothing in this film—he only reacted. He only went through the war and observed it."⁵ In case so passive and noncommittal a hero sounds like Hollywood equivocation, it helps to recall Tolstoy's Pierre in *War and Peace*, whom Vidor made even more central to his 1956 version.

Although discipline as such is important (Apperson must march off in step while Melisande searches), the theme of a "company of buddies"— so carefully worked through the comedy, and kept distinct from a later stress on tough discipline—finds its moral consummation after Apperson's riveter buddy Slim returns from a foray carrying the helmets of those whom he has killed, trophies like scalps. There's a certain admirable exuberance, which can be mistaken for hubris, about Slim's quiet prowess as a killer. When he casually shoots a sniper out of a tree during their march through the woods and spits with grinning satisfaction, it's without pathological ferocity, more with satisfaction in a task well done. He's a *worker*, who likes to see his bullets, like his spit and his rivets, end up where he aims them. As he lies dying out in no-man's-land, the erstwhile playboy is inspired by a compound of self-sacrificial rashness ("greater love hath no man") and its antithesis, a revengeful rage. Disobeying orders, Apperson leaps out of his trench (fig. 31) in an act of insubordination later routine in Hollywood military movies, presumably to prove that the hero's acceptance of authority has not crushed his independent individualism. But the man whom he finds in no-man's-land is a wounded German—perhaps the man by whom Slim was killed. Apperson's humanity triumphs over his rage in a scene of sharp quick twists. He lights the German a cigarette, then bats away his face, which keeps coming to rest, doe-eyed, on his shoulder. The cigarette, which Apperson sensibly finishes after the German dies, reminds us that the poor little rich boy was taught the virility of chewing plugs of tobacco by the man he set out to avenge. It's oddly acid, flip, and eerie, quite unlike the shellhole dialogue between the soldier and the dead foe in *All Quiet on the Western Front*.

In this assertion of human compassion some might see a condemnation of war, others merely homage to the spirit of the Geneva Convention. And it's probably worth bearing in mind, cynically no doubt, that a substantial proportion of American spectators were of not-so-remote German descent, and, war fervor over, would appreciate Apperson's humanity. Before Pearl Harbor, Louis B. Mayer was insistent on showing a captured Luftwaffe pilot (in *Mrs. Miniver*) as a "good guy," thus forcing William Wyler to argue that given two Germans he could show one good one, but only one German meant he had to be a nasty Nazi. Presumably Mayer had German-Americans on his mind—and the German market MGM, unlike some other majors, still retained. All very relevant to *The*

Figure 31. The Big Parade. *John Gilbert as James Apperson, shouting vengeance. [Frame enlargement.]*

Big Parade. At any rate, the majority of spectators would admire *both* the murderousness of Slim *and* the forbearance of his friend. Vidor may be a post-puritan, but he's no party-liner about the "correct" attitude. Morality means different strokes for different folks. As Blake said, "One Law for the Lion and Ox is oppression."

Spiritual education always comes expensive, and can ask you to risk life itself. The war leaves Apperson shorn of a leg and embittered in spirit. "You look great, Jim, old man," enthuses his dishonest brother. "Don't try to kid me. I know what I look like," he replies. His mother, seeing her mutilated son, weeps, and her honesty elicits his confession of love for another woman: "There's a girl, in France . . ." She sets him to it: "Then you must find her. Nothing else matters." Truth, tears, purpose, faith: his mother's power flows into him. The audacious staging of the mother-son relationship (lingering mouth kisses; cradling him in her lap [fig. 32b]) echoes John Gilbert's mother fixation in Monta Bell's astonishing *Man, Woman and Sin.* If Apperson once seemed in danger of becoming merely a ladies' man, it was also because femaleness has a power his generously impressionable (not crudely "tough") maleness has the caliber to accept. His manhood now affirmed, and injured, and in the midst of masculine

a
b

Figure 32.   Mothers and sons on the Home Front. a: Bud's Recruit *(1918);*
b: The Big Parade *(1925).*

sycophancy, female strength revives the life force in him. His mother's
command could seem *merely* optimistic, but silent-film titles are never
literal. They're situational, and Mom's freedom from jealousy and xenophobia, and faith in her son's ability to defy his mutilation, would not be
lost on family audiences then or since.

Earlier, when Apperson's regiment moves off from its billet to the front
line, Melisande clings to the truck until he throws his boot from his pack,
as if he knows she will not let go without a token or totem. She clasps it
to her breast, sitting in the middle of the suddenly empty road (fig. 33a–
b). It's another prefiguring of harsher issues. Apperson sacrifices not a
mere symbol but an earthly "para-body" (which he may well need). It's a
prophetic sacrifice, since it's not just the Germans, but his search for
Melisande after he's hospitalized that loses him the leg. But what woman
inspires man to lose, she consoles him for: Mom sends her son, limping
but dogged, across French fields to find the woman. His body is *expendable.* The story is a ricochet of renunciations and sacrifices: by the son,
the hometown girl, the wartime love, the mother . . . *

The conclusion yields its fuller meaning when contrasted with Apperson's earlier attempt to find Melisande. Half-delirious, he struggles up
from bed while, behind him, a patient so crazy that he's been tied down (a
detail too savage for the British censor) is like his doppelgänger. But his
attempt is futile, and it is not until he has returned to mother that the
current can flow and, defying his new bitterness, he finds his beloved. It
shouldn't be easy, and yet it's as if by magic. The combination of delir-
ium, madness, and the church-as-hospital setting also creates an aura of

---

*An orthodox Freudian might read symbolic castration here (a leg for a phallus), but
the "English school" psychoanalyst Melanie Klein would read the phallus as a symbol for
the breast, first font of pleasure and power.

a   b

Figure 33.   The Big Parade. *Renée Adorée as Melisande.*

supernatural forces. Whatever their good works, Christianity, or the offi-
cial versions, are sterile compared with the family circuit that compels the
universe to respond, not perhaps with a miracle, but with a concession.
Desire is natural and supernatural. It's not so far from here to a certain
surrealism (cf. Ado Kyrou's *Amour-Erotisme et cinéma*),[6] nor indeed to
the vernacular vitalism to which Napoleon appealed when he asked of a
candidate for generalship, "Does he have *luck?*" Something in some
people's, not *will* exactly, but spirit, works with nature, like Orpheus
with his lute.

And this seems to us the film's overall sense, rather than an affirmation
of peace and love as against war (which, after all, enabled Apperson to
meet his Melisande). Why go to war? Because it's there—or, rather, because man must not just *test* but *perfect* himself one way or another. That's
not militarism. Apperson's indifference may well echo, not the audience's
indifference exactly, but isolationist feelings, which could mix with pacifism. Thomas Ince's *Civilization* was avowedly anti-interventionist, and
some such sentiment might well underlie the apotheosis of Griffith's *Intolerance,* with the masses of soldiers throwing down their rifles (both
were released in 1916, the year between the sinking of the *Lusitania* and
America's entry into the war). Even in 1918 Griffith's *Hearts of the World,*
made as a propaganda effort for the British, seems torn between its interventionist plot and pacifist titles. Vidor's *Bud's Recruit* (1918) is more
typical fare, but it would be surprising if isolationism, as a traditional
American attitude, never found accommodation on the screen. (And at
least one neutral's film, Holger-Madsen's *Himmelskibet* [*The Sky Ship*;
1918], from Denmark, seems on balance both pacifist and pro-German,
not surprisingly, if one considers where its main market lay.)

A book about family tensions in American movies is long overdue, but
it's likely that the "mother" theme, here as in many American films and

songs of the twenties, is not just a facile exploitation of sentimentality. On the contrary, it attempts a desperately "inspirational" answer to specific social tensions: between immigrant parents and would-be all-American offspring; between European peasant notions of family and American individualism; between a stable homeland and America's accelerating social mobility, notably the massive "internal immigration" from depressed rural areas to the cities. In a sense, the military life is just a special form of that. But the tensions between mobile independence on one hand and the family on the other may account for a certain American vehemence (sentimentality? hysteria?) in relating military machismo to family pieties. Vidor belongs to the same generation as that other great sentimentalist, Frank Borzage. In his documentary *Marines*, François Reichenbach mentions the vulgar-Freudian hypothesis that, if so many young Americans readily volunteer for harshly disciplined training, it's in order to assert their manhood against Momism. But film examples apart, it's obviously schizoid to assume, as in attacks on sentimentality we too often do, that by becoming part of an army you cease to be your mother's son, any more than you cease to be your wife's husband. Having raised the point, we needn't dwell on it. Certainly the triangle (mother-son-toughness) is obsessive in gangster movies like *Scarface, Little Caesar, The Public Enemy*, and *White Heat*, and in the first two of these the immigrant theme is absolutely clear. *The Big Parade* inverts the theme: the American WASP finds a foreign wife.

Just as Slim teaches Apperson to chew tobacco, so Apperson teaches Melisande to chew gum, and maybe there's a kind of "inheritance," or hierarchy of virility there (counterpointed by Slim's death and Melisande's biff-bang response to a mistimed kiss). Chewing tobacco, gum, and kiss are all initiations; and the series of oral acceptances is continued by the cigarette Apperson gives his dying enemy. As compassion, relenting, valediction, it's a *reverse* of initiation. The moment you become tough, you must learn not to be. It's the sort of "twist" that links drama as a dialectic with the paradoxes of philosophy (fig. 34a–d).

The change from baccy to gum also implies a switch from a nineteenth-century, he-man style to something softer, blander, slicker, more twentieth century. The chewing gum lesson finally eases Melisande into a successful kiss. It's a bit like some pioneer woman being tricked into a loss of integrity that is also a womanly fulfillment. The irony parallels the way Apperson is seduced from his aimless comforts into signing up—not by the justice of the cause, but by callow, fervid propaganda. And, by an irony about irony, that surrender to agitprop leads to faith. It was *right* for Apperson, and Melisande, to yield—even if the vulgarity of the means strikes a discordant note.

Figure 34. The Big Parade. *Oral acceptances; or, Melanie Klein at the Movies.
a: gum; b: kiss; c: tobacco; d: cigarette.*

This mixture of defeat and growth is the moral theme of the film. Apperson hardly thinks about being tough. The usual war-movie hero options—"death or glory," "be a coward or be a man"—don't arise as he drifts through his choices. That's not so far from Renoir, and Apperson anticipates the crippled, convalescing war hero Captain John in *The River,* who also finds himself tended by females, and takes new life force from them, though more chastely. Despite Hollywood's subsequent fixation on toughness, Vidor isn't alone in asserting the need for the "masculine" man's acceptance of female strength. However, *The Big Parade* is still remembered largely as an "antiwar" film, its family-sexual theme virtually forgotten. Is it America's evolution, or just the film-critical subculture, that's responsible for the eclipse of intimate roots?

If the comradely brawling strikes us as the film's real weakness, it may be because by the time we saw it everyone from Walsh to Ford had done all the variations on the Flagg-and-Quirt bit (a) more lyrically and (b) to death. Not that barrel-and-knuckle horseplay was our cup of tea to start with. What we like best about the pranks and pratfalls here is the studied mismatch of the faces and bodies between Karl Dane's "Slim" and John Gilbert. And Apperson's air of wide-open, friendly surprise at all this, and at his own involvement too. A passing tone in his eyes is oddly like Harry Langdon's. As Vidor's original notion suggested, Apperson is slightly bewildered, a little outside such European worlds, as are we in the audience. There's an actor/scenery mismatch too: John Gilbert in an Andrew Wyeth landscape!

The Belleau Wood sequence deploys what Vidor termed his "favorite obsession": "silent music."[7] It's an overall visual rhythm in which the cutting takes its cue from some strong rhythm of movement within the scene—so that it's an organic integration of mise-en-scène with montage. More than any American director, Vidor refines Griffith's quick movement-and-cutting into a counterpart of Russian montage. Three strategies: Eisenstein's, Murnau's, Vidor's. Murnau's cutting on the moving camera, on a steady "through movement" (a boat on a lake), melds with in-shot visual development (mise-en-scène again). Here, the Belleau Wood sequence, with its following shots of a rhythmically orchestrated steady advance, isn't so far from the Murnau style, whereas the air attack is closer to the in-shot aesthetic in Renoir and Wyler. Later, Vidor forgoes *both* cutting and camera movement for the three minutes of ensemble acting, unbroken even by titles, when Apperson demonstrates gum chewing to Melisande. It's as wise a bit of directorial restraint as any until Ford's extended two-shot of James Stewart and Richard Widmark on the riverbank in *Two Rode Together*.

In retrospect John Gilbert's association with Garbo imparts a further incongruity to his presence in the barrack-room world. But Gilbert was always willing to forsake, or subvert, his dashing-lover persona, as in his own scenario for Monta Bell's scathing *Downstairs* (1932). Vidor and Gilbert conspire in *The Big Parade* to undercut any such expectations— from Apperson picking his ear as his father lectures him to the flies on his face in the hospital. Gilbert's dark, lustrous, sensitive eyes suffice to give Apperson a sort of gallant femininity.

Apperson never loses his spiritual differences from his comrades, yet his contact with his spiritual antitheses—Slim, the deadly hardhat; Melisande, the peasant woman—is real. It is his having to bounce between such disparate milieux and values, between worlds signified by a hot towel, a funny barrel, and a crutch, that gives this film its crucial position—at the crossroads between the sleek toughness of Hawks, the robust toughness of Walsh, the male tearjerkers of Ford, the romanticism of Borzage, the bitterness of von Sternberg, the bouncy self-help of Wellman. *The Big Parade* charts a modern progress through a crazy world. Neither picaro nor pilgrim, Apperson drifts, marches, stumbles across a landscape he never made.

Figure 35.   The Big Parade.

La Bohème (1926)

In a left-bank rooming house in the 1830s live aspiring playwright Rodolphe (John Gilbert) and three equally impoverished artists, who survive by ingenuity and the benevolence of Musette (Renée Adorée). Above them in a drafty loft, the seamstress Mimi (Lillian Gish) is failing to eke out the rent. Rodolphe and Mimi's love blossoms with the spring. But her faith in his art provokes tragedy. To keep his inspiration unhindered, she toils nights to cover his editor's rejection of his hack work. He finally catches on, vowing to abandon his play and devote himself to nursing her back to health. But she flees into the fatal anonymity of factory work. Out of his "bitter despair" comes a "great play." On the night of his theatrical triumph, Mimi makes a heroic trek across the city, to die in her old room, near Rodolphe.

La Bohème has its defenders—and certainly its final reels are stunning—but it is hard to avoid a feeling that its plot sets Vidor a choice between two options—"bohemian" pretensions and Mimi's self-sacrifice—neither of which he admires.

For copyright reasons, the film lists its source as Henri Murger's *Scènes de la vie de Bohème,* though it switches between that, Murger's own dramatization of it, and Puccini's opera. Banished from the film is any hint of the teasing Mimi (in the novel) or of Rodolphe's scheming uncle, who wants a rich match for his nephew (in the play). The result is an independent Mimi, but so self-deprecating that she's half in love with death, a creature who (despite Vidor's claims) is close to Puccini's. If the playing is broad, perhaps influenced, after all, by something operatic, it needs only harsher light and angles to turn expressionist in the final sequences. A bright, low-angled light outlines the hook nose of an unconcerned doctor as he pinches snuff and pronounces that Mimi won't live through the night (fig. 36a). Perhaps overhearing, she pulls herself up for her last, dark journey across the city, dragging herself along by chains behind horse-drawn wagons (fig. 36b), and silhouetted struggling past featureless black spaces and De Chirico–angled high walls.

No other Vidor film has so self-conscious a painterly influence. It's a short history of fin de siècle French art: impressionism supplanted by expressionism. The spring picnic is a *déjeuner sur l'herbe,* with Mimi's nervous vivacity disrupting the tableau vivant; ballet dancers are beheaded with Degas framing from the theater box of would-be seducer Vicomte Paul, a foppish caricature out of Daumier.

If John Gilbert, in stills, looks like your archetypal ladies' man, his portrayals ripple with tensions between a certain likeable impishness, that soft-underbellied mother's-boy sensuality, and a half-disguised threat of something more ruthless and cunning. In *La Bohème,* his cute incorrigibility with his editor becomes a willful misunderstanding of Mimi's sacrifices—reinforced by his layabout friends ("These women! I never knew where Musette got her money either"). When his jealousy leads him to rip apart her carefully sewn finery and hit her across the face, the scene gets its power less from the stain of blood she coughs up onto rough

a   b
c   d

Figure 36.   La Bohème *(1926).* Mimi's Return Home. *d: On her deathbed, Mimi (Lillian Gish), with Musette (Renée Adorée) and Rodolphe (John Gilbert).*

floorboards than from Lillian Gish's projection of a *private* fear. Thus her escape from the roominghouse looks half like animal panic. Gilbert connects so compellingly with Renée Adorée in *The Big Parade* (as his few moments here with her Musette remind one) because of something mutual in their openness, in their strength as survivors. (That all three actors themselves proved just the reverse as survivors may show more than that you have to watch the dance, not the dancer. For the camera, a certain recklessness may translate as openness.)

. Perhaps it's not that Vidor distrusts self-sacrifice as such, so much as its needlessness here, and the disproportion of a life for a play (even from "the next Victor Hugo"). When Vidor holds nothing back in *Stella Dallas*, the persuasiveness of self-sacrifice is awesome, as, in other ways, are the death clutches of those postwar lovers in *Duel in the Sun* and *Ruby Gentry*. Passion vindicates all in those films. Mimi, too, has her passion, but interior and solitary anxiety is Gish's forte. Her fears of Rodolphe *are* justified, and make sense of her "generous deception." But the film comes really to life only with Mimi's dying struggle across town, a variation on Apperson's panicky struggle up from *his* sickbed and his final limping run across the French fields. Frank Borzage, with his sympathy for characters too weak for their world, might have given *La Bohème* a more stable hand.

No doubt *La Bohème* is more coherent from the angle of Gish's auteurism. In this, her first film for a major Hollywood studio, she supervised the script and overhauled costuming and rehearsal practices, much to the consternation of those used to the studio system. One need only place the film beside her second MGM project, *The Scarlet Letter*, directed by Victor Seastrom, to appreciate her control. Murger's and Hawthorne's novels have little in common but their completion in 1849. Murger's is an episodic chain of light immoralities, opposite in structure and intensity to *The Scarlet Letter*'s unrelenting fable. But both films stand or fall by Gish's conviction in her identical characterization: the self-sacrificial lover. The initial justifications for sacrifice in Rodolphe's "great play" and Dimmesdale's "good works" are forgotten next to the spectacle of Gish's endurance, which brushes aside equally the frivolity of Murger's Mimi and the passion of Hawthorne's Hester. While Seastrom's hard shadows and heavy playing are impossible to mistake for Vidor's flat light and buoyancy here, the two films arrive at identical symbolism—embroidery as Mimi/Hester's penance; woodland romp as their passion; caged birds as their emblems of fettered freedom.

When it comes to the final choice between self-sacrifice and artistic posturing, Vidor gives the edge to the latter, since it survives by resourcefulness, by literal monkey business ("What a man can't do, a monkey can," the artists discover in letting an organ-grinder's monkey hold out the beggar's cup to which they would never stoop). They survive by an ingenuity and insouciance entirely missing from Mimi's plodding all-nighters over the needle. Posturing is, at least, a joke among the artists themselves, as when the songwriter hits up Rodolphe for money by admiring his suffering eyes. Meanwhile, the rotund wife of the rooming-house superintendent takes Mimi in hand to advise the futility of her night work.

But commonsense solutions aren't the business of tragedy. The plot combines with the star-vehicle style to clear away obstacles to Henrik Sartov's soft-focus showcasing of Gish's heroism. Vidor's jackknife speed at times gears wonderfully with Gish's softer, fluttery kind of elaboration. Mimi, forced to resort to a municipal pawn shop for her month's rent, visually caresses each article of clothing with a little moment of hope, a smile, a half-attempt to speak its merit; then disappointment, resolution, and full circle back to hope for the next item—all with a gentleness undaunted by the faceless pawnbroker's brutally routine hands. Vidor sets up a tightly crowded mise-en-scène, and the chain of changing ideas in

Gish's face constitutes, in Eisenstein's profoundest sense, a montage of emotions. Charles Affron describes Gish warming herself near Rodolphe's stove, "turning around, exploiting the opportunity with a commitment that never suggests telegraphy or semaphore. The sign is clear, yet with nuance and timing it is broken up and reconstituted—the hands, the nose and the body ceaselessly redefine the space and the object—stove." Affron proceeds to eleven pages of admirable analysis of how Gish's acting and Vidor's continuity generate a series of surprises, contrasts, modulations.[8]

Griffith pitted Gish against outside evil—brutish fathers and unfaithful seducers. *La Bohème* does have a Griffithian pay-up-or-out landlord, and continues with Vicomte Paul's seducer complications, but the two are soon insignificant; and, with the play's wicked uncle missing, Mimi's fears can only turn inward to a sort of abstraction—Dostoyevski and class consciousness being too far away. Gish's careful nuances often rattle around in MGM's typically oversized and bright spaces (a problem Sartov overcame with Seastrom through spotlighting and shadowed backgrounds). Vidor's impatience over Mimi's sacrifice combines with MGM's visual denial of economic explanations to make her seem pathologically skittish. In place of Mimi running off at the first bark from Rodolphe's editor, it's easy to imagine a scene where Rodolphe talks him round into letting him keep his job, as we've seen him do before. It ought to be paradoxical that Gish's fluttery playing fits best with Seastrom's Nordic style, but in practice they balance out—he fashions just the right prisons for her panicky tours de force. Seastrom's *The Wind* becomes her masterpiece by shuttling her fears between a melodramatic seducer *and* pathologically projected phantoms. *The Scarlet Letter* suggests to us that *La Bohème* makes its best sense through an Americanized viewing of this Paris: Mimi's all-night hard work and fatal self-sacrifice is the harshest puritanical way out. His puritan streak notwithstanding, Vidor was too transcendent an optimist to look on Mimi's death without being irritated by its masochism.

The Crowd (1928)

John (James Murray) begins life with an indulgent father who means to give him all the advantages. But with his father's untimely death, he is precipitated down among the crowd. An obstinate, foolish, and admirable ambition sustains him in his office routine and through marriage to Mary (Eleanor Boardman) until, as his daughter lies dying, he convinces himself that she is only sleeping, and tries to quiet the traffic so that it won't wake her. But one can't expect to hush New York.

Demoralized, John loses his job and comes near to throwing himself in the path of a train, but is brought round by the open faith of his small son. He takes a job as a sandwich-board carrier, whom he had once, in his ebullient arrogance, thoughtlessly mocked. Dressed as a clown, he sports the legend: "I am happy because I always eat at Schneider's Grill." Visiting a vaudeville house with his family, he laughs at the pratfalling clowns with frank enjoyment, with neither bitterness nor superiority.

The Crowd belongs to an international wave of populist films, if we use "populism" in its film sense, as being about the *petits gens,* the lower middle classes and below. The cycle flourished from just before the beginning of sound until the mid thirties, when a mixture of economic stagnation and preparation for war shifted the emphasis different ways in different countries. Some German films—*Backstairs* and *The Last Laugh,* for example—tend to be too quickly subsumed under the label "expressionism," their other aspects remaining underrated. Much early populism may be grouped under "rural American" themes close to the political Populism of Vidor's first features; but Paul Fejos's *Lonesome,* Borzage's *Seventh Heaven,* and Vidor's *The Crowd* and *Street Scene* clearly belong to this wider international category. German populism also includes such fascinating films as *Berlin Alexanderplatz* (1931) and *Asphalt* (briefly reminiscent of Vidor in its bodily energetics). French populism remains the best remembered—with Vigo's *L'Atalante,* Clair's *Sous les toits de Paris* and *Le Quatorze juillet,* Renoir's *Toni* and *Le Crime de Monsieur Lange,* Carné's *Hôtel du nord* and *Le Jour se lève.* The same cinematic current was obscured by another label, "neorealism," after 1945, although Becker's *Antoine et Antoinette* indicates the continuance of the earlier strain. The late course of populism in the United States included such obvious descendants of *The Crowd* as *The Marrying Kind, Marty, Studs Lonigan, Christmas in July,* and *The Apartment,* the last two featuring the open-plan office of Vidor's film.

A particular motif of screen populism—the theme of the crowd—pervaded the cinema between the wars, for a variety of reasons (ranging from the European recognition that the poor are not a mob to the internal immigration within America from depressed rural areas to the cities). In Vidor's film, the crowd, while never exactly malevolent, intrudes—into a visual background otherwise quite blank—at moments of private distress. The first crowd clusters at the base of the expressionist staircase in John's childhood home as he catatonically learns of his father's death (fig. 40a). When, years later, his daughter has been run down by a truck—a victim of the city's weight and speed—the crowd, seen from above, is a vertiginous mass of heads pressing in toward the two (fig. 37a). The shot is hardly less disturbing than one identically angled and composed in Buñuel's *Un Chien andalou* of the same year, where a crowd gathers with

a   b

Figure 37.   The Crowd *(1928). One Death in the City: John Sims*
(James Murray).

commonplace curiosity around a girl poking a severed hand with a stick.
Little more empathy exists in Vidor's subsequent scene of the crowd
shoving behind John as he carries his limp daughter into their second-
story walkup (fig. 37b). Although Vidor attributes to New York none of
the positive cruelty that a thoroughgoing expressionist might have under-
lined, the scene still reads as: "With all the best will in the world, crowded
cities are pressure cookers of hysteria." Even at less traumatic moments,
as when oceanside sunbathers shout at John to stifle his ukulele and singing, groups of people can be as oppressive as the elevated trains that
rumble outside John and Mary's rooms.

The sense of the crowd as a dauntingly impersonal mechanism, swelling and subsiding in machine-speed routines, inspires Walter Ruttmann's
Berlin (1927), whose Hollywood equivalents are, amazingly enough,
such Busby Berkeley numbers as "I Only Have Eyes for You" and the
chorus-girls' aubade in *Dames.* What Ruttmann and Berkeley have in
common is a kind of semi-abstract cinema. Indeed, Berkeley qualifies as a
Broadway constructivist. What we think of as Berkeley's "visual choreography" is what Vidor called "silent music." And in both directors one
finds an inspired, unselfconscious eroticism born of a generalized exuberance. Berkeley ventures into social comment too, in the "Remember My
Forgotten Man" number in *Gold Diggers of 1933.* In *The Crowd* Vidor's
camera moves up an office building and then, to locate his hero, in through
one particular window among thousands—a device shared with Berkeley, as well as with René Clair. In *The Big Store* (Marx Brothers, 1940),
Tony Martin's rendering of "The Tenement Symphony" trivializes the
theme into sentimental operetta terms, only too characteristic of the
genre's decline in wartime Hollywood.

What distinguishes Vidor's film from its genre is the ways it captures everyday tensions of marriage and unemployment, the deadening habits in office routine, even the commonplace dreariness in romance. Only the slimmest of traditions existed for such an examination (although Paramount Studios generally, and even Vidor's first MGM films, found saleable satire in *upper-class* marriage), most prominently far back in the pre-Hollywood gag-formulas (as with the John Bunny/Flora Finch pairings and Edison's "Jones Family" series). James Cruze's comic *Welcome Home* (1925) satisfyingly enough reminds one how rare it is to expose marriage not via contrived issues but through an escalation of confined gestures of tension. *The Crowd*'s breakfast scene captures an undramatizable frustration, neatly displaced into tiny annoyances and angers— broken dishes, slammed cupboards, spilt milk (figs. 38 and 39).

While no blockbuster, neither was *The Crowd* an "artistic" write-off for MGM. It more than earned back its production, distribution, and advertising costs. Perhaps Vidor's entertainment secret was to infuse even commonplace anguish with a bouncy vitality that, as in his postwar excursions into *film noir*, gives the unhappy endings their exhilaration.

Figure 38.   The Crowd. *Eleanor Boardman and James Murray. Intertitle: "Your hair looks like Kelcy's cat!" [Frame enlargement.]*

Figure 39.   Intertitle: "Why can't you tell me when things are full?" [Frame enlargement.]

MGM, and Vidor too, were so nervous that at least seven different endings were written, at least three were shot, and it was offered to exhibitors with the choice of two. In the happy ending, John's advertising slogans have made him prosperous, and a joyous Christmas reunion gets even his awful in-laws to affirm great faith in his talent. Vidor was justifiably proud that only one exhibitor requested it. The film's source story, "The Clerk," written by Vidor with John V. A. Weaver nearly two years earlier, has the hero ending with modest independent success as a garage mechanic. Later in 1926, Vidor, solo, drafted a treatment called "March of Life" that followed John's suicide attempt with his ecstatic success as a real-estate salesman in charge of a suburban development, and ended with a strange coda of his death in satisfied old age. Troubled even with the final script, Vidor continued tinkering throughout the often improvisational location shooting, which may have led to the suspicious number of days Vidor is listed on location records as "ill," and resulted in anxious telegrams back to Thalberg from MGM's production assistant: "VIDOR UNCERTAIN WHAT TO SHOOT STOP CANNOT GET DEFINITE DECISION FROM HIM . . ."

Not that Vidor was breaking entirely new ground. Such location se-

a   b

Figure 40.   Expressionist and documentary perspective in The Crowd.

quences as John and Mary's ride on a double-deck open-air Fifth Avenue bus, where he mocks the little people below them, capture the grit of city life (fig. 40b). But streetcar sequences in the populist era frequently served as concise metaphors for city anomie, as in Hitchcock's *Rich and Strange* (1932), Augusto Genina's *Prix de beauté* (1930) or, in America, *Queen High* (1930). The shopgirl-jostled-on-subway scenes in two 1924 films, Allan Dwan's *Manhandled*, with Gloria Swanson, and Vidor's own *Happiness,* encapsulate everyday exasperations of urban existence into crisp gags. Such humor may be shadowed either toward sarcasm (as in Billy Wilder's tragicomic *The Apartment*) or cheerfulness (as in George Cukor's *The Marrying Kind,* which, sensitive as it is, renounces the depth its scenario makes possible). This common-enough entertainment device prevents realism from becoming too drab or depressing. While it may slightly vitiate some early passages in *The Crowd,* notably the honeymoon trainride to Niagara, it's sharpened by Vidor's characteristic energy and impregnated by all the latent possibilities established in the prologue. When the shift in tone comes, it is all the more devastating. On the whole, the gagsmanship formula serves to underline all the temptations into which *The Crowd* does *not* fall.

Its studiedly "average-life" storyline also retrieves dramatic tensions by balancing between styles, or rather by shifting among them with small visual surprises. If, as archetypal fable of "the man" and "the woman," *The Crowd* succeeds less well than the previous year's *Sunrise,* it's because Vidor won't make his locus of excitement and torment just "the city," exclusive of documentary specifics. In theory, there ought to be a ruinous clash between *The Crowd*'s expressionism and its documentary side. (Vidor occasionally used hidden cameras, which explains the perfectly puzzled double-takes from the "extras" who watch our hero's youthful dash through the streets.) But each has its primary domain—documentary shifting to expressionism when John's private oppression fills the world. City life has its own rhythms, which one can harmonize to or quixotically outshout, as several sets of parallel scenes underscore.

In opposition to the crowd stands the family. Without his son's and wife's faith, our hero would have ended as a wet spot between the rails (the same threat and salvation, apparently, as in Vidor's first feature, *The Turn in the Road*). Marriage brings out the best in Mary—who evolves from halfhearted flapper to resilient mother—though one can't say the same for John. He's more the passive victim than a creator of ad slogans. His single published work, "Sleight-O-Hand, the magic cleaner," is even worse than that winning slogan in Sturges's *Christmas in July*, "If you can't sleep, it isn't the coffee, it's the bunk." His impulsive first-date marriage proposal is inspired by a subway ad card, "You Furnish the Girl, We Furnish the Home." The identical slogan had inspired Buddy Rogers's proposal to Mary Pickford in her city-life film *My Best Girl* the year before. Impulsiveness is part of both heroes' energy, charm, openness—and, for Vidor, part of John's "typical" Americanism. If the film veers at times toward overgeneralization, there are still quirky qualifiers to the family-as-savior. John's extended family consists of Mary's hulky, bowler-hatted brothers and her bird-headed mother, who whisper and nudge over John's inadequacy. And the success story set against John's slide is no family man, but Bert (Bert Roach), a flapper-chasing pudgeball who starts at the next desk and ends as supervisor to John's supervisor. Beyond the nuclear family lie only the fringes of the crowd.

In its concern with morale, *The Crowd* parallels other films of the twenties, notably von Sternberg's *The Salvation Hunters, Underworld,* and *The Last Command* (1928) (another social fall: from czarist general to Hollywood extra). Such films may well have special reference to the difficulties of survival or cultural shock experienced by immigrants to the city, whether from across the Atlantic or from within America itself. A few other fascinating, forgotten American films of 1928—*A Ship Comes In* and *Jazz Mad*, for instance—are direct narratives of European immigrant ordeals in New York City. Mostly, however, the shock of big-city life is experienced by a stranger from the virtuously WASP Midwest. He poses fewer problems of identification, and perhaps, too, it was risky to criticize American city life from any perspective but that of an unimpeachably American type. One suspects that Emil Jannings' foreign angst (in *The Last Command* and elsewhere), like Rudolph Schildkraut's in *A Ship Comes In*, or Jean Hersholt's in *Jazz Mad*, or indeed like Garbo's, went increasingly against the American trend away from tragedy, which would be resented as "self-pity" if indulged in without some balance of hope or toughness. *The Crowd* certainly looks like a deliberate rejection of self-pity, its integrity lying in the extent to which it indulges it before the hero rallies his forces.

In Vidor's New York, immigrant childhoods undergo Hollywood's usual sea change upward into a native, middle-class detachment from the city. Still, an interethnic gang incongruously, but pointedly, appears in John's prosperous childhood, our hero undifferentiated on a fence-rail lineup. And he arrives in New York by boat, with an immigrant's wide-eyed enthusiasm over the skyscrapers (like the Eastern Europeans in the opening shots of Vidor's *An American Romance*). A rumpled and sad-eyed character behind him warns: "You've gotta be good in that town if you wanna beat the crowd." Like others briefly glimpsed later as John searches through train berths for his bride (a fat wife with two kids, a graybeard sleeping alone), this forgotten man seems one nightmare out of his possible futures. John fends off the curse of this ancient mariner with "All I need is an opportunity." But when he's fallen to his nadir, it's some-

Figure 41.   Employment line in The Crowd.

one else who chants that mantra with job-winning enthusiasm, and John whose face and dress double for the earlier specter. By its end, the film comes round to scenes rare enough even after the Crash: John, having recovered his will, fights for a place in job lines (fig. 41) and displays his juggling skills to win the sandwich-man position. Thalberg found the working title *One of the Mob* too suggestive of "a capital-labor conflict"—though that was the title-card that had introduced Swanson in *Manhandled*. (MGM first publicized the film as *The Mob*, but may have switched more out of concern for John Galsworthy's right to the title.) In the finished film, "capital" remains justly invisible, but Vidor does reduce the desk set to an assembly line and brings on those unemployment queues.

As with *La Bohème*, it's not the realism but the moments of expressionism that now come most unexpectedly. This strain in twenties Hollywood was stirred by several factors, among them emulation of the German art film and the influence of expressionist theater on all the dramatic arts. It may also have been owing to the connections between an individualist romanticism (whose middle- and lowbrow forms loom so large in the American cinema) and expressionism—if that's considered as romanticism shorn of its individualism, but still concerned with the cosmic in man's spirit, at bay against a stifling society. The rough pattern continues when the *film noir* evolves its tight-lipped expressionism to evoke the city's pressure on such deviant idealists as Raymond Chandler's Marlowe.

Nonetheless, American cinema expressionism remains relatively "deadpan," for expressionism proper requires an interaction of individual, social, and philosophical tension that Hollywood optimism and individualism restrict to certain mood-states or genres (horror films or private-eye thrillers). A rhapsodic expressionism appears only fitfully, as in *The Informer*, John Ford's study of guilt in war-torn Ireland. Orson Welles, in particular, blurs the boundary between lyricism and expressionism by studies of megalomania that can be taken as liberal, but also Nietzschean, criticisms of American ambition and individualism. With their expressionist staircases, *The Crowd* begins roughly where *The Magnificent Ambersons* leaves off: an oppressively well-to-do family's willful young scion gets thrown into the world, gets his comeuppance, and learns to make do.

While Welles is fascinated by a gigantic life force in hollowness or decay, and presents attained success as somehow monstrous, Vidor is more likely to celebrate normal parental love that seeks to bestow all the advantages upon its children. The ebullience of John's father is reflected in his prosperous station, normally enough, given a Horatio Alger optimism about worldly success. And the son shows the same energy and resilience, as well as an arrogance that, if it's a flaw, is a normal and not unlikable one. Struck by misfortune and then tragedy, it modulates into philosophic acceptance, a profounder spiritual fulfillment. It's "inspirationalist" rather than "reformist" in transcending the jealousy, bitterness, sadness, or protest other artists might feel appropriate. But this ultimate optimism is achieved after too much tragedy to be complacent. It's easy to see why Vidor's affirmation should have meant so much to Billy Wilder, Hollywood's most scintillating cynic.

It's a tribute to Vidor's daemon that he should at a glance have recognized his lead actor in James Murray, an inexperienced extra. Murray's life story exemplifies a systematic negation of Vidor's philosophy—with his defensiveness, apathy, and drift to a bum's condition, until he drowned eight years later in an accident or suicide, in Manhattan, aptly enough. It's as if something in his soul never recovered from the lowest point of John's depression. Nor could Vidor himself ever quite let go of *The Crowd*. In the sixties he worked on a contemporary sequel, *Mr. and Mrs. Bo Jo Jones* (eventually made without his participation as a telefeature). In the early seventies he tried to interest producers in another update, *Brother Jon,* and in a biographical film about Murray, *The Actor*.

It's not so paradoxical to cite the negation of a film's philosophy by its leading actor as an enhancement of its authenticity. At least it fits a neo-Freudian logic: your repression is your inspiration. But perhaps the common factor between Murray and "John" is just a certain recklessness, to which alternate courses were open. Perhaps, too, it was this that Vidor, most physical of directors, recognized at a glance, just as he insisted. What's love at first sight but the recognition of mind revealed in body and gesture?

Nothing in *The Crowd*'s ending (everybody laughs together) denies an earlier title-card: "The crowd laughs with you always . . . but it will cry with you only for a day." It's less a communal spirit than all of us being in the same boat. John's swift emotional reversal leaves a residue of despair, just as his flip from marital discord to bliss on hearing of his impending child remains troubling. One has to view the film as a fable of typicality not to find something disheartening in his sandwich-man future. Has he achieved fraternity in back-slapping his vaudeville-house neighbor? Was he then arrogant in his annoyance at the mass-deformed minds spewing pointless variants on "Washin' 'em up, eh?" in the company bathroom, like Tocqueville's worst nightmare about where American equality was leading its workers?[9] Qualms about the ending Vidor finally settled on don't deny the film's force—just the reverse. Its force is such that its ending can only purvey a momentary euphoria, which grows troubling in retrospect. *The Crowd* dissects the common man's pain with delirious integrity. In doing so, the film is rare in an always too rare genre.

Figure 42.   Shooting The Crowd *at Coney Island.*

The Marion Davies Comedies: *The Patsy* (1928), *Show People* (1928), and *Not So Dumb* (1930)

Vidor is hardly remembered as a director of comedy. But, with his feel for rhythm and the gestural, he could have been up there with Cukor, Sturges, and Minnelli. It was his bad luck to work the genre before talkies, and to have Marion Davies as his lead. Still, his three films for Davies converted her from heavier roles in period romances into a touchingly resilient screwball comedienne.

In even the best of her earlier films, the dramatic challenges tended to highlight her limitations. Sidney Franklin's *Quality Street*, on the *New York Times*'s ten-best list for 1927, is crafted to showcase a nonexistent range—Davies ages into a withered spinster, who rejuvenates by impersonating her niece. The loving close-ups are to little effect: for happy, we get prancing; for heartbroken, she throws herself face down on the floor. One can understand why Davies remains fated to be best known through Orson Welles's infectious slander as the talentless tootsie "Susan Alexander," foisted onto the opera-going public by her Citizen Kane, William Randolph Hearst. In Vidor's films, her vitality is her healthy defense against Kane-styled pretensions in high society and art.

Figure 43.   Marion Davies and King Vidor, 1928.

Figure 44.   The Patsy (1928). Marie Dressler and Dell Henderson.

Film historians' emphasis on the more stylized extremes of silent comedy (slapstick or Lubitsch) has tended to eclipse the mainstream of straightforward comedy that dips good-naturedly, but not unpointedly, into satire and near-drama—*The Patsy, Show People,* and their ilk. Vidor's first trick with *The Patsy* was to take the well-received drawing-room comedy of a few years earlier and, by casting Marie Dressler and Dell Henderson as Davies's parents, infuse a tradition of knockabout farce. Dressler and Henderson had been out of film acting for a decade before returning in 1927 and 1926 respectively, but both here display the broad gestures and timing mastered under Mack Sennett at Keystone. *The Patsy*'s Cinderella situation lends itself to all manner of treatments: an upper-middle-class family with aspirations to gentility push forward one daughter at the expense of the other, Pat (as in "patsy," played by Davies), whom they consent to drag along to yacht club dances but assign kitchen chores when prospective husbands appear. With more stress on family discord, it could resemble Mal St. Clair's *Are Parents People?* (1925); with more slapstick, it would presage Jerry Lewis's *Cinderfella* (1960).

Pretensions to status are deflated here by the family stepping not so much beyond their social station as beyond their physical limits. The rich playboy has a magician's deftness (twirling plates of crackers, catching dropped saucers in mid-flight). It's a smart skill (the rich aren't subhuman) *and* the physical correlative to his superficiality. The family, with the exception of the mean-spirited sister, are endearingly clumsy. In their mutual lack of pretension, Pat and her father share a bond of put-upon stupor that varies the film's pace while establishing its humanity—freeing it from a couple of the hazards of silent comedy. Likewise, the handsome object of the sister's rivalry is made worthy by his architectural dreams ("gas, electricity, sewers!"). Rolling out his blueprints in myopic ignorance of romantic schemes, he's lightweight brother to the builder heroes of *Love Never Dies, Proud Flesh, An American Romance,* and *The Fountainhead.*

The bulk of the film is a broad comedy of manners, of thwarted societal aspiration. Vidor choreographs the family's pre-dance preparations like a prizefight, the three women's heads bobbing for a spot in the mirror, Pa hoisted off his feet by Ma's energetic yank at his bow tie. When they arrive at the yacht club, one adept shot brings the relationships together. The camera dollies with the four down a long aisle, Pat traipsing in a too-long Spanish shawl passed down from her sister. Ma, distracted by greeting others with absurd (for Dressler) little finger-waves, steps on Pat's shawl and pulls it off; Pat turns round, slamming into the steamroller bulk of her mother, who's annoyed at her clumsy daughter; Pa saunters off unaware, the sister haughtily, as a waiter stoops for the shawl; and Ma turns with increased disgust to Pat: "Don't you know it's not good manners to be polite to a waiter." The title comes as topper, not an interruption, to the flow of physical comedy.

The Patsy's stage origins may account for the desperate look of its few exteriors and for the positive *lack* of sound. *The Crowd* could signify intrusive city-life cacophony in perfectly satisfactory ways. Here Pat tries for "personality" through self-help guides that require terrible title-card one-liners ("Always remember—Nature gives us many of our features, but she lets us pick our teeth"; "No thank you, Mr. Smith, work is the curse of the drinking classes"). Davies' impersonations, well-known San Simeon entertainment—here Mae Marsh, Lillian Gish, and Pola Negri— are amusing enough, but in a context considerably more forced than they would have been had Vidor saved them for *Show People* or *Not So Dumb*.

Stuck with a stage play he couldn't bear to finish reading, Vidor enlisted his new companion Wanda Tuchock (credited writer on five of his next six films) to help revise *Show People,* taking inspiration from the career of Gloria Swanson. Here Davies is aspiring starlet "Peggy Pepper," who begins as a butt for slapstick, rises to greater "artistic" dignity as "Patricia Pepoire," and is recalled to her down-to-earth senses when Billy Boone (William Haines), an actor she left toiling at the two-reeler treadmill, catches her in the face with a stream from a seltzer bottle (as a substitute for custard pies, in deference to Hearst's objections).

While the Hollywood setting generates the assumption of glamor, Vidor wryly documents the trash intruding on the high style, the grind of work behind the lightest slapstick. Hollywood is not exactly hoorayed for, but, given contemporary criticism of its immorality, it's no hothouse of folly either, just a sort of small town where all the usual moral flaws abound and get their usual retribution, or forgiveness. There's a wonderfully antisatirical, anti-Pirandellian scene where MGM stars, lunching at the MGM stars' table, all behave just like their screen selves. You don't have to get a Ph.D. in self-reflexivity to chuckle at the irony. Especially when Marion Davies as Peggy Pepper stares at Marion Davies as Marion Davies, and is visibly unimpressed. Earlier, Peggy and Billy linger in a moviehouse after the premiere of their Keystone-like comedy, and catch Vidor's (now lost) *Bardelys the Magnificent* (1926). When Billy mocks its riverbank love scene as "punk drama," Vidor isn't putting him down for it, nor demystifying his own movie, but acknowledging a reasonably down-to-earth viewpoint (figs. 45 and 46). Vidor can laugh at "himself," just as do Marion Davies and John (in *The Crowd*).

Southern belle Peggy and her father, Colonel Pepper (Dell Henderson again) have driven straight across the country from Georgia (as Vidor had from Texas) into this "golden spot on the map called Hollywood." Aspiring film actors wait outside the casting director's office, all slumped,

a   b

Figure 45.   Show People *(1928). William Haines (Billy) and Marion Davies (Peggy Pepper). Billy: "What do you want to see a punk drama for? Come on."*

a   b

Figure 46.   *Peggy: "That's the kind of acting I'm gonna do some day. That's real art!"*

patient or passive, in contrast to their peppy outfits (cowboys, strong-men, even a dog—with its head bowed). But spunky Peggy and her pa step right up to the hatch, won't take no for an answer, and do their stuff. It's all very Harold Lloyd in principle, not that Lloyd in *Movie Crazy* dwells on the distinction between laughter *at* or *with* him. Like Lloyd's, Peggy's stuff is as bad as bad can be. Still, her demonstration of different emotions ("Meditation," "Passion," "Anger," "Sorrow," "Joy") has its points—like its resourceful use of an unfolded handkerchief to corre-spond to a cut, and the casting office hatch as a close-up frame. It's such a mixture of the ingenious and the awful that the casting clerk can't help but stare, boggle, laugh, and let her in. All those losers might be very tal-ented, but talent without initiative is nothing, whereas initiative without talent can snatch a chance to prove itself something it didn't know it was (in this case, awful enough to be amusing). She gradually becomes good enough for Hollywood hokum ("Ah, my brave toreador, in all Spain there is none more skillful with the bull"). For Capra's slickness and Cukor's fluid warmth, Vidor substitutes a vital resilience from which a certain ruthlessness emerges. Yet Peggy and her father, each lost in a private pretension, also have a quiet patience, as if even self-centeredness could be a strength. In the end, inspiration and delusion are heads and tails.

Here, pretentiousness is Hollywood's main occupational hazard. It is the vice of Peggy's courage; it corresponds to the callowness that is the debased form of John's eventual resilience in *The Crowd*. With her pretentiousness comes languor, Vidor's most consistent emblem of moral defeat. Alongside "Andre" (formerly Andy, a waiter), her delicate new beau from "High Arts Studio," "Patricia Pepoire" lounges through a gossip interview until, puckering her mouth Swanson-style, she becomes too "fatigued." The line between an occupational hazard and criticism of a system (creative or social) is bound to be hazy, but Vidor's interest centers on the individual's response. In *Show People*, a *work*place like any other (except in being Vidor's) reconciles the individual to his community ("Take it on the chin," Billy advises Peggy after the shock of her first slapstick scene. "Success in this game means work"). Social criticism is secondary, so long as the system is free enough to allow individuals their choice, including the choice of opting out. Vidor's response to his workplace in 1928 could hardly be further from von Sternberg's in *The Last Command*, where the crowd of movie extras is exactly as bitter, and as lacking in freedom, as the prerevolutionary mass it impersonates. In the post–World War II period Vidor's concern moves nearer to social criticism, without quite arriving at it. But Vidor loves to notice how life high and low offers protections against pretentiousness. The commensalism of the stars' lunch together at the same table is one. (When we're all stars, no one is.) Vidor's affable ironies about *Bardelys the Magnificent* are another. And so is the slapstick director's shout to Billy after he has run into "Patricia" (on location for a French swashbuckler like *Bardelys*): "Come on, Billy—forget the sob squad and jump off that rock." Here, only the comic is consistently himself. His openness is communally reflected in "Mr. and Mrs. Audience" at the wildly successful preview of the slapstick feature (a scene that itself reprises the acceptance in *The Crowd*'s final emblem of audience hilarity).

Location shooting on the High Arts Studio's riverside love scene is disrupted by Billy's troupe's amazingly comic chase, where everything runs down the road, including a laid-out corpse, anticipating the more Boschian flights of Tex Avery (although this was, of course, the era of the necrophilic Fleischers and the great Ub Iwerks). There's such puncturing of filmland's pretensions in *Show People* that MGM's "Ars Gratia Artis" end logo comes across this time as somebody's smart-ass irony.

The story of *Not So Dumb* combines the social striving of *The Patsy* with the Hollywood satire of *Show People*. It must have looked a safe bet. But Davies's gifts, in mime and parody by mime, get suppressed in this early talkie. Her voice, at least as recorded by early equipment, is strident, though it doesn't jar with the drive-you-to-distraction persona established in the earlier comedies.

Not So Dumb, based on George S. Kaufman and Marc Connelly's *Dulcy* (also filmed in 1923 and 1940), is an early screwball comedy, unrelentingly paced and not yet in the classic mold. For all the technical advances in the half year since *Hallelujah*, in moving the camera and cutting within dialogue, Vidor's second sound film is never more than a competently transcribed stageplay. With too many medium shots constricting the more varied silent continuity, Davies's charm looks panicky. She plays Dulcy, a scatterbrain who one weekend fills her Los Angeles home with assorted quirky types and a certified lunatic (Donald Ogden Stewart in his single feature-film performance, one that may have convinced him to stick to writing). Her complicated scheming involves aiding her fiancé by marrying off his financier's daughter. All works out for the best, but despite her plans, belying the film's title.

Much as *The Patsy* is almost Marie Dressler's film, *Not So Dumb* gets stolen by Franklin Pangborn, in sporty knee-pants and argyle socks, as a babyfaced but self-important scenario writer, marked by Dulcy for the financier's daughter: "I beg your pardon, not 'scenario writer,' 'scenarist' really. . . . Yes, it's the more modern term. The scenarist of today is far different from the scenario writers of yesterday." What furthest exasperates the business-types is Pangborn's two-hour recounting of his upcoming picture, *Sin*, complete with cross-cutting pretensions: " . . . and to keep up the symbolism to the end, just as Jack and Coralie are kissing in Chicago, we show Marc Antony kissing Cleopatra in ancient Egypt, and George Washington kissing Martha Washington in Mt. Vernon, and so at the end of the dream trail we fade in to a long shot of Jack and Coralie once more in their South Sea bungalow with the faithful old Tootaheva waiting to greet them in the sunset, and fade out." With Pangborn disheveled and sweat-drenched by his high-art ordeal, it's quite the funniest bit in the film.

But it is amusing with none of the complex mixture of understanding and undercutting in *Show People*. *Not So Dumb* is recognizably a New Yorker's satire, a theatrical shot at the movies. And the *Intolerance* joke was staler by 1930 than it must have seemed on Broadway in 1922 (notwithstanding such ponderously cross-cut items as Curtiz's *Noah's Ark* [1929] and De Mille's *The Road to Yesterday* [1925]). Of Vidor's three films for Marion Davies (rather than vice versa), *Show People* remains the enduring success. Its smooth nuances, sharp characterizations and subtle self-consciousness allow it to be seen sixty years later with very little "making allowances," even of the sort one practices unconsciously.

5

1929 to 1935

"Looking Forth on Pavement and Land"

Vidor returned from Europe in 1928 worried about this new rage for talkies. "KING VIDOR DECRIES DIALOGUE FILMS," shouted a page-wide banner across the July 14th issue of *Motion Picture News*. "Sound pictures, those with dialogue that runs continuously, will do away entirely with the art of motion pictures," he predicted, while admitting that his months away made him "hardly qualified." But in August he completed his story for *Hallelujah,* and in an October radio interview in New York (where he was scouting black actors), he had converted: "There are all kinds of new developments and improvements just around the corner."

However, MGM was the slowest major to adopt such developments, with the result that *Hallelujah*'s location work in Tennessee and Arkansas was filmed silent and work begun even before Vidor could determine if the added sound would be on Warners-style Vitaphone disc or Fox-style Movietone film (the choice of which affected the framing aperture). He circumvented Mayer and Thalberg by taking the proposal for an all-black film directly to Nicholas Schenck (president of Loew's Inc., parent company of MGM), and it was accepted only after Vidor deferred his paper salary of $100,000 against any profits. (He was still writing MGM for correct accounting and payment in 1981!) Despite his promotional tour, there was spotty distribution in the South. In the thirties, Vidor briefly directed for a black theater group in New York, but, in spite of his efforts, he could never put together financing for another black film, and felt forced to reject Major Frank Capra's offer to have him direct *The Negro Soldier,* which would have interrupted his work on *An American Romance.*

Following *Not So Dumb* (1930), he was allowed another long-desired project, *Billy the Kid* (1930), the first movie version of this much-filmed legend and one of a cycle of experiments that year in 70-millimeter wide-screen photography. Authentic in its New Mexican locations, it was compromised in its casting. Vidor left MGM for the first time since its 1924 inception for Elmer Rice's *Street Scene* (1931), one of four films he directed in the thirties for independent producer Samuel Goldwyn (who had severed his connection with the old Goldwyn company before Vidor's silent films there).

Back at MGM, Vidor was assigned what he regarded as Frances Marion's "foolproof story"[1] for *The Champ* (1931), which allowed him to toy with improvisation and a more fluid acting style. RKO's new production chief, David O. Selznick, persuaded his father-in-law, Louis B. Mayer, to lend him Vidor for *Bird of Paradise* (1932). During its Hawaiian location shooting, plagued by storm delays, he began an affair with the film's script clerk, Elizabeth Hill. Eleanor Boardman was granted a divorce in 1933. Hill became Vidor's close collaborator on several scripts and even, uncredited, on direction. They married in 1937, after several years of rocky romance.

Following *Cynara* (1932), an unfaithful-husband drama for Samuel Goldwyn, came what we've labeled "the back-to-the-land trilogy": *The Stranger's Return* (1933) for MGM, Vidor's own production of *Our Daily Bread* (1934), and Goldwyn's *The Wedding Night* (1935). The farm cooperative idea that became *Our Daily Bread* was turned down for MGM by Thalberg and then by each of the other majors. Charlie Chaplin (who also helped revise the script construction) secured a pre-production release contract through United Artists. The relatively poor box office for these three films (and others in the post–*State Fair*, rural-life cycle) prompted *Variety*'s famous headline "STICKS NIX HICK PIX" in 1934. Not only did the midwestern "sticks" ignore these pictures, but the West Coast box office was particularly poor for *Our Daily Bread* and was hardly helped by a Hollywood premiere introduced by the socialist Democratic gubernatorial candidate, Upton Sinclair. Vidor shot the film on a self-financed budget of approximately $150,000. His claim that he "just about broke even"[2] is true only if one leaves out of account payment to himself.

Hallelujah (1929)

Zeke (Daniel L. Haynes) lives with his parents and siblings in a ram-shackle hut in South Carolina. When he goes upriver with a younger brother to sell the cotton crop, Zeke meets up with Chick (Nina Mae

McKinney), who rapidly presuades him to gamble his money away to her lover, Hot Shot. Zeke won't let his family be robbed so easily. But his very courage in struggling over Hot Shot's gun helps to get his brother accidentally shot. Zeke returns home with only a corpse to show for their year's work. Plunged into an ecstasy of grief and guilt, he discovers a vocation as a revivalist preacher. Chick comes to sneer and finds herself stirred. After Zeke has baptized her in the river, the two elope, Zeke finding work in a sawmill. Chick is bored by her day-long solitude and her man's poverty and fatigue, and she abandons him when Hot Shot returns. Zeke pursues them; the carriage sheers off a forest road. Chick, injured in the crash, dies in his arms, and he strangles Hot Shot after a chase through the swamp. Zeke serves his prison sentence and returns to his family—all passion spent, all crime purged, his conscience cleansed, strumming his banjo.

Vidor's long-cherished project about southern black life could only be realized when the advent of sound, the Broadway success of Mamoulian's *Porgy*, and word of a similar project at Fox (*Hearts in Dixie*) persuaded MGM to gamble on the popularity of spirituals and jazz as the film's accompaniment. While it both is and isn't a musical (since music accompanies rather than expresses most of the climaxes), *Hallelujah* initiates

Figure 47.   Cast and crew of Hallelujah *(1929).*

both Hollywood's sideline in "Negro" religiosity (*Green Pastures, Cabin in the Sky*), on the one hand, and its sexual operettas à la *Carmen Jones* on the other.

The cotton-picking black folk, contented on their little patch of land, don't carry Uncle Tom overtones, for Vidor celebrates the same life in the enterprising white community of *Our Daily Bread*. Even had he never made that film, the day-to-day anxiety and exhaustion of agrarian independence is encapsulated in Mammy's nightly whispered "Thank God" for her family safely at rest, and its seasonal uncertainty is paraphrased by a major plot point (the loss of crop dollars to city folk). If *Hallelujah* is to be faulted, it is for the *complete* exclusion of whites, even at the prison, and the subsequent imprecision about the family's relationship to the land they work. (Their poverty suggests sharecropping, but any owner share is omitted from the documentary tracing of cotton from field through gin and baler to riverboat.) The contrast of rustic frugality and slick cheaters corresponds to the city-country dichotomy in innumerable American films (from such Griffith one-reelers as *A Child of the Ghetto* through *Woman of the World, Sunrise, The Lights of New York*, and *Mr. Deeds Goes to Town* right on down to its rebuttals in the urban cowpokes unleashed by *Midnight Cowboy*), which featured more consistently in Vidor's work than in most. Zeke holds on tight to his family's money until Hot Shot nettles him with taunts of "country hick" and "dollar-and-a-half cotton picker." Certainly the film affirms the values of the family, the land, the rural community, and (at least in its emphasis on diligence, frugality, hard work, and family individualism) the puritan ethic—mediated through an Afro ethnicity.

Vidor once described the film in starkly melodramatic terms as a conflict between sex and religion, and a "struggle" between good and evil.[3] But interview remarks can't be taken as definitive, for a variety of reasons.* This description implies a far less interesting intricacy of factors than that given in his autobiography: namely, his sympathetic interest in Southern blacks—whom he had known as a youth—not only for "the sincerity and fervor of their religious expression" but also for "the honest simplicity of their sexual drives," such that "the intermingling of these two activities seemed to offer strikingly dramatic content."[4] We certainly

---

*First, nobody owes strangers the truth, the whole truth, and nothing but the truth. Second, the movie business, like any other, has its secrets, its confidences. Third, artists cannot always articulate their ideas except through their art. Fourth, the human memory is pretty fallible. Fifth, an artist may wish to please, or at least not upset, a critic-interviewer, especially when the latter is a cult-maker. Sixth, the interviewer's assumptions or personality may derail an artist. Seventh, it is difficult to recall subtle or crucial issues on the spur of the moment. Eighth, people change, as Vidor, at sixty, admitted: "I am aware that themes which might have intrigued me in my immature twenties could conceivably leave me cold today" (King Vidor, *A Tree Is a Tree* [New York: Harcourt, Brace, 1953], 272).

agree with the Catholic critic Henri Agel that, ferocious as Vidor's film is, it unleashes elemental forces rather than evil in its fundamentalist sense.[5] Charles Barr sees Vidor's film as a genuine tragedy—a conflict between two rights rather than between right and wrong.[6]

The scenario's obvious moral polarity, family affection versus an apparently passionate sexuality, isn't good versus evil exactly. For Agel, the "tragic flaw" of black vitality is a volatility of all passions, good and bad, so that Chick, Zeke, and even perhaps Hot Shot become, through the very strength of their passions, the childlike instruments of a natural force, half outside them. Agel was writing in the relatively innocent days of 1963, and his talk of racial childishness risks confusion with a now embarrassing anthropological position. After all, the Society of Friends were called Quakers, and early English Methodism was notorious for its hysteric congregations. A proper consideration of where the boundaries between racism, ethnicity, and culture lie is beyond our scope, especially given the enormous changes in ideology, sensibility, and mere terminology between 1928 and now. What *Hallelujah* would mean if Vidor had made it in 1980 is one of those questions that deserve no answer, like, why did Shakespeare ignore Freud? In 1928 many people thought "colored people" (the respectful word, as in NAACP) were excitable, not because they were childlike, but because they were passionate, like Spaniards and Italians. And they liked that, rather like whatever it is that Roberta Flack and Donny Hathaway mean when they sing, "Be real black for me." Emotional intensity characterizes Vidor's most interesting characters, and Slim the hardhat in *The Big Parade* and Colonel Rogers in *Northwest Passage* are as remorseless as their black blood brother in *Hallelujah*.

Zeke's revenge is a hinge situation in Vidor's morality. Revenge is both natural impulse and destructive project, and of varying legitimacy depending on its social context. Accepted as a duty in Wild West movies, its moral permissibility in a backwoods context in the twenties is bound to be less clear-cut than its illegality. Since it can also be inspired by mere *meanness*, ambivalence about it *should* be intense in anyone who, like Vidor, comes close to anarchism in the ways in which he combines individualism with spontaneous community. Pity and self-control (the restraints on revenge) are also universal moral matters for Vidor, not racial ones—a point strengthened by the swampland ferocity of Jewel, the *white* preacher, in *Ruby Gentry*. Vidor is clearly right in assuming that Zeke will retain *our* sympathies despite his crime.

Audiences of the eighties, accustomed to slower tempi or more forceful close-ups, may lose a quarter of an hour in adjusting to *Hallelujah*'s pace and relaxing their guard against sentimentality. Its masterly qualities are likely to be first apparent in Vidor's keen eye for supple vitality; for reli-

Figure 48. Hallelujah. *Zeke (Daniel L. Haynes) takes his vengeance on Hot Shot (William E. Fountaine) in the swamps.*

gious sentiment in its physical mode; for sexuality as an exasperated scream of the spirit; for the exuberance of the rascally and the ferocious. Alexander Walker would have it that *Hallelujah* is "undeniably better in intention than achievement."[7] But we find just the reverse: the scenario's simple melodrama is reinvigorated by the ambiguous detailing of the execution. In one scene, for instance, notable only for its apparent inconsequence (and for its addition late in production, after completion of the "final" shooting script), thematic tensions knock against each other in nervous gaps in the early-talkie dialogue. In the sparse kitchen of "Ezekiel the Prophet's" evangelical train, Mammy and her adopted daughter, Missy Rose (played by blues great Victoria Spivey), are talking all around the family catastrophe that looms in the evident attraction of Zeke for Chick at her baptism. Mammy does her best to relegate it to a hazard of the trade—they been lucky, that gal's the "first she-devil we run across" (fig. 49a). Missy Rose responds, with a hint of despair at a sexual threat, by remarking on Chick's "big eyes." Zeke enters, half-contrite, giving thanks to these two good women, who keep him on the straight-and-narrow. The closest the dialogue comes to opening onto the central issue is Missy Rose's plea, "What we goina do, brother?" (fig. 49b)—to which

a   b

Figure 49.   Hallelujah. *In the "Ezekiel the Prophet" train.*

Zeke responds with a proposal of marriage. All the film's tensions flit around the scene, with none quite pinned down. Is Zeke her brother or her husband? Which variant of female vitality (maternal, sexual, or wife-as-helpmate) does he most require? How exclusive are family stability, religious commitment, sexual passion? Missy Rose's tears "for happy" lend a closing irony to Zeke's solution.

Hallelujah replaces with indirection early sound film's double determinism of picture and voice. Likewise, its structure—four sections divided by titles—restrains passion. We don't see Zeke and Chick after they flee the church (with Missy Rose in anguished pursuit) until the "Months Later" title card surprises us. The strangulation of Hot Shot is left to our imagination (except in publicity stills: fig. 48). Thus the moments of highest ecstasy, violent or erotic, are denied us. It's possible to see this tantalizing avoidance as catering to an audience embarrassment at passion that, from all reports, was particularly touchy in the first years of sound (six weeks after *Hallelujah* came John Gilbert's infamously mirth-provoking "I love you's" in MGM's *His Glorious Night*). One might even see it as a way of restraining the too-soulful frenzy of black folk. (It's easy to forget the climate in which Vidor worked. Consider British critic James Agate: "Personally I don't care if it took Mr. Vidor ten years to train these niggers; all I know is that ten minutes is all I can stand of nigger ecstasy.")[8] The result of *Hallelujah*'s structure is that we never get *our* release until Zeke's own prison release.

Vidor experimented under the most hectic of conditions, as MGM rushed to complete a sound stage while he shot location sequences silent in October and November 1928. But the resulting forced displacement of sound from outdoor image imparts a striking expressionism, as in the rending snaps as Zeke tracks Hot Shot through the swamp, or in the mu-

Figure 50.   Vidor (third from left) on location for Hallelujah *in Arkansas.*

sical wailings when Zeke wagons home his brother's body (shockingly foreshortened, a Mantegna dead Christ, with worn shoes). Such aural expressionism may have been unavoidable, but has its visual counterpart, as when Zeke screams futilely into the night street for help for his gutshot brother, half the screen turning featureless black. Beyond its expressionist moments, *Hallelujah* anticipates the early Visconti variety of neorealism, with its authentic dialects, its quirky, slack, or overlapping dialogue, its inexperienced actors, its documentary interest in rural life, and its relentless analysis of the *crime passionnel.*

If the lower melodrama settles for good versus evil, the higher melodrama knows all about tragic conflicts between good and good. Here our sympathies are not so much split as doubled between an eroticism and a religious vocation, which (generated by family grief and frustrated infatuation) is really a counterfeit of the deeper, more ordinary piety of Zeke's community. His revivalist vocation is somewhat hysterical, and surely family love represents the *truer* spirit. Is this a general statement about religion on Vidor's part, or simply what's best for Zeke? The question stays open, but the repudiation of narrow, self-conscious religion is as prominent in his first feature as in his last.

The nature of this repudiation is suggested by Zeke's *crime passionnel* and its psychological consequences (or lack thereof). If we in the audience recognize Hot Shot for a low-down opportunist, we can also feel with Zeke's doubled rage against a man who must seem a demon, or fate, in running off with his woman *and* in being largely responsible for his brother's death. As Chick and Hot Shot, eloping, speed off into the forest in their horse-drawn carriage, Zeke blasts away with his shotgun, ready to risk killing the girl, whom he might have wanted to rescue. If Vidor is criticizing Zeke, he's also admiring a rage that, however hysterical, is a passionate hubris. His pursuit on foot of the carriage would be hopeless were his terrible willfulness not lending wings to his feet, for he runs with magic speed. (Vidor indulged in fast motion effects, just as he did at the end of *Our Daily Bread*.) Thus Zeke displays, not subhuman wildness, but a superhuman effort of the kind that compels fate (and corresponds to Apperson's limping pilgrimage after Melisande).

And so Vidor's ambivalence (the assertion of conflicting values between which Zeke is torn) is not a criticism of Zeke, but a *condition* of the scene's pity and terror. In retaliation, Zeke, like an agent of the Old Testament God, is both just and unjust. Hence the finale's terrible exhilaration—paralyzed Chick's screams to be pulled from the mud; Hot Shot's surprising return in concern for Chick, and his touchingly human stumbling; Zeke's cadenced pursuit. Anguish and satisfaction—which logically cancel each other out—escalate into a passionate acceptance of opposites, a "marriage of heaven and hell." And from this vicious circle (a.k.a. dialectic) Zeke emerges, by the boldest of twists, his crime expiated, his soul freed, his loyalties renewed.

The prison sentence asserted by the narrative is denied by the cinematic continuity, giving the finale—as it exists—a bold insolence. One assumes that jail gave Zeke a chance to come to terms with remorse and morality. But what we see after four brief shots of Zeke working a quarry is an almost insolently carefree murderer returning to the bosom of his family to live happily ever after. Prison couldn't break him either. Cut after at least partial filming was a chain-gang sequence, twenty pages of the 150-page continuity (figs. 51 and 52). In the release version, a hypothetical moral chastisement is denied by our experience of the last of a series of dramatic reversals. How far is Zeke's murderous fury childish? or childlike? or hysterical? or wrathfully puritanical? or a tragic (antisocial) flaw? And how far is his eventual insouciance a pre-moral resilience, or confidence in God's forgiving *crimes passionnels*? Many possibilities dance in our minds.

Figure 51.   Production still from the cut sequence of Hallelujah.

Figure 52.   Production stills from the cut sequence of Hallelujah. *A deadened Zeke works out his sentence in the chain-gang. As they sandbag against a flood, he says, "Let it drown us. What we got to live for anyway?" When the flood comes, the guards panic, abandoning the still-chained men. Zeke, unlocked at the time, knocks unconscious and perhaps kills a guard who had refused to go back to unlock the others. After freeing the surviving convicts and leading them to high ground, Zeke leads them again—in prayer. Thus he recovers a modest sense of religion, of leadership, of the worth of life (while further violating the Hays Code). Whatever we say won't stop archivists scouting,* Lost Horizon–*style, for footage that was abandoned by its director quite cheerfully, perhaps in this case because the further watery adventure moves away from otherwise central issues of family and eroticism.*

a   b

Figure 53.   Hallelujah. *Chick's death in the swamp.*

If the lower melodrama is merely vague (because its characters are so simple-minded), Vidor's type is more ambiguous. Even if the ambiguity doesn't show up in the narrative, it shimmers over the lines. Like Chick's dying cry: "I'ze broke in two already, Zeke!" (fig. 53a). It's a lovely line: so physical, and yet as if she's a toy; so resigned, and yet still pleading. Is this her feminine wheedling or her dying pain? As Agel says, she seems "washed of all perversity at the moment of quitting the earth, and filled with a childlike terror." [9] (Lewt dies like that in *Duel in the Sun.*) It's more complex than just sentimentalizing a double-dealing woman in her death scene (as Ford memorably treats Linda Darnell's death in *My Darling Clementine*). If we read Chick's death a little differently from Agel, it's in the same area: we see her freed of ego, so her energy becomes pure. Yet death is terror because she is selfish. We say, "because she is selfish," not "because she has sinned." She appeals for Zeke to save her from a palpably approaching "devil," in which as old-time fundamentalists they would both believe (fig. 53b). Her death isn't about being called to account for acts. By the process of dying, Chick is forgiven, and freed.

Zeke's fall from preacherhood is equally curious. Why shouldn't he marry Chick and carry on preaching? Couldn't she play the minister's wife, while his vocation brings in excitement and money? No doubt there are very real obstacles in her relationship with Zeke's brother's killer (so far as his family is concerned), in her scandalous past (known to a congregation that mutters, "That gal!" at her baptism), and in her fixation on city-slicker pressures. All this enables the incompatibility of his infatuation and his vocation to pass without question. But such incompatibilities, given Vidor's sense of Sturm und Drang, might exist only to be overcome.

The real obstacle is indicated by the details of Chick's and Zeke's succumbing, which reveal two key factors: Chick's dependence on immediate sensual excitement and Zeke's moral weakness. Ambivalent as is the ecstasy of her cries as he dips her into the waters of baptism, her "bad faith" is not of the gross kind we can contemptuously disown. Up to a point, Chick expresses a city treachery and greed (to contrast with rural diligence and thrift) such that her and Hot Shot's deaths are a case of the heathen being smitten hip and thigh—both excused by their background and predestined by it to a bad end. But she expresses a kind of truth also. Her conversion involves something that isn't quite bad faith at all. An important element in Chick's capitulation is the fact that she who came to mock the pious ("Betcha ten-to-one you can't save me, Brother Zekial!") is suddenly the only "sinner" who hasn't repented, which puts her in a position of acute social embarrassment. And Zeke's rhetorical presence is compounded by the exaltation of a whole community, a kind of meta-family, making her a little child again. Her conversion's ambivalence is encapsulated in the wry scene where she sings "Gimme That Ol' Time Religion" to the mirror while applying her makeup (fig. 54a). Hot Shot's subsequent struggle to keep her from church service ends with her solidly whacking him with a poker until only his moans show he's survived. "That's what I do to anybody stands in my path to glory!" (fig. 55). That violence in her sexuality, which Nina Mae McKinney carries off with ebullient spasms, has Zeke in open-nostriled, slack-jawed awe. When she bites deeply into his hand during the post-sermon frenzy (fig. 54b), he can only follow, without will, to the woods.

It might be said that Chick is driven by herd feelings and sensuality (two bad reasons) to a conversion that (because they *are* bad) ends tragically. But *are* they so unequivocally bad? How is community possible

a   b

Figure 54.   Hallelujah. *Nina Mae McKinney as Chick.*

Figure 55. Hallelujah. *"That's what I do to anybody stands in my path to glory!"* Nina Mae McKinney and William E. Fountaine.

without them? The baptismal cries called forth by her feigned (or sincere, or naturally overdetermined) sensations of regeneration by grace in Zeke's arms become ecstatic wails of love, of surrender, and—by no very great stretch of the imagination—orgasm. For sensuality lurks in the very temple of religion, perhaps because each plunges its roots so deep into human nature as to draw half its strength from the other. Which is why Vidor's solution is family affection.

But Chick isn't the only woman in *Hallelujah* whose inspiration becomes confusion. A middle-aged woman is overcome by hysteria and has to have a bucket of water flung in her face by two deacons standing ready for this everyday emergency. This "anti-baptism" is also a touch of comic relief, but, like much comic relief, it hints at a lifelong frustration of instinct by a harsh world. These purificatory immersions—erotic or comic—amidst meadowland contrast with Zeke's murder of Hot Shot in the marshy forest (and, in the cut sequence, of the guard in the floodwaters).

As the buckets of water may remind us, any revivalist preacher is aware of the all-too-human emotions involved in the conversion experience. So Chick is as much a victim of seduction by the whole revivalist situation as Zeke is by her sexual presence. His ministry abounds in images one may find appropriate to his flock, but that are also more akin to show business than soul saving. (Not that revivalism on its Marjoe Gortner level, or even fundamentalism on its Jerry Falwell one, worries much about so fine a distinction, but we'd hate to place Zeke in the cynical evangelist tradition of Capra's *The Miracle Woman*.) Zeke rides from his train on an ass, surrounded by children robed in white, waving American flags. Coming hard on his heartfelt inspiration, this *Green Pastures*–type production is shocking, one having expected a more modestly human commitment.

This is not to dismiss his evangelical style as *merely* a sham. The river baptism in front of the congregation expresses inspiration from community—the film's other moral pole. It finds its most stable and beautiful expression in the overcrowded shack when Mammy takes each of her younger children on her lap in turn and sings them to sleep (fig. 56a). The promptness of their response isn't just a gag (though it is that too, of the gentlest kind); it's also evidence of a magic power to bestow contentment, and a magic generosity going far beyond the grasp of jealousy. Man's real God is his earthly parents, and there's love enough for all their children to be soothed and content. When Zeke rocks Chick into the river of salvation (fig. 56b), he is touching on the same emotions in her, emotions that perhaps only a real family can satisfy. The Vidor family's not atypical southern experience with a continuity of "mammies" no doubt contributed here: the daughter of Vidor's mother's black nurse was young King's childhood nurse, and *her* daughter came out to Hollywood in 1918 to care for his and Florence Vidor's infant daughter. As Vidor reflected,

a   b

Figure 56.   Hallelujah. *Rock My Soul.*

much later, about his nurse, "I made this film for her. I should have dedicated it to her." [10]

Mammy has adopted Missy Rose, a friend's daughter, as her own (in a sidelong reference to the broken family patterns common since slavery), so that Zeke can grow alongside her, come to love her, and marry her. (The parallel with Mrs. Apperson's command is clear.) Later, Missy Rose sings Zeke to sleep, as his mother has done for his younger siblings. And on losing him, she clings to his knees or searches, wailing, through the forest (like Apperson's Melisande). Her womanly paroxysms and patience contrast with Chick's childlike, sensual, and impatient attack. After all, it is possible to imagine that, with a little more patience on Chick's part, the premature seduction in the forest would never have taken place, and that Zeke's "bad faith" would never have been revealed to him.

We may take this train of thought further. Chick's impulsiveness is honesty, a touchstone that reveals Zeke's *dis*honesty and frees him from a false vocation, making it possible for his real piety to emerge. But the film's individual confrontations are so powerful that it's easy to overlook the power of all scenes of community—the one-room home, the funeral, the baptism, and Zeke's return to the family. In contrast the city saloon crowd, at first jolly enough, scatters as soon as a shooting looks like trouble.

The feelings of community at the younger brother's funeral are also wildly orgiastic. But at this point of communal over-sympathy, error becomes so natural that one can see why Vidor's transcendentalism has to be founded on a dynamism of resilience, not on rationalist hopes of correct behavior. Here, perhaps, Vidor's vision reveals one of the tension points that are its inspiration. On one hand, humans need a strong community and a strong morality. On the other, community and morality both involve obligations that limit freedom. By and large, Vidor's heroes choose freedom rather than community; *The Wedding Night* condemns the sense of community *Hallelujah* upholds. The earlier film crosses the color bar, perhaps as an unconscious expression of nostalgia for community; for Vidor's own "ethnic" community—the one in *Our Daily Bread*—involves a pointed repudiation of the recent past. Indeed, a strong auteurist reading of *Hallelujah* is tempting (especially filtered through Melanie Klein). It would be a film about Vidor's own restless ambition, his own way of fusing religion with show biz, tempered by the Christian Science learned at his mother's knee and by something warmer remembered from his "mammy's" rocking. He's Zeke: a little different, but not much.

Henri Agel compares Chick's frailties to Eve's. Perhaps that's a Catholic reading; for puritan piety—more concentrated on the family and on teaching at mother's knee—isn't misogynous, even when it strengthens the good/bad girl divide, which, if the English school of psychoanalysis is correct, is natural before it's ideological. Vidor does toy with that metaphor for innocence-in-sin. "Adam and Eve," a middle-aged couple with eleven children, stop over to be married by the local *uninspired* preacher, Zeke's "Pappy." "Seems to me the damage is all done," he comments. While biblical patterns don't apply too exactly here, Agel's comparison nonetheless hits a fine Christian wavelength: enormously elastic forgiveness for certain sins as vitality's muddle-through response to an exasperating world. It counterpoints, as much as it contradicts, Ado Kyrou's surrealist, anti-Christian reading of *Hallelujah* as a celebration of desire.[11] (Compare Nina Mae McKinney's forked-lightning charm, as Chick, with her merely decorative presence in Zoltán Korda's *Sanders of the River*.)

If Vidor's sense of bodies is most easily recognized in its erotic mode, that's only part of a fuller range of physical sensibility. Money apart, Zeke is too tired by work in a sawmill to take Chick out nights for the fun she craves. And something as hard and familiar as fatigue in a workaday context was well on its way out of Hollywood's ken. Here the scenes stressing Zeke's sawmill fatigue follow a second little documentary, contrasting with the expressive possibilities of an earlier one on the process of cotton preparation. The forcefully cut cotton sequence matched Zeke at a moment when he was as exuberant as the Irving Berlin tune he sings to accompany it. Later, "natural" buzz-saw rips and a shrieking whistle reinforce the industrial vertigo created by a camera mounted behind Zeke on an oscillating lumber saw.

Vidor's interest in work is altogether more down to earth than usual in Hollywood, particularly MGM, at the time, as may be suggested by a comparison with Victor Fleming's *Red Dust*. There, exotic tourist interest—details of rubber preparation in the tropics—doubles, believe it or not, as a series of allusions to Jean Harlow's bosom. Roughly, the sense of prosaic physicality in American films follows a falling curve from the twenties through the thirties to a nadir in the forties, where its nearest equivalent is the emphasis on oppressive bourgeois interiors. The fifties brought it back, with Method acting and Elia Kazan.

If "the personal is political" can pass for a radical insight, it actually marks Marxism's passage from a political program to a religious one, to the same totalization of the personal by a belief. In *Hallelujah*, the personal is religious, the religious is erotic-physical. Orthodox religions are uncomfortable with that idea, seeking to control the physical in religion (shifting blood sacrifice to symbols, fertility rites to chastity, initiation to ceremony . . .). Vidor kept something wild and nervous. His films make every ideology (from sin-killing to Ayn Rand) physical, and that's why they can look so coarse to cerebral-liberal critics. Vidor's physicality

Figure 57.   Vidor on location for Hallelujah *in Tennessee, in a workplace familiar from his father's sawmills, deeper in the South.*

brings the spiritual with it. And that's what brings him so close to, believe it or not, Norman Mailer, in one fascinating respect. Vidor is "hip" in Mailer's sense in—what a title in this context!—*The White Negro* (1957).[12] Vidor must transcend a framework that is essentially rural, Texan, and "square," while Mailer's definition of "hip" stresses city anomie. Both converge, however, on a sense of nervous will, of violence and bodily resilience, of mind-body reflexes straining for unity with some over-harmony, of the difficult mixture of interchange with, and resistance to, surroundings.

If Chick on the town in glad rags isn't exactly a Cotton Club-er, she's as hip as a down-home soul sister could be. It's because both the hip *and* the pious ooze out of Chick's and Zeke's every pore that Agel can describe this film (for all its speed and discipline) as "baroque." The simultaneity of religious and erotic sensations during Chick's baptism by Zeke is both a hip insight and a transcendental one. The overlap may seem less bizarre if one thinks how Whitman's vitalism can be projected in one direction toward the ethic of nation- and character-building by work à la Sandburg and in the other direction toward polymorphous joys à la Ginsberg.

If *Hallelujah* is all about puritanism versus transcendentalism in black culture and in anybody's character, the definition of *puritan* poses problems. Vidor's puritanism would be at daggers drawn with the grim, original Puritanism, whereby only a repressive theocracy—and work considered as a curse, a curb, a duty, as well as redemption—can save man from his total depravity. In *Our Daily Bread,* Vidor's study of a tightly cohesive community, the sinner girl is allowed to make her getaway to the city, where presumably her little soul will be a lot happier. Liberty of escape is as central to Vidor as it is contrary to Calvin's double predestination.

Historically, puritanism was profoundly influenced by the wider Protestant belief in the possibility of direct access to the spirit. Its "pure" forms include Unitarianism and even blend with Deism, Freemasonry, romantic communion with nature, and, of course, Christian Science, which is almost Calvinism standing on its head. Despite certain doctrinal details, "evangelicalism" might do as a term for these optimistic puritanisms, while "fundamentalism" will do for Zeke's (or Billy Graham's or Pat Robertson's) compromise position, whereby a minimal sufficiency of faith and grace is always available, if not "in" you, then "to" you. It seems to suit the great American expansiveness, so that work can treble up, as worldly success *and* spiritual salvation *and* helping one's neighbor. From salvation by works to salvation by success . . . In this work-centeredness, too, Vidor stays with the primitive American cinema Hollywood all but smothered in stressing glamor, luxury, and escapism, until top hats outnumbered blue collars, tapshoes workboots, and six-guns monkey wrenches.

But when the French neo-Catholics of *Cahiers* called Vidor a puritan, they saw a grim, original Puritan, preoccupied with physical miracles and punishing the decadent, so that mad brother Jewel in *Ruby Gentry* would be King's alter ego. Such attitudes certainly abound in America, and Robert Aldrich pays them lip service in *Sodom and Gomorrah,* where the righteous rural Hebrews go their way while the slick cities get wiped out for effete self-indulgence.

Maybe *Moby Dick* is the movie Vidor should have attempted, for all the pitfalls we have noted in connection with film melodrama. Its mainspring is the conflict between the original Puritanism and a transcendentalist revisionism. Ahab becomes as evil as the Great White Whale, which may not be evil at all, but natural—like Blake's Tyger Tyger, Burning Bright, or (one step nearer to us) King Kong. John Huston could only go through the motions because, as faintly demonic and highly intelligent as he is, a believer by nature he isn't (with that gloatingly sardonic voice of his father's). A believer by nature Vidor is. Huston's is a father's intellect, Vidor's a mother's.

Jonathan Edwards's convolutions remind us how the grim Puritan's misanthropy involves complex spiritual acrobatics about hating the sin but loving the sinner. The transcendentalist has the same problems, reversed, even though they're rather masked by complacencies built into faith in progress and man. The smiling face of transcendentalism tends to remain silent before the jungle snarl of Social Darwinism, or the transmogrification of double predestination into Manifest Destiny. At any moment, therefore, transcendentalist confidence in freedom and faith in humanity can turn turtle, so that some particular evil—drink, communism, or "terrorism"—is at once absolutely everywhere and so alien as to be expellable only through a witchhunt—that is, the brief enforcement of a rigid theocracy. Transcendentalist expectations of high ideals may covertly imply puritanical dismissal of anything less than the ideal. "We needs must love the highest when we see it" can rapidly become a pretext for punishing those who need a longer acquaintance than one quick look. Maybe transcendentalism and Puritanism are natural bedfellows, happiest when neither can pull all the blankets onto its own side.

If Vidor shares the energy and optimism of transcendentalists from Emerson to Whitman, he also has a streak of the Social Darwinism that stopped American transcendentalism dead in its tracks. It's easy enough for a phrase like "self-reliance is God reliance" to imply or accommodate "and the devil take the hindmost," or Vidor's "I don't like failures." [13] (From the director of *The Crowd!*) In *The Big Parade* he admired both Apperson's forbearance and the riveter's killer instincts. In *Hallelujah* there's a genuine, inspired transcendentalism in Zeke's conversion at the funeral. He can free himself from guilt, or revenge, because he sees that his brother has been given to a Lord who is "the sky, and the moon, and the heavens, and the sun; and the Lord is the earth, and all the living things of the earth."* But almost without pausing for breath, he reduces this vision to show biz, then fist-pounding fundamentalism, then backlash violence, before, finally, becoming a natural man, neither as great as he could have been nor as guilty as he should be. Aren't Zeke's piety and his ferocity complementary, rather than contradictory, aspects of an underlying *élan vital?*

---

*Far from it being some "pathetic fallacy," some irrational anthropomorphism, perhaps Zeke experiences what Freud called the oceanic feeling. It comes, in a *generous* personality, as naturally as sympathizing, loving, embracing—comprehending. Compare Emerson's Harvard Divinity School address of 1838: "The world is not the product of manifold power, but of one will, of one mind; and that mind is everywhere active, in each ray of the star, in each wavelet of the pool. . . . The perception of this law of laws awakens in the mind a sentiment which we call the religious sentiment, and which makes our highest happiness. Wonderful is its power to charm and to command. It is the mountain air. . . . It makes the sky and the hills sublime" (Ralph Waldo Emerson, *Essays and Lectures, 1832–1860* [New York: Library of America, 1983], 77–78).

The Failure of Populism: *Street Scene* (1931), with Glances at *Billy the Kid* (1930) and *Cynara* (1932)

In the first years of sound, Vidor reexamined the populist world of *The Crowd*.

Billy the Kid (to which we'll return in connection with later Vidor studies in regional ferocity) is propelled by a conventionally political Populist plot, like so many Westerns (small ranchers versus monopolist). It's also a melting-pot Western, *Street Scene* on the range, stressing the diverse heritages of its emigrants to New Mexico—Danish, Scotch, Spanish, English, Irish, Mexican—for ethnic vignettes and good-natured rivalry. Billy the Kid's unsavory image early in the twentieth century, as propagated by Emerson Hough, was that of an anti–Rough Rider—a gunman who fell in with "this half-Spanish Civilization" that "the Anglo-Saxon Civilization was destined to overrun." [14] Perhaps because he sank so low, he inspired no films in the silent era. But he fits in neatly with the populist centerpiece of Vidor's film—varied nationalities besieged in a cabin and learning to band together. (Later Billies paraphrased despairs and crazy, mixed-up teenagers.) [15]

But, along with its production problems, *Billy the Kid* shows revisionist strains such as plagued *Heaven's Gate,* with its Eastern European immigrant ranchers. In *Street Scene* itself, Vidor's next film, set in New York City, he could be more direct, although it is particularly difficult to tell how much of it is his, how much is playwright Elmer Rice, how much is the original stage production, and how much is producer Samuel Goldwyn.*

The film version of *Street Scene* centers our concern on young Sam Kaplan (William Collier, Jr.), who must escape from the tenements, but can do so only by going through college. In his struggle for freedom, dignity, and self-betterment, his deadliest enemy is his love for his natural equal, the girl next door, Rose Maurrant (Sylvia Sidney). But his duty is to consecrate his fully developed talents to a newer, broader, younger America—an *American* America, without the ethnic divisions and other carryovers from tired old Europe, embodied in his father's ineffectual ranting and his neighbors' frustrated, stagnant, or confused lives. In the end, it is

---

*Goldwyn's work lends itself surprisingly well to the auteur theory. On the one hand he offers us the Goldwyn Girls—early epitome of deodorized and de-ethnicized American womanhood—and the spectacular musical. On the other hand, he produced slightly funky populist films like *Street Scene, The Wedding Night,* and *Porgy and Bess.* Both *Roman Scandals* and *The Secret Life of Walter Mitty* take the dichotomy into their own structure, cutting between melancholy reality and glamor-fantasy. Later, Goldwyn's concern with the family in *Street Scene* and *The Wedding Night* reappears in his suburban family series of 1946–52.

Figure 58.   Street Scene *(1931): Dane versus Italian (John Qualen and George Humbert).*

Rose who escapes, and thus forces him to keep faith with himself. Perhaps the surest guarantee that his individualism isn't mere selfishness is that his career-before-family decision cuts him to the quick.

Ethnic vignettes: a gloomy Dane and an operatic Italian perpetuate a pointless and backward-looking argument about whether Leif Ericsson or Columbus discovered America (fig. 58). The Italian and his German wife can't have babies, and the contemporary debates over racial reproduction rates and birth control would have honed the jokes about pullulating bambini to get a sad double-edge: none or many; you're damned if you do and damned if you don't. Rose's embittered mother, turning to adultery to live out a little of her frustrated life force, has considerable sympathy from the film (and prefigures *Beyond the Forest*). Another obstacle to Sam's self-emancipation is the example of his father, whose Old World socialist idealism has metamorphosed in America into something pathetic and defeated. Rose's burly father is restrained from punching out "the dirty Bolshevik" for the heathenish notion that "When private property is abolished, the family will no longer have any reason to exist" (fig. 59). The film implies that Maurrant's protest by fist, if anachronistically crude and legally wrong, is natural, traditional, healthy-hearted,

Figure 59.   Street Scene: *"Socialist vs. Pragmatist" (Max Montor as "Abe Kap-lan," in window; David Landau as "Maurrant," on stoop).*

and spiritually justified. It's the gut response of inarticulate honesty to all the insidious double-talk of intellectuals.

The original play is propelled by a melodrama that resists all this. Maurrant's murder of his wife and her milk-collector lover is the Grand Guignol coiled within Rice's naturalism (a style from which he was wont to take emergency exits). Maurrant's virile stand against "change," or his bluster that "What this country needs is a little more respect for law and order," is the Nixonian morality of *Stagecoach*'s thieving banker. Not that the revelation of Rose's father's true stripes vindicates the atheistic Marxism of his antagonist, old Abe Kaplan, who stands universally condemned—by Sam, by his neighbors, and by the film itself. Neither utopian *nor* Billy-the-Kid-style solutions mark the escape route for Sam and Rose. *Both* paternal codes are obsolescent.

As its genre-painting title implies, *Street Scene* is not only Sam and Rose's story, but also a cross-section, a slice of life, an omnibus film. In theory at least, it's a neatly unified dramatic structure: the young people's escape, the aids and obstacles contributed by their neighbors, and the big-city pressures that have frustrated those neighbors and may do the same to them. A film achieving this would have been exceptionally sophisticated for its time. As it is, Vidor's film comes so near as to provoke, in us at least, a wild impatience—an obsession with its cussedness. The individual pair and the wider canvas cross purposes rather than counterpoint each other. The film has the effect of being both direct and sidelong, deeply moving yet never quite memorable, neorealist in theme, yet profoundly anti-neorealist, almost anti-populist, in spirit. It's everything that irritates us about smart American art.

Oddly, Vidor felt he was hamstrung by Samuel Goldwyn's excessive *respect* for a prestigious stageplay (as Goldwyn seems to have had, later, for *Porgy and Bess*). Vidor found himself with a large, but single, set: the street and the front facade of a brownstone apartment. This spatial constraint couldn't be more contrary for tracing the interaction of family groups—though it did allow Vidor to shoot in sequence, and his camera movements and alternations of angle are as resourceful as one would expect. Faced with static characters jolted by a single spasm of violence, Vidor found that "the composition became the action." [16] There is, to be sure, a certain isolation about such flourishes as the bird's-eye shot of the cabdriver-bully, or the below-street-level view of the marvelously catty Mrs. Jones (Beulah Bondi in her first screen role), fidgeting with her

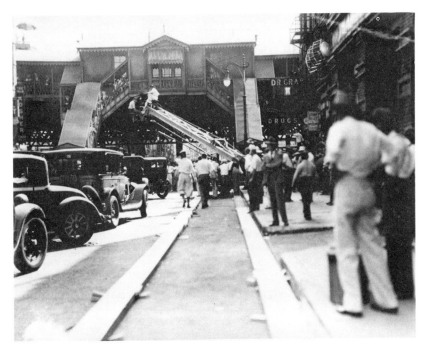

Figure 60.   Setting up a boom shot on the Street Scene *set.*

sweat-drenched underwear. The division into acts is palpable, with "director's cadenzas" between them. The handful of montage *accelerandi* are effective enough; and even Rose's descent from the "el" is more than a bravura boom-shot, since the structure over the street, the crowded life in the street, and the loved ones among the crowd are like a summation of all the forces that might hold Sam back.

The limitations within which Vidor has to work are indicated by Renoir's roughly comparable *Les Bas-fonds* (*The Lower Depths;* 1936). If the latter is hardly a tidy film, its bums and failures are both individuals and a group. The strong sense of negative interaction between separate, anomic individuals is eased by the in-depth structure of the several sets (a courtyard, a dormitory). Similarly, *Le Crime de Monsieur Lange* juxtaposes a printing works, a courtyard, and a laundry—three continuous areas dovetailing into one another.

New York tenement streets, stoops, and fire-escapes in summer could have been such a courtyard—as they were in the elaborate main set for a later Goldwyn-produced New York City film, Wyler's *Dead End* (despite its unlikely connection with the rich folk's townhouse). Or Vidor might have extended his tracking movements in *The Crowd* to group the apartment windows in a manner prefiguring Hitchcock's way with a similar hot-summer facade in *Rear Window* (with its neat side-alley *échappée* into the street beyond). But so voyeurist a vision of New York isolations may have cut against Vidor's grain. The temptation is there, in the elaborate track past a dozen windows, filled with small jokes on styles of waking, that separates *Street Scene*'s first two "acts." (The shot was borrowed, forty years later, to open the film of Rice's *The Adding Machine*.)

What is at issue is not, as the montage-versus-Bazin antipathy might suggest, a film-form imperative whereby the disunities of space and time must be observed or surmounted in some systematic fashion. The problem is rather one that Vidor, as a lyricist of individual energy, isn't temperamentally suited to resolve: the reconciliation of individual decisions with socio-environmental pressure, whose relentlessness is revealed through the enormous diversity of a cross-section. It's not merely "the individual versus the mass." Even to pose the issue in those terms is to forget *Hallelujah, Our Daily Bread,* and *Northwest Passage.* For in all three of those films the individual fulfills himself by surrendering his fate to a thoroughly cohesive group, in which he shares one common relationship (the family) or purpose (the military expedition). But *Street Scene* involves the *diversity* of purposes within an *apparent* group. The problem lies in the network of unity (everyone's common antagonist is "the city"), disunity (each separate apartment), and isolated conflict (as Sam surmounts temptations).

With Elmer Rice as screenwriter, buttressed by Goldwyn's respect for the text, the film maintains fidelity to the play. But on his copy of the script, Vidor penciled, as if in protest at its social subtext, "It is not our surroundings that defeat us." He grabs hold of Sam as a fragile guide through determinist jungles. Transmuted is Rice's fatalistic Sam (one of whose methods for escaping with Rose is for both to take "ten cents worth of carbolic acid") [17] into an aesthete whose visionary optimism is held at bay by the city. *The Crowd*'s office notwithstanding, it's hard to imagine what Vidor could have made of *The Adding Machine*, another Rice drama of marital hatreds and domestic murder, whose characters, even after death, wallow on with their self-destruction. Twenty years later, in his *noir* night of the soul, Vidor will get there, and cover it, but never cross-sectionally.

When Rose asks Sam to recite her a poem, Rice's filmscript, like his play, gave Whitman's elegy, "When Lilacs Last in the Dooryard Bloom'd." But Vidor, jotting "Change" in his script's margin, substituted a more expansionist Whitman, "Passage to India": "Sail forth—steer for the deep waters only. . . . And we will risk the ship, ourselves and all." Could American society be so constrictive as to allow no way out for the passionate? So, Rose's response to Whitman isn't Rice's deflating irony: "Yes, that's it! That's just what I felt like doing—breaking off a little bunch of flowers. But then I thought, maybe a policeman or somebody would see me, and then I'd get into trouble; so I didn't." [18] It's: "Yes, that's it! That's just what I felt, like risking everything, and not being afraid!" In the post–World War II years, Vidor's still not-quite-*noir* heart will go with those who risk all and meet disaster with, if not courage, then *spirit*.

Street Scene has a "collective hero"—it's an omnibus version of John's fate in *The Crowd*. But our focus on Sam and Rose makes for a struggle of two individuals, with the minor characters as a fringe of failures. Vidor separates this couple from the crowd by reserving for them the majority of shots closer than full body. No doubt this was also his defense against the broad gestural and vocal style of a primarily stage-trained cast. And William Collier's mumbling, nervous performance as Sam does make comic naturalist sense of Rose's mother's Social Darwinist dismissal of a sympathetic minor character: "He's an awful nice young fella. Nice and gentle. It makes you feel sort of sorry for him." But these minor characters are cameos, too limited in their spiritual potential to be either tragic or relevant. Rose's faithless mother isn't quite what Rose might be, or overreact against, if Sam abandons her forever and she marries another. We identify with Sam's rebellion, but hardly with his father's pain. And so on. A major film becomes a minor one, but a major minor one—that is, teasingly implying more than it can ever quite say.

Behind its problems lie a long American tradition, whereby America's expansionist sense of greatness and its individualist creed reinforce each other to impose confusions on studies of groups or communities. *Street*

Scene is the down-market, melting-pot equivalent of *Winesburg, Ohio* or *Our Town,* which also conspicuously lack a functioning social network. They are studies in loneliness, or else the dead awaken, so that a moral-cosmic reference occludes cross-purpose social patterns. *Street Scene's* alter ego is O'Neill's *The Iceman Cometh,* rigorously confined within a New York bar, whose melting-pot dregs devise convoluted excuses to remain. *Iceman's* dynamo proselytizer for ambition and motivation, the positive-thinking father-figure to them all, likewise reveals his true stripes in the murder of his wife. Even more so than Sherwood Anderson's and Thornton Wilder's, O'Neill's closed community is socially inert, an anatomy of loneliness. Just as *Street Scene's* running gag about Danish versus Italian versions of history stands in for (and conceals) the more violent interracial running battles, so O'Neill's immigrants daily refight the Boer War and other safely lost or won or sidetracked causes.

European minds and films were then more drawn to cross-sections and coexistences, whether urban-pastoral (*Le Quatorze juillet*) or pessimistic (*Hôtel du nord*) or gravely mellow (*It Always Rains on Sunday*). Wyler's, and Goldwyn's, *The Best Years of Our Lives* is something of a tour de force in its adaptation of a European theme to American styles. (Its mix of virtuosity, moral solidity, and an out-of-fashion, but admirable, bourgeois caution deserves several essays in itself.) Still, so far as social issues go, Clair, Carné, and Hamer are remoter than Capra or Vidor. The oddity is that a certain Hollywood populism faded in the mid thirties just as its European counterpart ascended—the French with the Popular Front, then the English with wartime films such as *Millions Like Us,* followed by Italian neorealism in the postwar years, until Hollywood remembered a genre, a *strategy,* it had almost forgotten. *Street Scene* betrays the reservations that brought Hollywood populism into eclipse.

In Vidor's next film for Samuel Goldwyn, *Cynara* (1932), these reservations are painfully evident. With Goldwyn again imposing what Vidor considered a deplorable degree of respect for the stage original, the film's working title, *I Have Been Faithful . . . ,* must have been annoyingly ironic. Both play and film recount the consequences of a seven-year-itch on the part of a British barrister, James Warlock (Ronald Colman). His affair with a shopgirl, Doris, leads to her suicide and his disgrace. The rare satisfying scenes in Vidor's *Cynara* are those that stray from the play to ask: what would a repressed character like Warlock make of the crowd? Warlock is dragged, half-protestingly as always, by his reprobate friend Sir John Tring, along with two shopgirls, to a movie theater, where we watch them watching *A Dog's Life*—the scene where Chaplin shoves his dog down his trousers to sneak it into a cabaret. Vidor's boom-shot over the wildly laughing audience again evokes the conclusion of *The Crowd,* where John accepts that revitalizing human fraternity by laughing at "himself." Now his camera picks out Doris with Warlock, who, chuckling mildly, is as far gone into a slumming unselfconsciousness as he is ever to get, but separate, in dress and demeanor, from the audience. How could he ever identify with Chaplin's tramp-clown?—notwithstanding the pornographic perfection of the animal-in-his-pants metaphor for Warlock's passive desire, as Doris reaches for his hand.

His other encounter with the workaday world comes when Tring maneuvers him into judging a local bathing-beauty pageant. His improvised speech mixes moral homilies with his refrain, "No class distinctions here." It's a joke, but not his. Where *Street Scene*'s camera prowls along the sidewalk, *Cynara* finds its visual keynote in vertical movement along staircases, aptly enough, since shifting between levels, class levels, is its subject.

As a film, *Cynara*'s new theme is: what can a man like Warlock make of the man (or woman) in the street? The answer is: not much. And it lets him off the hook. The events aren't tragic; they're a cautionary tale. Upstairs and downstairs, never the twain shall meet. Worse, it's *his* story, told (as in the play) through a flashback frame. The film makes much of his moral fortitude in refusing to answer questions at the inquest about Doris's sexual experience (thus leaving himself open to the onus of ruining a virgin), but little of his moral cowardice in shucking her off with a rational letter ("I hope you will have a happy life . . ."). This is heroism at its most passive, and matches his resolution to recover from class myopia by self-banishment to South Africa. The ship-out solution forgets such bright moments as when an Italian restaurateur throws open his palms and apologizes to the two British gentlemen over "these foreigners!" who have smashed a slot-machine in quick anger. Moments of anger or desire punctuate the film with counterexamples to Warlock's introvert dilemma.

Perhaps the American pitch for screen populism was further queered by America's extreme ethno-cultural plurality. Set in faraway, fuddy-duddy Britain, *Cynara* could allow class facts lethal consequences. Hollywood substituted ethnic or cultural conflict, with the melting pot providing a ready-made resolution. (Among the rare exceptions: von Sternberg's *An American Tragedy* and Stevens's *A Place in the Sun*—the same story, though twice cut down to aesthetically elegant mood pieces.) America's cultural plurality drove Hollywood to its expert stereotypage and to replacing real social frictions by stylized high-class WASP settings or individualist social vacuums. *Street Scene* is hard hit, forcing it to raise issues it must encapsulate in cameo or jest.

Melting-pot theories were optimistic about all the cultural possibilities: reciprocal adaptation, assimilation, pluralism. But the metaphor inadvertently gives itself away. To be tossed into a melting pot would be a quick and horrible death (for all its astoundingly literal two-color depiction in the finale of *King of Jazz* [1930]). In fact, *The Melting Pot* wouldn't be too bad a title for *The Crowd*. Its sense of failure and pain typifies a little cycle of silent films that includes von Sternberg's *Underworld*, which, in the terms of the gangster genre, catches the process whereby an especially tough individual becomes the spiritual champion of his demoralized group.

One can trace a movement through the thirties away from such pain of assimilation. The flavor of the silent-era melting pot lingers in von Sternberg's *Shanghai Express* and *Blonde Venus* (both 1932). The former, particularly, stresses Marlene less than one might expect, and the Shanghai Express itself functions as a melting pot, in that initially self-obsessed individuals of diverse origin come to respect and help one another. The Chinese woman in the film (Anna May Wong) typifies a recurring device. She is differentiated from the villainous patriots of her own race, and even kills one for the sake of her American friend (a device that tops out much later with the American Nisei of *Go for Broke* yearning to slaughter Japanese in the Pacific instead of Nazis in Italy).

Simultaneously in the early thirties, the gangster film indicates trickier patterns: (1) swarthy exotics (Paul Muni, Edward G. Robinson) make foreground villains who contrast with law-abiding communities (the gangster's ma); (2) as for James Cagney (for the Irish gangsters), however heinous his crimes, or deranged his psychology, he's lovable enough to identify with. Even in *Street Scene*, Maurrant's tough-guy style, all looming hulk and meaty fists, harks back to an older Irish-bruiser style—represented by George Bancroft in *Underworld*, and even more anachronistically perpetuated through the blarney (not to say kitsch) of John Ford's Victor McLaglen. Later, the suburbanization of the Irish is undergone by Louis B. Mayer's Mickey Rooney. Indeed, the Bancroft-Cagney-Rooney progression arouses the suspicion that the thirties cycle of films about happily cozy Victorian families represents an escape not only from Depression insecurities but also from the vexation of heroes having immigrant families.

Given America's isolationist and un-European policies between the wars, it's difficult to see why audiences should have been so interested in "foreign" themes except as sentimental or exotic melodramas of internal social processes. Geoffrey Gorer sensibly theorizes that American-born immigrants' sons rejected the alien, old-fashioned ways of the foreign community.[19] This would correspond not simply to Sam Kaplan's rejection of his Yiddish newspaper–reading father, but to Hollywood's ambivalence about Paul Muni (European father-figure Louis Pasteur *and* Scarface) and Edward G. Robinson (European father-figure Dr. Ehrlich *and* Little Caesar); both Jews, their dark, complicated faces and psychologies are virtual identikits of the non-WASP who, although he has become partly assimilated, remains "different."

Melting-pot themes get drawn relentlessly away from any American street-populist genre into the American gangster film. The idea of a Chicago gangster loving his ma's spaghetti strikes some audiences today as absolutely hilarious, but at least it indicates the generation gap between first-generation ethnicity and second-generation descent, fists and blackjacks flying, into the seamy side of the Social Darwinist jungle. *Street Scene* (self-improvement) and *Dead End* (gang delinquency) are two sides of the same coin: youths' responses to city pressures and to the obsolescence of parental codes. In Vidor's film Sylvia Sidney must abandon her college-bound boy friend. But remember the fate of her other lovers, who choose the other career, in *Fury* and *You Only Live Once*.

Does *Street Scene*'s "bracing morality" imply a certain elitism or disdain? Does it lend itself to right-wing arguments that environment explains nothing, because some people are able to escape from it; those who cannot are discards. In the unyielding terms of Jonathan Edwards, which Vidor cites approvingly in *Truth and Illusion* (1964), the material universe exists only in the mind. This turns soft "environmentalist" reformism against itself thus: "To excuse people on the grounds that they are victims *of* their environment is to imply that they are as corrupt *as* their environment." Or, in Old Testament terms: "Every citizen of Sodom and Gomorrah deserved death because his character was shaped by Sodom and Gomorrah, and any civic virtues he may have possessed were either only apparent or outweighed by corruption." It's the "collective guilt" argument against the Germans of 1939–45, and it's also that Marxist slogan, "The bourgeoisie, whatever it does, is always wrong." All are logically related to optimism. If human perfectability is easy, the imperfect are expendable.

No such condemnation appears in *Street Scene*, explicitly or implicitly; nor could it, without enraging its audience. Still, this film's close identification with Sam and Rose, mixed with its prevalent longshots of everyone else, constitutes a careful withdrawal of interest from those who are either insufficiently dynamic or undeserving. In contrast to its European equivalents, the film seems to condemn most of its characters, to see them as sticks-in-the-mud deficient in life force, and to give them some quick pity, maybe, but little interest in savoring their quirks—in the way that Marcel Pagnol, say, savors those of Raimu in the *Marius* trilogy. And in this falling off from *The Crowd* we see one reason for the drying up of American populism in favor of crime films and the Rooney-Garland healthy pasteurization. Still, the tenement creatures are cramped and sad, in the teeth of anti-immigrant prejudice. So, *Street Scene*'s very *subject* may itself be an affirmation.

The Champ (1931)

Regularly, a has-been boxer (Wallace Beery) begins his long climb back up the championship ladder. And, as regularly, falls two rungs back, into a Tijuana saloon, despite the efforts of his son Dink (Jackie Cooper) and Dink's gang. But the ex-champ's sallies into the gambling saloon do win him a racehorse. At the track, Dink meets his mother, though neither recognizes the other. Long estranged from the boy's fa-ther, she has married a prosperous businessman, who bribes the champ to let her see the boy. The threat of losing Dink spurs the champ on to a supreme effort, and he wins a fight, which proves to be his last. He dies of a heart attack in the dressing room, and Dink, wailing "I want the champ," is swept up in his mother's arms.

The Champ is a latecomer among the waif stories that abounded in Hollywood's early days. One thinks of Griffith's *Broken Blossoms* with Lillian Gish, of most of Mary Pickford's films, of Vidor's own *The Jack-Knife Man*. Its clear model is Chaplin's *The Kid* (1921), with the latter's Jackie Coogan passing the dustrag to Jackie Cooper, who maintains the orderly room for his less mature parent. The class powerlessness of down-and-out men, reinforced by the social powerlessness of children, create a pair of "buddy films" that rise above the male bonding of that otherwise so conventional genre. Recent three-handkerchief screenings argue that *The Champ* remains an exceptionally durable entry in that underesti-mated genre, the male weepie.

Thematically, its closest relatives are *Stella Dallas* (a parent, coming to grips with his/her own inadequacy, must force class status and wealth on the unwilling child) and *Street Scene* or Vidor's silents with Laurette Tay-lor (against his or her will, a child must leave a home background for a strange new social world whose powers can develop a fuller, truer self). Although Vidor celebrates individual freedom, the antithesis—of spiri-tual growth by failure, by constraint, by fate—is never far away.

The Champ was made before the repeal of Prohibition, and the story belongs a little more naturally in some pre-Prohibition American city. But a natural acceptance of illegal gambling and drinking would arouse pressure-group outcries or goad Prohibitionist audiences into misreading its principal characters as criminal riffraff. So the movie takes place in Tijuana—which is almost America anyway—and apart from an opening mention of the Mexican setting, and one brief shot of a Mexican police-man, one might as well be in pre- or post-Prohibition America.

Vidor called *The Champ* "one of the . . . conventional films" he felt obliged to make after "experimental" ones like *Street Scene*, but allowed as how "It turned out well." [20] The roots of its sentiment plunge into a popular iconography that seems to have appeared first in American newspaper comic sections after 1890 and rapidly spread into the movies. A big, burly, kind-hearted brute is either unintentionally destructive or hilariously slow witted. The spiritual kith and kin of this uncouth, but protective, father-figure range from many Lon Chaney and George Bancroft characters in their silents to King Kong and Lennie in *Of Mice and Men*. And Dink's pals borrow from and contribute to the movie tradition of the inter-ethnic kids' gang—from Vidor's own Judge Brown series, through Hal Roach's "Our Gang" (in which Jackie Cooper had played) and the Dead End Kids, with their mutation into the Bowery Boys.

The marriage between Linda and the champ was apparently a hasty, romantic affair between cultural incompatibles: the bride a wealthy WASP who has now outgrown her bold-flapper's pseudo-romanticism; the bridegroom, rejected by the socialite world because of his failures in the ring, now returning to the asphalt jungle whence he came. The film thus involves itself in a cultural schism a bit more topical than the champ's claim that "I wasn't in her class." At least we pick up the *other* meaning of that phrase. This clash—between wealthy, rustic-suburban do-gooders and the struggling asphalt junglers—recurs, for instance, in *Dames* (1934). But in *The Champ* both types are generous and well-meaning, and the conflict is poignant precisely because their life-styles are mutually exclusive, the story being a tragic conflict between two mixtures of right and wrong.

So far as moral impeccability goes toward winning our sympathies (which isn't very far), Linda and her husband would win hands down; but that's a less vital matter than the warm loyalty of father and son. Dink is distinctly unimpressed by what Linda's lifestyle offers, and his subjec-

Figure 61.   The Champ *(1931). Tony (Hale Hamilton) and Linda (Irene Rich) versus Dink (Jackie Cooper) and the champ (Wallace Beery).*

tivity largely determines our rooting interest. We have a double stake in their world: his father's success, and its effects on them both. Our sense of that world's temptations (drinking, gambling) is balanced by the obviously viable freedom of Dink's life. He gets it straight when he first visits his mother's home: "Gee, this ain't a bad dump you got here. . . . The champ and I ain't fixed up as swell as this; [pause; glances around] but our joint's more lively." Our involvement in the champ's success demands that we accept the terms of the world upon which it depends, so that—by one of those logical paradoxes with which dramatic structures abound—the dangers of the city world endear it to us against the exhortations of moral prudence. Better to live dangerously than too wisely.

This balance is very lightly emphasized by two minor details. First: the courts have given the champ custody of the child; perhaps a plot convenience, this implies desertion or misconduct by the mother. Linda's new husband doesn't contradict the champ's version: "She washed the both of us up a long time ago." Second: the husband's appearance (sleek, smoothly mustached, smilingly complacent) puts him somewhere among the rich villains of the cinema's innocent age, the B-feature rancher or the Douglass Dumbrille type in the Marx Brothers' *A Day at the Races* and *The Big Store*. The champ's mutter to him in the same conversation, ". . . and then you came along," hints at a tawdry triangle at odds with the husband's public openness. All the same, Linda has clearly lived down her wild-oats irresponsibility, and Dink's prospective father behaves very well. Pointedly, the film makes nothing of the tempting theme of the asphalt jungle potentially corrupting the son as well as the father.

The film also repudiates a venerable reverse pattern, most memorable through the *sinister* moral crusaders in *Traffic in Souls* (1913) and the *malevolent* do-gooders in the present-day sequences of *Intolerance* who separate the waif from her child. In one lovely scene in *The Champ*, a bored and tired Dink leaves his childishly optimistic father at the craps table, finds an abandoned roulette table, swings up onto it with the aplomb of long experience, stretches out, tilts his Stetson forward over his eyes, and immediately falls asleep (fig. 62a–c). It could look like a classic example of atrocious childhood environment. Yet family love survives under such makeshift conditions, as superbly as it does in Zeke's shack in *Hallelujah*. Linda's husband, who happens to be there, looks down on the boy and discretely switches off the light against which Dink's hat imperfectly shades his eyes (fig. 62d). In that unpossessive concern, that quiet acceptance, that neat control over environment, Dink's father-to-be is established as a man who generously cherishes his wife's mistakes as his own. The film is both wise and tragic in accepting that love and kindness may exist in radically incompatible terms. As obvious as that may be, it

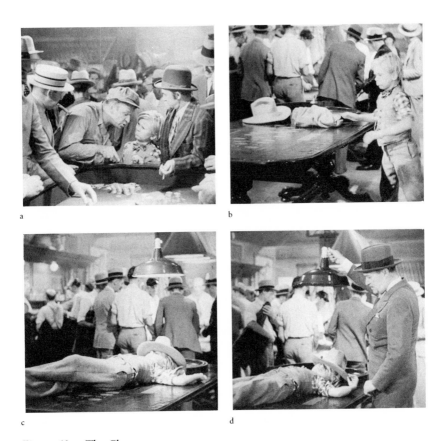

Figure 62. The Champ.

wasn't so common in Hollywood during the next thirty years, in part because of the Hays Code ban on sympathy going to immoral characters.

While accepting (as the "wets" would also have done) that alcohol destroys many people's lives, the film attains a similar moral balance about gambling, also a contentious issue. Yes, the champ gambles away the racehorse he's given to Dink; but that's how he won it in the first place. Maybe because his hopes are associated with luck rather than with the discipline of physical training, luck cancels itself out. After galloping with the fast motion of (the boy's) inspired will, the horse falls and loses the race. Luck giveth, and luck taketh away. Nonetheless, it is at the race that Dink meets his mother. So maybe a modest degree of moral effort is rewarded by providence—although in disruptive ways.

Meanwhile, Linda's husband keeps the champ going. A close-up emphasizes the hand-out theme. Is decent welfare to the deserving poor preferable to the pseudo self-reliance of gambling? Do the rich have a responsibility to their poor cousins, even when the poor aren't especially deserving? Or are we watching the furtive reliance of the old, boisterous, now degraded America on a step-family representing an alliance of only apparently innocent do-gooders and only apparently smooth big business?

Hints of military school if Dink goes with his mother may threaten American liberty more than they promise to firm up American manliness. (Vidor "hated" the one he attended in San Antonio.)[21] Dink's roulette-table bed is at least freer and easier than Linda's husband's glowing description of a military-school future: "You'll get riding, and drilling, and target practice!" Which sounds only slightly less bleak than the champ's version: "Well, it's just like a prison. Everybody wears uniforms." The champ's death in triumph makes the film something of an elegy to a lost, rascally America, in which Wallace Beery's female equivalent would be Mae West. The parallel argument to this nostalgia can be found in Gregory La Cava's *My Man Godfrey* (1936): that progressivism and big business must provide planned housing for those who may *seem* just bums, but who, given half a chance, won't be. It's just about how the balance works out in *The Champ*. Dink's future is with the charitable rich, even though their military academy may constitute too orderly a future for him. But if Vidor accepts that moral worth has nothing to do with the usual do-gooder notions of it, there's still no sign of his seeing any obligations beyond the ones within the biological-adoptive family. The handout close-up also has that note of shame, even in Depression times, and it's doubtful how far "charity" extends in a welfare sense.

The Champ again relates to the pain of immigration: its theme of the improvised or asymmetrical family complements the family disruptions in the melting-pot films discussed in connection with *Street Scene*. Dink understands life, and society, and has adapted to them rather better than the older generation as incarnated in the "Irish" Wallace Beery. It's the boy who acts as the father's (tolerant) conscience about heavy drinking; who trains alongside him to keep him going; who even drives their car. Whatever the Mexican driving laws were at the time, the impression of rascally anomaly seems related to the simultaneous discussion of whether Dink *accepted* sweets from his mother (which the champ would resent as a bribe, and which Dink would disdain as charity from a dame) or *swiped* them (which both men would agree is all right).

The scene of the actual theft is punctilious in its detail. Dink muses aloud as if to reassure us that he's stealing to give to his friends as much as for himself; and this absence of distinction between friends and self redeems the equal absence of distinction between the property of others and his own. The child-father relationship is a heroic disorder, a tour de force

Figure 63. The Champ's *Makeshift Family: Dad's drunk again. Jesse Scott (Jonah), Wallace Beery, and Jackie Cooper.*

that's finally defeated and resolved by the tragic twist that makes the little man a child again, as he "should" be. Paroxysmally, he cries "I want the champ!" (like a crowd's "We want the champ!"), and can find no consolation until his mother's arm, swooping around him to sweep him away, seems visually to promise a gradual consolation and a new hope.

In terms of movie cycles, it's easy enough to see in Dink a median term between the silent-era waifs and the precocious, adult-manipulating moppets of Shirley Temple and Mickey Rooney. Those child-moppet love duos are anticipated when Dink meets his half-sister. Though we may be reading back from later pseudo-precocities, the girl's provocative interest and the boy's disdain of "Dames!" do sexualize the scene gently, and a little incestuously. Dink goes on to treat his mother with the same disdain. "I don't kiss dames," he announces matter-of-factly and pats her on the back. When she starts to kiss his mouth, he takes her face in his small hands and turns her mouth to his cheek. We are almost in that ambiguous area explored by Goldwyn's *Kid Millions*, when the plug-ugly who's pretending to be Eddie Cantor's long-lost father goes to kiss him on the mouth. This peasant family salutation (normal enough at moments of intensity) seems to have become increasingly embarrassing, presumably because WASP scruples had made the mouth kiss exclusively sexual in America by this time. Family contacts were becoming dephysicalized.

Family physicality (not to be confused with homosexuality!) finds another little motif. In an early scene, the boy strips his drunk father down to his long johns. Later, when the father begins to undress the tired-out boy, Dink asserts his independence—more than his modesty—by undressing himself. The undressing theme is capped when Dink lets his mother remove his shirt, but objects as she's about to drop his pants; and she very sensibly respects his frail, manly modesty, rather than follow the expected rigid middle-class line about not sleeping in the day's underwear.

The absurdities in boxing's ritualized rough touching made it ripe for Chaplin (*City Lights*), Keaton (*Battling Butler*), and Lloyd (*The Milky Way*). The milieu puts an edge of brutality around this father-son symbiosis. But the fullest expression of physical contact occurs when father and son, both in their underwear, share a bed. The father, rolling over in his sleep, captures all the blankets (fig. 64a); the boy mutters irritably, rolls around to dovetail himself into his father's form from shoulder to ankle and then pats his father's shoulder with a slight physical awkwardness that redoubles the effect of emphatic fraternity (fig. 64b). It's simple, it's everyday, and it's full of decisions and surprises, including that acceptance of the other's oblivious egotism, which (once more) makes the child Dink the parent. The comic topper, come the dawn, finds Dink with all the blankets recaptured—fraternity matched by self-sufficiency. And the scene is doubly moving for rejecting the already developing taboo on nonsexual physical contact.

Conversely, after the racehorse falls, the champ reassures the boy that

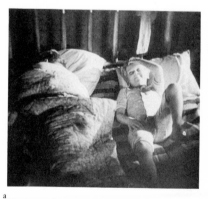 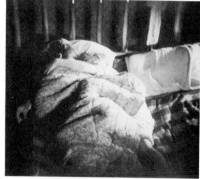

a   b

Figure 64.   The Champ.

the horse is all right, long before either he or we can possibly be certain of it. This mixture of lies (peace at any price) and protectiveness is also quite beautiful. All these contacts and distance-keepings build toward the boy's final collapse in the dressing room. For the champ's moral triumph—as much for the boy's sake as his own—and his own death reduce Dink to his mother's boy at last.

Against its nostalgia for naughty-bawdy-sporty Tijuana is the film's moral, which is broadly progressive and reformist. It involves several specific references to controversies about the effects of environment on character that were raging at the time. Wellman's *The Public Enemy* (1931) makes this clear: Cagney has a virtuous brother, a plot construction to insist that general social environment is only part of the story, that Cagney is responsible for his own psychopathy. In much the same spirit, Dink and his pals have—so far at least—survived with their essential innocence untainted. Without any anomaly, Vidor could have penciled the same note on *The Champ* as on his *Street Scene* script: "It is not our surroundings that defeat us." But there is nothing to stop spectators from seeing the theft of sweets and cigarettes as leading to delinquency and maybe Father Flanagan's *Boys Town*, or Dink's disdain of the maternal principle leading him toward the territory inhabited by Lewt (Gregory Peck) in *Duel in the Sun*. Certainly the champ's death is felt as a traditional tragedy, and *The Champ* (like *The Crowd*) is moving in part because Vidor's sense of the city carries both social pressure and individual freedom.

The images here also recall the grubby realism of *The Crowd* and *Street Scene*. And the space, although free enough to be appropriated at the characters' own discretion, is subject to quick, fluid camera movements of the sort one finds in contemporary films by Lewis Milestone and Jean Renoir (as improved sound equipment allowed the camera to revel once more in an earlier fluidity). The result is a fascinating conjunction of smooth, sharp, no-nonsense tracks and pans, which evoke city-busyness, and of the city's subservience to the film's characters when their will or feelings take command.

Dink's clambering over balconies and signaling from rooftops at his mother's California home is partly hooligan freedom and partly the appropriation of a home to whose spaciousness he is unaccustomed. He finally reaches an apex from which he can signal to his father, dozing at the wheel of their car. This exploration of rooftop freedom edges toward that of the rebels in Jean Vigo's *Zéro de conduite* and Lindsay Anderson's *If . . .* , and it doubtless expresses the spirit with which Dink will greet his brave new military academy. (Did a "bad" environment protect his freedom? Very likely.) Confronting his mother in her living room, Dink appropriates "his" space defensively by throwing his cowboy hat across the sofa and then holding a cushion over his knees as if to keep her at bay; meanwhile, her body visibly craves to touch him (in a prefigurement of the undressing scene).

Only environmental sounds are used throughout the film, until the last, quick, convulsive swelling of a snatch of "There's No Place Like Home." As Dink lies in bed he hears mellow ragtime played on a piano, and later alludes to his pleasure in hearing the music as he drifts off to sleep (another of the natural beauties of an environment fuller in vitality than the pious can understand; when offered later "a good home, decent environment, friends," Dink's polite response is that he's "full up" with "environment" already). During the pre-fight ceremonies, the only sound is the roar of the crowd. The context gives this noise an ambivalence characteristic of Vidor films, in which sympathy and indifference, good and evil, are so often inextricably mixed. The crowd likes the champ, and they want a ferocious fight—a contradiction, or balance, of the sort that sport and life are all about.

The champ's triumph and death form a pair so long expected that Vidor and his scriptwriters prepared surprises to enliven them. First, Dink's horse, Little Champ, *has* lost the race, so we're not completely certain that the champ won't lose this fight. Second, the champ's physical vulnerability has been on our minds from the beginning of the film, and is clearly stated by an unconcerned doctor just before the fight—but Little Champ lives, and our champ may too. Throughout the fight, Vidor plays cat and mouse with us over the heart attack, delaying until the fight is well over and the champ has seen the horse returned to Dink. After the delay, the death occurs abruptly (a sudden fall in the corridor, interrupting a natural movement). It's climaxed by a quick, grubby "funeral procession" onto his rubbing-table bier.

For luck, the boy spits on his father's cash-in-hand, on his fists, on his gloves. The gesture is laden with the characteristic ambiguities of a struggling class. While spitting expresses contempt, to be spat upon by a friend bestows preemptive expiation and, through the energy of insolence, bestows *his* strength too. During the fight, Vidor spares us those typical, boring shots of the interested party rooting at ringside; here Dink is made a "second" and given things to do: yes, spitting on the champ's glove, but also holding his rinsing bowl and nearly throwing in the towel for pity's sake—all of which is as slick and quick and precariously balanced as anything Hitchcock ever contrived to enliven an expected climax. But Vidor (or his way with his writers' master scenes) gives this succession of twists a sense of impulse unlike Hitchcock's colder calculation.

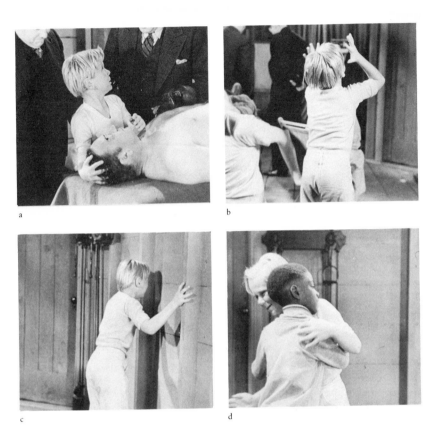

a   b

c   d

Figure 65.   The death of the champ.

In Dink's visit to his mother's house, Linda woos the boy, her back almost quivering as if to curve and enfold him against her breast. Yet she only briefly holds his hand, which he soon pulls away. At last, in the dressing room, Linda's long arm scoops across the space between them. In prison after his arrest for a drunken brawl, the despondent champ has smashed visiting Dink across the mouth in a gesture whose sudden, fierce, offhand diagonal curve across the screen is all but the converse of the mother's embracing arm. She pulls him to her side of the frame; the champ knocks Dink into a shot alone at its bottom edge. When the champ lies dead, and no one dares tell the boy, he screams with all the protest of his love against the truth, and beats his little body against the dressing room wall (fig. 65a–c), just as the champ has smashed his own guilty hand against the prison cell's stone wall. In his grief, the boy circles the

a   b

Figure 66.   The Champ.

dressing room, confronting one person after another and soothed by none—although he's almost calmed, for a few seconds, by his black friend Jonah (fig. 65d).

Vidor's camera has unflinching precision in this climax, tracking forward, at Dink's height, with Jackie Cooper transmitting an impotent protest, an incredulous futility, via spasmodic back, quivering fists and convulsive feet. Only after beating against the wall does he turn to face us, and the shot tracks back past ever more consoling figures (Jonah, Linda's husband [fig. 66a], and finally Linda [fig. 66b]). Her sweep down relieves him, and us, but the gesture brings with it a final unsettling ambiguity—a consolation, yes; but also a reminder of the scene where Dink, awakened from his roulette-table sleep, protests his independence with "I got legs!" against the champ's attempt to carry him home. The elaborate shot, like others in the film, validates Vidor's "flowing composition," that fluid, mid-range style developed while at MGM as a defense against "the over-ambitious editor or producer." At a time when Hollywood theory proscribed cutting while the camera was moving, Vidor's practice ruled out the options of cut-in close-ups or covering shots of the set and paralleled Ford's practice of "cutting in the camera."

Paradoxically, *The Champ*'s age shows mainly in its acting. Gaps hang too long within the dialogue. Wallace Beery's soft voice purveys feelings a little more broadly than we are used to. Jackie Cooper seems just a little too unsoiled and, as it were, presuburbanized. Sponge (Roscoe Ates), with his stammer, smacks of Runyonesque kitsch. Still, styles of physical behavior change as fast as anything else, and we have to be tentative about making judgments, even if we suspect which way Hollywood stylization was likely to err. And what *do* most of us know (except from films!) about the gestures and cadences characteristic of America in this era, and about significant deviations from any norm? *The Champ*'s slack dialogue, its repeated phrases and halting delivery, allows an improvisational naturalism. Whatever their individual excesses (and, to judge from Jackie Cooper's autobiography, personal animosity),[22] Beery and Cooper play perfectly together, as their dinner table conversation in pig-Latin underscores. With *The Crowd* and *Billy the Kid*, Vidor and MGM had been so uncertain about structure that the films had gone out to theaters with multiple endings. With this "foolproof" story, he could experiment with improvisation, including the sequence of Dink stealing cigarettes and sweets while talking and singing.

The Champ's emotional wallop survives our awareness of Hollywood formulae. Within its limits, the improvisational wit and sly sentiment of this "conventional" melodrama succeed much better than *Street Scene*. Certainly it numbers among the best city-life films of the populist cycle.

Bird of Paradise (1932)

Abandoning his shipmates, Johnny (Joel McCrea) "goes native" with Luana (Dolores Del Rio), a South Sea islander who has rescued him from tangled underwater rigging. For a time, they coexist in "Paradise," a cottage isolated from both Western culture and the native community. Eventually, however, volcano worship demands the sacrifice of a young beauty, and Luana accepts the call.

The trashy implausibility of *Bird of Paradise* must have been clear from the moment Vidor accepted the framework from RKO chief David O. Selznick: any South Sea adventure, so long as it contained three love scenes "like you had in *The Big Parade* and *Bardelys the Magnificent*," and climaxed with the girl tossed into a volcano.[23] Initial freedom gave way to amused desperation as the limited availability of the two stars made Vidor and writer Wells Root set sail for the Hawaiian location without a completed script. After a few days shooting backgrounds and native customs, they were obliged to settle on the dialogue.

The standard Polynesian motifs—festive outriggers greeting the white men, gunfire as black magic . . .—would have had more plausibility set in the eighteenth century, as in *Mutiny on the Bounty* or *Hawaii*. Vidor's fascination with conflicts of cultures, languages, and races is pared down to "civilization" versus sexuality. There is at least a certain equality within the (male *and* female) fantasy of a pre-Code woman at once sexually eager and inexperienced: for their second love scene, Luana does demand to straddle Johnny as they lie on their bed of roses, she gesturing toward her mouth to get more of this kissing business. Although no one

Figure 67.   Bird of Paradise *(1932). Dolores Del Rio and Joel McCrea in* "Paradise."

could argue with Vidor's dismissal of *Bird of Paradise* as "a potboiler,"[24] its lack of pretension to Rousseauian solemnity is engaging as formula turned tongue-in-cheek (not to be confused with modern "camp").

The early thirties started a little cycle of tropical-tribal exotica—African and Indian, as well as South Sea "Goona-Goona" (so called by the trade papers after the 1932 film of that title, an "Authentic Melodrama of the Island of Bali," which had high ethnological ambitions but ended playing grind houses, where the bare-breasted maidens were highly appreciated). F. W. Murnau and Robert Flaherty's *Tabu* (1931) and the perennial *Tarzan* (who returned as Johnny Weissmuller in 1932, as Buster Crabbe in 1933) mark the highbrow and lowbrow limits of the cycle, which set the sexual idyll of "savages" against tribal oppressiveness. *Bird of Paradise,* which toys with both the natives' abandon and the representatives of civilization, lies somewhere between the cycle's idyllic progenitor, Flaherty's *Moana* (1926), and the adventure-filled *King Kong* (1933). We might surmise that the southern hemisphere cycle filled the gap in "noble savagery" and alien encounters left by the retreat of the "A" Western in the thirties. Likewise these films parallel America's switch from celibate rural virtue to a new promiscuity, at least on the level of "petting in the park." So *Bird of Paradise* is a sort of anti-puritan Western, with whites entertained in the village by wild dances and strange food ("Poi or girl, I wouldn't like it," as one of the crew says, and the script's desperation is almost winning: "You know, apple poi, blackberry poi . . ."). Eventually the natives revert to traditional Injunism, basting the lovers over a fire before the deep fry of the volcano.

Vidor enjoys the sexuality/civilization clash. Although the natives succumb to cruel ignorance, they possess something like rural honesty in contrast to the goofy pleasure-cruise tourists, who respond to the free eroticism with nervous jokes about the "Virgin" islands. The divergent appeals of primitive religious fervor, sexually charged dancing, and the restraints of civilization recall *Hallelujah*, where the conflict acquires psychological tragedy by being contained within individual "Afro-Americans" rather than acted out, Western-movie style, between two races. There is amusing overstatement to Johnny's defenses of "civilization, where we don't have any crazy, superstitious ideas . . . where things are happening . . . parties, football games, dances, speedboats, airplanes roaring through the air." Luana, rightly, falls asleep on this frivoling Whitman. To Johnny's explanation of the wonders of the electric light, she responds with unanswerable sexual provocation that she likes the dark. And the film's near-final sequence does contain a touchingly desperate moment. After the two have been rescued by the returning Americans, Johnny lies recovering in a berth and whispers to Luana his need for water. She can only run her hands along the drops left in the galley sink and futilely shake a water cooler. In the end, it's less the strength of native culture than the heartless mysteries of shining brass that consign her to her religious duty in this formula—scapegoat.

Vidor's script troubles and dance sequence director Busby Berkeley's booms combine to overdetermine a pageant style. Only the final chases and an opening channel-crossing sequence break free with spacious montage. Elsewhere, ceremonies of marriage, or human sacrifice or good fishing all merge with ethnological indifference into rings of bare-chested maidens with safely glued-down leis, dancing with the open eroticism common to Berkeley and Vidor. In the context of a pageantry on land and (in swimming sequences) under sea, the slow reactions of the film's stars add a fatal weight. Joel McCrea's earnestness clearly needs, not just the ironic distance it gets here, but a certain surrounding speed to turn either comic (*Sullivan's Travels*) or into a bedrock of heroism (*Foreign Correspondent*).

The "tragic" conclusion of *Bird of Paradise* clashes strangely with its overriding optimism. Although boom-shot pageantry can be pushed into fatalism (for example, in Orson Welles's *Touch of Evil*, or the films of

Miklós Jancsó), that's not the option here, and nothing prepares us for Selznick's volcano sacrifice. Even the bizarre Old Testament logic of John Ford's late entry in the savage-paradise cycle, *Hurricane,* is relatively more satisfying—with the disaster wrought, somehow, by stiff European racism against the idyllic Polynesian couple. In Vidor's other films of this time, the past and Old World cultures are there for Americans, and their lovers, to transcend. In the discussion on deck among the Americans about the couple's chances, a sententious fatalist has it that "East is East, and West is West, and never the twain shall meet." More typical of Vidor is the bright mockery he gets: "Yeah, Mac, what's the dope on the North and the South?" If the film renounces miscegenation, that's not Vidor's fault. It yearns the other way. But the strictures against miscegenation were so strong that fatalism is built into the premise. Certainly that's hinted at by the furor over Barbara Stanwyck's erotic fantasies about an oriental in Capra's *The Bitter Tea of General Yen* (1933)—although there is, no doubt, some difference between American *men* lusting after Asians and American women doing so. Not until Selznick and Vidor next worked together, with the postwar *Duel in the Sun* and *its* racially crossed lovers' deaths, did Vidor's altered spirit mesh with Selznick's perennial fondness for tragic melodrama.

Back to the Land:
The Stranger's Return (1933),
Our Daily Bread (1934),
and *The Wedding Night* (1935)

The first impulse of Vidor's career came in the political Populism of the country-life silents. Capital-P-Populism's antithesis came in the city-life populism of the projects in the years around the conversion to sound. This loose trilogy tries for a higher synthesis.

The protagonists of all three films return to the country, though "country" is defined as "anti-city," as an escape to family-owned land, away from modern economic and spiritual troubles. It's a Jeffersonian conception of American opportunities, restated by Franklin Roosevelt in his first inaugural address, four months before the release of the first film in this series: "We must frankly recognize the overbalance of population in our industrial centers and, by engaging on a national scale in a redistribution, endeavor to provide a better use for the land." Clearly the pattern held great appeal for Vidor, while each of the three approaches owes much to its production situation. MGM's *The Stranger's Return* is a superior entertainment construct. *Our Daily Bread* is politics straight from the heart, and with a freedom allowed only by independent production. Samuel

Goldwyn's *The Wedding Night,* most uneven of the three, does starkly synthesize city anomie, immigrant struggles, and rural renewal.

The Stranger's Return

Divorced New Yorker Louise Storr (Miriam Hopkins) travels west to the prosperous Iowa farm of an 85-year-old grandfather she has never met (Lionel Barrymore). Grandpa Storr's distant relatives, who have long lived on the farm—his nephew's widow, Beatrice (Beulah Bondi); his step-daughter by a third marriage; and her husband—treat her solicitously, but distantly. She's attracted to the married owner of the next farm over, Guy Crane (Franchot Tone), an Iowan schooled in the East, with whom Grandpa ritualistically bickers over boundary responsibilities. Louise's easy dismissal of Beatrice's catty moralism seems mirrored in the placid unconcern of Guy's wife.

Grandpa's evident preference for blood-kin Louise over his extended family brings tensions. When his mind seems to snap and he obsessively plans Civil War fortifications, the three relatives call in the Insane Commission to certify him eligible for the "County Farm." But his illness is an elaborate charade, and the examining doctors serve as witnesses to the changes in his will, which disinherit the three schemers and leave the farm to Louise. His house in order, Grandpa dies. A few days later, Guy drives over to announce he's returning East to teach agriculture at his old alma mater, and Louise takes her place on a horse to ride alongside her workers.

The Stranger's Return is more Restoration comedy than rural realism, despite the waves of grain and harvesting scenes. *Le Malade imaginaire* in the rye. Still, our outline suggests an uneasier mixture of inspirationalism and entertainment machinery than the film itself actually is.*

As performance, *The Stranger's Return* has it all over *Our Daily Bread.* If gray-bearded Lionel Barrymore is his patented crotchety geezer, he plays sharply off Miriam Hopkins. The bright-witted sophistication she also brought to Lubitsch here complicates the romantic sheen, as in her response after Guy grabs a kiss (fig. 68a): "Should I be the woman amazed? or the woman afraid, or insulted, or compassionate, or just unknowingly wronged?" (fig. 68b). While for Lubitsch Hopkins's force is feminine impulsiveness, Vidor strengthens it into willpower, thus making sense of her ultimate commitment to the land, overcoming what ought to be prohibitive restraints of the city-girl type.

No doubt, the fascination of *The Stranger's Return* owes something to

---

*It is Simmon's candidate for Vidor's most underrated movie. Durgnat awards that melancholy honor to *Ruby Gentry.*

a   b

Figure 68.   The Stranger's Return *(1933). Miriam Hopkins and Franchot Tone.*

hindsight about Vidor's subsequent films. *Our Daily Bread* opens with a
lightly played prologue of desperate city economics—John bartering his
ukulele for a laughably meatless chicken. The MGM film, more consistently cheerful, substitutes Louise's sketchy tale of her father's death, her
divorce, her exhaustion, until "there just weren't any more jobs."

She arrives as a mere visitor, the last in a long line of relatives to grab
Depression refuge at the patriarch's farm. The film moves toward the
commitment that *Our Daily Bread* takes as its premise. Irving Thalberg's
response to the idea for *Our Daily Bread* ("He just couldn't see a picture
about a bunch of out-of-work people,"[25] according to Vidor) suggests
why *The Stranger's Return* must end where the independent film starts,
and why it hedges Depression agriculture in all the ways it does. It's as if
the price MGM extracts for the uncaricatured rural milieu in *The Stranger's Return* is that both pictured farms remain safely and equally boun-
tiful. So, that's made a point of plot. It's a squabble over something worth
inheriting. Even allowing for MGM's high style (fig. 69), the world of *The
Stranger's Return* was quite anomalous for the studio. Not since Vidor's
own *Hallelujah* had it ventured as close to the contemporary land—although the film has none of *Hallelujah*'s lingering visual documentaries
(the cotton gin, the lumber mill). The coalition of neighbors in *The
Stranger's Return* who band together for harvests and expensive threshers
are "the company"—a safe enough distance from the collective Vidor's
next film celebrates.

The oxymoron of the title hints at some convolutions in the city/coun-
try clash. With Chick in *Hallelujah* and later with Sally in *Our Daily
Bread,* Vidor uses the city-girl-in-the-country in her standard disruptive
mode. Here Louise can share in that conception of the West, generally
reserved for men and for Westerns, as a safety valve from the limitations
of the old East. Her blond curls and flirtatious ways with gruff Grandpa

Figure 69.   The Stranger's Return. MGM *in the Heartland: Franchot Tone in overalls.*

might mark her as the standard type, were it not for her irony ("the prodigal daughter returning from the great city"). To Grandpa's shrewd perception of a "farm girl underneath," she demurs that her muscles come from "lifting highballs and a little tennis." By convention, her rivalry should be with Guy's wife, who turns out to be neither easy victim nor deserving shrew. In everything that counts here—honesty, strength of will, optimism, and, well, beauty—she's Louise's uncultured reflection. The match between these sisters under the skin goes with a shift to weakness in the male. Louise awakens Guy's own unresolved East/West conflict. He stares with embarrassment at his fields as his wife proudly drags out his Cornell thesis, *Small Crops as Supplementary Sources of Farm Revenue.*

The harvesters' supper scene is crucial to the city girl's progress into rural life, and thus into her inheritance. In the local tradition, each household's womenfolk work to outdo the others by making the grandest meal for the men during their harvest day at each farm. In rapid panning shots and seamless cutting-on-movement, we watch Louise run ever faster to keep up with the farmers' mock-polite demands for more chicken, or more water, or more crab-apples, or more butter (fig. 70a–b). It's a game, a joke, a test, a ritual, which Louise plays in the traditional waitress ways. But the crux comes in the contrastingly static topper where, after all are sated, one man hints he didn't get *quite* enough pie (fig. 70c). With a smile, Louise says, "Oh, there's more out in the kitchen, but if I go

Figure 70.   The supper scene in The Stranger's Return.

and get it for you, you'll have to eat every bite of it, if I have to push it down your throat, honey." Which she then does (fig. 70d). It's a moment when she proves, to herself as much as to the men, that her spirit has not been broken by the city, that she has an inherent sense about when to follow rustic conventions and when to rebel. As Grandpa laughingly explains to an aghast Beatrice, "Louise has just behaved in no way befittin' a lady." That stepping out of her sexual role qualifies her as "boss" in the film's final line.

The scene may ring familiar as a variation on a well-known pattern. In Vidor's *Ruby Gentry*, Jennifer Jones, serving the hunters at her father's lodge, shows something of that spirit in deeply scratching the face of a hot-handed Charlton Heston. And in *Duel in the Sun*, she pushes jellied bread into a sexually insinuating Gregory Peck's face. Vidor's women have a spunky soul sister in Murnau's *City Girl* (originally titled *Our Daily Bread*). There, the farm son's new wife from the city, where her waitressing might have been expected to harden her, meets her match when she tries to serve the leering harvest workers.

The harsh way that Murnau plays this situation reinforces how *The Stranger's Return* isn't about woman-as-prey at all. That issue has been disposed of earlier, when Grandpa's hired hand Simon (Stu Erwin) fist-fights to defend Louise from sexual innuendo. What earlier scandalizes the townswomen is her refusal to be conventionally furtive about her attraction to Guy. She responds to Beatrice's advice about how her dancing is causing "talk" by asking him for more dances. If she's *ready* for the supper scene, which finally poses the issue of a woman's independence within a traditional society, it's because of such earlier scenes. At the dance, she takes the initiative, quite naturally, without gender tabu.

Just as Fox's *Hearts in Dixie* helped prompt MGM's atypical *Hallelujah*, so word of Fox's *State Fair* probably suggested *The Stranger's Return*, based on another Phil Stong novel of midwestern life. Indeed, *The Stranger's Return* is a battle between the bucolic world of *State Fair* and the vicious world of a third Phil Stong film, *Village Tale*, directed by John Cromwell in 1935, where a passel of the town's old boys hang around the general store concocting vengeful schemes they can only carry out as a mob. Guy's wife tells Louise that Pittsville is "a friendly little town," although that may be one more expression of her own guilelessness. There are edgy small-town undercurrents all over. The solicitude Louise encounters in her relatives at "Storrhaven" comes to translate as "Don't think you can stay." Grandpa interprets their attentive midnight welcome: "Think they'd miss a chance of seeing a relative that ain't living with her husband?"

This pattern of small-community insularity comes up again with the

Polish-Americans of *The Wedding Night*. Not that Vidor limits suspicion and envy to the countryside. Beulah Bondi's casting as Beatrice suggests an affinity with Bondi's city gossip in *Street Scene*. And that the type's small-mindedness is most concisely *expressed* as a rural trait is evident in the surprising Russian moment in Fritz Lang's *Fury* when the gossiping women's heads dissolve into clucking chickens. In this film Bondi is at her most sexually envious as she pumps the butter churn while insinuating that, with the added burden of Grandpa's illness, they will not be able to carry a "city girl" too.

By that time Louise has moved from city reflexes to a distanced admiration for country ways. A pair of scenes, subtler than they first look, chart the progression. On the night of her arrival, Louise is shown to the guest room by Beatrice, and Simon carries up her luggage. A well-bred New Yorker, Louise fishes money out of her purse for him (fig. 71a). At this urban violation of hospitality, Simon mutters that Grandpa pays his salary. But the scene continues with Beatrice scowling at Simon (fig. 71b), who grabs up the money: "Here, give it to me, I'll try to earn it." The city/country tensions aren't quite clear: Beatrice's scowl can mean, "Take the money—it's impolite to embarrass Louise" or "Take it—only a fool

a   b

c   d

Figure 71.   The Stranger's Return.

refuses money." The balance is tipped toward the latter only as we get closer to Beatrice.

A second sequence likewise promises a simple clash. Grandpa, who hasn't missed Sunday church in years, asks Louise if she goes "regular." "Well, I used to go to a little French church on Fourth Avenue. I wanted to learn the accent." Grandpa grumbles inaudibly, and the silence looks like another awkward moment of city superficiality. But the bloated preacher's Calvinist sermon (about measuring one's righteousness by God's absolute standard, not by comparison with one's neighbors) makes sense of the "rest and peace" Grandpa claims to find in religion—he's asleep before the preacher's first sonorous sentence is out (fig. 71c–d). Vidor, consistently wry about established religion, lingers on a mongrel dog that wanders in from the fields and also finds such rest and peace beneath a pew. All the same, Louise's smile at Grandpa's bowed head reminds us that the ritual of bodily peace *is* important for such a puritan worker, who won't slow down without a reason, and not in the superficial way his step-daughter takes the "unusually beautiful sermon this morning."

Here, small-mindedness only veils the true community spirit—*State Fair* finally triumphs over *Village Tale*. Grandpa and Guy's quarrels are of the good-fences-make-good-neighbors type, homey rituals of individualist friendship. The film opts for this goodtime cornbelt world opposite from both *Village Tale* (where white trash envy grows from wide class distinctions altogether missing here) and from a literary tradition represented in Hamlin Garland's bleak plains of isolation ("Up the Coulee" gives a very different view of a New York prodigal returning to the family farm).[26] *Days of Heaven* (1978), joining class envy to Garland-like isolation, has it that sexual tensions aren't so neatly resolved by one party motoring off to Cornell.

The conflict *within* the rural world is between those whom Grandpa dismisses as "little town folk," like his parasitic relatives, and those who were born close to the land. One's side in the struggle is determined less by birth certificates, however, than by wisdom, to judge by the meditative walks Grandpa takes with Louise through the family farm, which he feels to be "part of our minds." She's New York born, but of "Storr blood." Even Simon is grudgingly admitted to this side, the bond of the three ritualized by surreptitious smoking. In a traditionally peasant way, Grandpa cannot distinguish his sense of family from his sense of history. Thus he tells Louise, "You were born back here, a hundred years ago." With such a transcendent vision of the world, his "insanity"—where Civil War past turns present—is so small a leap that the audience, too, is taken in by the ruse.

Things work out with such comic perfection that one can, almost, ignore how identical Lionel Barrymore's stance is to the one he will destructively take in *Duel in the Sun*. His Senator McCanles, another first-generation pioneer with memories of Indian fighting, likewise cherishes blood kin and damns all the rest. Both men would find nothing amiss about *Village Tale*'s worldview: "It's all a matter of blood, good and bad, and when you got good blood nothing matters. And when you got bad blood, you ain't got sense enough to close the door after you." The tragic distinction in *Duel in the Sun* is that the vital new woman who enters the family is, as part Indian, consigned immediately to the bad blood side and stands on the receiving end of Barrymore's characteristic intolerance: "'Pearl,' huh? Whoever named you couldn't a had much eye for color. Better Pocahontas, or Minnie-Ha-Ha."

Although *The Stranger's Return* wraps up absurdly neatly, its classical plotting is a pleasurable mechanism. Ben Jonson's *Volpone* is an antecedent. Sycophants crowd round Volpone's "deathbed" when he fakes a fatal illness, hoping to worm out an inheritance. Grandpa's Civil War–prompted lunacy (as melodramatic as that of the grandfather back in *Wild Oranges*) dupes equally eager-to-be-deceived parasites. The hierarchy of evil among the three co-conspirators has the mousey, bow-tied, repossession-case lawyer and his wife following Beatrice's lead. But, typically for Vidor, weak will becomes nearly indistinguishable from malevolence. While Volpone's unquenchable pride in his acting skill finally gives away his masquerade, Grandpa's is so successful that there's retrospective irony in Louise and Guy's earlier nostalgia over the lost city pleasures of great acting—including *Ethel* Barrymore's. Grandpa's characterization of the three relatives as "the cat, the pig and the donkey" is as harsh as Jonson's subhuman names for Volpone's parasites (Mosca, Voltore, Corvino, and so on).

Parallels between the film and *Volpone* probably arise from a common heritage in beast fables like "The Fox Who Feigned Death" or the farcical tradition of doctor/patient tales. Volpone, with no sense of when to end his bluff, outwits himself. But for the finale of Barrymore's blood-kin obsession, we have to wait for *Duel in the Sun*, where the set-my-house-in-order plot turns in on itself. In place of the serenely composed shot of an exhausted Barrymore walking slowly out to his front porch, *Duel* substitutes a confused and lonely Barrymore sitting by a hill, wondering to old pioneering friend Harry Carey how family-centered plans can go so wrong. *The Stranger's Return* makes us admire Grandpa's need to fight a "civil" war to "cinch down tight" family continuity. In *Duel*, Senator McCanles's sin is a patriarchal ego that sets him against both state and family.

The traditional comic resolution of marriage is subverted by some-

Figure 72.   Vidor and Miriam Hopkins on location for The Stranger's Return; *Chino, California.*

thing in Louise's character, something that balances between stoic self-sacrifice for a deserving other woman (wait for *Stella Dallas* for the pure melodramatic form) and a more satisfying commitment to work, continuity, and the land (for the pure form, wait for *Our Daily Bread*). But as the sly reference to Ethel Barrymore hints, Vidor's film relishes its structure and symmetry. "It was all comedy," Grandpa declares of his charade. "Strange pattern it makes, doesn't it?" comments Guy on leaving for the East while Louise stays in the West. Two breakfast scenes frame the tale; Louise, in the closing one, inherits Grandpa's chair and prayer: "Father in heaven, we thank Thee that Thou has provided this our daily bread." It's a touching moment precisely because of her demonstrated denial of formal Christianity. But she has understood Grandpa's rituals, and intones this litany of continuity. She describes Storrhaven in terms others use "for Iowa or America," and that expansive commitment is something like early National Recovery Act resolution. The breakfast prayer leads into *Our Daily Bread* through the figure of a strong woman, increasingly key to Vidor.

Our Daily Bread

John (Tom Keene) and Mary (Karen Morley) are a young city couple brimful of cheerful drive. Comes the Depression. But at last they have the stroke of luck apathetic or embittered souls would let slip through their fingers. Her rich uncle offers them a spot of land that conditions have rendered worthless to him, and they have the guts to go out and try to make it pay. They pick up fellow dropouts and fugitives of all kinds, until the twosome has become a cooperative. John is willing to make over control of his land to the group, but, despite one man's forceful advocacy of a majority vote system, the group acclaims the idea of a strong leader—John, who has contributed the vision, the initiative, the property, and the faith in others.

Rapidly the cooperative runs into difficulties, some internal, some external. A bully tries to corner some land, but is cowed by a tough escaped convict who becomes the community's unofficial cop. The banks are altogether unsympathetic, and the community has to struggle along with so little money that the convict offers to give himself up for the reward. The community won't hear of it, but his idea is taken up by Sally, an attractive, perfidious city girl who means to keep the reward for herself and for John, on whom she's set her sights. As everyone's spirits flag, John becomes infatuated with her and even flees the co-op, utterly demoralized. But he returns after seeing a vision of the self-sacrificing convict. And as a seemingly interminable drought dooms the crop, he initiates the digging of an irrigation ditch from the nearby canal during the forty-eight hours after which the corn must die.

This outline bristles with implications that are not merely ideological but directly political. *Our Daily Bread* is usually regarded as vaguely left wing, and at release was criticized as such by the Hearst press. But it was also widely damned as right wing by certain elements on the left (*New Theatre* thought it moved in "an unmistakable fascist direction").[27] Most left criticism was less acrimonious, since the film satisfied earlier complaints about Vidor's subjects—such as a 1931 piece in *Experimental Cinema*: "In a world grappling with the problems of unemployment, hunger and capitalist exploitation, the American cinema offers films like *Hallelujah* and *Billy the Kid*."[28] If *Our Daily Bread* was too ambivalent to win first prize at the 1935 Soviet International Exposition of Film, it *was* awarded a certificate of merit.

Vidor's clear need with such a politically charged subject was to unite as broad a spectrum of belief as possible. But to leave matters thus would be boring. Unalloyed consensus so severely restricts dramatic conflict that Hollywood knows better strategies. One such is so to stack the points that converse political stances cancel out ideologically yet produce a double surprise dramatically. *Our Daily Bread* is a treasure trove of ingenious examples, as follows. (Our description employs the terms "left" and "right" in the rough-and-ready, but generally received, sense whereby the right emphasizes the individual's right to property and the left an egalitarian community spirit.)

1. John is ready to cede ownership of the land to the cooperative (a very left-wing gesture), which the cooperative feels it would be ungrateful to accept (a proudly anti-welfare attitude). Those reciprocal concessions generate an atmosphere of dynamic goodwill, and the dramatic surprises turn political ambiguity into generous sacrifice—and political challenge.

2. John is ready to abide by a majority vote (a left-wing principle), but the cooperative demands a strong leader (a right-wing attitude, although the left normally agrees to it in a crisis).

3. The advocate of democratic principles is pompous and demagogic (democracy as demagoguery being a right-wing criticism), but the demagoguery is democratically rejected. The orator's porcine jowls and blustery fist-pounding ("I suggest, my friends, that we bind ourselves together in SACRED COVENANT and establish an IMMORTAL DEMOCRACY!") (fig. 73a) could suggest Republican ultraidealism *or* the corrupt vote-catching targeted by Republican denunciations of (a) Democratic city machines like Tammany Hall and (b) Southern Democratic corruption.

The film touches on the implication that the whole American democratic system is corrupt and should be left behind by this community

a   b

Figure 73.   Our Daily Bread *(1934). A* Campfire Convention: democrat versus socialist.

("Ah, it was that kinda talk that got us here in the first place"). This might be apolitical (idealism turned desperate), or a form of Republican *immobilisme* as against Roosevelt's New Deal (in which government intervention loomed controversially large). As in Capra's *Mr. Deeds Goes to Town,* private enterprise has both the means and the will to pull itself up by its own bootstraps and put the poor back on their own two feet. In this there is nothing specifically anti-Democratic, since the New Deal was thoroughly eclectic and pragmatic. But so long as a need for government intervention isn't raised—as it never is in the finished film—*Our Daily Bread,* closely read, can't really be said to support the New Deal if it supports only those aspects of it to which even its opponents didn't object. All the same, audiences go by moods as much as small print, and Democratic audiences could, very easily, read "radical enthusiasm" as support for FDR.

The advocate of democracy is countered by a socialist (fig. 73b), whose outside occupation as an undertaker probably was Vidor's judgment on the "things must get worse before they get better," gloom-and-doom, revolutionary left. The community's one real farmer, Chris (John Qualen), cuts across their big words by demanding a "big boss" for a "big job." This hint of dictatorship was also dynamic consensus, especially during the 1932–34 years, which were producing a cycle of ineffectual-president dramas, notably *Gabriel over the White House,* where President Walter Huston is nudged from weakling to dictator by God's angel. It's just Executive Privilege if he must disband Congress and fill judicial loopholes with a Hammurabic Code. Hearst himself rewrote a number of the president's remarkable speeches in *Gabriel*—usually read as a fascist film, but apparently intended as a tribute to Roosevelt. Indeed, support for a strong leader was very much the property of left *and* right, which accounts for the now bizarre-seeming alliance between Hearst and FDR.

Amidst all this, ceding control back to John looks like a sensible middle road, as he's previously shown flexibility in abandoning his desire to choose ten men with usable farm trades in place of accepting all comers (undertaker, violinist, pants presser, cigar salesman . . .). The switch shows both his "rightist" moralism (faith in character over skills) and "leftist" softness (he can't say no). (Perhaps the latter is his admirable weakness, the weakness a man *should* be tempted by.) When Chris shouts, "John Sims is fella fer boss!" John's name reminds us of his pep-talk comparison of their situation with that of Captain John Smith and the early settlers—both left alone with the land and free to make of it what they will. His analogy, shunning outside forces (market or governmental) seems to put them beyond the New Deal. But not against it.

The film may seem left wing insofar as the banks feature prominently as villains. In fact, this attack on big business was one reason the studios refused to back the film, forcing Vidor to find his own money (though he eventually secured a $125,000 completion loan late in production from the Bank of America, with his home and the film itself as collateral). Criticism of big business is a popular plank of the Democratic platform, as it was of the Populist movement, which might indeed have taken up socialism if it hadn't become incorporated into the Democratic party instead.

But our left/right, Republican/Democratic dichotomy breaks down insofar as, in America, a radical criticism of big business is also a right-wing tradition (of which we'll say more in connection with *The Fountainhead*). And *Our Daily Bread* asserts (as the John Smith analogy first hints) not the need for some sort of "anti-trust" control of the banks by the government, but the poor man's self-help—a voluntary, corporate, morally inspired form of rugged individualism. To that extent, the film seems to align its city-versus-country theme with a Populism that asserts a "little man's," farmers' and artisans' individualism against the tentacles of banks and big business. Thus it asserts an old, perhaps obsolescent, grass-roots conservatism against what T. W. Adorno called the "pseudo-conservatism" that preaches "What's good for General Motors is good for America."[29] Finally, the film is ambiguous as to whether the community represents some kind of dropping out of the big-business-dominated system altogether, or whether it represents an *internal* counterweight within the system itself.

The film's genesis suggests the movement of Vidor's thought. His autobiography mentions that a *Reader's Digest* article caught his eye and prompted the project.[30] Most likely it was a June 1932 item, "An Agricultural Army," but he probably also noticed another a few months later, "Back to the Land?" whose author cites the fortunes of a city couple who attempt to live off the land. Vidor ignores, or reverses, its dire warnings: "For these are *city* people. . . . These newcomers will inevitably sink to the bottom."[31]

In the film's initial conception, in 1932 (from when the first budgets date), the community gets government help. Much of Vidor's 75-page story (the unpublished "Our Daily Bread" by "Karl Wallis") is set in Washington, where the Capraesque hero, Hank, lobbies overfed senators for an "Agricultural Army" bill to aid the unemployed. Congress sees the light only after our hero's own Virginia cooperative, Hanktown, overcomes all the setbacks, including the drought, that survive into the finished film. The agricultural bill passes, with Hank "risen to a national figure." In an early script, titled "The Ant Hill," the success has become more modest, although John Sims receives a congratulatory telegram from the secretary of the interior: HAVE WATCHED YOUR EXPERIMENT WITH GREAT INTEREST STOP IT IS IN DIRECT LINE WITH OUR OWN PLANS FOR ESTABLISHING SELF SUPPORTING RURAL COMMUNITIES . . . STOP COULD YOU COME TO WASHINGTON AT ONCE FOR CONFERENCE. A similarly spirited sequence, actually filmed, but cut before release, may well have been as unconvincing as it was anticlimactic. After the irrigation ditch is dug, the source canal runs dry. The power plant that supplies it "ain't runnin' . . . during the Depression," as a maintenance man tells the co-op men when they break in. But after a few calls to Washington, John is reading a telegram signed "FDR" when water is restored.

The final film has backed away from any government contribution, to be more keenly balanced about withdrawal from society. Nonetheless, its hope in something unconventional and nonindividualistic remains New Deal–like in *spirit*. As Vidor wrote in an October 1934 letter to White House assistant Stephen Early on learning that Roosevelt had screened the film: "I have felt since I first planned to do this picture two years ago that the idea projected was in line with the President's plan of subsistence homesteads."[32] (Apparently FDR enjoyed it; Early wrote back, with politician's caution, that "The President told me I could say to you confidentially that he was greatly interested.")

Vidor's Populist streak interacts in complex ways with his mixture of Emersonian transcendentalism and rugged individualism. There is, after all, a broad compatibility between Populism and Social Darwinism, for all the former's insistence on "a fair chance" and the latter's hereditarian callousness. Possibly, the forces making for competitive ideology in America prevented Populism from becoming socialist or fascist—like some European counterparts—despite its waverings in both directions. The coincidence of ownership and leadership in *Our Daily Bread* may just be a convenience for the purposes of political ambiguity; but that fusion itself owes something to Jeffersonian democracy, which put its faith in the yeoman farmer, distrusted Eastern mercantilism, and anticipated later reactions against big business and demagoguery.

Figure 74. Filming Our Daily Bread. *Vidor, in sweater-vest, is next to the camera.*

Populism's weakness when it comes to large-scale planning appears in the film's basic plot gambit. Everything depends on the cooperative producing an abundant corn crop during the Depression, but that was a period of catastrophically *low* demand. Farmers were notoriously burning the very crop Vidor's cooperative labors so mightily to produce. Certainly, not all Republicans were branding government interference in the market as socialistic. It was Republican President Hoover whose unending faith in self-help cooperatives led to the Federal Farm Board, which actually fueled the primary Depression disaster—collapsing commodity prices—by such actions as lending half a million dollars to boost the yield of the hundreds of members of the Cooperative Wheat Growers of Kansas City. (How apt that Hoover's former chairman of the Federal Farm Board should have written that dully realistic and unhopeful *Reader's Digest* piece, "Back to the Land?")

Had the film followed its John Smith analogy more closely and centered on a more self-supporting community, it might have been economically more realistic. But it would presumably have offered less scope for that love of expansion, that act of faith in, if not the *big* business system, at least the *American* system. And it would have registered as a negative withdrawal rather than an exhilarating expansion. In fact, attempts at producers' cooperatives had been a feature of American history, but (as in England) had mostly foundered, perhaps because independence from economic systems isn't easily attained.

Notwithstanding Vidor's admiration for the New Deal spirit, the film's combination of extreme precision about property rights and extreme vagueness about market forces suggests a right-wing basis to his (and his audience's) thought. It is the vagueness of Populism itself, which went in for grand schemes of currency reform in preference to accommodation to the market. In the film's least convincing sequence, the bank orders an on-site delinquent-mortgage sale, but the co-op's men muscle out the slick, serious bidders without the sheriff catching on, and buy it back for $1.85. The scene has proven perennially irresistible, reappearing recently as the climax of *Country* (1984), when the FmHA auctioneers are muscled out by the band of neighbors who refuse to bid at all. That the sale in *Our Daily Bread* comes as a shock to John and Mary hints that they, too, are hazy about the relationship of bank mortgages to property, since her rich uncle had stressed that they must make the land "pay."

The cooperative is morally redemptive, as the criminal's self-sacrifice suggests. In all three panels of this triptych, Vidor evokes that American tradition in which the land offers a fresh start to anyone frustrated, debased, or perverted by the city jungle. By reason of his clear political use, we have labeled the tradition after Jefferson, but it is as central to material success as outlined by Ben Franklin or to moral success as per Whitman.[33] Vidor's short story "Our Daily Bread" is explicit here, with cooperative "Hanktown" a measured alternative to the revolutionary ferment in "Hooverville" shanties. The film's hard case is slinky young Sally, playing city music (jazz) on her phonograph a few hours after her father's death (fig. 75a). Her heartlessness is a shock, and the phonograph as a frivolous luxury contrasts with John's having bartered his ukulele to begin some primitive economic chain—uke for emaciated chicken, to feed rich uncle, who offers land . . . (Already, in *Bird of Paradise,* a phonograph is the first thing Johnny barters away when he needs a canoe.) Sally's solitary, supine, passive, indoor listening contrasts both with the community's lively dancing and the spacious evening simplicities of the violinist on a hill. John mentions that the convict/cop has caught someone sneaking off to sell community goods: "His wife wanted a *radio!* Can you beat that! With that kinda stuff we'd last about a week." There's moral, as much as financial, laxity in such mechanical connections to the city. When John pushes a cart through the fields singing, "I'm going back to Oregon / With my banjo on my knee," music returns as pure spirit.

Sally proves incorrigible, and quits. Here Vidor asserts his usual resistance to dramas that set up villains as scapegoats. Nor is Sally the one rotten apple that rots the whole barrel. If John is attracted to her, it's because his own resolution is weakening. Their relationship parallels that of Zeke and Chick in *Hallelujah*—a by-product of "bad faith," eventually resolved not simply by success in the vulgar sense, but by hard-earned moral success. This is one of the reasons why the brief final images of rustic joviality seem so overheated. By trying to transform a *Saturday Evening Post* success image into an expression of spiritual vitality, while also capping the preceding climax, Vidor inadvertently produces an incongruous blend of Brueghelesque romp, midwestern prosperity, and gospel fervor. With the power-plant sequence excised, the film could have afforded a gently anticlimactic note, stressing contentment rather than uproarious success (which was established anyway, in the acrobatic rejoicing as the flowing waters refresh the parched crops).

If the vamp/good woman dichotomy now seems out-of-key in the hardy Hollywood manner, it's also Vidor's way of talking about what qualities America needs, more than any put-down of sex and independence. After all, *The Stranger's Return,* which backs away from all the social confrontations in *Our Daily Bread,* neatly converts *its* blond city flirt into a bedrock of rural independence. No doubt political constraints at MGM left room for pushing unconventionality elsewhere. In *Our Daily Bread,* the hero's choice between glamor and the homelier, sturdier virtues, like loyalty, is short-circuited by the penciled eyebrows and creamy skin given John's wife (Karen Morley, a fascinating figure, who was later blacklisted [fig. 75b]). Still, if Vidor gives the good, aproned

a   b

Figure 75.   Our Daily Bread. *Bad Girl/Good Woman: Sally and Mary (Barbara Pepper and Karen Morley).*

wife a Hollywood face, he allows more than a hint that it's for the community, not Mary alone, that John renounces whatever is special about Sally's attractions. Thus, in the final shot, the couple's bliss seems a dependent form of communal loyalty, rather than the root of it. In this respect the film keeps its discreet, but welcome, distance from the suburban ideal, where a community is built out of couples.

"John and Mary Sims" return from *The Crowd* (without their son— another truck accident?), but *Our Daily Bread* is a sequel only in the loosest sense of seeing what an average man and woman can make of the next decade. (Just before release, Vidor cut a *Crowd*-like sequence of John's search for work in the city.) As played here by Tom Keene, John has a charge-ahead superficiality in his lunkish walk and expletives ("That's a humdinger!" "Holy smoke!") that parallels his quick enthusiasms over new ideas and people, as well as his equally quick discouragement. He learned what little he knows of the country in the Boy Scouts, and something of the scoutmaster lingers in his leadership. The convict keenly has the reward check made out to *Mrs.* John Sims. It's not just that she's been shown as one inspiration of his gallantry; he apparently anticipates the fatal combination of John's streak of weakness + money + Sally. ("My gosh, ain't you anticipatory!" she rightly exclaims to the convict during her first meal in the community when he warns her to keep her distance from John.)

Today's audiences are sure to laugh, Freudian wise, as John and Mary watch their little shoot sprouting. But the scene celebrates fertility in the truer sense—the shoot is no more a phallic symbol than the phallus is a vegetation symbol. In a brief pause during the race to irrigate the crop, Mary hands John a mug of coffee; and, as he gazes at her gratefully, the steam from the coffee, mingling with his breath in the cold night air, is like the steam from the nostrils of a bull. It's more than a simple celebration of virility and the romanticism of lust (which, certainly, is not absent from Vidor's films). It's as if John's work had imbued him with a steadfast maleness, where passion has no need of the vamp, but grows from his own labor, toward the woman. Nor is the woman restricted to a responsive role; for her sisters, like the pioneer matriarchs of old, hold their torches high for their menfolk to work through the night, and wield shovel and pickaxe by their side (fig. 77a). The image of John as stud stallion carries the opposite sense from that which fifties-and-after morality is too quick to read into it.

Our Daily Bread is Vidor's shortest sound film. It zips along on a fluid camera, with quick pans, bodies filling the frame with energy, sequences split apart with angular wipes. If the speed may be a defense against audience expectations of a tedious subject, it's of a piece with the time-lapse sprout and the undercranked irrigation ditch sequence. The style highlights some sharp shifts, as when bodies walk off frame and leave us contemplating the earth, or when the camera backtracks from the convict coming with notice of the sheriff's land sale. Likewise, the fluidity transforms the few heavy gestures into commentary. Chris throws his arms above him when he sees the first plants, and shouts, "It's comin' UP!"; the same odd gesture pantheistically signifies the community's unity when the carpenter leads the group in prayer; and recurs when a surveyor stands high on a hill plotting the route of the crop-saving ditch (fig. 76b). Insofar as the film is a sequel to *The Crowd*, the gesture is the transcendent response to the urban psychosis John embodied there in raising up his arms to silence the city for his dying daughter.

"I believe that the climax of *Our Daily Bread* . . . is an example of film sense in its most comprehensive form," writes Vidor.[34] "Digging a long ditch in straight pictorial action" is the problem with which his climax is faced. And it is virtually impossible to do justice to the inventiveness and variety of his mise-en-scène without at least one frame enlargement of every setup. Vidor, going far beyond Hollywood's professional rules of thumb here, reveals himself as a formalist in the class of Eisenstein or Pabst. In strictly realistic terms, the action has its implausibilities—the route is still being surveyed after digging has begun. But the movement is as strictly rhythmed as any of Busby Berkeley's production numbers; the lines of sweating men correspond to *les girls*—or to his forgotten men. The onward thrust is counterpointed by Vidor's astonishingly varied succession of topography, activities, postures, and movements. It's a ballet of manual labor, built on contrasts. The crocodile of bending and straightening men advances as steadily as a Macedonian phalanx (fig. 76a). The surveyors and advance tree-cutters assert stiff, immobile verticals (fig. 76b–c). The *laborioso* of the digging is diversified suddenly by the *allegretto* of

Figure 76. Our Daily Bread.

Figure 77. From the climax of Our Daily Bread. *The man shouting for water (b) is Vidor.*

the women rushing with flickering torches. The straight, to-and-fro horizontal of a two-man handsaw (fig. 76d) sets a visual motif on which an automobile's fast swerve and halt is a lively variation. The lithe speed of men rushing downhill, keeping pace with the first wave, is broken up by the monumentality of John pushing an aqueduct up from beneath (fig. 77c) and a bare-torsoed muscleman crouching over the boulder he is lifting from the stream (fig. 77d) (anticipating the everyday heroism of FDR's Farm Security Administration photographic style).

The co-op's triumph is celebrated in an animal-vegetable-mineral-machine symbiosis by men somersaulting in the irrigated soil, or lurching motorcycles through it, as if copulating with the fertile mud. (It's almost an inversion of the images of the copulating couple in *L'Age d'or*, and certainly a spiritual antithesis of other Vidor swamp images: the deaths in *Hallelujah, Ruby Gentry,* and *Wild Oranges.*) If *Our Daily Bread* allows a man to abandon himself, childishly, a little crazily, to the embrace of Mother Earth, it's by way of recompense for his effort of will against the desert. As Charles Barr observes, earlier John and Mary settle down to sleep, but cannot do so until their bodies are touching; and the image is immediately followed by John's spade digging the earth.[35] The link is hardly a Freudian symbol; rather, it suggests the systole and diastole of emotion and will, contentment and work.

It's easy to be cynical, and to complete both the film's title, and the moral of its climax, with a much later film about big city life: Edward Dmytryk's *Give Us This Day*, whose hero dies in the wet cement pouring on him in a building accident. Actually, Vidor's celebration of an ideal, honest-to-goodness peasant capitalism goes beyond any specific political or social position, and hymns the relationship of humans, work, and earth. In its more nervous way, it joins the heavy classics of the Russian silent cinema.

In 1930 Eisenstein screened *The General Line* at Vidor's home. Whatever impression it made on him, the disparity of rhythms between *Our Daily Bread* and *The General Line* is crucial: as crucial as the contrasts, *within* Eisenstein's film, between Cubo-Futurist speed (the cream separator, the dynamized numbers) and those glum, suspicious, stick-in-the-mud peasant physiognomies, lit like Rembrandts and verging on Brueghelesque caricature. Populism's attempt to perpetuate past virtues in the present included assertive adaptations; and *Our Daily Bread*, like *The General Line*, is a hymn to mechanization. Not tractors here, but the "caterpillar tracks" of men with picks and shovels, moving relentlessly across the countryside, are not just a gang but pointedly reminiscent of a factory conveyor belt, a mass production line. Here John Henry calls on Taylorism to match the steam drill's speed. The line of men come over the brow of a hill almost as strangely as the tank in Pabst's *Westfront 1918*.

Implausible as it may be, the simultaneity of surveying and digging is inspired by the same appeal to industrial speed. Here rustic America learns
a trick, but without selling its soul. In this respect, *Our Daily Bread*
evokes Disney's insistence on the jollity of modern methods when prop-
erly domesticated by Mickey Mouse—rather than the feeding machine of
Modern Times.

Yes, of course, all three filmmakers are working from different view-
points: Vidor from a rural Populism, Disney from a somehow suburban-
ized eupepsia, and Chaplin from his anarcho-leftism. Odd as this range of
auteurs may seem, it's natural that societies' modes of self-transformation
should recur throughout a range of films and genres. One would have to
add, after all, the Eisenstein film, Clair's *A nous la liberté,* Lang's *Metrop-
olis,* and the high-speed slapstick of Mack Sennett. When mechanization
took command, it galvanized the popular imagination, not only as a
theme in itself, but as a measure dominating the vision of other themes.
Eventually, Cyd Charisse's ironical remark in *It's Always Fair Weather*—
"Yes, of course, I'm a machine"—points to Andy Warhol's "I wish I was a
machine" and to Robert Wilson's epic dramas of mechanized humanity.

Oddly enough, in the two most dynamic nations, the United States and
the USSR, anything like a realistic picture of labor virtually disappears in
the early thirties (a few 1932 Warners melodramas come closest, largely
by default—*Tiger Shark, Taxi!* and the early scenes of *I Am a Fugitive
from a Chain Gang*). Truck drivers and steelmen take pride of place in a
few films between 1935 and 1945, such as *They Drive by Night, Man-
power, Pittsburgh,* and Vidor's own *An American Romance;* but the setting is usually a pretext for melodrama or war-effort pieties, and interest
in the experience of manual labor is conspicuous by its absence. Tay Garnett's knockabout melodrama *Wild Harvest* (1947), with its battles between rival teams of mechanized harvest workers, qualifies, enjoyably
enough, as a perversion of Vidor's long-cherished project, an epic of
wheat. The only tools to interest postwar Hollywood are small arms
(*Winchester '73, Colt .45,* the Bowie knife). The last Hollywood incarnation of American proletarian tensions is the boxer (*The Set-Up,
Champion, Body and Soul*), until Elia Kazan presents the ex-boxer-
turned-docker of *On the Waterfront.* The small cycle thus sparked off
were really post-Kefauver films about labor racketeering, not labor. Hollywood's proletariat sometimes resembled "two nations," of consumers
and gangsters, and most productive work happens at office level. For any
real sense of workers working one has to turn to renegade productions
like Vidor's film, Dmytryk's *Give Us This Day,* Herbert J. Biberman's *Salt
of the Earth,* and maybe Cy Endfield's *Hell Drivers* and *Sea Fury,* which,
despite their ostensibly English settings, do indicate the rage and cyni-

cism of proletarian life as described by a writer like Charles Bukowski. Not that Hollywood's labor musical *The Pajama Game* doesn't have enormous charms. But even a semi- or post-Hollywood American cinema continues to be rather tricksy about labor, so that even such diversely fine films as *Nothing but a Man* (1964) and *Blue Collar* (1978) subordinate the laboring life to race, crime, and violence. Yet what a subject, for Vidor or anyone else, exists, for example, in Edmund Wilson's account of the Iroquois who became construction workers![36]

Our Daily Bread justifiably congratulates itself in its title-card as "Inspired by the Headlines of Today." In which regard, it anticipates the WPA "Living Newspaper" theater pieces, begun in 1935, which also culled from headlines a compressed, charged drama of the average man buffeted by social forces. The nearest films in spirit to Vidor's come much later, from John Ford and Jean Renoir.* *The Grapes of Wrath* (1940) emphasizes the dignity of the manual worker, his expropriation from the land, and his reduction to the servility of working for others. The continuity is personified by actor John Qualen, whose immigrant farmer reveres the earth in *Our Daily Bread* and anguishes at its loss in *The Grapes of Wrath*. Renoir's *The Southerner* (1945), least lyrical of the three, compensates with its dourly realistic social and dramatic process: the growth of a guarded, cynical neighborliness, entwined with a *consumers'* cooperative (which, in real American history, succeeded as regularly as producers' cooperatives failed).

Our Daily Bread's cooperative is an association of people who have freed themselves from the past. It's a fascinating converse to the past-rootedness of *The Sun Shines Bright* (1953), as personal to Ford as *Our Daily Bread* is to Vidor. Diverse as they are, these two films afford a remarkable set of opposite points of view across a common territory.

Both films concern themselves with the problem of moral leadership and mobocracy. In *The Sun Shines Bright* Judge Priest ruins his chances for reelection by alienating every group in turn; he stops the Tornado boys from lynching a black man, and he alienates the righteous by giving a prostitute a decent burial. The dead girl turns out to come from a respectable family, and the Tornado mob support Judge Priest because "He saved us from ourselves." Judge Priest, like all Ford's leaders, is delibera-

---

*The resurgence of interest in the theme led to two odd offers to Vidor in 1940. Astor Pictures re-released *Our Daily Bread* under the amazing title *Hell's Crossroads*. And Vidor accepted an NBC offer that made *Our Daily Bread* one of the first theatrical films to be televised in the United States ("We could pay a maximum of $150 for a one time screening. . . . This transmission might be expected to reach 1,800 television screens in the New York metropolitan area"); King Vidor papers, cited p. 325 below.

tive, slow, self-assured, inner-directed, concerned with reconciliation and equity. Ford's leaders are at once relaxed and cynical; they accept, and all but relish, demagoguery as part of the traditional political game. John Sims, like Vidor's leaders generally, asserts a quick, spontaneous rightness. He's impressionable, inconsistent, weak, and works from responses rather than memory; while politics elicits Vidor's impatience. The two films stage similar scenes of holding an angry mob at bay, but while Judge Priest overcomes via the guns-and-butter of a folksy shaming plus a quick draw, John wins by infectious inspiration (see fig. 106, p. 228).

Ford deploys all the paraphernalia of rural Americanism: the flag, parlor hymns, six-guns, sexual chivalry, the puritan *gravitas* of Abraham Lincoln and Wyatt Earp. Yet he divests them of their Americanist prejudices to achieve something different. The mountain men in *The Sun Shines Bright* stand in for any group of no-good scruffies—that is, ultra-WASPs for immigrants. Judge Priest insists on the human dignity of moral failures when he follows the prostitute's hearse. And Ford takes the same attitude toward the unemployed of *The Grapes of Wrath* and the "white trash" of *Tobacco Road*. Judge Priest achieves a fascinating balance between the Abraham Lincoln image and the Tammany Hall–type demagoguery of *The Last Hurrah*, which may be why *The Sun Shines Bright* was Ford's own favorite among his films. And although critics were charmed out of their wits by the military nostalgias of the Seventh Cavalry (Ford's ersatz community spirit, whose civilian forms had become curiously elusive), the Civil War veterans' organizations of Judge Priest's old Kentucky home are carefully demilitarized by the switches to fraternity between the now-reconciled veterans. Vidor keeps looking for a sort of spontaneous combustion of togetherness, whether ignited by the agricultural triumph of *Our Daily Bread* or, in other films, anything from a long marriage to sudden reconciliations at the split second of death.

Both Ford and Vidor are careful to gratify both the hero-principle of the individual and a belief in the responsible decency, at bedrock level, of the crowd. Where Vidor emphasizes superhuman efforts crowned with success, Judge Priest's last line is "I gotta take my medicine; I gotta get my heart started." He walks slowly away from us through a recession of dark doorways, as the image both counterpoints the dialogue to assert staying alive as a lonely duty and recalls Young Mr. Lincoln's acceptance of his personal loneliness and his political destiny. Earlier Judge Priest threatens to do what the law forbids a judge to do by swearing himself in as a deputy and carrying out a citizen's arrest, a line whose hilarious ingenuity moves us aesthetically, intellectually, and morally—partly for outrageously exploiting the letter of the law, lynch-mob style, and partly for profoundly respecting the spirit of the law. The prevailing implication seems to be that the law as it stands is perfectly adequate for all decent

Figure 78. *Barbara Pepper in a promotional shot for* Our Daily Bread.

purposes, and that more sweeping powers would betray America's traditional liberties.

In other words, *The Sun Shines Bright* is a defense of the Constitution against the revisions and negligence promulgated by the McCarthy spirit, which was still riding high when Ford made this (veiled) protest against it, in the very terms most likely to move McCarthy's supporters. Ford's film, like his sense of the past, is as much moral example as it is mere nostalgia; his general position would seem to be a Democratic conservatism. Ford's nostalgia is thus more topical than it seems, being a continuing restatement of America's liberal-democratic roots. Vidor's topicality in *Our Daily Bread* is more traditional, or archaic, than *it* seems, for it depends on the assumption that America retains a primitive, "pre-Constitutional" vigor, spontaneously creating its own forms in response to circumstance.

Both directors have their generation's "respect" for women, although Ford's Victorian gallantry differs from Vidor's suffragette-era awareness of their force. Ford's heroes are often solitary and celibate, or soft-hearted men's men, or moral steel like Lincoln and Priest—almost Calvinistic "monks in the world." Ford's concealed model may be an Irish, priestly celibacy transposed into a WASP key. The whore is a lady at heart, or is at least to be treated with that courtesy. And the woman-taming antics of *The Quiet Man* are a one-sided set piece, vapid compared with the ambivalence of Vidor's heroes toward their women, whether as inspiration, temptation, or Amazonian challenge. Vidor's dynamism recognizes that only through temptation can a spirit grow, and that fear and rancor are as pointless as remorse. His responsiveness goes with a veneration for an identical life force coursing through both sexes.

True, Ford's film is twenty years younger (that is, older) than Vidor's. In 1934 Ford hadn't reached his later, more profound, more oblique, very cautious overtones. His fifties nostalgias are really a restatement of American ideals, suddenly made archaic by the cynicism of the *film noir and* the pseudo-conservative backlash. Postwar *film noir* wrenches Vidor out of his thirties affirmations into exacerbated violence. Sketchy as our comparison is, *Our Daily Bread* and *The Sun Shines Bright* separate out two intertwined, continuing streaks in American conservatism.

The Wedding Night

Author Tony Barrett (Gary Cooper), short of money, retreats from Manhattan to his inherited Connecticut farm, salving an ego mortified by his publisher's rejection of his latest novel. He is attracted to Manya (Anna Sten) and to a community of Polish immigrants who band together to buy his land. At first, she, and the simple life of her hospitable family,

seem an idyllic alternative to the city smart set. His new-found humility
helps him to stop resenting criticism of his facile writing and to find in-
spiration for a new novel in the community's country customs.

An ominous note is introduced at an immigrants' meal, during which
the children sit hungrily watching until, their elders having finished, they
are allowed to rush to the table. The tips of the horns of Old World author-
itarianism are rapidly followed by the remainder of the beast. Manya's fa-
ther and her Polish fiancé are paranoid and jealous of the smooth writer.
His wife finally returns for him, scaring off Manya, and revealing the hon-
esty underlying an urban sophistication that is merely skin deep. On
Manya's wedding night, her drunken groom is bestial to the point of rape,
and murderously vengeful against Barrett. After warning Tony, Manya
dies in a tragic accident, still in love with him. But life, and art, go on . . .

In light of the finished film, the first intentions are astonishing: producer Samuel Goldwyn bought Paul Green and Edwin Knopf's story
"Broken Soil" and retitled it *The Wedding Night* with the hope of du-
plicating the success of *It Happened One Night.* But as Vidor reworked
the script with Edith Fitzgerald, it became the final panel in his rural
trilogy.

Tony Barrett approaches Manya with slick seduction ("Don't be so
moral; it doesn't go with those eyes"), and gets a slap for his efforts. His
next attempt respects country ways—he borrows her woodaxe to "see if
I've forgotten how." He has. And doesn't take it up again. Barrett returns
to family land, but this time Vidor's back-to-the-land theme is self-
consciously twisted into artist's terms. Manya, as Barrett's rural conscience, squats to milk a cow, and leans around with a wry smile for his
writer's block: "I pity my poor cow, if I didn't get in the 'mood' to milk
her." Her gentle sarcasm moves him to post another phrase of hers, slightly
altered, in his study: "YOU MAKE YOUR LIVING AT IT—YOUR PEN IS YOUR
PLOW." In the script, and in directing Gary Cooper, Vidor modeled the
hard-drinking Barrett, who can no longer draw from the reputation of his
early novels, on F. Scott Fitzgerald—perhaps as retort to the latter's
less-than-flattering fictionalization of Vidor in "Crazy Sunday." Vidor's
roughly contemporaneous recourse to psychoanalysis hints that Fitzgerald had no monopoly on monitoring artistic and marital crack-ups. And
it wouldn't be surprising if Vidor too, at forty, felt himself the aging boy
wonder, caught up in production systems. From what we hear of Barrett's
novel, *Earth's Return* (titled after Whitman), an autobiographical romance about recovering one's moral spirit through the country, it seems
to turn full circle back to *The Stranger's Return.* That Barrett never regrets selling off his land is reasonable, considering his Depression-era financial woes. What he draws from the land bears fruit only in his art.
Already in *Show People,* Vidor had taken pains to demonstrate a tradi-

tional work morality in his own much-maligned occupation ("Success in this game means work"). In *The Wedding Night,* the highflying writer learns it all over again, from immigrant peasants renewing the American experience.

Vidor's autobiography expounds some of his problems with the different acting styles of Gary Cooper and Anna Sten, and the result is a conventional passion we take on trust more than feel. Goldwyn's goal of promoting "the next Garbo" set up Sten for easy ridicule, but her hesitations here, or Vidor's direction of them, balance touchingly between Old World reserve and sexual magnetism, between stolid peasant and Jefferson's "natural aristocrat," between oppression and vitality. Perhaps by the time of this "Goldwyn's Last Sten," he'd found a role tailored to her limitations.

The film's inapt title emblemizes the romantic holdovers from its origin. From a Goldwyn perspective, it could look like one of his dramas of marital or sexual anguish, a second *Cynara.* Once again the unfaithful husband extricates himself with troubling lightness from the "other's woman's" death. Barrett must have it on his conscience, however, that, though Manya helped him find himself, he abandoned her to a life that her glimpse of American liberty, through him, would have rendered unbearable to her. Vidor's back-to-the-land trilogy is also an adultery trilogy. All those stark marriages throughout Vidor's work can't be written off to Hollywood.

Here it's the city wife who, as tactic, but truthfully too, reminds Manya that she has no "common ground" with Barrett. She repeats the rationalizing words of *Cynara*'s Warlock, which here reaffirm her condescension toward the immigrant community as a whole: "Well, we certainly have delightful neighbors. We *must* have them up to dinner sometime." She lingers before returning to the city to spend the land money only long enough to mock the ancestral portraits on the walls ("Are you the one that cleared the land with your own bare hands; well, bless your heart"). Meanwhile, their Japanese servant enacts a gothic joke version of the immigrant's fearful traditionalism by glancing back over his shoulders for the ghosts of "an-chest-ahs." Between an obsolescent patriarchy and "sophisticated" gag put-downs, Gary Cooper's Barrett picks his half-authentic, half-cagey way.

This minor film in the Vidor canon has a particular interest for venturing into the shadows into which Hollywood's bright lights plunged an important part of America's evolution. In Barrett, city and artistic individualism has encouraged a petty egoism; the Polish poor have community, but it's overly restrictive. The golden mean is a mixture of mobility and rootedness. The writer must relate sophistication (the city) and simplicity (the country), and it's all too easy for him to be evasive and self-

Figure 79.   The Wedding Night *(1935). Frederik (Ralph Bellamy), Manya (Anna Sten), and Barrett (Gary Cooper).*

deluding. But he contrives, with Manya's help, to synthesize a fuller art. In a sense, Manya is the *substitute* victim of his mobility. True, the film emphasizes another cause of her tragedy: the bestial near-rape and accidental murder that could be taken as the logical conclusion of the immigrant group's cohesiveness, as its essence, as its Old World decadence unveiled. The spectator may of course prefer an alternative reading: that Manya's fate reflects the community's *real* spirit as little as do the land-lusting conspirators of *The Stranger's Return*.* Every norm has its abuses, but brutal sex is patriarchy gone wrong, not patriarchy as such.

*Fred Zinnemann's *Oklahoma!* (1955) is a fascinating example of the difficulties here. In this idyllic slice of Americana, the nasty subplot involving Rod Steiger sticks out like a sore thumb. Maybe it's because the film, like the show, concedes, honestly enough, that rustic life can have its lonely, ugly, warped side; but it doesn't know how to relate it to the positive side. So it emphasizes the bad guy while abstracting him from any community pressure. It's a haunting equivocation. All by himself Steiger's "poor Judd" carries the vices distributed through the various little people in Thornton Wilder's *Our Town*. He is also a descendant of various rural Mephistopheleses, like the devil who tries to drive a bargain with Daniel Webster in *All That Money Can Buy*. The tangle of good and evil in rural life, and the problem of its implications for America, is easier to deal with when the American system isn't in question—for example, in Frank Borzage's *Moonrise*, Sydney Pollack's *This Property Is Condemned*, and John Schlesinger's *Midnight Cowboy*.

It's hard to say how far Goldwyn, or Vidor, wanted Polish "alienness" to bear the brunt of the blame. Our suspicion is that spectators whose immigrant family experience is fresh in memory would treat Manya's fate as a tragic anomaly, while others (and these will be the majority) would have veered nearer the anti-Polish response. To wit: "While Polish immigrants may eventually be capable of aspiring to Americanism (as young Manya does), old Polish ways are not merely different, or out-of-place, but in themselves bad." If Manya is a tragic figure and not a vamp, as a coarser film might have made her, it's because her natural goodness has already responded to the possibilities of America. If she isn't exactly a "good Injun," her plight comes over as entirely her community's fault.

Now that we're more sensitive to "roots," we're more likely to wish for a more complex moral movement, whereby, however alien and harsh the old Polish culture may initially seem, Barrett comes to respect its raison d'être. In this light, his feelings for Manya would be a response not, as here, to the American-style glamor that sets her so far apart from her fellow Poles, but for those qualities of hers that could only grow in their culture. And to which Barrett, being what he is, can come no closer than nostalgia. Which exiles him forever from Manhattan glitz, or anywhere else, so that he is at home nowhere, and everywhere.

Maybe it's unfair to expect some such sophistication from the film at a time when rural America, ravaged by the Depression, rejected renewed immigration so violently that the Johnson-Reed Act virtually stopped further immigration after 1929. *The Wedding Night* doesn't explicitly question those overly optimistic melting-pot theories whereby the diversity of immigrant talents painlessly concocts a uniquely American richness. But it asserts that cultural shock would be longer and more painful than melting-pot theory had supposed (a position too often confused with racism).

One respects *The Wedding Night* for raising the issue of new immigrant cultures at all, and it's one of those unjust ironies of critical response that the film's near uniqueness (as far as we know) makes us steadily more irritated as the minority culture is steadily blackened to conform to spectator prejudice. Beyond those earlier titles mentioned in connection with *Street Scene*, only a handful of sound-era films face the issues of white immigrant groups at all straightforwardly, most of them in the postwar years. Joseph L. Mankiewicz's *House of Strangers* (1949), a variation on the *King Lear* theme, looks with some compassion on the founder of an Italian bank who can't adapt to American legalism. Around the same time, a sentimentally liberal, but likable, acceptance of ethnocultural plurality informs several of Dore Schary's B productions at MGM (*Glory Alley, My Man and I, A Lady without Passport*). But such films are in a minority. Tough, tight-lipped heroes rule the postwar decade:

nomadic monads, reluctant to reveal their emotions or weaknesses—or roots. Kazan was particularly conscious of immigrant subcultures, from *Panic in the Streets*, through the Eli Wallach–Karl Malden confrontation in *Baby Doll*, to *America, America*. By the mid sixties, it looked as if a New York Jewish nerviness had been accepted as a sort of portmanteau non-WASP style (much as the New York Irish style had been so accepted thirty years earlier), possibly for good reasons (Jewishness as a well-adapted urban style) as well as an ultra-cautious one ("Some of the smartest people . . .").

Through the seventies, Italians muscled in on the Jewish monopoly on non-WASP styles, compellingly so in the outsider rage of the Robert De Niro of Scorsese, Coppola, Cimino, and early De Palma—a pattern coming full circle with De Niro's ostensibly Jewish gangster for Sergio Leone. But immigrant themes were buried under a macho, Catholic angst; and a nostalgia for first-generation immigrant life pastelized even the edges of *The Godfather(s)*. The enormous disparity between the immigrant experience in America and its rare appearance on screen has remained a Hollywood constant. Louis Malle's Vietnamese-immigrant drama *Alamo Bay* is the most sympathetic of a southern "Fortress America" cycle in the eighties, which also included the (tellingly titled) *Borderline* and *The Border*, both of which cover their bets with documentary pity and cynicism ("Sleep tight, America—your tax dollars are hard at work").

George Seaton's *Anything Can Happen* (1952) is one of the few films to endow its immigrant with the quirky remnants of Old World habits so often missing from more solemnly goodhearted treatments like *A Ship Comes In* and, alas, Vidor's *An American Romance*. Seaton has discussed the problem of essaying an immigrant theme a little too clearly:

> Do you remember a film called *Anything Can Happen?* It was about George Papashvily, a Georgian, a little man (played brilliantly, I thought, by José Ferrer) who didn't belong in his own country but so desperately wanted to belong somewhere. It won a United Nations Organization award; the corps of foreign correspondents in the United States loved it; and on the whole it got good critical notices. But it was a colossal commercial failure. People actually came out of their homes and went down to the local theatres where it was playing just to stand outside and say, "Let's *not* go in." I should know, because I made it.
>
> And having made it, and having seen how completely I failed to communicate with a mass audience, I quit film-making for a while to try to find the reason why. I worked for the International Refugee Organization of the U.N., and one of the refugees it was my duty to receive was an old man from Poland, whose sister had been living in the States for several years.
>
> Everything, I thought, would be easy. There would be a happy family reunion, and I would do a quick dissolve into the background. How wrong

I was! The facts were that the sister didn't want him. She had actually sent him a letter saying, "We Americans don't want any more foreigners, so go back where you come from."

I learnt the sad lesson that no one is more anti-foreigner than those who until recently were "foreign" themselves. My film had come too near to reality. I had identified too closely. Too many Americans saw themselves and their immediate family on the screen; and instead of feeling pity, they felt animosity.[37]

Seaton's story explains a good deal about *The Wedding Night*. Samuel Goldwyn was himself a Polish immigrant. Joseph Losey's rare concern for his Polish-American hero in *The Big Night* (1951) becomes more meaningful when one relates it to the about-to-dawn era of Polish jokes and other ethnic sickies. ("Why are there only two pallbearers at a Polish funeral?"—"Because a garbage can only has two handles.") Ironically, such obnoxious cracks may have indicated the emergence of a crucial shift from tabu into frankness.

The Polish spelling of Vidor's name is "Wajda," but any connection is indirect, for Vidor is primarily a Magyar name. King's Budapest-born grandfather came to America as a press agent for a Hungarian violinist, and stayed, no doubt thankful to escape the repressive Austrian rule. For all the longstanding frictions between Poles and Hungarians in Europe, it's reasonable to assume that Vidor's Americanism was independent of any inherited animosity; and there is no reason to assume that he had been involved in a Central European authoritarianism like that depicted in *The Wedding Night*.

All the same, cultural tendencies often continue more deeply than their inheritors realize, and it's perfectly possible that Vidor's Texas expansionism wasn't without its family-transmitted, European immigrant undercurrent. Back in the Eastern European forests and plains, no natural boundaries protected ethno-cultural groups. During centuries of struggle or occupation, they preserved their identity and community only through cavalry audacity or by communal *will*. With the collapse of the Austro-Hungarian empire, that tradition, which with its sense of "communal imperative" can seem so arbitrary, contributed, perhaps, to that Eastern European sense of the absurd. If the muscular and nervous tone of Vidor's transcendentalism differs so profoundly from Emerson's, it may well have a double, rather than a single, source—from the Eastern European plains, as well as the Texas ones.

Where we might expect Vidor to share with Capra some "fantasy of goodwill," he counts, rather, on a spontaneous identity of individual and community interest. His communities, even when they're argued out, as in *Our Daily Bread*, feel less like "love," or even "enlightened self-interest," than a sudden coalescence into an atavistically instinctive cohesion. The communities—how diverse!—of *Hallelujah, Our Daily Bread, The Texas Rangers,* and *Northwest Passage* are all communities of the spirit, of the *will,* where initially laborious effort is rewarded with a sort of magic transcendence. Vidor is conscious of their economic infrastructure (hence his films should interest Marxists), but its importance is regularly presented as an expression of moral fiber (which defuses any economic materialism).

The hypothesis of an inherited European influence on Vidor can be made only tentatively, and we risk it because we fear that ancestry is still so touchy a subject that we're less likely to mislead anybody if we're wrong than to be dismissed too rapidly if we're right. But social anthropologists seem to have the feeling that older cultural patterns subsist under newer forms rather more persistently than had once been thought, or leave a kind of spiritual void if they don't.

The European/American conflict in *The Wedding Night* is the antithesis of that in *The Big Parade.* There, love crosses all boundaries; here it is frustrated by them. Where *The Stranger's Return* and *Our Daily Bread* assert an escape into rustic community, *The Wedding Night* asserts a tragic failure to escape from it—at least from Manya's immigrant perspective. The various positions aren't inconsistent, given the differing nature of the communities. The Polish community of *The Wedding Night* looks backward into peasant feudalism. The cooperators of *Our Daily Bread* look to the future, emancipated from their past. Tony Barrett's New York coterie abounds in petty egotists and constitutes a spiritually infested society. But at least one can escape from the city, and revive an inspirational *idea* of community.

6

1935 to 1944:

"Through Dim Lulls
of Unapparent Growth"

King Vidor's truest success in these years was off-film. Troubled by the director's waning power within the production system, he explored the possibility of a new union. In late 1935 thirteen (possibly fourteen) directors met for final discussions at Vidor's home—among them Herbert Biberman, Frank Borzage, Howard Hawks, Henry King, Ernst Lubitsch, Rouben Mamoulian, Lewis Milestone, and William Wellman. In January 1936 the Screen Directors Guild was incorporated, with twenty-nine founding members and Vidor as its first president. Two years later, it had grown to some six hundred, including virtually every active director and assistant director. Under the name it took in 1960 (after incorporating television directors), the Directors Guild of America remains a key Hollywood bargaining and professional unit.

In these ten years all Vidor's own films were compromised by their production situations or by his uncertainties. And a growing number of projects were abandoned in pre-production.

After *The Wedding Night*, Ernst Lubitsch, newly appointed production chief at Paramount, approached Vidor to film *So Red the Rose* (1935), a bestseller with a southern perspective on the Civil War. Vidor himself initiated his second historical epic for Paramount, *The Texas Rangers* (1936). Although Paramount got behind epics at a time when other studios abandoned them, neither film proved commercially successful. Indeed, *So Red the Rose* was widely cited as proof that *Gone with the Wind* would flop. Nevertheless, Paramount, urging Vidor to stay, offered him another Texas epic, *Sam Houston*, which he turned down in a letter to production head William LeBaron (who replaced Lubitsch in 1936):

"As we discussed before, I've such a belly-full of Texas after the Rangers that I find myself not caring whether Sam Houston takes Texas from the Mexicans or lets them keep it."

Instead, Vidor returned to Samuel Goldwyn for a 1937 remake of the producer's silent melodrama, *Stella Dallas*. Goldwyn disrupted shooting by announcing to the cast that they were universally "terrible" and would be replaced. "It was very painful," Vidor recalled. At the end of principal photography, Vidor posted a vow above his desk: "No More Goldwyn Pictures!" But he was nonetheless able to supervise the final cut and was pleased with the result.

Although the Screen Directors Guild imposed itself successfully, it had to make more compromises than Vidor first envisioned. Following *Stella Dallas*, he promoted a directors' cooperative—"Screen Directors, Inc."—composed of four directors, each drawing a relatively small up-front salary and large profit percentage. The colleagues most actively committed to the plan were Lewis Milestone and Gregory La Cava (although Vidor was not keen on the latter's participation: "Hawks is more reliable than La Cava," he wrote to Milestone). Despite start-up financing and release agreements from RKO, the plan fell apart. But it would not be Vidor's last attempt at such a cooperative.

Perhaps it was the disappointments over the cooperative, as well as the production tensions of *Stella Dallas,* that sent Vidor back to the MGM fold exclusively for five pictures released between 1938 and 1944, under a contract beginning at $3,500 dollars a week. He had turned down two offers (in 1934 and 1937) from David O. Selznick to direct *The Adventures of Tom Sawyer,* despite the fascination of the Mississippi milieu. It was also in 1937 that Vidor's announced engagement with Hollywood columnist Sheilah Graham was broken off, either (as Vidor said) because she had met F. Scott Fitzgerald, or (as she said) because Vidor had taken up again with Elizabeth Hill (whom he was soon to marry).

The Citadel (1938) was his first MGM film under the new contract and the studio's second British co-production, with a script coauthored by Elizabeth Hill. Working outside America for the first time, he hired Pare Lorentz to assist with the documentary feel of the Welsh mining sequences. Back in Hollywood, Vidor briefly considered Selznick's request to assume direction of *Gone with the Wind* after the firing of George Cukor. Instead, he completed the final three weeks of shooting on MGM's *The Wizard of Oz,* thereby freeing Victor Fleming for *Gone with the Wind.* It's a happy irony that Vidor, who never had his much desired chance at a true musical, nevertheless directed (without credit) Hollywood's most fondly remembered musical number, "Over the Rainbow." He was responsible for most of the black-and-white "Kansas" frame (fig. 80) and for small bits of the Technicolor center (including the last leg

Figure 80.   From Vidor's sequences of The Wizard of Oz *(1939). Judy Garland and Bert Lahr.*

of the Yellow Brick Road, where the travelers are enchanted into sleep within sight of Oz).

His many uncompleted projects in these MGM years included *National Velvet* and *The Yearling*, both of which ultimately went to Clarence Brown. For six months in 1939 and 1940 Vidor prepared *The Witch in the Wilderness*, a high-passion Amazon-river adventure with a ship of fools who crash their boat far from civilization. "As it has been my baby from the beginning, I intend to make it very much my responsibility to finish," he wrote. But the equally complex pre-production for *Northwest Passage* (1940) took precedence. Concerned by the weather and falling lake levels, he left in July 1939 for what became eight weeks of Idaho location work (made particularly cumbersome by Technicolor cameras; fig. 81), carrying what he believed was the first half of the script. But the original conception was destroyed by studio decisions to abandon the second half, and the ending was tacked on by a substitute director, Jack Conway.

The routine political comedy *Comrade X* (1940) was a minor relaxation.* More personal was the film of J. P. Marquand's *H. M. Pulham, Esq.* (1941), for which Vidor and Elizabeth Hill shared script credit. (Much later, probably in 1953, he and Marquand failed to persuade Charles Lindbergh that they were the right team to film *The Spirit of St. Louis*.)

Preferring not to join a military film unit in World War II, Vidor threw his soul into a patriotic saga of industrial and immigrant success, "an ideal of American democracy." The result, after three years and an uncountable number of scripts, was *An American Romance* (1944), which

---

*Briefly discussed in the filmography only.

Figure 81. Tracking shot with an 800-pound, three-strip Technicolor camera and dolly on location for Northwest Passage; *Payette Lake, Idaho.*

turned into his deepest disappointment. Originally fashioned for Spencer Tracy, Ingrid Bergman, and Joseph Cotten, the eventual cast may have been ruinous. But MGM also cut thirty minutes soon after release, without Vidor's assistance and based on patterns in the soundtrack music. Returning only to collect his belongings, Vidor left the MGM lot for good, "deeply discouraged."

Regional Barbarism: *So Red the Rose* (1935), *The Texas Rangers* (1936), and *Northwest Passage* (1940), with a Glance Back at *Billy the Kid* (1930)

In the middle of a forgettable fifties Western (*Escape from Ft. Bravo*), troopers conduct a twenty-questions inquiry into the mysterious past of a new woman in camp. She's not from out west; she's not from back east, not from up north, and not from down south. "Must be from Texas!"

one brightly concludes. It's a moment Vidor might have enjoyed, what with his keen sense of American regionalism and his home-grown feel for Texas. Indeed, on a model drawn from his Westerns, one could sort out Vidor's Easterns (e.g., *The Crowd, Street Scene, H. M. Pulham, Esq.*), Northerns (*An American Romance, Beyond the Forest, Northwest Passage*), Midwesterns (*Our Daily Bread, The Stranger's Return*, and many of the pre-MGM silents), and Southerns. Oddly, in four of the six periods into which we've lopped his career, Vidor followed a Southern with a Western: *The Jack-Knife Man* before *The Sky Pilot, Hallelujah* before *Billy the Kid* (with *Not So Dumb* intervening), *Ruby Gentry* before *Man without a Star*. And, in the period we take up now, *So Red the Rose* before *The Texas Rangers*.

The most involving of these regional studies relish the violent excesses typically identified with his postwar melodramas. But such passion is just what's sadly lacking in this pair of Paramount historical sagas, as if they were smoothing the way for the gray, professional responsibility of *The Citadel* and *H. M. Pulham, Esq.* It is *Billy the Kid*, back before the 1933 Production Code, and *Northwest Passage*, as World War II loomed, that—however deep their production flaws—grapple with the spirit in which battles, military and/or spiritual, might be waged. Of all Vidor's films, *Northwest Passage* explores the lurid zone where vitalism shades into the variety of Social Darwinism, red in tooth and claw, one may call patriotic, chauvinistic, jingoistic, or genocidal—depending on whether one is an American, a Frenchman, an Englishman, or an Indian.

So Red the Rose

This southern Civil War saga is overshadowed by *Gone with the Wind* (which, even as a novel, it anticipates) on the one hand and by *The Birth of a Nation* on the other. Vidor's film, at just over a third the length of its famous counterparts, feels like their breakneck essence. Riders with news of Fort Sumter excite the Bedford family's plantation, "Portobello," with rhetorical visions of Lincoln hung from the tallest oak. The pacifism—or is it one-nation Americanism?—of cousin Duncan (Randolph Scott) disgusts the belle, Vallette (Margaret Sullavan), who sees her less cherished beaus ride off to duty. As horror arrives in letters from the front, even Duncan enlists, while Vallette channels her spirit into quelling a slave revolt. But she, her mother, and a female slave are no match for Sherman's march, which puts the torch to Portobello—and toughens them into survivors, who cook over an open fire and toil in the fields.

So Red the Rose touches, in its mild, tamed way, on the paradoxes of conflict between moral equals—the individual northern and southern soldiers of the Civil War. In addition, it introduces a visiting Texan (Rob-

Figure 82.   On the set of So Red the Rose *(1935). Margaret Sullavan (Vallette) and Elizabeth Hill, uncredited assistant director and, subsequently, Vidor's
third wife.*

ert Cummings, who claimed to be Texan at the time) into its Mississippi
cotton plantation, thus clashing two distinct southern regional responses
to political insult.

As nearly as *The Birth of a Nation*, Vidor's is an unrepentant—unreconstructed—Southern. It's also the last unselfconscious, pre-gothic
Southern before Wyler and Selznick, with their Jezebels and Scarletts and
sundry little foxes, led the way for Tennessee Williams. It does shift some
way from *Birth*'s aristocratic viewpoint toward a common man's skepticism about the paternalistic plantation "massah," Malcolm Bedford
("I've never been a bad master, and you've never been bad slaves"). He's
somewhat diminished, too, from his models, St. Claire in *Uncle Tom's
Cabin* and Griffith's porch-settin', julep-sippin' "kindly master." Virgin-
ians of the Old South would have disdained him as a "cotton snob"—a
first-generation "aristocrat" who hadn't quite succeeded in rounding off
the rough edges of the pioneer. As W. J. Cash observes in *The Mind of the
South*, everything about his world would conspire to blind such a Mississippi cotton snob to its social tensions: the lack of class pressure from
blacks *or* whites below him, the otherworldliness of his evangelistic religion, and the scapegoating of changes for the worse onto Yankee swine.[1]

Figure 83.   So Red the Rose. *Malcolm Bedford (Walter Connelly) with a death-grip on his mint julep.*

Bedford has settled into an aristocratic complacency from which the film derives its rather facile comic moments, as in his alcoholic fury at locating only ludicrous hats to go with his ornate battle uniform. But the film comes round to sentimentalizing him too. As he dies, a close-up frames his hand, a "Confederate States of America" belt buckle, a spilt julep (fig. 83).

And yet, *because* of its stock figures, *So Red the Rose* can play around with traditions. As W. J. Cash hints, the Civil War was never a battle between an inflexible northern puritanism and some mellower southern living, but between *two* puritanisms—the South's evangelism having turned harsh at the same time that religious participation became a social requirement. Whatever the comedy in the Southerner's rhetorical bluster, Vidor, like Hollywood generally, had no hesitation in choosing the more dynamic of the two puritanisms. As Buster Keaton said (in connection with *The General*), "You can't make a villain out of the South." The southern melodrama of *Wild Oranges* and the baptist ecstasy of *Hallelujah* converge in the bloodlust that overtakes the Bedford plantation.

The visiting Texan, bringing to the mansion his competing frontier mythology, remains unmoved by Mrs. Bedford's effort to "convert" him "to our calm way of doing things." He's impatient with the formalities of vengeance, and rides off, six-guns blazing, on the night of the Fort Sumter news. His Mississippi schoolfriend, family scion Edward Bedford, apologizes: "Don't think I'm *trying* to stay behind." Chivalric *and* frontier honor meet insults with violence—a duel just takes a good deal more arranging than a showdown. Only within this doubled violence ethic—southern and Texan—does Duncan look a pacifist. He turns soldier along with the rest of the family, but with neither social mythology. (In *Gone with the Wind* his counterpart in reasonableness is Ashley Wilkes.)

Duncan returns to the mansion for Vidor to rephrase the dialectic of vengeance and compassion. *The Big Parade* put Apperson in a foxhole with a dying German. The question here is whether Duncan will hand over for execution a wounded northern boy Vallette has taken pity on and disguised as a Confederate. (Griffith used the situation in *The Fugitive* [1910] and *In Old Kentucky* [1909].) It's Apperson's dilemma drawn out, with silences and reversals (that is, it's played for suspense, not surprise) until humanity wins out, just, over war-forged cruelty. Painfully, Duncan finds his way back to his original position. That little moral battle in the manor is forced to stand in for the convention of an equal North/South sacrifice on the battlefield that the film hasn't time, or budget, to otherwise explore. "I don't believe Americans should fight Americans" is Duncan's credo. The structure's mainspring is a neat, but still drastic, irony: Duncan's and Vallette's war experiences flip-flop *both* their ideals, leaving them (until the final resolution) just as far apart.

When, early in the war, she charges spunkily into a barnful of rabble-roused slaves, we are hit with the depth of the film's southern sentimentality. She takes over the cotton-bale podium from the slave Cato, who's been promising a "freedom" of "no work" and "sittin' round in coats and brass buttons." She turns them round with a speech that slyly mixes belle-sentiment (how one family's kindness has transcended the peculiar institution) and puritan logic ("I don't say you should be slaves, but I say you have to go on working if you want to eat"). Thus she embodies, demurely, that iron southern paternalism that, at least during Andrew Johnson's brief presidency, restored the spirit of slavery through a matrix of "vagrancy" laws. She's a descendant of Harriet Beecher Stowe's Little Eva, knocking the slaves witless with her fine ways. The underlying economics is uncovered by a happy accident of film casting. Here Clarence Muse as Cato bows to Vallette's argument and turns misty-eyed over her little brother's reminder of the rabbit trap he's promised to build (fig. 84). Thus he consigns himself to reappear, like his own grandson, in Michael Curtiz's *Cabin in the Cotton* (1932), where Muse is a blind sharecropper ever further in hock (at 40 percent interest) to the owner's store.*

---

* Curtiz's film is something of a white *Hallelujah* (down to its use of footage from Vidor's film), with blacks a picturesque footnote of deeper oppression. Its solution to white "peckerwood" sharecroppers taking the crops they figure they've earned is the unpersuasive compromise of a planter/tenant cooperative.

Figure 84.   So Red the Rose. *So long, Nat Turner. Clarence Muse (Cato), Dickie Moore, and Margaret Sullavan.*

Nevertheless, Vallette's tactics keep the community surviving. War transforms her from a belle who spouted passion for "youth" and "Byron," and who was as dreamy about war as Apperson's hometown girl, into a woman who leans on her hoe as confidently as Melisande on her plow. The direct aristo-slave symbiosis (the film excludes "white trash") gives its subsistence-farm finale the allure of Rousseauian pastoralism, as if the family has dug back into some arcadian peasant, not peckerwood, simplicity. Duncan returns to a flexible, pastoral family in place of the patriarch's "continuity" of slaveholders. For all the decency of the Old South, this New South is better off in every spiritual way for having weathered the death of a sham aristocracy.

Billy the Kid and The Texas Rangers

Billy the Kid stumbles into its exploration of social violence. It's a deeply flawed film, overly sentimental in its casting of Johnny Mack Brown as Billy and Wallace Beery as his nemesis, Sheriff Pat Garrett. But it enjoyed the good fortune to have been made before the tightening of the Production Code in 1933. For twenty years thereafter, Westerns were fated to easy moral dichotomies between white Stetsons and black. *Billy*

Figure 85.   Widescreen composition in the 70mm version of Billy the Kid *(1930). Unlike other large-screen experiments around this time, MGM's reduced the camera negative for release in masked 35mm. Although MGM was far and away the leading studio in preservation of its output,* Billy the Kid *has apparently survived only in the standard format, except for a few frames Vidor himself kept, including the one above. Evidence of the panoramic location work remains—in the cattleherd duststorms, Billy's sheer-walled canyon hideout (in which Vidor stands in the cover photograph), and particularly the authentic recreation of the tawdry spaciousness of Lincoln, New Mexico.*

the Kid cleaves to the old silent tradition, where white and black dwell in the soul of the lone rider, but brings it into the era of vehement gangster-film killings. It's a fascinating mix of archaic indulgence and modern murder.

The Texas Rangers, in 1936, tries for a mellower variation, with its outlaw/lawman lead (a part written and publicized for Gary Cooper, which went instead to Fred MacMurray). While Billy the Kid shuttles between being a justified and a near-psychotic murderer, MacMurray's "Jim Hawkins" *matures* rationally from outlaw to G-man. Even back in 1930, Vidor had trouble "convincing Thalberg that all the Kid's murders were understandable, if not entirely excusable."[2] If Billy's revenging a murdered father-figure and his protection of immigrant small ranchers are morally unimpeachable in principle, his *methods* are out of kilter with the Code of the West. When an accomplice tries to instruct him in the appropriate strategy for drawing their antagonists out of the saloon into the street for a High-Noon showdown, Billy interrupts, "Won't be no standup, Tom. I'll just go in and shoot down any of them that's there, come on back out. Won't be no trouble and no violence."

The Texas Rangers avoids that deadpan tone. A light morality tale, it follows three outlaws (MacMurray, Jack Oakie, and Lloyd Nolan). The

Figure 86.   New Mexico, standing in for Texas, in The Texas Rangers *(1936).*

first two join the Rangers out of cunning desperation, but come to see the honor of their job and end by hunting down the third. Its moral conflict—"friendship versus duty"—is stated, just that baldly, in a note from Oakie to MacMurray in jail, before Oakie rides out after their reprobate ex-friend. Thus the two Rangers begin outside society, then join it, then acknowledge a *duty* to maintain it—a pious, and dull, progression. *Billy*

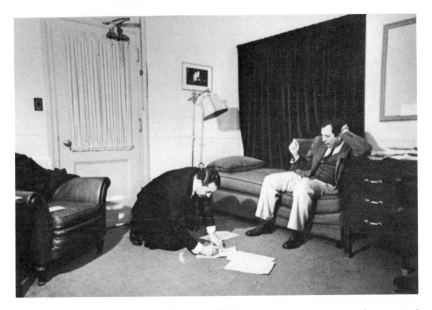

Figure 87.   Louis Stevens, on floor, and Vidor, yawning, at work on the script of The Texas Rangers.

the Kid's happy ending* matches *Stagecoach*'s satisfyingly "illegalist" conclusion (lawman turns his back while good-badman heads for the border with new-found ladylove). Not that Billy's private vengeance quite so honorably matches up with community service as John Wayne's.

Some following Vidor films (*The Citadel, Northwest Passage,* and *An American Romance*) suggest that he was becoming sympathetic to the responsibility for remaking civilization, a widespread mood of the late 1930s, not only in the land of the New Deal. And the shift that appears in Vidor's two Westerns is observable throughout thirties America moviemaking. Nick Roddick, in his study of Warner Brothers in the thirties, traces it through the Edward G. Robinson and James Cagney gangster films—from the complex morality of *Little Caesar* and *The Public Enemy* (both released shortly after *Billy the Kid*) to *Bullets or Ballots* and *G-Men* (both released shortly before *The Texas Rangers*), in which Robinson and Cagney are tamed into heroic government agents.[3] In the course of *G-Men*, Cagney grows from outlaw to FBI man—the contemporary version of *The Texas Rangers*' pattern.

We've elaborated elsewhere on gangster and Western movies as complementary genres—unsynthesized thesis and antithesis, as it were.[4] If

---

*Vidor initially shot an ending truer to the legend, where Garrett takes advantage of Billy being backlit to gun him down. It played in some European theaters.

they continue separate existences, it's not only because of the city/country dichotomy traditional in American thinking, but also to spare everyone involved the controversies that might arise were their synthesis achieved.* *Billy the Kid*'s strange synthesis of Western innocence and gangster morality makes it the "missing link" in the movies' sociology, and constitutes its challenge to the audience. Thalberg objected that the public would never take to a hero committing "too many murders,"[5] and when Vidor and Laurence Stallings urged the contrary, they may well have had the career of Al Capone in mind. Around 1930, who didn't? With the 1929 St. Valentine's Day Massacre and the formation of the Justice Department's "Untouchables" under Eliot Ness, Capone's fame had reached its height, even as his days were numbered. But, especially with his grandiose food giveaways in 1930, Capone never stopped being a hero to some immigrant groups. Billy sends in a bullet before he first walks on screen, just as does Howard Hawks's gangster, Scarface, two years later. Billy shoots a bully who was poised for an easier showdown, who (like us) never saw him coming, and Vidor plays the entrance as heroic introduction. John Ford, much later, plays such a murderous intervention in somebody else's High Noon quite differently, when John Wayne shoots Lee Marvin's Liberty Valance. There, it's a very uneasy, legend-questioning revelation. Johnny Mack Brown hasn't a prayer of pulling off the vengeance-justification-by-force-of-personality key to the Cagney/Robinson gangster cycle, so that our rooting interest is distanced, and would be even more so were there any rival centers of attention around. Murders from charismatic, hyped-up, sharp-tongued ethnic gangsters are emotionally compelling. From clean-shaven, rational-voiced Billy, it's something else again. *The Public Enemy* digs up a wild corollary of the vengeance ethic when Cagney, fresh from the funeral of his sharpie boss, buys the racehorse responsible for his death, shoots it, and storms out of the stall, horseblanket in hand. Vidor's Billy is never quite mad, never even really wrong, but is progressively disconcerting. With Johnny Mack Brown's Alabama accent, Billy is like some calm, smiling, gray-suited evangelist, reasoning step by plausible step from "God is Love" to Hellfire for all. Billy, on his terms, is always right. But Sheriff Pat Garrett is more right—the New Testament to Billy's Mosaic Law, one might say. Do two

---

*Such a synthesis would sooner or later involve many of the very touchy social issues traced in Kenneth Allsop's *The Bootleggers* (London: Hutchinson, 1968), Andrew Sinclair's *Prohibition: The Era of Excess* (Boston: Little, Brown, 1962), and the chapter on "Crime as an American Way of Life" in Daniel Bell's *The End of Ideology* (New York: Free Press, 1960). The closest the two genres came to that synthesis—Spaghetti Westerns—proved unduplicatable in America (Sergio Leone's own *Once upon a Time in America* notwithstanding). Intermittently, fragments of the synthesis appear from Hollywood: a Western baron imports his most evil gunmen from the city; a bank robbed by Bonnie and Clyde (rural WASP gangsters) has just foreclosed on a tenant farmer.

rights make a wrong? Our theories of tragedy would say so. And the tragedy of the anarcho-right is close to Vidor's nerve.

Ultimately, *Billy the Kid* becomes the anti–*Little Caesar*, through its demonstration of the historical context in which smooth and smiling killings are OK. There is moral shock in the gangster-cycle murders (Little Caesar's no-nonsense execution on cathedral steps of a would-be confessor; the easy banter of the "Public Enemy" with victim "Putty Nose"), but the deaths themselves are perfunctory. Vidor never slickens the killings in *Billy the Kid*. When they occur on-screen, life chokes out before any touchingly comprehensible last words, but after the screams of agony. It may not be possible to carry off (at least with an actor like Roscoe Ates) the shifts between jokiness and realism that Vidor stabs at. But he undercuts the moral acceptability of murder in Westerns through a frightening staging.

After these shocking deaths, *The Texas Rangers*' lack of any but a pictorial realism is a letdown. It turns passably crisp only at its conclusion, when the two friends turn against the third. The death of Wahoo (Jack Oakie) is staged, at least, for unclichéd surprise: Sam (Lloyd Nolan), having discovered the double-cross, sits opposite Wahoo and flips cards to tell his (bad) fortune; we hear a shot, see smoke rising from under the table, notice Sam's been fortune-telling with only one hand. The shock comes also from it being a very rare violation of the convention in Western films that the buffoon figure doesn't die. (The previous year, Fox had shot a new ending to *Call of the Wild* after previews revealed that Jack Oakie could not acceptably be killed off.)

Thalberg agreed to *Billy the Kid* at a time when the death of the Western was widely predicted in the wake of sound; MGM's eye was probably on the widescreen possibilities. At the start of the decade, nervous major studios took on only established classics (*The Virginian, The Spoilers*) or pumped up every other story into an epic, a style that weighs uncomfortably on Vidor's historically insignificant outlaw. Despite *Cimarron's* best-picture Oscar in 1931, the A Western was, as predicted, moribund between 1931 and 1939—or perhaps it was held siege by the nearly one thousand B Westerns of those years. The resulting atmosphere permeated the structure of *The Texas Rangers* (an A Western, although its budget was reduced from $625,000 to $450,000 when Gary Cooper was replaced). Between the parentheses of introducing and disposing of its characters, it contains what amount to two B Westerns: "The Texas Rangers Wipe Out the Injuns" and "The Texas Rangers Wipe Out a Monopolist."

The Indians charge in with B speed, encircling a homestead and massacring the family in less screen time than that taken for the father's dying paean to pioneers. And they're killed off with the B feature's ludicrous ease—though not before they've rolled boulders onto the Rangers down

Figure 88.   The Texas Rangers besieged by boulders: "Only an Indian could think that up!" Jack Oakie (Wahoo), at left, and Fred MacMurray (Jim Hawkins).

some stark cliffs (fig. 88). Within the conventions of the genre, the Indian and monopolist episodes neatly split the film into right and left wings, while sketching trial cartoons for *Northwest Passage*'s savage anti-Injunism and *Duel in the Sun*'s comeuppance of a belligerent Texan. Here the town boss is led blustering to a fifty-year sentence once the slick Ranger coaxes Judge Gabby Hayes through the motions of a barroom trial. The episode isn't nearly as pointed as Republic's *Winds of the Wasteland* the same year, with its Depression parable of a monopolist stageline owner defeated by a small town's restored "confidence." But the Ranger's courtroom summary is a pep-talk to the citizens of the jury to be worthy of their nation.

Vidor and Elizabeth Hill claimed that *The Texas Rangers* was based on Walter Prescott Webb's history, but it comes across as entirely too quirky to pass as anything resembling truth. Such vague historical trappings appear in many self-consciously defensive A Westerns of the mid thirties (*The Plainsman, Sutter's Gold, Wells Fargo*). Vidor's film is an awkward compromise. It has too much history to join the wonderful subgenre of Westerns "classically" structured and comically undercut (*Along*

Came Jones, Dwan's *Trail of the Vigilantes*), but too little to connect with the reality of Texas itself. "Texas" inspires only the limp framing narration, and a few jokes about size (actually, the sheer cliffs mark the location landscape as well to the west). If the story's central conceit resembles Ford's *Three Bad Men* or the oft-filmed *Three Godfathers*, the tone seems borrowed more from the "Three Mesquiteers," whose jokey comradery took hold in 1935. The casting of MacMurray, Oakie, and Nolan further subverts the solemnity, all three being previously identified as city lounge lizards.

Like its characterizations, *Billy the Kid*'s deadpan comedy erupts in wilder mood shifts within scenes and even single shots. Early sound films were quicker to allow comedy to crash into genres than movies have been since. In Raoul Walsh's *The Big Trail*, another 1930 widescreen epic, solemnity is punctured by one wagoner's mother-in-law troubles; the 1929 version of *The Virginian* retains the cowpoke hi-jinx of switching babies at the mass christening. Vidor ricochets between comedy, violence, and a down-home patriotism about law-and-order.

Whatever the mere publicity value of having William S. Hart as advisor on the set, and of his giving Johnny Mack Brown guns allegedly owned by the real Billy the Kid, the archaic spirit of Hart's Westerns (essentially dead with the public by 1921) is pervasive in *Billy the Kid* (fig. 89). Its archaic style comes both from choice and from unavoidable early-talkie constrictions. Close-ups are virtually nonexistent and titles are dotted throughout. Like Victor Fleming before him in *The Virginian*, Vidor does find a few occasions for virtuoso outdoor tracking shots. But the harsh voices and noises, the avoidance of background music, and the restriction of camera movement during dialogue all make *Billy the Kid* more "authentic" than its creators could have predicted. William S. Hart's spirit returns not least in *Billy the Kid*'s recapitulation of the perennial Hart plot: the chivalric redemption of a good-badman. Alas, everything to do with Billy's awe over his father-figure Tunston's fiancée rings conventional, especially with her fussy moralism. (In MGM's 1941 remake, this is almost the only issue: can the kid, scared by tough childhood, be brought round to the side of good by angelic woman and old pal?) Billy's gangster counterparts came complete with spaghetti-toting mamas, and with a parallel need (his own mother having been murdered), he finds himself too many mother surrogates, especially "Mother" McSween and Tunston's fiancée. But when the latter seeks him out as a lover, it's a cool reversal leaving Billy slackjawed. (We'd like to think that Bonnie, picking up her Clyde in Texas in 1930, stopped off to enjoy *Billy the Kid*.)

Vidor emblemizes this clash between the outlaw and high feminine culture in a piano (the emblem reappears in *Duel in the Sun* and *Man without a Star* to come, and gets its most rococo treatments in Huston's

Figure 89.   Presentation of Billy the Kid's six-guns. Johnny Mack Brown, Vidor, William S. Hart.

The Unforgiven and Nicholas Ray's *Johnny Guitar*). As Tunston's fiancée sits down at the piano, Billy examines his guns; he steps out to kill a man off-screen, and returns in time to appreciate the end of her mellow song. Later that night, he gets up from noodling at the piano to sneak out of the house with guns drawn, and turns savagely on the fiancée for "backlighting" him. At the siege, when Garrett's men have the McSween house surrounded, "Mother" McSween frets over their lives: "That's all that matters—except my piano." Which is to say that the battle would hardly be won with civilization lost. By the time of *The Texas Rangers,* the domestic or suburban Western looms, urged on by De Mille's *The Plainsman* (also 1936) and Wyler's *The Westerner* (1940) to reach its height, if that's the word, in the postwar forties. Our Rangers stand much in awe of the

Figure 90. Billy the Kid framed outside the McSweens' familial doorway (Searchers-*style).*

regiment commandant's daughter (a figure who, in the person of Shirley Temple, comes near to scuttling Ford's most nuanced cavalry film, *Fort Apache*). Here she reduces Jim and Wahoo to stammering impotence when they invade her dining room to gripe over her "sissifying" the surviving son of the massacred family. Like Calamity Jane in *The Plainsman*, Jim talks tough against the opposite sex, but when it comes down to it, accepting "apron strings" is what verifies his redemption.

Unconventionally, *Billy the Kid* and *The Texas Rangers* both place their major battles at the midpoint, but both succumb to the genre's gun law. *The Texas Rangers* pauses to admire the paternal commander's office with its shrine of dead Ranger photos, mounted alongside their six-guns. Until its midpoint, *Billy the Kid* centers on the wider issues surrounding the Populist siege, only then narrowing—and how regrettably—to an elite rivalry between Billy and Garrett (comparing bullet holes in ever smaller coins—I'll show you mine if you show me yours). But Vidor goes, pointedly, beyond genre in provoking a sado-shudder with Billy's gleeful technical thrill in having shot a man when he "couldn't see but a quarter inch of his skull." Which points straight to the carnivorous streak in *Northwest Passage*.

Northwest Passage

By the end of the thirties, Hollywood was reviving the Indian wars, and in lavish Technicolor. Ford's *Drums along the Mohawk* and De Mille's *North-West Mounted Police* loomed large in the resurgence of A Westerns generally. If its comeback owed a little to Technicolor landscapes, it probably owed more to less edifying considerations. First, gangster violence had been castrated by the controversies of its city setting, which implicated big business, ethnicity, delinquency, and crime. The Western's blood-and-thunder was reassuringly mythic, rural, and "puritan." Second, the middle classes accepted the new Westerns—perhaps regearing themselves to a pre–World War II hawkishness. The crescendo of violence reveals a premonition of *film noir*. Indeed, it was two *film noir* Westerns, *The Outlaw* and *Duel in the Sun*, that, well ahead of their time, defied the Production Code and the pressure groups it represented.

Billy the Kid had put Vidor ahead of the pack in a new, if qualified, admiration for violence. *Northwest Passage,* the single most ferocious prewar film we know, says it again, with bells on. It's also a Western of sorts, though far from "classic," being set in prerevolutionary America, when the Indian federations were still strong, more like nations than guerrilla bands. As a title, *Northwest Passage* is misleading, being normally associated with exploration around Hudson's Bay; for this French and Indian War saga the more appropriate title would be *Northwest Territory.*

The full screen title—*Northwest Passage (Book 1: Rogers' Rangers)*—suggests Vidor's production disappointments. "The second part was never made because of the producers' lack of courage. In the first part Rogers [Spencer Tracy] was a tremendous hero, but the second part showed his disintegration, and I guess they feared audiences of that time wouldn't accept that. Anyhow, we kept enlarging the first half so much

Figure 91.   Vidor and Spencer Tracy on location in 1939 for Northwest Passage.

that it became a full-length picture, and it was always anticipated that I would continue on to do the second part. We even kept the actors on salary for a couple of weeks. But that became a myth and someone else— [Jack] Conway, I think—shot the ending on it. . . . The producer called me up [in New York] and asked if it was all right. I was so disheartened that we weren't going on with the whole film that I said, 'Go ahead and shoot it.'" [6]

The film as released follows an escalation of backwoods ordeals through which artist and Harvard drop-out Langdon Towne (Robert Young) toughens into a cartographer and survivor as he and Rogers' other rangers fight for the English against the French and Iroquois. The second half would have dwelt on the flaws evident in Rogers' heroism when he returns to civilization, but was left unfilmed despite treatments beginning with Frances Marion's in 1937, a witty if diffuse script by Robert E. Sherwood, and revisions by Jules Furthman, Sidney Howard, and Richard Schayer. Rogers would have been seen *promoting* his fame, with a media boost from Towne's heroic paintings, toward the goal of persuading King George to finance his search for the Northwest Passage. In the process, Rogers leaves a trail of debts and dishonor across two continents, until banner headlines cry: "Fall of a Hero! Impending Court Martial of Major Rogers! A Moral Tragedy!" When he's finally able to clear himself and set out for the West, Towne's commentary (in the Sherwood script) is that Rogers "has done everything he had to do, honorable and dishonorable, to carry out his tremendous ambition." It's a more finely measured coda than as filmed: ". . . for that man will never die."

As produced, *Northwest Passage* certainly hit a new mood, deploying what were to become favorite motifs of later war films. Its use of the novel's original title, *Rogers' Rangers,* as its subtitle underlines its ancestry of Sam Fuller's *Merrill's Marauders.* As Spencer Tracy's men fight and trek their way through Injun-infested forests up from the Adirondacks, so Jeff Chandler's slog and slug it out through the Nip-infested jungles of the Pacific islands. Once our green-clad tough guys get into action, they'll slaughter redskins or yellowbellies before you can say *genocide.* Like all succeeding screen high-rankers, Rogers' virtues include an eagle-eyed interest in each and every one of his men (more plausible in this small unit than in all those mom-reassuring epics of World War II and since). Still, there's something weirdly inhuman in Rogers' "personal" touch: it's the way each loss increases his bland satisfaction in having a smaller, leaner, tougher outfit. Towne's wound goads Rogers to a startling array of paternal attitudes. He wheedles ("What's a little piece of lead to a great big husky fellow like you?"), taunts ("Say, you've got a sweetheart back home, haven't you? Now what are you going to do, lie here and rot and let some other fellow take her?"), commands ("Left! Right! Left! Right!") to make him, temporarily, an automaton of reflex obedience, a soldier briefly, for his own good.

The *real* battle is the grueling long haul of the will against fatigue, hunger, rage, weakness, insubordination, and an excess of zeal expressed through one man's reversion to cannibalism. A Ranger maddened by his physical suffering secretes an Indian head in his kit and nibbles at it for subsistence, sharing with his buddies what they think is animal meat. As a madman, he has to die, but Rogers salutes him as a brave soldier for whose mental wound no one, or only the enemy, can be held responsible. Also more dangerous than Rogers' enemies are his allies, the weak and treacherous English, some of whom wouldn't mind too much if these independent-minded Americans were scalped in their tents by the unreliable Mohawk guides.

The quick, exceptionally violent battle halfway through takes the form of a surprise attack so sudden that it's almost a massacre.* It's so pitiless that one might have expected some prior justification in Indian atrocities vividly shown. But the film is satisfied with astonishing rhetoric ("They tore my brother's arms out of him; they chopped the ends of his ribs away from his backbone and pried them out through the skin one by one . . ."). Cannons are fired into sleeping officers' rooms (fig. 92a), tents are set ablaze while their occupants sleep (fig. 92b), and the others are herded into a square so that volley after volley may be poured into a virtually defenseless mass of flesh (fig. 92c). The whole sequence is so tightly rhythmed that it might almost have been planned with a metronome and a drum like the "silent music" of *The Big Parade*. Only this time we're dishing it out instead of taking it, an experience more exhilarating, or more disturbing, or both, according to moral taste.

Both the atrocities in the attack and the demoralized, mind-numbing retreat evoke something of Miklós Jancsó's Hungarian vision of nihilistic braveries. It's in the long retreat home that most of the grimmer *internal* questions of military necessity arise. Should one slaughter one's wounded or leave them to the enemy's torture? Can one bully one's demoralized men through the swamps? How to reconcile the military autocracy implicit in the corps' names (Rogers', Merrill's) with democracy? Vidor's film, like Fuller's, now suggests a bloodlust not unrelated to *Why Are We in Vietnam?* It retains anomalies intended to tie into the second half, hint-

---

**Billy the Kid and *The Texas Rangers* also situate their *apparent* climax (some big action set piece) halfway through, and then follow its consequences "compressively" (in terms of internal psychology) rather than "expansively" (some even bigger action). *Gone with the Wind* is the key example. It's an unconventional form, not, as critics can too quickly assume, an incompetent one. In fact, we are tempted to press the argument that the real spiritual climax of many Hollywood movies comes in the pre-credit sequence, where they establish cultural fears, including *realities*, that the rest of the film exists to see put right.

Figure 92.   Northwest Passage. *Apologies to the Iroquois? d: "Crofton, haven't you had enough!?"*

ing at a Lieutenant Calley comeuppance for the unquestioned discipline behind sweating, stumbling, savage killing.

The Vidor/Laurence Stallings script for *Northwest Passage* provides a tougher variation on the theme of their *The Big Parade,* with fate reduced to human moral purpose and morale.* But with this new emphasis—on the place of wartime leadership within democracy. When there is widespread disagreement with the hitherto autocratic Rogers, he accedes to the calls of "Take a vote! Take a vote!" and is defeated. As a result, a quarter of the men are lost, horribly tortured by the Frenchmen's Indians. The preference for a strong leader as against a pettifogging democracy in *Our Daily Bread* is reaffirmed. Rogers doesn't merely save his men, but

---

*When Vidor was assigned to *Northwest Passage* in late 1938 (succeeding W. S. Van Dyke), he commissioned Laurence Stallings to collaborate on a rewrite of the first half. (Stallings had performed a similar role in the rewrite of Maxwell Anderson's version of *So Red the Rose.*) But Stallings, according to Vidor, was "an impulsive idea man" (DGA), who left after a few weeks' work. Vidor kept revising the script on location, collaborating with the second credited writer, Talbot Jennings, despite increasingly peremptory telegrams from producer Hunt Stromberg that Jennings return to Hollywood.

makes them more than men: "We've always done things they thought were impossible in the past, and I don't propose to stop now." Any criticism of the democratic principle is cancelled out by the special contexts—military discipline, the requirements of specialist knowledge (Rogers'), the number of volunteer scoundrels who accepted the expedition's conditions—and would have been further qualified in the second half's critical eye on Rogers. Nevertheless, the majority-rule principle is questioned, and the film clearly intends to inflict on the audience the exhilarating shock that so often distinguishes the entertainer-artist from the mere entertainer. (John Boorman's *Deliverance*—another lush green film with its battle at midpoint and its test of will to follow—inflicts just the mirror-image shock. The men's faith in an argument for the "democracy" of a quick vote over a mountain man's body justifies a murder conspiracy after the fact.) In equating democracy with insubordination, and insubordination with weakness, Vidor is challenging the *sentimental* resolution of the conflict between wartime leadership and democracy, whereby (as in *The Big Parade*) an insubordinate streak expresses a virile independence.

Given its prerevolutionary setting, Vidor's film celebrates the early American gift for radical improvisation in matters of government. Tragic mistakes are made; their cost is heavy. But adaptation prevails over the dead hand of principle—even though the pragmatic mind has to brace itself for "brutilitarianism." After the McCarthy period, it's difficult to forget the affinities between this aspect of the pioneer spirit and the revisionism toward constitutional rights still aggressively maintained by various right-wing think tanks. The reciprocation in *Northwest Passage* is impeccable: Rogers accedes to the majority-rule principle, just as John in *Our Daily Bread* is ready to cede his property rights. In the context of the *Northwest Passage* story, no democrat who isn't also a dogmatic anarchist will object to the expedition's autocracy. Nevertheless, the thought here includes the kind of Nietzschean elitism presented still more emphatically in *The Fountainhead*—albeit there's all the difference between elitism in a democratic context and an elitist authoritarianism.*

---

*Postwar anticommunist crusades tended to mute American criticism of the principle of unreserved democracy. But such criticism was not so rare *between* the wars, when Walter Lippmann denounced "that purely mystical concept of democracy which encourages the illusion that ten million amateur thinkers talking themselves incompetently to death sound like the music of the spheres. . . . We do not want people to know everything about everything all the time, because it is impossible. We do not want the people to make up their minds on specialized problems, because that is asking too much. We do not want to see them given as individuals a false notion of their freedom in society, and have them paralyze action with the infinite din of their amateur judgments. In particular we do not want to see encouraged a din in which the people's own best interests cannot be heard" (*The Phantom Public* [New York: Macmillan, 1925]). Lippmann was rationalist and elitist, Vidor inspirationalist and Populist, but they overlap in their pragmatism. However, the Lippmann passage, with its ingenious confusion of specialized knowledge with general social awareness, indicates how the pragmatic principle can be used in a demagogic fashion against a democratic one.

Towne, the artist-mapmaker civilian, evokes *The Big Parade*'s Apperson, *So Red the Rose*'s Duncan, and *War and Peace*'s Pierre, men of peace caught up in war. Rogers will take moments away from battle preparations to reassure Towne ("I know just how you feel. It's nothing to be ashamed of"). But the quality of *mercy* to be found in *The Big Parade* is conspicuous by its absence here. Rogers' assurance comes from his killer's instinct—in his first battle, "my old musket . . . kept firing by itself. Killed six Indians and never pulled the trigger."

One wonders if there's a topical relevance: if *Northwest Passage* is urging Americans to brace themselves against an extremely ferocious enemy, Nazi Germany. On the other hand, Rogers' extremely unreliable allies are the English, and his perfidious enemies include the French—so that the moral might equally be isolationist. This ambiguity would prevent steering too close to any particular contemporary parallel. One reason why patriotic epics regularly revert to the past is that unwelcome contemporary dissensions fade in an air of traditional unity, as with *Henry V, Alexander Nevsky* et al. The old-fangled, bewigged, Tory style of the English in *Northwest Passage* ensures that British audiences won't identify with them either: they're yesterday's tyrants for Britain as well as America. Considering how grim its military adventure is, *Northwest Passage* might be less a call to arms than a caution: true patriotism entails America *über alles*—or, to use a more neutral slogan of the time: America First. It's easy to forget that isolationism was a serious U.S. option, even if we distinguish it from nonmilitary interventionism. It was so prevalent as late as 1941 that Britain's Ministry of Information commissioned Michael Powell's *49th Parallel* (another story of the Canadian border) to combat it, and Hitchcock was undoubtedly doing his British duty in making *Foreign Correspondent* (1940), for Walter Wanger, a Hollywood interventionist. Vidor's personal sympathies made him, at the least, a "premature anti-fascist" in financial support of Spanish loyalist causes, including Joris Ivens' production of *The Spanish Earth* (1937) and Hemingway's "Emergency Ambulance Committee." All in all, *Northwest Passage* is probably impeccably balanced between isolation and intervention: each spectator could select, and weigh, the historical parallels as he liked.

It's not easy to spirit oneself back and know how 1940 audiences would have received the savagery of *Northwest Passage*. After all, today's reactions don't represent posterity—only another, maybe less relevant, era. What *is* clear is that the audience of *Northwest Passage*'s time was less used to wholesale slaughter than is today's. We've a suspicion that a year later, in *Sergeant York*, Howard Hawks took some trouble to prepare a mise-en-scène in which the ex-pacifist war hero picks off unsuspecting Germans slightly from behind, but still very much to one side,

Figure 93. Northwest Passage. *The artist in action. Robert Young as Langdon Towne.*

rather than shooting them right in the back, which the Western code didn't allow, although the rules of war do. Vidor's film is similarly entangled. A dawn raid is militarily normal, and that's all these rangers carry out when they attack the Iroquois village. But they don't take prisoners—not even the women. And some spin-off from the Code of the West (though it only applied among whites anyway) makes us uneasy about killing men as they sleep. Hence we're all shocked by the close-up of Brando's face at the end of *The Missouri Breaks:* "You know what just woke you up, Lee? You've just had your throat cut." Vidor's film has a curious position, hung between horror and relish, cruelty and duty. Where Hawks notes the tensions, but minimally, Vidor upfronts them. The Hawks is abstract; this much more fleshy.

Northwest Passage ushers in the thirty-year period during which Ford, Hawks, and Hollywood generally keep returning to the military detachment as the symbol of community. Ford turns to the Seventh Cavalry, softpedaling its true function (to harry the Indians), but borrowing its ceremonies and traditions. Vidor opts for an ad hoc military, the Texas Rangers and Rogers' Rangers, neither of which had flag or uniform, and thus seem all the readier to dissolve into plainclothes spontaneity. His depiction of the Texas Rangers as more a collection of cowboys than a cavalry rings, for once, historically true. But *discipline* is as prominent in *Northwest Passage* as it was pointedly absent in the 1936 film. Rogers consoles himself for the death of rangers with the reflection that "I'd make this expedition with fifty men; yes, with ten men, and I'd do more with those ten than with two hundred who didn't obey orders." Disturbing, that triumph of disciplined will; yet as two French fascists, Maurice Bardèche and Robert Brasillach, wrote of Renoir's *Grand Illusion*, "It is neither [Renoir's] fault nor ours if some men were able to experience [in war] something which they have been unable to experience since."[7] Even so, *Northwest Passage* leaves the spectator shaken by its violence in a way that, say, the exuberantly choreographed bloodbath near the end of *Stagecoach* and the highly moralized Injun-killing by the heroic civilian community in *Drums along the Mohawk* do not. Which is probably to its credit.

Our hunch would be that, in its time, this carnage provoked exhilaration and triumph, but accompanied by an undertow of horror that, while too weak to reverse sympathies, evoked a sense of excess, of hubris, such that it's not just the squeamish who feel something is amiss. That cannibalism on the long march home could be one of the clues to the second half's disquiet about the military virtues. Cannibalism is a more eccentric atrocity than those warfare regularly unleashes. In American culture it's intermittently an emblem for the savage in us all, and perhaps there's an associative slide from the red meat in the pouch here to the savage use made of a slaughtered Indian woman's breast in *Nevada Smith* and the slaughter of Indian women as My Lai–look-alikes in *Soldier Blue*. The cannibal theme intermittently appears in American literature, notably in Melville's *Typee*, as the catch-22 in the psyche of the noble savage; through it, Melville subverts American romanticism, turning back toward a Calvinist notion of human depravity—or maybe just a commonsense one.

In *Northwest Passage*, the enemies of the new Americans are an alliance of the overcivilized (the French and some of the English) with ignoble savages (Iroquois and Mohawks). Between these two extremes the Americans, if they're hardly a golden mean, do just contrive to hold a natural norm. Vidor's Indians are in equally bad moral odor whichever side they're on—savage enemies and treacherous friends. And no American-versus-British lesson is intended when we say that it's a relief to turn from all the moral half-truths of the American movie tradition (Vidor-Ford-Fuller-Peckinpah) to Peter Watkins' *Culloden*, which takes a tragic, accusatory view of WASP civilization versus "savages" (the Scottish clans parallel the Indian tribes).

Since Vidor disliked the final scene, shot by Jack Conway, it's difficult to know how to take the dialogue (which draws from several scripts) or, just as significant, the swelling music and the actors' rhetorical tone of voice, as the mapmaker longs to leave his bride and to set off on another (carnivorous?) expedition. When Towne's bride questions whether this Northwest Passage exists, Rogers boasts, "Before I'm done, I'll load a canoe with the goods of Japan and end up by coming down the Hudson River to New York." Which blatantly contradicts his earlier dismissal of such a water route across America: "Of course they failed. There is no short cut. . . . The only true route to the western ocean will be found by men who break trails and follow rivers and fight Indians." Fascinating, this puritanical reason why the Northwest Passage can't exist. It would make life too easy.

Before the conclusion at least, a certain responsiveness in Tracy's dialogue style makes Rogers altogether different from the man John Wayne, say, would have created. A pity, then, that when Tracy is earlier required to say that his troops will set off "when the last glow of the sun has left the western sky," he nervously resorts to a quick grin, as if sensing that this touch of an old poetic *gravitas*, which has somehow remained in the script, had outlived its time. Griffith could fuse this dignity, at least in the battle scenes of *The Birth of a Nation,* with a sense that both sides are somehow honorable.

Part of the tragedy may indeed be that the Americans, the French, the English, and the Indians are all behaving according to different senses of "honor"—a concept key to the split between Texans and Southerners in *So Red the Rose* and to the convoluted justifications for murder in *Billy the Kid.* By its alliance with an expansionist puritanism, even transcendentalism can come to identify everything alien with the morally inferior who are destined for the scrap heap of history. For just as the apparent "acceptance" of pantheism may lead to an "acceptance" of amoral Sturm und Drang, so doctrines of wise resignation to fate may lead to a "wise" acceptance of one's own side's atrocities. Transcendentalism and Social Darwinism may call on each other's rhetoric for mutual camouflage.

The artists whose work, in its challenge and frankness, makes us most uneasy are often those who best help us to live out aspects of problems no moral philosopher has settled yet. *Northwest Passage* comes close to denying us the complacency of imagining we can derive some general rule about the spirit in which war should be waged.

Stella Dallas (1937)

Working-class Stella Martin (Barbara Stanwyck) plots to catch dapper young Stephen Dallas (John Boles), manager in the plant that employs her father and brother. Although reduced by his millionaire father's bank-ruptcy, Stephen Dallas still looks to be her ticket away from a drab, au-thoritarian home. They marry, but with the birth of their daughter, Lau-rel, all of their differences widen—differences of taste, of manners, of class, of vitality. Stephen frames their clash into one of morality, espe-cially when he repeatedly finds his wife with the lively, boorish Ed Munn (Alan Hale). Stella and Stephen separate, their daughter becoming the ex-clusive focus of Stella's devotion. When Stephen eventually marries a rich childhood acquaintance, Laurel becomes immersed in the Massachusetts socialite world. Stella finally removes herself as a social embarrassment to her daughter by feigning an immoral escapade. But she returns to watch her daughter's elegant wedding from the anonymity of rain-drenched streets.

"See silent picture," Vidor noted to himself among his revisions of the script of *Stella Dallas*. And clearly he made a detailed study of Henry King's original (also produced by Samuel Goldwyn). Certain sequences (such as Stella's visit to her daughter's "new mother") are identically cut, shot, and staged—right down to gestures. Yet, owing perhaps to his con-fidence in only subtly altering and then translating into sound terms those moments that clicked in the silent, Vidor's *Stella Dallas* surpasses its original.

On the level of Frank Borzage and John Stahl, Vidor was a Hollywood master of the fine art, or craft, of wringing audience tears. (Never mind if in interviews he disparaged the skill and listed *The Champ* and *Stella Dallas* among his dues-paying commercial assignments.) Film culture, re-cently finding ways to grapple with melodrama, has turned *Stella Dallas* into a key text.[8] Back in 1961 Pauline Kael's essay "Fantasies of the Art-House Audience" astutely polemicized against the covert sentimentali-ties of highbrow cinema—which provoked tears galore but exorcised, by "art," the terrible guilt of wallowing in emotion.[9] Still, hers is a shout from the street against what Charles Affron incidentally redeems in *Cin-ema and Sentiment* in connection with Bresson's "melodramatic" sub-jects—a pubescent girl's suicide; a cancer-ridden priest; a scapegoat don-key.[10] Film critics, low on culture's totem pole, are hypochondriacs about their vulnerability to bad taste—whence the long neglect of Stahl and Borzage, and Bresson's success with a meditative circumvention of high-brow defenses.

Vidor's tactics come to a head in *Stella Dallas*'s final sequence, rivaled only by *The Champ* for its parting gut punch. Stella muscles her way through a mass of black umbrellas and gazes, alone and forgotten, through a cast-iron fencerail and picture window at her daughter's high-society wedding. She lingers, biting on a handkerchief, as a street cop breaks up the crowd (fig. 94). The sequence is copied from Henry King's version,

Figure 94.   Barbara Stanwyck as Stella Dallas.

even to the use of the window as something like a cinema screen and the tearful Stella as audience surrogate (the parallel preoccupies much recent discussion of Vidor's film). And yet it's not the "same" sequence at all. While the earlier version cuts between Stella in the rain and interior shots of the wedding preparations and ceremony, in the remake Stella's arrival marks the end of interior shots and indeed of our interest in the wedding, except insofar as it touches Stella. The changes owe something to the remake being a star vehicle for Barbara Stanwyck, more so than the original was for Belle Bennett. But the new emphasis is also the culmination of Vidor's empathy with this brassy woman. The respective concluding shots are *almost* identical, but where Henry King cuts through 90° to follow Bennett walking off parallel to the house, Vidor cuts through 180° and tracks back in front of Stanwyck, as her stride strengthens. Visually, mother and daughter barely separate, and it's easy to accept Stella's resilient joy in remaining transcendently "with" her daughter.[11]

Was the film's spirit obsolescent by 1937? Certainly, class anguish recast as fashion gaucherie looked more central an issue in the year of the original, 1925, as when Clarence Brown's *The Goose Woman* worked other changes on a sacrificing mom in ridiculous styles, thoroughly embarrassing a Jazz Age son. Indeed, however much Vidor "copied" the final sequence, he had already staged a virtually identical ending back in 1920 in *The Jack-Knife Man,* where Booge, the waif's real father, watches (through ivy bower instead of fencerail and plateglass) the honeymoon embrace of "the Jack-Knife Man" and "the Widow Potter," his son's new parents, with their home and money and stability that his wandering can't provide.

Still, the set-up could be reinvigorated in the thirties, as it is in Raymond Bernard's epic *Les Misérables* (1934), when Harry Baur's Jean Valjean gazes in through a plate-glass window at the marriage of *his* (adoptive) daughter. This high-society wedding, again made possible only by a parent's exile to dank streets, reaffirms that such melodramatic sacrifices are less economic than social-status matters. If *Stella Dallas* annoys some spectators, it's owing less to the old-fashioned intensity of upper-class uptightness than to a disparity between cause and reaction. Wearing out-of-date dresses and enjoying herself too noisily makes Stella nearly as criminal an outcast as Jean Valjean. If the disguised paradigm looks like high-school behavior, it is, after all, Stella's daughter's snooty high-school pals who first mock Stella's outfits.

Vidor's impatience with unnecessary self-denial (as in *La Bohème*) came up against the preponderance of sacrifice (from moms and other women, for kids and lovers) throughout thirties weepies. And no doubt the function of weepies is to paraphrase a far wider range of disappointments and, in the thirties, the common folks' trials.[12] The sacrificing moms of the forties filtered life's sadness through stiffer-lipped styles—bitterness, criminal desperation. But sacrifice for children remains a commonly enough expressed working-class and immigrant ambition, underrepresented on the screen since this film's time. Certainly Stella's mid-film scrimping (firing her maid; sewing clothes for her daughter in ever dingier surroundings) ought to have endeared her to 1937 audiences living in an apparently permanent Depression, especially considering the riches of the widow the already-prosperous Stephen Dallas intends for his second wife. As Stella peels potatoes with rising speed, daughter Laurel prattles on with suburban dreams of "a little tiny house . . . with our own front door, and a garden, and a room for each of us," and about the graces of her father's new woman ("Well, she reminds me of a flower that grows up in Maine, all pale and delicate, but strong too"). The focus remains on *Stella's* sacrifice, all the more remarkable for being directed at an object so shallow. Her considerable energies have been diverted into a dauntingly sacrificial strain of motherhood: "I don't think there's a man living that could get me goin' anymore. Oh I don't know, I guess Lolly just uses up all the feelings I got and I don't seem to have any left for anybody else." Hers is a traditional sexual politics, with children as the single post-marital avenue for upward striving.

In a startling scene, Stella offers her daughter to her husband's intended new wife (". . . you being Mrs. Stephen Dallas, everybody would naturally think she was your little girl"). It's motivated by Stella overhearing that she's the laughingstock of her daughter's new high-school tennis-and-tea circuit. Taken straight, the spectacle of Stella denying maternal ties because she wears the wrong clothes and makeup is likely only to infuriate us with her, but the whole sequence picks up the particularly American attitude that the social circuit is female, that the wife determines one's social class. Stella's economic rationalization of her sacrifice ("There's lots of things Lolly ought to be havin'") is a facesaver for the two women, who are equally gracious and equally attuned to the unspoken. Unlike dull men. Hubby John Boles retains a pursed-face embarrassment throughout his years with Stella, as when he ever-so-neatly drapes her coat over his arm, blinking impatiently as he waits for her to leave the dance floor. Edmund Goulding's *That Certain Woman* (also 1937) provides a yardstick for Vidor's success with that outrageous motif, the tainted and the fashionable woman topping one another in self-sacrifice while a shared husband (there, Henry Fonda) watches in dim incomprehension. Bette Davis remains too worldly to be convincingly broken by giving up her child.

Stella Dallas bears every mark of an object lesson about upward mobility. There's some sense that she gets the life she deserved right from the moment of plotting her first lunch with Stephen and fingering the material of his coat when he leaves the office. But her penance stops short of the tragedy in George Stevens' postwar *A Place in the Sun.* Stella's wide, if tearful, smile in the last shot registers satisfaction in having successfully stage-managed the charade (of a purported South American escapade with Ed Munn) that earns her standing room in the audience for her daughter's wedding. It's true that the forties do make room for a happy-ending mirror-image of *Stella Dallas* in Mitchell Leisen's *To Each His Own.** But *Mildred Pierce* strikes closer to the hard lesson given postwar sacrificing moms.

The unresolved problem of Vidor's film remains the strange transitions between a Stella who's cunning enough to capture her man and stage-manage the lives of two families and a Stella who's absolutely obtuse about the social impression she creates. Perhaps the *new* money she apparently receives after visiting her husband's lawyer late in the film lets her fatally overload with her self-admired "stacks of style." In place of hand-sewn dresses, she brings to the posh hotel "a trunkful a' new clothes my skin is just itchin' to get next to."

---

*Olivia de Havilland delivers her infant over to a rival, but after years of suffering—years of unsatisfying business success—she's rewarded with the chance to witness his wedding, an event that leads to recognition and reunion.

Barbara Stanwyck's performance is a knockout. And to judge by sniffles at recent screenings, *Stella Dallas* has lost little of its power to bring tears. Yet, compelling as Stanwyck's performance is, she never finds a bridge between the worldly-wise and the socially obtuse Stellas. Partly, her performance is retrospectively subverted by a somewhat later Stanwyck persona. When she goes wide-eyed or helpless, it looks like a familiar prelude to the scheming *faux-naïfs* of *The Lady Eve, The File on Thelma Jordon,* or *Double Indemnity.* However, even back in her formative early-thirties roles at Columbia, she was most convincing when mockingly self-aware. Typically she was cast as the lower-class goodtime girl, to which she returns in *Stella Dallas.* And already men begin to "correct" her manner of dressing. *Shopworn* (1932), a dull film energized entirely by Stanwyck, begins with "sensible shoes" advised in place of flashy heels. Capra's *Ladies of Leisure* (1930) plays variations on the pattern when a railroad heir picks up Stanwyck ("a party girl, that's my racket"). Soon enough, he's showing her magazine illustrations of tailored suits and complaining that her makeup covers the spirit that he's trying to capture in a painting entitled "Hope" (his hope being that he can remold her). Stanwyck comes across knowing and arch when she smiles up at this stiff man with "Oh, I getcha; you want me in character."

Stella Dallas remains obsessively watchable as another of those endlessly fascinating films about women "redressed" by men. Fashion is just the opening metaphor for a tyranny born of men's demands and women's ambitions (syndromes oversimplified in recent debates about desire and "the gaze"). If *Pygmalion* set the dramatic pattern, Hitchcock gave it its creepiest twist with *Vertigo*—in James Stewart's passive insistence that the "second" Kim Novak remake herself in the image of the first. His love returns in grotesque increments as clothes, hairstyle, and makeup convert the saucy brunette shopgirl back into a blond, tailored-suited ice-goddess. With her "second death," does Stewart, too, get the object lesson he deserves? To Stella's husband's complaints about gaudy jewelry, she replies, "Now Stephen, I'm perfectly willing for you to tell me how to act and how to talk, but please don't give me pointers on how to dress." But packaging is the social key (as McLuhan's *The Mechanical Bride* early made clear).[13] To judge only from the Capra and Hitchcock, "talking" and "acting" follow easily from the redressings.

Stella's problem in adapting to her new upper-class milieu isn't uncommon. Hence the film's resonance with daydreams of upward mobility and, indeed, problems of everyday embarrassments. But Stella's devolution from worldly wisdom to social obtuseness is all the more troubling because of such knowing moments as one late in the film when Stephen makes a surprise visit—and Stella quickly wipes away lipstick and scissors frills from her dress. Instantly she's the "high-class" woman he was always desiring. Her inability to continue along this line is owing less to any martyr complex than to individualist spunk. "Mechanical" bride she's not. Here, too, a drunk Ed Munn enters behind the couple and diverts everybody's attention. But Stella clearly has the wherewithal to remake *herself* in her poker-faced husband's ideal image. Isn't that, in its way, even more frightening than *Vertigo?*

At her most outlandishly dressed, Stanwyck resorts to copying Belle Bennett's waddle-walk down the hotel's garden paths, but (as Richard Roud comments)[14] Bennett achieves a vulgarity that Stanwyck keeps genteelly distant. Maybe Vidor retains so much sympathy for his Stella that he can't help but subvert her transformation. Perhaps, too, there's a certain conflict between the weepie and Vidor's admiration for female vitality bursting social bonds—although tears *can* be an index of self-respect, of recuperation, hence "a good cry" for the audience to share. After 1945 Vidor's women weep fewer tears (or only tears of anger), and turn more quickly to the shotgun, the riding crop, or the checkbook than to piles of exquisitely laundered handkerchiefs.

As in so many women's dramas, the men are an unlucky assortment, either too much or not enough. Stella's earthy male counterpart Ed Munn ("a good judge of horseflesh") is too hearty, too much the drinker and the prankster (right down to itching powder on the train—"Things are just a little too quiet around here"). John Boles is so smug a husband that he makes Vidor's H. M. Pulham, Esq., look like Leo Gorcey. His Stephen Dallas is another of his moral weakling roles, as in John Stahl's *Only Yesterday* and *Back Street* (where his announcement that "I've given birth to two children" is a hilarious arrogance in the context of another sacrificing-woman melodrama). When Ed Munn disrupts his tentative reconciliation with his wife, Stephen goes silent, then lies about being unable to get Stella a seat with him on the train.

Stella Dallas lines up among the "pure" weepies. It's never really a battle of the sexes, since the husband is expendable.* But, as so often with Vidor in the thirties, marriage itself gets a rough going over. He fought for the stark view of the institution in *The Wedding Night, The Stranger's Return,* and *H. M. Pulham, Esq.,* a feature of those films he considered among their most personal. Indeed, within Hollywood ideology and happy-endism, we can't think of another director whose portrayal of marriage is so bleak. This skeptical romanticism leads from the domestic ten-

---

*Vidor's involvement in the final editing also led to a closer focus on Stella. Among the sequences shot and cut before release was one taking up the first sixteen pages of the script, which began (as does the silent version) with Stephen Dallas's youthful romance with the woman who eventually becomes his second wife. As Vidor wrote in advocating the proposed cut in a memo to Goldwyn the month before release, "Some of Dallas, Jr.'s background may be lost, but I believe the personality, or lack of it, on the part of John Boles supersedes any conviction that one or two opening scenes would give us."

sions of the silents through the half-hearted adulteries of his thirties films and on into the wild sexual struggles of Vidor's postwar melodramas.

MGM's Good, Gray Responsibility: The Citadel (1938) and H. M. Pulham, Esq. (1941)

If we take *The Big Parade, The Crowd, Hallelujah,* and *Our Daily Bread* as the most personal of Vidor's surviving films from before World War II, they imply that the individual's relationship with the social system is a dialectic of acquiescence and resistance to its routines. The system is not the primary responsibility of the individual; he must play his part in it, but can do so only by following the logic of his own growth. And it's a common transcendentalist act of faith that a kind of moral egoism may be socially cohesive in the long run, even if it imposes something like dropping out—to Walden or civil-disobedience prison—in the short run. On the other hand, the individual requires community—be it old Concord, Mass., or new Brook Farm—and what distinguishes a free community from a despotic one seems to be whether that community cherishes or stunts the individual's growth. If, at its best, America's community system cherishes individualism more than any other, then at its worst it abandons the individual to his own devices—as in *Our Daily Bread* and *The Crowd.* Nonetheless, it allows response and escape, whether to a new community or to moral spaces within the system. In both respects it differs from the old European community of *The Wedding Night.*

There is thus a constant tension between eluding the system and contributing to it. In *The Citadel,* "the good old system" is an Old World one—the British medical Old Boy network. In *H. M. Pulham, Esq.,* it's the closest American equivalent of British manners—*New* England's old-money rectitude. Both MGM films were highly regarded in their day, and they earned Vidor his best reviews since his MGM silents. But Vidor's chastened, subdued affirmations in these films chime well with certain complacent sentimentalities to which MGM clung well into the postwar years, when every other studio had long known their day was done. And both films' hope of what the individual might accomplish is a sober rather than a heroic one.

The Citadel

A naive idealism has inspired young Manson (Robert Donat) to his doctor's vocation. His disillusionment begins, while an assistant in a Welsh mining village, with his discovery of the insanitary conditions tol-

erated by the obfuscating bureaucracy. One evening he and a colleague, Denny (Ralph Richardson), intoxicated and inspired, dynamite the village's most virulent sewer. The miserliness of his dying employer's wife pushes him, with his bride (Rosalind Russell), on to a more promising position in a brighter town. But when the miners themselves turn on him, fired by superstitious fears of his research into black lung silicosis, he moves on again, to London.

There, his practice falls to poverty cases and ear piercings until a chance encounter with a medical school chum (Rex Harrison) leads to his quiet seduction by the medical establishment, whose only concern is fashionability among the rich. When Denny returns from the colonies full of plans for a doctor's cooperative to benefit the poor, a now effete Manson shows more interest in a new sports car. The drunkenly disappointed Denny is struck down in the street, and an incompetent poseur kills him with a botched operation. Manson wanders through London suicidally until reawakened by memories of Denny's enthusiasm. He helps an unlicensed American expert save a young girl and denounces his "smart" colleagues at the medical board inquiry into his actions. He strides from the hearing room without awaiting their decision.

The sobriety of *The Citadel* may represent a standoff between Vidor's heroic optimism and A. J. Cronin's dour English view (in the source novel) of the slowness of change. The film does keep faith with Cronin's attack on the mercenary spirit of the medical profession and, in some respects, sharpens it. For once, a film cannot be accused of betraying its literary source through happy-endism. Just the reverse. In the novel, the enthusiastic description by Denny (still alive and well) of experiments in a small, rural clinic is enough to inspire Manson, who also ends fully vindicated by the inquiry board. "I was careful to have my ending all worked out and OKed before I left Hollywood," Vidor noted at the time of release.[15] His longstanding fascination with Christian Science may well have encouraged his new ending, where his hero walks proudly away from the medical profession.

Given Hollywood's freely admitted dislike of controversy, it's unlikely that MGM would have considered making an equally incisive attack on American medicine. Even at that distance, a cold-feet title card informs us that the film "is in no way intended as a reflection on the great medical profession which has done so much towards beating back those forces of nature. . . ." *The Citadel* exemplifies the intermittent American genre in which components of the American scene that make good dramatic material but might cause resentment are palmed off onto the Old World, a tactic we first noted in connection with Vidor's pre–*Big Parade* "Jazz Youth" dramas at MGM. Later essays in the genre include Stanley Kubrick's *Paths of Glory*, Swinging London sex mores films, and Sidney

Figure 95.   Shooting The Citadel *(1938) in Britain.*

Lumet's *The Hill* (the last using the British military setting to say in the overground cinema what *The Brig* said about the U.S. Marines in the underground one). Some spectators will take the point, and mutter, "If the shoe fits . . ." Others can allow their conviction of America's general moral superiority to override any parallel.

Vidor's film is something of a link between two cycles: Warners' biographies of medical idealists (notably Doctors Pasteur, Ehrlich, and, as *film noir* looms, Clitterhouse) and two other films about Welsh mining, Ford's *How Green Was My Valley* and Carol Reed's *The Stars Look Down,* both of which *The Citadel* anticipates. Ford sees his Welsh villagers as Irish-American pioneer folk; Vidor relates them to hardcore Bible Belters. Reed's film veers to the left, Vidor's to the right. In *The Citadel* the principal obstacles to the miners' health are bureaucracy and the miners' own superstitions, rather than the healthy capitalistic instincts of the mine owners, which carry the weight of the blame in Reed's film. The idea of a doctor's cooperative as a solution to the problem of medicine for the poor isn't simply a paraphrase of the idea of a National Health Service (introduced in Britain seven years later). Taking a cue from a developing system ("the panel"), it's an *alternative* to it—a demonstration that socialism will be unnecessary if only the medical profession will follow an "inspirationalist" change of heart.

After Vidor's preceding films, the big surprise in *The Citadel* is the failure of its idealistic cooperative, and of the common people, whose benightedness destroys it. In a manner wildly at odds with Welsh trade unionism, and "chapel" culture, the miners become a mob who wreck a laboratory (in a plot feature presumably derived from the Priestley riots of over a century earlier). Any hope of progress would seem to lie, not in "the people," but in a technical medical breakthrough by an inspired individual. Manson recovers his verve, but only in relation to an individual experimenter, and in certain respects his fine denunciation is negative, something Ayn Rand might have appreciated. *The Citadel* is pretty negative about everything—with this all-important proviso: its mixture of moral verve and concern speaks louder than the plot's fine print, and it was always accepted as a strong, socially conscious film.

What overcomes British inertia is not finally any doctors' cooperative but American initiative. Manson saves the life of the Italian girl by snatching her from the hospital of another bumbling London doctor to "Mr. Stillman's" country clinic. Stillman, an American who has galvanized the benevolence of "Sir Herbert Cranston . . . the motorcar manufacturer," is the ultimate expression of impatience with medical bureaucracies. He's been so busy with advances in lung work, he "never got around to taking a medical degree." Like Lend-Lease to come, and indeed like this MGM/British co-production itself, the New World brings saving expertise; Denny's cooperative plan is verified as "working . . . several places in the States."

The cooperative ideal is the middle way between the dangers of socialism and the problems of an aggressively mercenary medical service—an issue to which Vidor returned in *Beyond the Forest* a decade later. But the hour of *film noir* had yet to strike. Moral victory and social defeat combine to mark an intermediate stage between the affirmation of *Our Daily Bread* and the more somber conclusions of *Beyond the Forest*. The co-op here is pointedly an *ideal,* not put into practice following Denny's death. The medical plan in Manson's second town *might* look like democratic salvation: the "company" pays, but a worker stays with any doctor only so long as he's satisfied. "All of which you'll agree is very fair, even though it sounds a little aggressive." Very aggressive, if the miners' superstitions ensure survival of only the most backward doctors.

The film's style, like that of *H. M. Pulham, Esq.,* is quite sober—almost as if in both films Vidor were retreating into himself, no longer so confident in his earlier affirmations, yet refusing to renounce a sense of internal freedom. Perhaps that accounts for *The Citadel* drawing, not without technical mastery, on such diverse styles. The camera tracks as smoothly as Rex Harrison's diction down long white hospital corridors as Manson is overwhelmed by the ease of bilking high society through its nervous complaints. Such scenes contrast in every way with the quickly

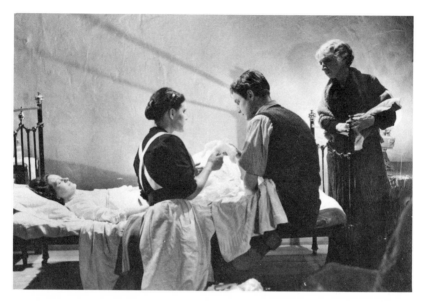

Figure 96. The Citadel. *Manson committed . . .*

Figure 97. . . . *and seduced. Rosalind Russell, Rex Harrison, and Robert Donat.*

cut, dark, tight close-ups of impassive faces that press in on him during his first Welsh cases. The film's somber mood might have more consistently suggested stuffy, oppressive interiors as its visual key, picking up on the staircase of *The Crowd*. Instead, it plunges into *The Crowd*'s visuals only for a sequence that reprises its plot: Denny's auto-accident death leads to Manson's nightmarish wandering through city streets and onto a bridge, until at the last moment he relents of suicide. In general, *The Citadel* places its characters within whitish, loose space. Vidor is reserving their right to move in any emotional or moral direction they may choose, rather than making it seem natural (as a more consistent expressionism would have) for them to succumb to atmospheric pressures. The groupings and the acting similarly stress individual distinctness rather than the Old Boy network, and Vidor tends to watch his redoubtably expert actors being fascinatingly English instead of tailoring their styles to his continuity (as he regularly does in his "American" films). Robert Donat's reserve is the opposite of the unselfconscious enthusiasm with which *Our Daily Bread*'s John pushes blindly ahead with *his* cooperative.

There's a similar sense of space in *The Fountainhead*, despite its lonelier and gloomier key. In both films, Vidor allows a certain visual "instability" that indicates both moral freedom and moral uneasiness. Rosalind Russell introduces a curiously American note by admiring the hero's ambitions as if he were her little boy doing well on Prize Day, and the beautiful Vidorian theme of female-maternal power sinks almost without a trace under forties Momism. (Margaret Sullavan, Vidor's first choice for the wife, might have provided some fiery inspiration for Manson.)

Vidor's caveats about the intoxication of inspiration are indicated by two scenes. In the first, the two young G.P.'s are inspired by alcohol to blow up the pestilential sewer. In the second, Manson revives a (really or apparently) dead baby, partly because its mother's serene love inspires him to do his best, and partly to live up to his own reassuring bedside-manner lie, which he makes true (fig. 96). His idealism transcends the defeatist faith of the grandmother: "It is God's will; let it alone." It's as if *his* frenzied will, shocking the infant to life with slaps and plunges into hot and cold water, exorcises the measured pace of death. Love and desire ricochet from one person to another in a community separate from a deceptive system—using its forms, yet redeeming them. The film refers to these two intoxications without convulsion of style, perhaps because it is in the nature of medicine, as of any true vocation, to link the sacred and the routine, the magic and the everyday. The theme of a "secret transcendence" of routine would be taken even further in *H. M. Pulham, Esq.*

The Citadel seems a hybrid between Vidor's most personal films and his assignments. And its inspiration remains at a similar level: half and half. In the intriguing half, certainly, would be Manson and Denny's dy-

Figure 98. The Citadel. *Neophyte terrorists: Manson (Robert Donat) and Denny (Ralph Richardson).*

namiting of the unhealthy sewer (fig. 98), an act that fits almost any political position you please (except legalism). It's the most constructive form of direct action, a quick and noisy impulse shared by anarchisms from left to right, elitists and populists, Wild West heroes and everyday opportunists. If you can get away with it, all the best luck to you (but don't say we said so). Vidor's homage to recklessness is in strange tension with Manson's concluding patience. Somewhere under its pale, methodical, almost bland visuals, there's a Nietzschean film here: pessimistic, crazy . . .

H. M. Pulham, Esq.

Each morning Harry Pulham (Robert Young) performs his complacent, middle-aged routine. Fussily he turns his breakfast egg in its cup and slices off its shell. The deathlike clicking of the clock only underlines the distance between his wife (Ruth Hussey) and himself.

An invitation to a reunion with his Harvard companions sets him to writing a biographical note and reviewing, in flashback, his past life, which hardly seems more inspiring than his present one. He reviews his conflicts with his prosperous father (Charles Coburn): his college hopes and his gradual disillusionment; and his affair with Marvin Myles (Hedy Lamarr), an immigrant's daughter working ambitiously with him in a New York advertising office. She, at least, is determined not to remain a face in the crowd, but her hectic New York worldliness finally cannot mesh with Harry's Bostonian reserve and quietly stuffy existence.

Perhaps, in the end, Harry's weakness reveals itself as an involuntary expression of integrity. Deadened as he has become, it takes only a gesture from his wife for him to realize that he need only become alive to her to recover a modicum of happiness and self-respect.

This film's challenge is precisely its abstention from revolt. It asserts a suburban routine and its sedate virtues, when *deliberately* chosen, as a form of freedom. Its whole structure is dedicated to this twist. Its deft, rapid flashbacks *seem* to be leading up to some liberation (whether by new romance, or by flight, or maybe by a gesture of rebellion in the spirit of J. B. Priestley's *Last Holiday*), but Harry Pulham's very nostalgia absolves him from the destructive renunciations that haunt *The Citadel*.

The choice of an ultra-WASP hero—or rather anti-hero, since Harry could be interpreted as a man without individual qualities—is pointed. Helped by the Depression's passing, Vidor looks at another variety of his average man. "I'm as happy as the average man could hope to be," is Harry's opening self-consolation. The humdrum discontent that has imprisoned him in the sense of a lifetime lost may come from his being a poor little rich boy—a John never drawn down into the liberating vulgarity of the crowd. The brief scene of Harry's birth reprises John's in *The Crowd*—proud papas making grand plans for minute-old sons. However, *this* fade-in to adolescence finds Harry's father still hearty, and Harry taking the place at "St. Swithin's Academy" reserved for him by telegram on the day of his birth. Still, one doesn't need to be ruined to change. Harry's final acquiescence in what he has become is not an easy surrender to passive conformity, but a rebirth as crucial as John's laughter at the clown. *Plus c'est la même chose . . .*

Some of Vidor's favorite themes are clear enough. Harry learns to prefer his home and spiritual roots to the city girl. His rediscovered life force makes his plain wife as fetching as the other woman. Vidor's script (written with *his* wife, Elizabeth Hill) stresses Harry's self-conception as an "average man"; in J. P. Marquand's novel he's annoyed that his Harvard classmates think him "the norm." [16] But Vidor's Harry is such a bundle of puritan strengths and flaws that his self-conscious retreat to average-man

Figure 99.   H. M. Pulham, Esq. *(1941). "Don't* Crowd," *indeed—another sort of average man. Harry Pulham (Robert Young) before his marriage to Kay Motford (Ruth Hussey), left; with Marvin Myles (Hedy Lamarr).*

status stays troubling. It's as if he has grabbed the consolation offered by Emerson in his most complacent essay, "Compensation" (which Harry's sister reads to their mother after their father's death). Although Emerson separates his "law of compensation" from a "doctrine of indifference," it seems to matter little what choices an individual makes; the natural world will counter with an opposite reaction.

Harry moves from his spacious, slow, patriarchal boyhood home, filled with statuary and applied columns, through the crucible of World War I, into a New York of tiny, blank-walled offices and apartments. There he's stunned to find a woman driven by a zeal he's known, and then only infrequently, in men. The city's social leveling makes him useful for gauging "the average person's" reaction to ad layouts. His temporary immersions in the crowd are free of the supercilious condescension of the barrister back in *Cynara.* There, the friendly catcall of "Puritan!" at the barrister was far off the mark if it implied that he was ruled by any sense of personal destiny. H. M. Pulham is made of sterner, or more consistent, stuff. His patrician directness prompts a testimonial to a new brand of soap even from a suspicious German-American housewife. Or, rather, the teamwork of his dry Boston Brahminism and Marvin Myles's New York dynamism talks her round (fig. 100). But Vidor also respects the New England world into which Harry finally retreats. *With* awareness of its insularity—as in Harry's mother's "joke" about pronouncing Iowa as "Ohio," or her classifying Marvin as a "really nice girl" because she's read Emerson.

A droll puritan reasoning underlies Harry's father's marriage: "I was sitting in a barrel in the marshes shooting ducks, . . . and I realized that I was all alone, that I ought to be doing something for someone." It's passed along to Harry via successive close-ups of gripping hands, the last being his father's deathbed clasp, which hints at an inheritance closer to the oppressive "continuity" of *So Red the Rose* than to the liberating re-newal of *The Stranger's Return.* Like Apperson in *The Big Parade,* an-other privileged everyman with a doting mother, Harry has occasion in the trench-fighting of the Great War to offer a German a cigarette. But

Figure 100.   H. M. Pulham, Esq. *Hybrid Americanism conquers immigrant fear. Marvin (Hedy Lamarr) jots down the hausfrau's testimonial to Coza Soap Flakes.*

this time it's Lieutenant Pulham's response to a formal demand for his platoon's surrender. It's democratic nonchalance, donned for the occasion, but also truer than we know. Those of his men who want to may surrender; for him, "the right thing" is to fight on, to carry on his father's ideas about "common decency, civilization, and human liberty" with admirable puritan cool.

A dissolve from battlefield to bubblebath wryly marks the price of Harry's return to inherited values. He returns to precisely the hot towels that signify Apperson's temptation to languor. A peppy college pal, Bill King (Van Heflin), who leads Harry into the advertising game, compares him to an insect that can't alter its reactions to an altered environment. He's his girl's man in New York because he was his mother's boy in Boston (dabbing cologne on Mom's handkerchief because "you always do it so nicely"). If it's to his credit that he rebels from falling into life as "husband of the Woman's Copy Department at Bullard's," there's a conservatism there too, a disingenuous limiting of his city options. Marvin Myles's faults are evident enough—a certain selfishness, acquisitiveness, a studied desire for the knickknacks of high style ("Someday I'm going to have a butler, and I want to know how they work"). But she takes an immigrant's daughter's justified pride in her hard-earned economic independence. The fault is Harry's; Vidor never looks down on Marvin's refusal to trade in her career. What her role as Harry's wife would have been is suggested when, in his parents' home, she asks for a drink with the men, and Harry embarrassedly ushers out the butler.

As an essay in troubled conformity, *H. M. Pulham, Esq.* marks a midpoint between *Babbitt* (1922) and *The Organization Man* (1956).[17] In film terms, it's an early entry in a genre whose best-known example is *The Man in the Gray Flannel Suit*. Closer yet, in both films, a man with a set of principles he fears have become outdated must compose an essay that becomes a moral self-examination—the last expression, almost, of the diary-keeping New England conscience. Harry performs his self-investigation to present his biography to the Harvard reunion. Nunnally Johnson's hero, Tom Rath, must invade his own privacy by constructing a factitious autobiography for a prospective employer; the small voice of the diary may be obliterated by the publicity image. Rath, more inner-directed than he seems, thinks hard, and proudly, and achieves success by becoming average—and private. Pulham, confronted with the advertising girl, also withdraws.

These two films move in their own orbits around a common problem. Pulham's world *has* survived, notwithstanding his friend Bill King's predictions. But he has survived into an America in which the Sams (of *Street Scene*) and the Marvin Myleses have created their brighter, more anomic city world. City America has triumphed. The virgin forest has become a well-manicured park, through which Harry walks each morning, throwing bread to the squirrels. And individual integrity is thought to be stuffy or suicidal in the executive suites, where insect world metaphors apply, where opportunism seems fittest to survive. In its elegiac aspect, *H. M. Pulham, Esq.* relates also to a little cycle of domestic dramas (notably *The Magnificent Ambersons, Citizen Kane,* and *The Little Foxes*) set against the background of stuffily respectable upper-middle-class life, whose bleak, exclusive values are menaced by commercial vulgarities and cynicism—qualities these films present as newer than economic historians might agree.

Citizen Kane is yet another review—not by a diary but by mass-media exteriority ("News on the March") and a private-eye figure (the reporter). There, the good, gray spiritual cousin to Harry Pulham and Tom Rath is Kane's drama reviewer, Jed Leland, who represents integrity, and who is also tested by the writing of an essay, in his case about a performer (Susan Alexander Kane) who is both another of Kane's alter egos and a puppet of publicity. (It's easy to imagine Joseph Cotten as Pulham.) Sharing both a year of release (1941) and the flashback form, *Citizen Kane* and *H. M. Pulham, Esq.* survey intersecting slices of Americana. No doubt Welles's verdict on Pulham would have been just as corrosive as his onslaught on Kane. (His film has no sympathy, no pity—a heart of darkness indeed.) Welles scarcely concerns himself with the Johns and Marys and Pulhams—Vidor's humble, yet transcendental, people. He prefers (and in this respect he's authentically liberal) to cut moguls down to mediocre size. Vidor rarely seems preoccupied with "the great" because he thinks adjustment is a sort of heroism in itself.

Perhaps the clearest variation on Vidor's *Pulham* is Albert Lewin's *The Moon and Sixpence* (1943), whose hero renounces his gray-flannel existence for South Sea exoticism—for the realm of *Bird of Paradise,* or, at least, a related myth. For Vidor's noble and healthy savages, Lewin substitutes a more decadent, Wildean, realm (worlds apart from the contemporaneous degradation of Polynesia into forties kitsch on the Dorothy Lamour/Maria Montez/Betty Grable level). *The Moon and Sixpence* shares with *Pulham* the white, flat lighting that occupied the opposite end of the spectrum from the dark, more oppressive, palettes of Welles and Wyler (for reasons touched on in discussing *The Citadel*). Whiteness keys *Pulham*'s brief ventures into physical sensation—the love scene in the snow, the sudden appearance of a naked newborn babe. As in *The Crowd,* the babe who enters this world trailing clouds of potentiality all but fails in his self-appointed task, and yet saves his soul, which is, after all, a corner of the universe. *Il faut cultiver son âme.* In this respect it reiterates, quietly, Manson's public defeat and private victory in *The Citadel.* The challenge here lies in the subtlety with which self-salvation counterfeits

Figure 101.   H. M. Pulham, Esq. *Gray Harry Pulham and Marvin Myles, remembering passion.*

conformity. That Harry's renunciation of the constraints of the past occurs within the confines of his home may seem evasive or challenging, complacent or profound, by comparison with, say, Kurosawa's *Ikiru*.

All the same, Robert Young's emotionless playing allows a harsher reading. Harry's wedding is a perfumed nightmare, less flamboyant, but much more chilling, than Spencer Tracy's in *Father of the Bride*. The minister's hair-tufted Adam's-apple is Harry's purest wedding-day memory; "and why was he asking me if I would . . . keep her in sickness and in health? Doesn't he know that I always do the right, the honorable thing?" Even more, the final phrase in the film's dialogue is double-edged: to his wife's suggestion that they renew their love in the Berkshires, Harry says, "Why, yes, Kay. Of course." The phrase has been his consistent hedge against commitment. On their wedding night his wife protests his soothing of her doubts about their love by his repeating, "Of course." And, when Marvin asks if he's going to leave her, he says, "No, of course not." The protest-too-much phrase is as close to lying as this puritan ever gets.*

---

*Vidor later commented on the wedding scene: "I think I got by with that because I was my own producer on that film. I just put it in, and it was too late when they found out about it. . . . I am not sure if it is a happy ending or not" (DGA).

The film's bland tone is of a piece with its virtues. Its respect, from a distance, for New England values allows it neither enthusiasm for, nor satire of, Harry. It doesn't hit upon any outcrop of involuntary, underlying *strength*. And, though the dialogue touches on this New England quiet desperation, the acting doesn't bring out the stresses underlying the rigid defenses that bind their victim to everyday habits. Robert Young and Hedy Lamarr seem to float around each other, so that the remembrance of passion is drained almost to the level of the present marriage. Young's casting makes Harry's moments of fortitude ring less true than his spinelessness; and Marvin's complaint that Harry acts like Ethan Frome lingers.* Despite Vidor's conscious purpose, his temperament sees this life as a sad half-life . . .

Responding to Harry's self-centeredness, the camera places him at the center of *every* scene (the converse of Welles's distance from Kane). There's still room for a counter plot—Harry's wife Kay's own secret passion, apparently for Bill King. But that twist is more a tit-for-tat than an expression of patience, suffering, and duty. *Pulham*'s egoistic perspective overwhelms its critical angles (much as *Kane*'s critical angles overwhelm Kane's own perspective). Made too much in its hero's image ("Pulham on Pulham"), the film remains a minor challenge. Another Marquand novel, *The Late George Apley*, found in Joseph L. Mankiewicz a director more at home with its unlyrical coolness, confined interiors, and literary irony. The 1947 film involves another man's crisis of confidence in insular moralities, again brought on by an incursion of New York vitality—this time, the daughter's lover, a Yale Ph.D. whose lectures pump some life into "the carcass of the late Ralph Waldo Emerson."

It's tempting to suggest that *H. M. Pulham, Esq.* is an attempt by Vidor to vindicate an aspect of his own career—the turn it had been taking at MGM. It's a vindication of impersonality. As *The Crowd* alone makes quite clear, Vidor never demanded worldly success, or some nonconformist posture. Still less would one expect the transcendentalist Vidor, however sustantial his puritan streak, to consider America so corrupt that an acquiescence in its ordinary aspects would be a moral surrender. Furthermore, *Pulham* is a film of its time: a newsboy's insistent shouting about war casualties through the car window as Harry and his wife make their reconciliation is a detail that feels like the call of an outward-looking director's conscience.

---

*This impression would have been reduced by Vidor's original choices for Pulham. "CAN SEE NO ONE PLAYING THE PART BUT YOU," he telegraphed Gary Cooper, who wired back his acceptance. When this fell through, Vidor disingenuously wrote James Stewart, "Am having difficulty seeing anyone else play this part." J. P. Marquand wrote Vidor with general praise for the film, but said: "Between you and me, I was not entirely pleased with Robert Young."

Figure 102.   The Organization Man? Vidor with costume boards and a copy of Marquand's H. M. Pulham, Esquire.

Taking another 1941 film, Preston Sturges's *Sullivan's Travels,* as inspiration, one could mock up a scenario about Vidor's reverse trajectory—a film director lionized at MGM in the looser production days of *The Big Parade* who was bold enough to shuttle between studios or quit them altogether to make *Our Daily Bread* for himself, but who now, in the more tightly knit forties under Louis B. Mayer, found himself going to work in the mornings like H. M. Pulham . . . Our scenario may well be a figment of the critical imagination, but it would suggest how the repudiation of misgivings, in a man like Pulham, could lead to the strenuously affirmative project of *An American Romance*.

An American Romance (1944)

In the 1890s Stefan Dangosbiblichek (Brian Donlevy) is fresh off the boat, four dollars in kronen in his pocket. He must walk the thousand miles to join his cousin (John Qualen) as a miner in Minnesota's Mesabi range, where he's assigned the name Steve Dangos. Inquiring and restless, he leaves behind a new-found love, Anna O'Roarke (Ann Richards), and grabs a job in the steel mills. He sends for Anna, and the growth of his family parallels his rise in the steel industry. In partnership with an inventive schoolteacher, he moves on to Detroit to manufacture an advanced, safe automobile. Eventually, he's forced out of management because of his intransigence against a union shop, but returns from retirement to run a San Diego aircraft plant. We last see him in the contemporary World War II years, standing proudly with his family, watching a plane roll out every five minutes with efficient, assembly-line speed.

Vidor's autobiography defends *An American Romance* in Whitmanesque cadences, and brings on a gushing Louis B. Mayer to call it "the greatest picture our company has ever made."[18] Notwithstanding, MGM quickly chopped half an hour from its two-and-a-half-hour running time.

The film tunes in to a wartime mood—rearmament and prosperity. Its virtues do stand out by contrast with other essays in the genre, like Lew Seiler's *Pittsburgh* (1942), which also elevates its struggling heroes (John Wayne and Randolph Scott) from lowly coal miners to managers of the steel industry and purveyors of patriotic cornucopias. In recounting their heroes' prewar years, these industrial films treat hardship as merely the catalyst of triumph, forgetting union battles or recollecting such tensions in tranquility. The tone *now* plays as capitalist schmaltz, but in its time it stood for something, sustaining morale and confidence for audiences with tensions enough in the war itself.

It is true that some of Vidor's most personal projects only freed themselves from wild optimism by the skin of their teeth. The first draft of *Our Daily Bread* ended with uproarious success that catapults the co-op's leader into the U.S. vice presidency. And even in the finished version, its solution to the problems of Depression agriculture is an irrational enthusiasm: "No one's buying our goods—Let's double our output!" But with wartime munitions, overproduction becomes impossible. Reality, and *An*

Figure 103.   Brian Donlevy as immigrant Stefan Dangosbiblichek in an early promotion for An American Romance, *under its working title,* America.

American Romance with it, can latch onto a longstanding inspiration-alist myth.

Vidor had never abandoned the general idea of an industrial epic. At MGM in 1926, he had planned a film on the building of the Panama Canal (*The Big Ditch* or *The Glory Diggers*). In 1939, he sent MGM studio manager Eddie Mannix a memo ("Subject: An American Story") proposing a film about a world-changing lawyer: "The picture would not have one iota of obvious propaganda, flag-waving or 'Star-Spangled Banner-ing,' but I would hope to have everyone thinking, as they left the theater . . . 'I'm glad to be an American.'" He toyed with a number of other storylines (one celebrating a woman world-shaker, "The Cannie Morris Turnipseed Story") until settling, in early 1941, on the three-page outline for *An American Romance,* although without an immigrant at its center. After that addition, Vidor wired Louis Adamic, author of memoirs and studies of the immigrant experience,[19] who drafted the first sections of the script. The writing credit on the film ("Screenplay by Herbert Dalmas and William Ludwig; based on a story by King Vidor") conceals a chaos of revisions, extreme even by Hollywood standards.* Perhaps it was the multitude of hands that stripped the dialogue of much quirky individuality.

Vidor was deeply disappointed by losing Spencer Tracy, whom he'd kept in mind through the early stages of the writing. Possibly Tracy was less enthusiastic about working with Vidor again after *The Yearling* had been cancelled, following two weeks of location shooting in Florida (though, by all accounts, the problems arose from the casting of the boy and an unforeseen shortage of young deer at that time of year). Whatever the reasons, Vidor's *On Film Making* cites the switch from Tracy to Brian Donlevy to show how miscasting can ruin a film.[20] In *Boom Town* and *Sea of Grass,* Tracy defends capitalist acquisitiveness with a soft-spoken self-assurance and challenge to doubters quite beyond Donlevy, who specialized in blunt and blustering characters. Vidor cites Preston Sturges's *The Great McGinty* (1940), where Donlevy plays a crooked governor undone by a moment's honesty, as a sample of the associations he was working against. Perhaps Fritz Lang's *Hangmen Also Die* (1943) softened Vidor's resistance, persuading him that the Irish Donlevy could be right for his Eastern European. Donlevy's forte was a bullheaded perversity, wonderful in its place, as in a scene in *Brigham Young* (1940). When the Mormon prophet spots the site of the future Salt Lake City and utters his immortal "This is the place," Donlevy is the one shouting to the rest of the wagon train, "This isn't the *place!*"

The last-minute title switch from *America* to *An American Romance* upfronts Vidor's purpose, and argues, like Hawthorne's grumbling dis-

---

*The chronology is, approximately, as follows: Norman Foster and John Fante wrote a treatment (as *Man of Tomorrow*) based on Vidor's story (7/41); James Hill revised it (12/41); Tom Treanor and Wessel Smitter made separate additional revisions (2/42); Louis Adamic wrote the first part of the script and Vidor himself completed it (3/42); Ross B. Wills and Renata Oppenheimer wrote a new treatment (4/42); Herbert Dalmas and Vidor rewrote the script (as *The Magic Land*), with subsequent changes by Wessel Smitter (5/42); Vidor wrote a new outline, retitled *America* (9/42), and rewrote the script again with Herbert Dalmas (11/42); Gordon Kahn wrote a few additional pages and made changes on the latest script (1/43); then it went to Frances Marion and to Vincent Lawrence who added some dialogue (2/43); shortly before production began in April 1943, William Ludwig joined Dalmas and Vidor for another full rewrite; after principal photography ended in August 1943, some reshooting dialogue was written by Robert Andrews. Whew!

claimer to *The Blithedale Romance*, that the work not be judged by the
strict social realism that comes so easily to critics. Vidor toyed with another title that made the same argument—*The Magic Land*. Perhaps,
too, the final title is a rejoinder to Dreiser's *An American Tragedy*, with
its nix on class mobility. The conflicts of ambition and the nitty-gritty of
industrial struggle are both astonishingly muted in Steve Dangos's virtually oppositionless rise. His life's text is: "Yes, Steve Dangos, your son
can be president of the United States." (Typical of the setbacks—his first-
born is a daughter.) In *The Crowd*, John mocks the sandwich-board
clown: "Bet his father thought he'd be president!" "Blessed are the poor
and ambitious" is the credo of the 1944 film, for America allows them
satisfactions unknown to the silver-spoon births, like John's or H. M.
Pulham's. Romance's pastoral nostalgia masks even the horrors of late-
nineteenth-century mining—underground shafts are convivial, communal places, soon superseded by the open pit. Here history and romance
cohabit as uncomfortably as in Scott's footnotes to *Ivanhoe*.

Steve Dangos plays his part in two American dramas: industrial growth
to wartime triumph and revitalization by immigrant blood. What tends
to get submerged in this epic swirl is the fragile drama of marriage and
family, Steve's justification for ambition and egoism. His wife is indulgent, capable, and inspiring, Ann Richards's Australian accent providing
the hint of patrician tolerance of her tycoon. Her Momism pulls him back
when his drive turns inhuman. It's a smooth *Bringing Up Father* family
saga with the bumps coming from college-educated second son Teddy
Roosevelt Dangos's support for the union men, and first-born George
Washington Dangos's death in World War I, fatalistically anticipated and
tied to the price of citizenship. The confluence of epic + domesticity +
romance merges into what Leslie Fiedler labels "white romanticism" (to
distinguish it from the gothic), where hope is the keynote, and where
natural laws get a little confused with bourgeois culture.[21]

The film's speed brings other genres to mind. Its biopix plotting of a
hero's rapid rise recalls the wartime musical—without the music. Its
broadly physical good spirits recall the comedy—without a guffaw. Our
go-getter immigrant's first encounter with American machinery, a steam
shovel, is a jolly metaphor for mechanization discomfiting man (fig. 104).
If, now, one squirms rather than laughs, it's not only because we're quicker
to see open-pit mining steam shovels in the rape-of-the-landscape terms
of Godfrey Reggio's *Koyaanisqatsi* (1982) (which, just as sentimentally,
cuts from steel forge to A-bomb), but, even more, because Vidor's episode confuses foreignness with childishness and whitewashes industrial
accidents.

At its best, *An American Romance* earns its name through its magical
faith in opportunity. Meanwhile, the genre conflicts among the epic,

Figure 104. An American Romance *(1944). Dangos (Brian Donlevy), Dube-chek (John Qualen), and "Big Nellie."*

a

b

c

d

Figure 105.   An American Romance. *"Fill up the shovels—let's make steel."*

documentary, family drama, musical, and comedy fill in for the lack of plot tension, and provide a string of stylistic surprises. In such a sequence at the smelting plant, a dimly lit circle of men trudge rhythmically, throwing shovelfuls of ore into a hearth (fig. 105a). As realism, it's absurdly inefficient, although the gleamy bare-chested workers have visual precedent in Office of War Information propaganda. It's as if we've stepped into some Germanic epic or infernal musical. When a flare-up from the hearth burns the foreman, apparently severely (fig. 105b), the men show no emotion, hardly any interest. Steve looks around, picks up the foreman's protective goggles (fig. 105c), orders four men to carry his body out, and takes his place, intoning ritualistically the foreman's words: "Fill up the shovels—let's make steel." It's a remarkable sequence—part magical romance, part allegory, part epic, part musical choreography, part documentary—tying the strands of Vidor's film into a moment that stylistically matches the faith behind it. Only the briefest of Brian Donlevy's side-glances before retrieving the goggles hints that he's making a pretty egoistic, hard, and nasty move, pure self-promotion (especially compared to British films, where bosses were responsible for accidents and heroes tried, at least briefly, to champion the men). The qualification is reinforced by the subdued sequence that follows, where a bartender must explain to him the spirit of Christmas (as if it were a holiday unknown in Europe, or unknown within capitalism, à la Scrooge) (fig. 105d).

America is a rainbow—American industry, American capitalism, American opportunity, American democracy. It's a Couéist mantra: in every day in every way, things are getting better and better. We wouldn't put it down to war propaganda, even in the face of dialogue like, "Efficient production demands cooperation between labor and management." To do so would ignore the conviction Vidor put into it. The film reviews the years since his birth through the new American conservatism evident in the 1942 congressional elections. The past is marshaled against questions some intellectuals found inappropriate leisure to ask. And answer uncomfortably. Joseph Schumpeter's *Capitalism, Socialism, and Democracy* (1943) asked, "Can capitalism survive?" and thought not.[22] Vidor's response comes closer to Peter Drucker's *The Future of Industrial Man* (1942): "The central fact of the social crisis of our time is that the industrial plant has become the basic social unit, but that it is not yet a social institution. . . . The only solution which makes possible both a free and functioning society is the development of the plant as a self-governing community. . . . And the time to start this is now when workers and management, producers and consumers are united in the one purpose of winning the war."[23] If Vidor had so accepted the industrial plant as a social model, he could have put it where John Ford put the cavalry, and his documentary could have meshed neatly with his social drama. In the event, the American working class went the suburban way. Perhaps that's what leaves Vidor's factory, like Ford's cavalry, in such isolation.

The muckraking tradition behind *The Citadel* is inapplicable to the radiantly healthy miners here. When Steve and his partner build a prototype of their new auto, they are forced to form a cooperative with their workers. Despite the return of John Qualen from the Mesabi mines (and from *Our Daily Bread*) with his life savings rolled into his pants cuffs and hatband, this time the co-op is "a gamble" with "a chance of hitting the jackpot" (figs. 106 and 107).

Likewise shunted aside are the cultural conflicts of *Street Scene* and *The Wedding Night*. This immigrant resembles nothing so much as a very bright child, reborn at Ellis Island and eager for new skills. When he tells his future wife that he thinks no more of the girls back home, it's a rare reference to his past and a characteristic denial of it. By the next generation, even the idea of ancestry is gone—once Teddy Roosevelt Dangos

Figure 106.   The evolution of cooperatives: John Qualen (left) with Tom Keene in Our Daily Bread . . .

Figure 107.   . . . and Qualen with Brian Donlevy in An American Romance.

Figure 108.   An American Romance. *Visionary inventors (from left, Walter Abel and Brian Donlevy) and complacent capitalists.*

has "seen enough cathedrals to last the rest of my life," Europe can be relegated to a Baedeker dream.* It was observant of Vidor to put men with Irish names (Murphy, O'Roarke) just above this next round of Eastern European immigrants, but the film's central conceit, "making men and metal analogous," as he put it,[24] puns support for the melting pot. Arthur Penn's notations on the immigrant's reception suggests a counterpoint: the father in *Four Friends* returning to Yugoslavia, or, in *Mickey One*, the title character being tossed his Americanized name with sleazy scorn.

At his career's height Steve faces token opposition. The venture capitalists want his automobile patents only to sit on them until the "time seems opportune." Their ornate, Europeanized office gives away their moral flabbiness (fig. 108) (as will such architectural backsliding in *The Fountainhead*). Steve's ideas are "much too radical" for them—which will be his own feeling about unionizing workers. He has stuck too long

---

*All of which reminds us of *My Girl Tisa* (1948), a charmingly absurd saga in which T.R. as deus-ex-rough-rider arrives on Ellis Island just in time to save deserving immigrant Lilli Palmer from deportation and to shout "Bully!" for her spunk.

to his triumphant individualism, and hereabouts the film comes down clearly on the side of the unions (though we're given pause by a snakelike chalk line on a blackboard, which the camera picks out and follows toward the first organizational notice). The issue projects back into the thirties the battles for union recognition (rather than wages) in the flourishing armament industry early in the war, where violent strikes had even less public backing than Depression labor wars had had. Under censorship from Roosevelt's Bureau of Motion Pictures, the shooting script of *An American Romance* cut the use of tear gas against Steve's unionizing workers. Indeed, we don't actually *see* anyone striking, still less the tear gas, machine guns, or bayoneted workers, as at North American Aviation in 1941.* In a sense, even this aspect of the film is a conservative answer to the renegade production *Native Land* (1942).

Bracing wartime physicality relegates transcendental spirit to feminine wiles (Anna's coquetry about "the sun, the sky and, oh!, the trees"), to leisure when work is done (Steve's treasured leaf Anna has given him) or to a son's curiosity (over a butterfly's metamorphosis). Disney's *Nature's Half Acre* is an apter confine than Walden Pond for "white romanticism's" deity, which Anna describes thus: "God is being born, and living, and kindness, and being happy, and helping others."

However, if the story is evasive, the film's beauty lies in its skin. And in particular, its Technicolor. Michael Powell's *The Life and Death of Colonel Blimp* (1943) was, by a year, the first cooling of only too "glorious Technicolor" (as contemporary credits ran). The, rarely shown, original Technicolor prints of *An American Romance* establish Vidor's collateral pioneering. He had learned something about color from *Northwest Passage,* and had taken up painting soon after. Not that *An American Romance*'s palette is consistent: several studio interiors, especially the sentimental courtship of the nature-loving schoolmistress, are as overly glossy and bright as any Fox or Joe Pasternak musical. But the film's first scene is a stunner. In a gray mist, a gray steamship seems to hang upon the ocean, with a cool half-rainbow in the clouds. Promised land/virgin continent apart, the asymmetrical, unfinished space sings like a Wyeth. Certain sequences glory in a white so pure, so luminous, that, poetically speaking, it's supernatural, even when snow shares the shot with a thin crust of industrial grime, and all the more when it's cut directly against a violently, industrially red sunset. The steam shovel sequence is composed in beige, black, and brown, and in the quarry the colored strata of soil and rock are as delicately etched as the veins in a leaf. Delicacy, sometimes ethereality, keys the modern industrial colors, from the high-key primaries

*Clayton R. Koppes and Gregory D. Black in *Hollywood Goes to War* (New York: Free Press, 1987) examine the OWI/Bureau of Motion Pictures pressure on *An American Romance.* The intention was to "moderate" the script's perceived anti-union bias; the result was to make the script even more blandly consensual.

Figure 109. *Vidor filming* An American Romance *in an iron ore pit; Mesabi range, Minnesota.*

of Dangos's automobile production line to his aircraft assembly shops, where the bombers' silver skins reflect the pastel greens of the factory walls, but transmute them into emerald threads and skeins (echoing the earlier strata and snow). Vidor was justly proud of this careful progression, which excluded hot colors until the climaxes.*

The visual movements are carefully finessed. When Dangos first experiences a mine elevator, the shot's framing leads one to expect it to go up. When it goes abruptly down, we're as disoriented as he is. The trudging ring of men at the blast furnace contrasts with the impersonal, erratic, comic fits and starts of "Big Nellie," the steam shovel that, pictorially, *chases* Dangos out of his myopic, manual world into the schoolhouse. This dialectic of harshly purposeful human labor and mechanization taking control is optimally resolved in Dangos's ideal factories. At the climax, a clock hand "crashes" five minutes each time a completed bomber whomps out; it's a deliberately artificial presentation, combining the mechanisms of factory, clock, and film. If it reminds one of Dziga Vertov, that figures. It's a bourgeois capitalist equivalent of Vertov's theme. But where the Bolshevik envisioned man's happiness in becoming an enthusiastic cog in the Stalinist machine, Vidor's gentler, more reflective film stresses a pastoral (hence those greens) factory, as per that wonderful thirties oxymoron, the "garden city." The celerity of riveting shots is followed by a surprise tableau of women comfortably riveting; and when comic-oily faces bob up from various bits of a half-built bomber, it's a happy jigsaw, the optimum synthesis of the dull and dreary circle and the coldly complicated machine. The schizo-alienation of *Modern Times* ends here.

The critical reaction to the film was overwhelmingly negative. MGM responded by cutting ten sequences totaling twenty-eight minutes, including several that read interestingly (a black man on a barge singing a gospel song with lyrics by Vidor; Steve's confrontation with his workers at a union meeting). Since the cuts were made *after* the release prints had been struck, a main consideration was to avoid breaking into the background score—not exactly a rationale to produce coherence—and evidence of the haste remains in half-chopped lap-dissolves. The film had occupied Vidor for nearly three years, and was intended by MGM, too, as a grand epic (Vidor's own budget at the start of shooting was $1,950,000 for a three-hour film; he went half a million over that figure). In some real way, the experience altered Vidor's spirit. His postwar films are turbulent, spiritually almost desperate.

---

*The visual description of thin, tired agricultural soil reminds one that Vidor gave substantial help, in funds and purloined film, to documentarist Pare Lorentz, famous for his studies of soil erosion, *The Plow That Broke the Plains* (1936) and *The River* (1937).

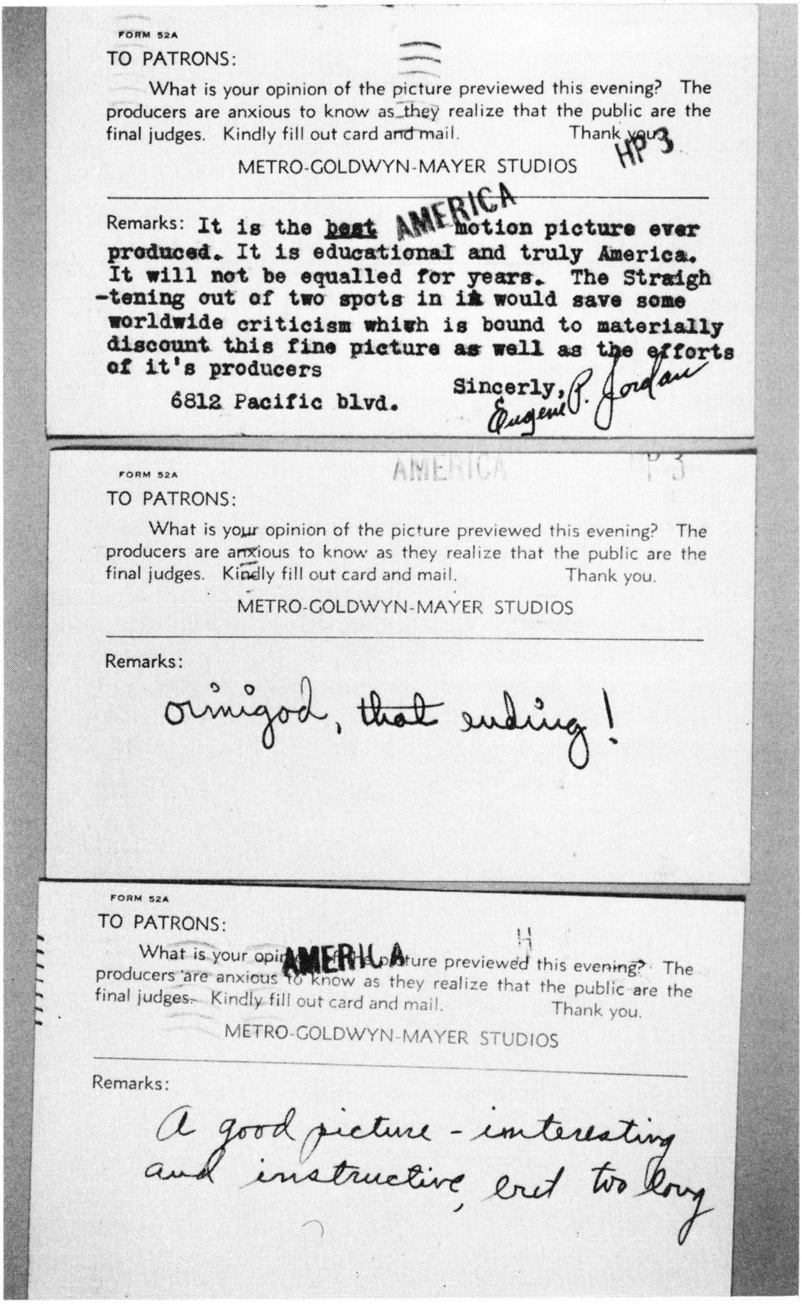

FORM 52A

TO PATRONS:

What is your opinion of the picture previewed this evening? The producers are anxious to know as they realize that the public are the final judges. Kindly fill out card and mail. Thank you.

METRO-GOLDWYN-MAYER STUDIOS

Remarks: **It is the best AMERICA motion picture ever produced. It is educational and truly America. It will not be equalled for years. The Straigh -tening out of two spots in it would save some worldwide criticism which is bound to materially discount this fine picture as well as the efforts of it's producers**

6812 Pacific blvd.

Sincerely, *Eugene P. Jordan*

FORM 52A

TO PATRONS:

What is your opinion of the picture previewed this evening? The producers are anxious to know as they realize that the public are the final judges. Kindly fill out card and mail. Thank you.

METRO-GOLDWYN-MAYER STUDIOS

Remarks:

oimigod, that ending!

FORM 52A

TO PATRONS:

What is your opinion of the picture previewed this evening? The producers are anxious to know as they realize that the public are the final judges. Kindly fill out card and mail. Thank you.

METRO-GOLDWYN-MAYER STUDIOS

Remarks:

A good picture - interesting and instructive, but too long

Figure 110. Preview cards for An American Romance *(stamped with the working title* America).

The important *New York Times* review, from Bosley Crowther, was only slightly harsher than most: "A wonderful opportunity, plus considerable money and time was squandered in a most distressing way. . . . For Mr. Vidor made a great big color picture with an abundance of vivid American scenes but with a story so banal and tedious that the whole film seems one massive platitude."[25] Vidor found himself doing something he seldom did, answering critics and jotting off notes of praise to the "perceptive" reviewers (including one to *The Daily Worker!*). His most astonishing reaction came in a letter written in Vidor's own hand, but which was evidently intended to go out under someone else's signature: "I have just read your review in the Oct. 16 issue of *Time* on the new film *An American Romance*. Last evening I saw this picture at the RKO Albee Theater, Cincinnati, and I emphatically do not agree with your reviewer's opinions. The film could be called long or slow, even ponderous, but certainly not a one-alarm fire. . . . I thoroughly enjoyed every minute of this very American film as it unrolled before me, and the audience all around me seemed to be enjoying it as much as I. It is a film we had been hoping a long, long time to see."

There is much that is touching in this dishonest letter. And one can see Vidor's spirit shifting to a (momentary or deep?) despondency when, four months later, he responded to a fan letter for *An American Romance:* "I am completely bewildered by the reception of the picture, and have decided to go into the familiar formula of two men and a girl, with heavy emphasis on the sex, for my next venture."

7

1945 to 1955

"Sing the Body Electric"

From Hollywood's angle, Vidor's career in these years charted a sad decline through ever less prestigious studios, and included suspiciously frequent run-ins with producers and stars. From an artistic perspective, however, severing the bond with MGM was just the needed jolt.

In late 1944 he cast around for projects, holding talks about directing for the New York stage, talks with David O. Selznick about a remake of *Wild Oranges* (for Ingrid Bergman and Gregory Peck), even talks with Sam Goldwyn—despite Vidor's vow after *Stella Dallas*. He also began to plan again for a directors' cooperative, whose participants this time would have included Leo McCarey and Clarence Brown. But the contract he signed was for *Duel in the Sun* (initially for twenty weeks' work, at $100,000), which included a commitment to rewrite the script and an unrealistic starting date of January 1945. Ronald Haver has unraveled the tangled production history of the film, not released until December 1946 and not widely until May 1947.[1] In short, after confrontations and a mountain of memos from producer (and credited screenwriter) David O. Selznick, Vidor walked off location with what he claimed was two days of principal photography remaining. But Selznick kept expanding the Western, using *eight* other directors, himself included, and Vidor had no say in the final cut. The bitterness seems not to have been long lived. Selznick was something like an advisory producer on *Ruby Gentry* because of his wife Jennifer Jones's participation, although his long and astonishingly abusive memos were more easily ignored that time around. Vidor also filmed two segments of Selznick's television production "Light's

Diamond Jubilee" in 1954, and held later discussions with him about a film to have been based on stories of Hermann Hesse.

Following the back-to-back production disasters of *An American Romance* and *Duel in the Sun*, Vidor put some time and distance between himself and Hollywood. In 1946 he bought his Willow Creek Ranch on 1,200 acres near Paso Robles, California. "I wasn't tired of filmmaking, but I was tired of all the people who just seemed to get in the way," he later said. Inspired by such apparent successes as Capra, Wyler, and George Stevens' Liberty Films, Vidor made yet another attempt to organize a directors' cooperative. This latest one, which included Howard Hawks, Tay Garnett, and Victor Fleming, was conceived as involving joint participation on individual films, but it, too, fell apart, with Vidor placing the blame on Hawks. A final effort in the same direction involved the short-lived Enterprise Studios.

Vidor put in four weeks of shooting on the omnibus *A Miracle Can Happen* (1948).* *Variety* reported a curious project ("King Vidor Making Oater for Video"), a 26-episode serial Western for television, to have been shot in 16mm at his ranch.[2] But just then a proposal to direct Ayn Rand's *The Fountainhead* (1949) came from Warner Brothers after Gary Cooper had been signed, and Vidor was immediately keen on it. He discarded the script as unsatisfactory and asked Rand to write one herself. The relatively happy production experience led him to sign an additional two-picture contract with Warners. *Beyond the Forest* (1949) also came to him with the star set. Although Vidor wasn't aware of it until after the shooting, Bette Davis had asked Jack Warner to have him fired. (Her threats to quit backfired; they were apparently an opportunity Warners had been seeking, and the film was her last at the studio, for which she had worked for seventeen years.) Not until he caught the film in a theater did Vidor realize that Jack Warner had had its abortion sequence removed from release prints. Although he sought *The African Queen*, then owned by Warners, his final film in the contract was a Texas mystery, *Lightning Strikes Twice* (1951).

For producer Joseph Bernhard, Vidor made *Japanese War Bride* (1952), and they continued together by co-producing *Ruby Gentry* (1952) on a relative shoestring. As with *Hallelujah*, Vidor deferred his entire salary, but this time against a 25 percent share of the profits. The pre-release budget was very tight ($572,000, of which $333,000 was deferred), which necessitated substituting his ranch for the "North Carolina" backwoods and, after Jennifer Jones broke her hand in a slap-down scene with Charlton Heston, eliminating some scripted sequences.

Much of the following year was spent continuing to revise, with Laurence Stallings, and to promote, unsuccessfully, the remake of *The Turn*

---

*Briefly discussed in the filmography only.

COME IN

KING VIDOR

... and make yourself at home. We're happy
to welcome you to our studios to direct
"The Fountainhead"—the star Gary Cooper,
the producer Henry Blanke.

Warner Bros Studios

Figure 111.

in the Road. Vidor's next film, completed on a four-week shoot, was
Man without a Star (1955), an Aaron Rosenberg Western at Universal-
International.

Duel in the Sun (1946)

*Following her father's execution for the murder of her Indian mother,
young Pearl Chavez (Jennifer Jones) comes to live at the vast Texas cattle*

Figure 112.   Duel in the Sun; *or,* Gone with the Wind *goes West. [Frame enlargement.]*

ranch of "Senator" McCanles (Lionel Barrymore) and his wife, Laura Belle (Lillian Gish). Pearl's blossoming sensuality lures both McCanles sons—Jess (Joseph Cotten), an Eastern-schooled lawyer who has inherited his mother's refinement, and Lewt (Gregory Peck), a hell-raising chip off the old block. The independent McCanles, long crippled since a fall from his horse while jealously pursuing his wife, faces his severest test from the new railroad. Eventually, tracks are laid through his property, though not before precipitating another fall from his horse and a breach with the civic-minded Jess. After Jess's exile, Pearl succumbs to a passionate attachment with Lewt, who refuses to acknowledge her publicly. When Pearl half-retaliates and half-recovers by accepting marriage with the older Sam Pierce (Charles Bickford), Lewt guns him down in a barroom. Ever his father's son, Lewt derails an explosives train as it crosses McCanles land; and when Jess returns with his new fiancée to bring Pearl back with them to Austin, Lewt shoots his brother as well. Faced with Lewt's continuing threats to the convalescing Jess, Pearl agrees to rendezvous with Lewt in the distant desert mountains—where she shoulders a rifle to initiate their mutually destructive duel in the sun.

David O. Selznick bought the screen rights to Niven Busch's novel in 1944, and began planning a modest Western, which expanded as he went along, until he proclaimed his ambition "to go whole hog" and "top"

Gone with the Wind.[3] When Vidor started reworking a preliminary script by Oliver H. P. Garrett in late 1944, his comments were unenthusiastic. "Dull, dull" is typical marginalia. Vidor conceived "an intense new angle on a Western situation—a small, really small frame."[4] No doubt willful self-deception played a part in his expecting any such thing once Selznick got going. Vidor was particularly exasperated by Selznick's repeated breathless arrivals on the set bringing script revisions of scenes just shot. Eventually Vidor withdrew, amidst mutual recrimination. Selznick had brought in Josef von Sternberg as consultant for photography and lighting (in which matter Vidor's films generally vary with the cameraman), and, for major additional scenes, William Dieterle. Selznick piled on the sex (Hollywood's first French kiss), violence, and spectacle, and made Lewt progressively more wicked—too much so, Vidor felt, for the film's tensions to work.

A notebook in which Vidor recorded his dreams throughout 1945 reveals how troubled he was at having felt the need to quit. Selznick haunted him, literally. In one nightmare, Selznick has taken over direction (as he did, for a few scenes) and electric cables transmute into snakes, strangling cast and crew; in another, Selznick talks Vidor into accompanying him to a hospital that turns out to be a lunatic asylum. There was Directors Guild arbitration before Vidor emerged with sole credit. Even so, he deplored later additions such as the scene where Lewt, having dynamited a train and apparently killed the crew, rides away singing "I've Been Working on the Railroad." (Vidor noted a preview audience's dislike for the scene,[5] and presumably further revision occurred, for in the release version a shot shows the stunned but not too badly injured men scrambling from the cab, implying no harm done except to "the company," so we can relish this "fun" sabotage.)

Vidor's film was to have opened with the very confined scene in which Pearl's father receives his death sentence (fig. 113a). The garish saloon dance (fig. 113b) and prologue were a Selznick afterthought, inspired by his *The Garden of Allah* (likewise directed by Dieterle and danced by Tilly Losch). Selznick assigned to von Sternberg the duty of supereroticizing Jennifer Jones, and Vidor recalled "von" throwing buckets of water over her to imbue her with just the right excess of glistening sweat. (All a far cry from that icy creation, Marlene—clearly "von" had more than one string to his erotic bow.) One suspects that Selznick himself dreamed up certain tableaulike extreme longshots (fig. 112), given similar night silhouettes in *Gone with the Wind.*

It's traditional to look with suspicion on the products of collaboration. But *Duel* is hardly alone in enabling us to recognize the work of many hands. Von Sternberg's moody shadows; Vidor's free, rather unstable, space and bodily exuberance; and Selznick's opulence and tableaux take

a   b

Figure 113.   The two opening scenes of Duel in the Sun. *a: Vidor's; b: Dieterle's.*

turns in dominating, or even work together. Dieterle is the man most likely to be eclipsed in all this, partly because he was so often Selznick's right-hand man, partly because he was a versatile craftsman with a gift for moving actors, a *metteur-en-scène* in the best sense. *Duel in the Sun* is concerto, not solo.*

As for Selznick, his fine-tuned antennae for the feelings of female movie-goers coexisted with a streak of creative fury that could lift soap opera to the level of *amour fou*. As the French surrealist Ado Kyrou points out, the Selznick-Dieterle *Portrait of Jennie* really is surrealist about love communicating with a parallel universe beyond death.[6] Selznick had spotted—or felt in himself—a trend in women's dramas, away from the sentimental, Borzage-style yearnings of the thirties, toward the clashes of egoism, the love/hate themes to come; a trend marked by (1) his own *Gone with the Wind* (1939), (2) the Goldwyn-Wyler *Wuthering Heights* (1939), and (3) their country cousin, Howard Hughes's *The Outlaw* (1943) (which Selznick had seen before he bought the rights to *Duel*). If *The Outlaw* survives as rather listless fun, a very interesting case of celibate sado-misogyny combined with complicated macho-paranoid homophilia, *Duel* is almost its reverse angle: flamboyantly heterosexual and familial, with

---

*The difficulties in sorting out a single filmmaker's contribution are indicated by comparison with a much later feature. Had Selznick's or Vidor's name appeared on *The Unforgiven* (1960), auteurists would have an easy time of it. John Huston's film features Audrey Hepburn as another orphan half-breed, again reared with two foster brothers, and once again the foster mother is Lillian Gish, once again associated with a grand piano. And just as Pearl must shoot Lewt, the most deeply loved and hated of her foster brothers, so Audrey Hepburn has to shoot her real Indian brother in the face when his war party attacks her foster mother's log cabin. In the earlier film, a lanky, itinerant "sin-killer" points out that the half-breed girl means trouble; and in *The Unforgiven* a lanky mist-enshrouded rider says much the same thing. If, surprisingly, the Huston movie can't hold a candle to the Selznick/Vidor, it's partly because the battle against the Indians eclipses the internal tensions for which *Duel* provides neither scapegoat nor counterattraction.

misogyny a *cause* of the tragedy.* Both films were the product of a determined producer hiring directors right and left as if possessed by a vision.

Duel's flaming bad taste—which earned it the trade nickname "Lust in the Dust"—was entirely unlike the family classics and love stories with which Selznick's name was so long associated. Yet, he had, after all, been the executive producer, way back, of *King Kong* and Vidor's own *Bird of Paradise*. If *Duel* is a Selznick film, in its heart of hearts (we like that plurality), it's sufficiently a Vidor text. While Vidor had no control over its final form, the film remains key to his evolution from an affirmative to a pessimistic emphasis. It's clear that he experienced distress when the Selznick/von Sternberg/Dieterle consortium allowed sensuality to blossom into the film's least negative emblem of the life force. Apparently surprised, but impressed, by the public's acceptance of the film's balance of moral forces, Vidor repeated elements from it in his subsequent films, but in quite different contexts. *Duel*'s love/hate exasperation, its theme of American ideals gone rotten and turning lovers' embraces into bags of snakes, its slaps and dragging death-agonies, set Vidor's thematic and stylistic agenda for the next ten years. *The Fountainhead* and *Beyond the Forest* lead directly into *Ruby Gentry*, which is all but "Duel in the Swamp."

If Vidor's films of this period delighted Kyrou, the Marxists of *Positif*, and a renegade talent like Curtis Harrington,[7] most Anglo-American critics were shocked. What had happened to the robust spiritual health of *The Big Parade?* the liberal momentum behind *Hallelujah?* the social activism of *Our Daily Bread?* As we've suggested, the answer may be that the liberal Vidor and Vidor *en noir* were quite closely related, like hope and disillusionment. The destructive possibilities the earlier films joyously, though not without struggle, overcame, are here unleashed.

Duel in the Sun weirdly conjoins (a) the long tradition of romantic excess; (b) a thoroughly Victorian bourgeois tragedy of love through two generations; (c) the epic Western; and (d) something "modern"—that is, nervous and neurotic. The aspect of melodrama of particular interest in relation to this film is what melodrama owed to romanticism—for example, the stress on lifelong fidelity to passionate commitments, even in terrible solitudes, in such godparents of the genre as Hugo, Dumas, and Emily Brontë. *Duel* is almost the last sunset of a current of popular romanticism of which certain romantic movies (for instance, *Portrait of Jennie*) represent one strain and the Western genre another. *Duel* draws

---

*Feminist critics often underplay the extent to which the "misogynistic" *film noir* generally acknowledges its heroes' misogyny as a disease, albeit one so endemic as to be only normally abnormal. Rita Hayworth's celebrated song in *Gilda* (also 1946), "Put the Blame on Mame," is altogether ironical, a counterattack on Glenn Ford's (not entirely unjustified) suspicions about her behavior.

The Degradation Scene

as played by

JENNIFER JONES · GREGORY PECK

in

A Memorable Moment *in the* SELZNICK INTERNATIONAL
All-Star Technicolor Production

Figure 114.   Selznick's pre-release publicity for "a memorable moment": "The Degradation Scene."

from both strains, and asks to be compared to everything—*Wuthering Heights*, D. W. Griffith, Nietzsche, "Dallas" . . .

It marks a shift from weepie to, shall we say, slappie, and thus to *film noir*, which regularly had an interest in neurotic violence and in vindicating a "notorious" woman. (It was probably the second *film noir* in Technicolor, after *Leave Her to Heaven*.) Pearl's ride out to exterminate Lewt anticipates the cycle of revenge Westerns (with Randolph Scott for Budd Boetticher and James Stewart for Anthony Mann) that reoriented and revitalized the genre. It looks back to *Destry Rides Again* and *The Outlaw* in its mixture of the Western with "women's themes," and looks forward to another fifties cycle, matriarchal tales of *female* McCanleses (noted further in connection with Vidor's own entry in the cycle, *Man without a Star*). *Duel* also precedes by a year or two the little cycle of "liberal" films like *Pinky* and *Gentleman's Agreement* that marked a new, cautious, liberalization of Hollywood's attitudes to America's assorted racial prejudices. The race barriers are in this film, not because race is exactly its subject, but so as to top all the other barriers that impede passion (class in *Cynara*, background in *The Wedding Night* . . .).* To an extent, the film accommodates the "I told you so" of misgivings about miscegenation. But it's racist in the interesting sense of especially admiring a *different* ethnicity. Pearl Chavez's "half-breed" blood is rich blood, not bad blood, and whatever strain of passion she has too much of, the McCanleses have too little of.

The thirties had been an era of driving action, or tears, the psychology being frisky and mercurial rather than profound. The new brooding over passions and the past (*Wuthering Heights, Rebecca, Citizen Kane*) were a first phase of *noir*, which led in turn to Hollywood's discovery of depth psychology (to which another Selznick-Peck picture, Hitchcock's *Spellbound*, had given the fillip the year before). Selznick was thus encouraging "new" Freudian ideas with one hand while reviving "old" lurid melodrama with the other. The power of *Duel in the Sun* comes from its hybrid nature, its Janus soul.

Within the finished film's sprawl, it's still possible to discern Vidor's intent: an intimate scrutiny of a handful of characters cut off from the communities whose values they represent. Senator McCanles's story is a big-scale Texan tragedy: the individualist turned patriarchal magnate.

---

*It touches on two other minorities. Butterfly McQueen's dimwitted black maid isn't an anti-black icon but a period idea of comic relief on a principal theme, race. Doubtless it's now as offensive to many as Stepin Fetchit. As Jess cuts the barbed wire to let the railroad through his father's land, Chinese coolies (who had nearly been shot down by McCanles's men) stand close by him. Here the racial implication is clearly progressive.

His wife Belle represents an older South, with her southern-belle elegance and culture. But what looks like a culture clash, with the dominant culture in the wrong, turns out to be less simple. McCanles's harshness to his wife contains a chicken-and-egg riddle: somewhere along the line his possessiveness goes with a passionate vulnerability. In classic Hollywood style, a life-shaping event is recapitulated not by flashback but by recurrence. McCanles's second fall from his horse occurs after he has lined up his gunmen against the railroad, and then, seeing the U.S. flag under which he fought in the Civil War, called the battle off. His megalomania directs his rage against Belle's favorite of their sons, Jess, who has taken the side of the railroads. McCanles's double fall from the saddle suggests, in old melodramatic terms, poetic justice, and in new Freudian ones, accident proneness (i.e., self-punishment), earning him our sympathy for his frustrated vulnerability. And we can regret the noble surrender of this personal era before the impersonal conjunction of railroad officials and government troops (in full Selznick spectacle).

McCanles's meditative, hillside discussion at sunset with an old friend (Harry Carey) sets the film's thesis: the pioneering ideal has lost itself in coarseness and brutality on the way to modern America. McCanles's favorite son, Lewt, and the "half-breed" adopted into their family, Pearl Chavez, might, for Vidor, both be victims of impulsive sensuality arising from their isolation: Lewt as oppressively spoiled son, Pearl as underdog and orphan. As daughter of an Indian dancer and a hanged aristocrat, Pearl has a justifying aspiration upward; but the rich man's son is just as much the victim of "nature or nurture." Both heroine and "anti-hero" are equally deprived of steadying family, community, and life task, Pearl for flamboyant reasons (a "broken home" being an understatement), Lewt for subtle ones (to do with the mental violence between his parents). But Pearl recognizes the right values when Belle offers them, and on this point the film comes near a Quaker optimism about decent treatment meeting a quick response. Vidor generally finds the roots of stable feelings within community, and, from that angle, it looks as if Lewt's and Pearl's bad environments lead them to become infatuated with an unsuitable "other"— like the attraction between Chick and Zeke in *Hallelujah;* between H. M. Pulham, Esq., and the sleekly ambitious office girl; between *Cynara's* barrister and shopgirl; or between the New York writer and the Polish immigrant of *The Wedding Night.*

Maybe Vidor, at least early on, was thinking along the lines of *The Champ.* The do-gooder, Jess, is in sharp (but still fraternal) rivalry with the fighter, Lewt, who gradually becomes as savage as Billy the Kid (another nice, winning brat, with escalating violence). But as Selznick developed the film, the sense of the Code of the West as some sort of norm was lost, *and* Lewt's aggressiveness sharpened. Vidor, pushing the character more toward the past, drew from *Hallelujah*'s Hot Shot and suggested to Gregory Peck the shamble and drawl, the hat slouched over one eye. When Lewt starts killing friends and family for so casual a relationship with Pearl, it looks like pure petulance. Still, his charm—Gregory Peck's charm—stands for something, for his potential.

Jess represents the America to whom the future belongs. His androgynous Christian name isn't an insignificant detail, given his closeness to his mother. And his concern with the rights of the "little man" is liberalism and Progressivism in the form Populism was most likely to accept. When he sides with the flag and the railroad (identified as making Texas a land of opportunity for little men) against his father, his motive isn't a bold, manly, flag-waving patriotism. It's a result of several other things: his impersonal eastern legal training; his mother's gentleness; his Populist sympathy for the smaller homesteaders; and his putting principles before family loyalty. He incarnates an attitude it's altogether in character for Old Man McCanles to detest as schoolmarmish, cold, unfilial, even unpatriotic. Similarly, Robert Frost once defined a liberal as a man who can't take his own side in an argument (that is, the earnestly moral aren't very virile as compared with good old red-blooded selfishness). When Jess goes to the showdown against Lewt without taking guns, his act has almost all the virtues: it's brave and it's principled, an act of faith in family goodwill, a fraternal solicitude over his brother's criminal record. But it's also crypto-pacifist, the sort of "unilateral disarmament" that doesn't realize that when people threaten you, they may mean it.

When, eventually, Jess returns from exile in Austin to his father's ranch, it is on the train with a quiet, delicate-featured eastern woman, who has the idea of building a spur line to facilitate the transport of cattle. Thus, without bloodshed, the McCanles empire can continue to grow. It's a Vidorian solution (individualism + acquiescence + enterprise = American fertility = the opposite of the desert). Not that there hasn't somewhere along the line been a sad loss of the boundless individualism that inspires McCanles's pioneering *and* Pearl's love. Jess's bride comes from the world of H. M. Pulham, and it's part of Jess's sadness that, in resisting the McCanles egoism, he seems short on passion. When, earlier, he rejects Pearl for her sexual weakness with Lewt, it's in the hard, cold, stiff style of a do-gooder. Vidor's hesitations over Jess anticipate John Ford's qualified admiration of James Stewart's lawyer in *The Man Who Shot Liberty Valance*, another rationalist heir to the individualist's West. And Jess's spiritual grandson appears in Kazan's *Wild River*, with Montgomery Clift as the New Deal federal agent who tries to persuade a proud old matriarch (a female McCanles) to give up her land. We're drawn by Jess and Lewt alternately, and the result is a continuous moral suspense. In the following year's *Monsieur Verdoux*, Chaplin achieved a very complex

Figure 115.   Duel in the Sun. *Jess (Joseph Cotten) cutting his father's barbed wire for the railroad's men (Otto Kruger, left, and Harry Carey).*

mixture of Jess (the good, gray, domesticated lover) and Lewt (the psychopathic murderer) that is all the more disturbing for involving, invisibly but omnipresently, his renowned, and then renounced, tramp persona.

Crucial to Vidor's more intimate tale is the half-Indian Pearl's status as our identification figure. In accordance with melodrama's romantic ancestry, the film casts her inner conflicts in an archaic, nonanalytic mode. Part-Indian, part-Spanish, she's an earthy, unassimilated, lumpen outsider: every kind of underrace and underclass. There are just two sides to her character. Her good side (she thinks, and we agree) comes from her father, Scott Chavez. As incarnated by Herbert Marshall, his ways are those of an English gentleman, while his patronym evokes the Spanish colonial aristocracy, twice defeated (by the Mexicans, then by the Americans). Too refined, haughty, and unproductive for the greedy West, he has sunk in the world and married the Indian saloon girl who subjects him to the infidelities so luridly evident in the Dieterle prologue. Pearl wants desperately to be her father's girl, although she is also, as she knows, her mother's daughter. But the two brothers force *both* sides to blossom, and the contradiction tears her apart.

While responding to Belle's faith, Pearl can't help responding also to Lewt's contempt. She's eager to prove to Lewt that she can ride and shoot, as if to be like him—a companion, a partner, *not* sexual. Her eagerness to prove it is childish, no doubt. But his unfair tricks not only obscure her demonstration, but throw her back into a helplessness that resexualizes her. The twist is part of the climax: she *can* ride (she finds his desert hide-out) and she *can* shoot (she kills him). Pearl may look now like a feminist claiming the right to lust, just like a man, a revolutionary underclass trembling on the edge of an anti-American crusade, if only she'd read Marx—like, by the way, Polanski's *Tess* (of the D'Urbervilles), with whom Pearl has blood ties, through romanticism and Hardy's taste for melodrama (so pitiable to Henry James). As the film sends out its branches, backward and forward in time, we almost begin to wonder: is it, in some uncouth way, a classic?

Simple, almost stock, as the tale and characters of *Duel in the Sun* may seem, they're developed with a careful eye for contradictions. If any event resolves an issue, it does so only to open up another, related one. A pair of scenes may clarify the ways in which the film provokes psychological issues that, in a melodramatic idiom, it doesn't "discuss."

When Pearl promises her condemned father that she'll learn to be a lady with Belle, the fervor with which she does so has an intensity that may be natural (he's about to die) and complicatedly Oedipal (he's killed her mother, her unladylike side). It also suggests a volatility that might undermine her resolution. The possibilities—sincerity or volatility, natural feeling or protesting too much—foreshadow the events to come; they don't predetermine them. This opening establishes Pearl as her parents' daughter, and her vehemence suggests childishness, which recurs in her natural nervousness in the scene where she arrives in Paradise Flats. Jess has come to meet her, and expects, for some reason, "a little southern tot" (perhaps a vestige of Niven Busch's novel, where she joins the family at age twelve). When he finally approaches her, she assumes it's a sexual pickup, and insults him (fig. 116a–b), although eventually his serious politeness reassures her. Pearl's anxiety to be her father's girl and not like her mother makes her humiliate Jess as her mother humiliated her father, a parallel reinforced by the gentlemanly styles common to Joseph Cotten and Herbert Marshall. Insofar as Jess is the *least* deserving target for such an attitude, it also marks her as paranoid (although it's normal for people from tough lives to be paranoid about sweetly reasonable middle-class courtesy, which strikes them as creepy and inexplicable and therefore doubly sinister). This opening encounter is a simple situation, a trivial hiccup, hardly worthy of being called part of the plot (since what would happen happens anyway), but it creates a delicate balance. The kindly man and the spirited woman may make a fine pair, or she may prove too much for him.

In a later scene, the gentle southern Christian, Belle, worried by Pearl's misbehavior, and slightly misunderstanding it, turns for help to an itinerant "sin-killer" (Walter Huston). Roused from sleep, Pearl appears hastily wrapped in an off-the-shoulder Indian blanket, like a statue of temptation unabashed. Belle, foolishly trusting in religion's power to good, doesn't see that "the sin-killer" just transposes her husband's brutality onto the religious plane. She exposes the bewildered Pearl to this Ahab of the outback, who snakes around her, half-tempted himself, pounding his fist on tables, blustering in evangelical cadences about "a full-blossomed woman built by the devil to drive men crazy" (fig. 116c–d). Pearl's hasty protection of her modesty looks like outrageous provocation. The pattern of misunderstanding corresponds to her first meeting with Jess, only here their common subject is her sexuality rather than her childishness. Is this a criticism of do-gooder trustfulness in general (behind every do-gooder, a tyrant)? or of Belle's human fallibility? Is it dramatic irony? or an ac-

a

b

c

d

Figure 116. Duel in the Sun. *Pearl (Jennifer Jones) meeting Jess (Joseph Cotten) (a–b) and the "sin-killer" (Walter Huston) (c–d).*

cusation of puritan insidiousness? The scene reads all four ways, a characteristic of well-constructed melodrama, where finely judged excess works against *everybody's* norms and intents.

The twists in these two minor scenes aren't merely tricks. They correspond exactly to Eisenstein's conception of the dialectic. Two ideas create a third, which is all the more forceful for being unstated. As Eisenstein quite rightly insisted, the dialectic of montage displays no sign, being the product of the mind leaping to conclusions about the connection between adjacent signs.[8] That melodramas operate in this way has been disguised by the high-culture assumption that the cinema spectator is merely passive to what happens on the screen. But such an assumption can't even account for *suspense*. For this depends on the continuous and vivid existence in the spectator's mind of things that *don't* happen. The hero's car doesn't swerve off the cliff as shot A suggests it might, but gets back on course in shot B. During shot A, therefore, the spectator invents what he thinks shot B will be: the deduced and signless idea A + non-B. This element is visually nonexistent but it's a strong psychological reality; it's the *suspense* we remember, and the film must quickly start another *possibility*, in shot B + 1, or better yet, in phase 2 of shot B. Similarly, temptation plots depend on the spectator anticipating the character doing what he hasn't done yet, or may never do, or may do in an unforeseen manner. Hollywood's professional skills lie in substituting possibility for prediction and ensuring that if what is foreseen actually happens, it happens in a surprising way, or after circumstances have changed around it.

Just as *Duel* upfronts the conflicts within its stereotypes, so it exemplifies the old melodramatic strategy of pushing action and reaction, equal and opposite excess, to the point of paradox and irony. It doesn't claim to offer explanations—still less the bewildering variety thereof notably flaunted by Henry James—but its structure seeks to generate a sort of brooding amazement whose challenge is more perverse, but less pretentious. It assumes that human nature works less from single, precise reasons than from *balances* of drives.

In the—oh so infamous—climax, Pearl shoots Lewt as he welcomes her to his mountain hideout, and he retaliates. But when he realizes his wound is fatal, and wails her name, sounding like a spoiled boy, might he just want a mother figure to cuddle him as he dies? Or has imminent death liberated him from his egoism, so that, with everything lost, he can yield to love at last? Or could *both* motives apply? Simultaneously, there's suspense as to whether (a) Lewt is only tricking Pearl again, in which case we hope she won't expose herself by trusting him, or (b) Lewt is sincere, in which case we hope she won't distrust him. The suspense isn't a simple "will she/won't she" matter. We're torn between two contradictory hypotheses and two contradictory emotions. And when at last we're reas-

Figure 117.   The duel in the sun (Jennifer Jones and Gregory Peck).

sured (mainly by Lewt's sitting sideways to what would be his normal shooting position), and Pearl crawls painfully toward him, the sequence still isn't a simple affirmation, since a new question appears: will she reach him before he dies, and what will happen when she gets to him, or his body? (fig. 117a–d). After his death we are no less anxious that she *should* die too, an attitude not exactly devoid of paradox. The film is carefully not quite clear as to what Lewt realizes before dying.

The finale on the mountaintop is further complicated by its parallels to the earlier, indoor, deathbed confrontation, in the older generation, between Belle and Senator McCanles. This earlier scene is itself the climax of another love story, which happens before the film opens, an apparent triangle between McCanles, Belle, and Pearl's father, Scott Chavez. McCanles believes that, years before, Belle left him to elope with Scott Chavez. Galloping in pursuit, McCanles fell and was crippled for life. His remorseful wife returned to him, only to find the domineering ways from which she had fled compounded by bitter jealousy. But, as Belle lies dying, she assures McCanles that, though she fled, it was not to Scott, nor any other man, and, with her hair hanging as loosely and wildly as

a   b

c   d

Figure 118.   . . . and in the shade (Lionel Barrymore and Lillian Gish).

Pearl's, she crawls the length of her bed to her husband in his wheelchair (fig. 118a–d). Thus the edge of his jealousy is taken off, and their love can be *almost* freely declared in one of those deathbed reconciliations whose spiritual meaning isn't merely sentimentality.

It's fitting, in a way one almost never finds outside of art, that D. W. Griffith visited the set to watch this scene between his old Biograph players Lillian Gish and Lionel Barrymore—although he made Barrymore so nervous that Vidor finally had to ask him to leave. Isn't this deathbed scene the American cinema's last great burst of Griffithian sentiment? And doesn't *Duel in the Sun*'s physical, lyrical, "pre-rational" psychology belong more to the silent cinema than the sound? The dying Belle's struggling movement (across her bed toward her husband, paralyzed by his jealousy) anticipates Pearl's dying movement (across the sand toward her demon lover, who is immobilized also, by his stomach wound). Vidor (who shot both sequences) reverses the movements: Belle going right to left, Pearl left to right. A transitional scene (planned by Vidor and shot by von Sternberg), also indoors and at night, occurs when Pearl, clinging in her soft nightdress to her departing lover's leg, allows herself to be dragged pleadingly across the floor, in a gesture Vidor would no more despise than he despises Melisande's desperate clinging to the departing Apperson in *The Big Parade*.

Belle expects McCanles to look at her as she dies. But, whether through shame or residual obstinacy, he cannot. It is this *incomplete* reconciliation that the mountaintop finale finally completes. The love/hate theme, common to both stories, suggests not only that the older generation's tragedy is the cause of the younger people's, but that both tragedies arise from unnecessary conflicts between regional, cultural, or racial distinctions and a male egoism that has turned overdominant, destroying the more conciliatory female principle.

Within the complex audience psychology toward the stark options of film melodrama, a certain time is often required for the spectator to think of the various possibilities, so that what an uninvolved critic construes as "flabby" cutting may, in fact, be essential if the next shot is not to intervene before subsequent alternatives (like hope-against-hope) have had time to form in the spectator's mind. Opposite excesses can present themselves simultaneously—Pearl may be too unsuspicious *or* too suspicious of the dying Lewt. Thus shot A generates A + non-B (1) and A + non-B (2) although both are not only different from, but mutually exclude, each other. To overlook these "ghost" shots is to read as "sadomasochistic wallowing" what is in fact a crucial and tragic moment, love triumphing over paranoia, but only *after* death has obliterated egoism. In this structure of excesses, melodrama's very abstention from individual psychologizing accommodates a play of shifting influences, balances, and repermutations. All "motivations" apart, Pearl's ride out to kill Lewt is a tragic strophe: revenge as duty, hatred, sacrifice, suicide, all in one. Pearl becomes pure superego, the savage avenging conscience of classical Freudian theory. However, the final, forgiving embrace is a simultaneous reversal of that, like the "classical" tragic hero, whose last, greatest, power is to provoke, forgive, and accept what cannot be understood or justified.

If the refined spectator allows the film's lurid elements to provoke an alienating contempt and paralyze imaginative participation, if he lies in wait for "the texture of lived experience" or a high-density text that spells everything out, then this melodrama, like any, remains impenetrable. *Duel* proceeds from a naïveté, not in the moral sense (it demands criticism of *all* its heroes), but in the sense of a generous response to a "post-folk" low-culture predicament.*

---

*Our comments on the "logical" structure of melodrama here follow the analyses of dramatic structures in Durgnat's *Films and Feelings* (Cambridge, MA: MIT Press, 1967). They are entirely incompatible with structuralism à la Lévi-Strauss, whose resort to structuralist linguistics à la Saussure brutally flattens differences and repermutations into oppositions. But they're compatible with the paradigms for structure in Anthony Wilden's *System*

Duel in the Sun isn't exactly an apple of discord story: McCanles and Belle, Lewt and Jess, were bitterly divided even before Pearl's arrival. Her role is more passive than active, and, before the finale, her action is rather restricted. She's unconnected with the McCanles/railroad/Texas theme, which is less a story than a spectacular, if historically momentous, episode. In itself, the Pearl-Lewt story is a modestly immodest affair, coming perilously close to eternal problems like "How far should teenage girls go when necking?" and "Should a girl go swimming without a chaperon?" Not that 1946 censorship facilitated understanding which variations on heavy petting, sexual intercourse, or rape are occurring between Pearl and Lewt. But that's not the sole cause of the film's pretty bad case of what dramatists call act 2 troubles. It also neglects to introduce the gunfight-and-outlaw theme, which dominates its second half, after its very sudden eruption when Lewt challenges Pearl's "intended," Sam Pierce, in his first vicious abuse of the Code of the West. Similarly, there's a lack of a positive opportunity for Pearl in the McCanles family. If she'd had some specific project, as well as simply becoming "a good girl" instead of herself, the film could have integrated itself around the, characteristically Vidorian, possibility of a woman finding a role alongside a man. Whatever the confusions of the film's genesis, the final cut has a "classical" linear progression. Its fault is that it's too plodding, like Selznick's script for *The Paradine Case*. This combination of improvisational method and too-methodical result isn't so paradoxical. Working piecemeal and in a hurry, one tends to repeat things, so as to be sure one has said them.

If the film survives its lapses, it's partly because the wild, fast opening and the thematic spread set an episodic pace, which the spectacle and a lively filmic style sustain. And it's partly because of another, thoroughly theatrical, component: the appeal to the *actor*. This can function without any straining for "psychology"; it can be as simple as physiognomy and physique. It may follow an actor through varied roles, like their common denominator, so that the star remains our "old friend in a new guise." In this regard, *Duel* is a cannily subversive old shocker: before then, Jennifer Jones had been Saint Bernadette and Gregory Peck was best known as the saintly Father Chisholm in *The Keys of the Kingdom*. But it's not a matter of actor-as-star, for spectators respond to it in unknowns. It relates to terms like "personality," "chemistry," "the semiotics of appearance," and "the presentation of self in everyday life." It owes as much to the acting

and Structure (London: Tavistock, 1972) and Jean Piaget's emphasis on transformations in *Structuralism* (London: Routledge & Kegan Paul, 1971). But perhaps the best introduction to *Duel in the Sun* is C. S. Lewis's *An Experiment in Criticism* (Cambridge: Cambridge University Press, 1961).

craft as to the camera's supposed penetrating power, and gives Selznick's perfectionist mania about his wife's screen appearance every justification.

To be sure, Jennifer Jones isn't really very Mexican; but then Bambi isn't very like a real deer, and the Cowardly Lion wouldn't convince a zoologist (still less an animal psychologist). The essence of Pearl Chavez is not what a documentarist might have observed, had any existed around Paradise Flats in the 1880s, but a resonant stock figure. She's a metaphor, partly for increasingly repressed impulses, partly for other, high-chic, things, which the actress brings with her: her softly salient cheekbones, eyebrows radiant with the larger confidence of forties affluence, a fine restless mouth, and a loose-limbed yet nervous body that dominated her directors' styles, keeping the camera in long follow shots in an era tending to tight close-ups and talking heads. Often Pearl's face is obscured by von Sternberg's secretive lighting (fig. 119b), and although we see her expression partially, or by glimpses, we must often guess at her feelings by the tension of her clothes, the nervous twist of her hip, going far beyond Jane Russell's cleavage in the hay. That Jennifer Jones's pantherine streak is too graceful, too poised, too mature for a lumpen girl of sixteen isn't a fault of expressiveness; it's precisely what the film is really *about*—Pearl's *potential*.

Lewt is oddly served by Gregory Peck's soft, thoughtful, handsome features, which carried the liberal gentleman's problems of conscience so smartly through films like Elia Kazan's *Gentleman's Agreement* and Nunnally Johnson's *The Man in the Gray Flannel Suit*. Such "idealizing" casting can find a kind of common ground between an extreme hero and the normal spectator. While Peck's casting as Lewt doesn't psychoanalyze his perversity, it does sum up the character's odd mix of sensitivity and savagery. It would not have been hard to write a scenario in which Lewt—

a   b

Figure 119.   Duel in the Sun. *Pearl at her duel with Lewt in shots directed by Vidor (a) and von Sternberg (b).*

played by some higher-strung actor, perhaps John Garfield or Robert Walker—amazed us by hysterically *alternating* atrocities with finer and family feelings (as in *The Public Enemy*, where another charming psychopath is contrasted with a sober brother, insults women, and is simultaneously condemned and indulged by his parents). But the *continuous* sensitivity in Peck's screen persona is another way of fulfilling this function, and creating a continuous *ostinato* of sympathy in counterpoint to his escalation into self-destruction.* Lewt rejects and possesses Pearl, serenades and rapes her, all with Peck's winning smile and kind eyes. (The suave brute was another forties emphasis: if Rhett Butler was their godfather, Britain's James Mason was their apotheosis.)

The film's final balance is very ambiguous. For though Lewt's insanely excessive individualism is unreservedly deplored, it is *his* love, not Jess's, that Mother Nature honors with a pagan miracle. Jess's world is the world of *Pulham* and *Cynara*—a gray, dull place. Lewt and Pearl's dying thrust and parry is Nietzsche's *amor fati* at its purest. Their yin and yang machine is as curious as Shinoda's *Double Suicide;* as sharply balanced as Cocteau's witty admiration of *l'amour fou* in the double death finale of *L'Aigle à deux têtes* (two years later), set on a grand staircase instead of a mountaintop. In Buñuel terms, Lewt and Pearl crawl through rough sand and stone, like the scorpions of *L'Age d'or*, and sting each other to death.

Film Noir at Warners: The Fountainhead (1949), Beyond the Forest (1949), and Lightning Strikes Twice (1951)

Duel in the Sun and the gathering bitterness of the *film noir* set Vidor a double challenge. America (or Hollywood) seemed to have lost its faith in the transcendent energy that had brought his heroes *moral* success, from the laughing acceptance of the clown in *The Crowd* to military discipline in *Northwest Passage*. But the postwar years accentuated black moods and violence, or bland materialism. *Duel in the Sun* had achieved a violence *beyond* bitterness. Yet its violence suggested that America had come to the point when questions about the connection between a vital drive and an amoral ferocity had to be taken up again. And Vidor's fear seems to have been that the newly prevalent answers allowed too much of Jess's

---

*In *The Big Country*, William Wyler's essay in a Vidorian key, Peck is cast more conventionally as the pacifist, i.e., the "herbivorous" character, corresponding to Jess, and Charlton Heston plays the "carnivorous" one corresponding to Lewt. The support can be cast ad lib, starting with Carroll Baker as a WASPy Jennifer Jones.

weakness and too little of Pearl's strength—or too much of H. M. Pulham, Esq., and too little of Billy the Kid.

As Vidor delicately observed, "Morality is only the first level,"[9] which may explain how the director of some extremely violent sequences maintained his lifelong sympathy with Christian Science. After all, a secularized puritanism might well combine with an Emersonian transcendentalism to produce a vitalism whose "second level" stresses spiritual energy over moral correctness. In general, Vidor's films are less concerned with right and wrong than with the harmony of soul and action. As for victims and losers, resilience is a better protection than strict justice, whose meticulous observance would destroy energy in everybody. To be sure, Vidor's transcendentalism is only too vulnerable to Social Darwinism and to amoral irresponsibility; similar points have been pressed against Nietzsche ad nauseam, and doubtless would be against William Blake, were his imagery less oblique. Not that Vidor's Hollywood films could consent to the flagrant violation of justice, but his primary object remains the affirmation, in winner and loser alike, of a good that is expansive rather than pious, inspiring rather than scrupulous, pragmatic rather than neurotic, jubilant in destruction and free of self-pity in defeat.

Thus Vidor must have wanted to show some constructive resolution to *Duel in the Sun*, to craft *his* version of a project taken from his hands. *The Fountainhead, Beyond the Forest*, and, later, *Ruby Gentry* can each be seen as *responses* to *Duel in the Sun*.

In a sense, the Selznick film is innocuous enough: a tragic conflict between two rights, each excessive. But in the course of that last discussion between McCanles and his friend from their pioneering days (Harry Carey), who has chosen the side of the railroads, the conflict is quite explicitly enlarged to a question of America's past versus America's future; and in this context, both rights come close to being radically wrong. The Code of the West, gun law, is also psychopathic. Yet Jess's "gray-flannel" law has no place for the wild Pearl. She might have stood alongside McCanles himself in his log-cabin youth (better perhaps than Belle), or toiled like an Amazon in the rugged community of *Our Daily Bread*. But by midcentury, as Vidor had been learning from the impossibility of placing either the remake of *The Turn in the Road* or another "Farm Story" about average man John Sims (now a war veteran), few in Hollywood were interested in Arcadias, or in testing urban morality by the rural touchstone of so many of his thirties films. The railroad was everywhere, and which side of the tracks you came from mattered more than the crops beside them.

In the films to come, the negative possibilities implicit in *The Crowd* emerge, not according to older liberal/academic notions of "the tragic spirit" but with a Jacobean sense of cynicism and scandal and of idealism perverted into revenge.

The Fountainhead

*Howard Roark (Gary Cooper) is a genius among architects, but his visionary schemes are mocked or resented by everyone except his old architect-mentor, whose death from drink and despair leaves him with only one, dangerously lukewarm, friend, Peter Keating (Kent Smith), spokesman for the commonsense path of "compromise." Roark's projects make him the butt of a newspaper campaign ("*BUILDING OUTRAGE EXPOSED: *While many are starving, . . .") led by publishing tycoon Gail Wynand (Raymond Massey), who can see no further than profit and power. But Roark finds another insidious half-ally in Keating's fiancée, Dominique (Patricia Neal). She chose Keating because, being of the superior kind, she felt she could never fall in love, and so selected a convenient mediocrity. Dominique warms to Roark's work, and to his tough, honest way with her cold scorn, but with her egoism threatened by her desire, she flees into a marriage with Wynand.*

When Keating, also an architect, finds himself faced with a public housing project that obliges him to admit his inadequacy, he begs Roark for help; and Roark, unconcerned with fame or money, agrees, stipulating only that his designs be carried out without alteration. Eventually, the project IS *compromised. Roark persuades Dominique to help him dynamite it and faces trial. When Wynand mobilizes his newspaper in Roark's defense, the masses—roused by an architecture critic—turn against them and the paper is ruined. But Roark's impassioned defense of the individualistic principle behind his admittedly illegal actions convinces the jury. Twelve good men and true stand firm against mass hysteria. Wynand commits suicide, but not before acknowledging Roark's worth with a massive memorial—the Wynand building. The film concludes with Roark standing atop the towering structure, and an external elevator whisks Dominique up to nestle by his side.*

With *The Fountainhead* Vidor took up Ayn Rand for his first wildly grueling reply to *Duel in the Sun*. Monstrous egoism, it argues, needn't be destructive of America, of others, or of oneself. Indeed, only such egoism can integrate them all. Rand in her writing, and Vidor in this film's urgent style, both seem to have thought that these difficulties surrounding American individualism, always formidable, were greater than ever in the postwar period. The film style knocks aside workaday restraints to storm "the citadel." (The earlier title is newly appropriate. Like those doctors, this architect responds with dynamite to bureaucratic mismanagement of public works, and the pestilential Hell's Kitchen is razed for the Wynand Building.)

Once, big business, with its trusts and cartels, had made an obvious target, and Populism had carried a vestige of socialism. But as rampant

Figure 120.   A rightist cabal? Vidor, Ayn Rand, and Gary Cooper.

McCarthyism smeared even moderate liberalism with the communist brush, and as liberals celebrated responsible capitalism and "the end of ideology," any radical questioning of the big business spirit was a bold enterprise. Ayn Rand, attacking from the super-capitalist (not fascist) right, was freer to criticize what capitalism had become than liberals were to make such relatively commonsense points. Particularly this one: if you continued to preach the self-made man as an ideal, just as power was centralizing in what Eisenhower later called "the military-industrial complex," then widespread self-hatred, therefore bitterness, therefore nihilism and violence must result. Meanwhile, enough Americans clung to the pioneer myth to make a massive bestseller out of Rand's novel (which rests like a tombstone under the film credits). Rand's popularity resurged in the Reagan-era eighties, which renewed those conflicts between the pioneer myth and the big business ethos.

Drafted in 1938, the novel's rage seems directed at the New Deal, with its streaks of an older, Progressive-tinged Populism, proponents of which are damned as "collectivist . . . parasites" in Roark's summation to the jury. Rand's cult of genius goes with an encompassing contempt for "the man in the street." Roark's teacher gazes down at the crowd from their office in a New York skyscraper only to assure him: "I don't care what they think of architecture—or anything else." But, not surprisingly, the film omits his "fear" of "the people in the street" [10]—after all, Vidor had made *The Crowd*, and the people in the street are also the people in the cinema seats. Vidor's ambivalence about elitism would explain why this guru's countenance, at this moment, reminds us of mafioso Humphrey Bogart in *Racket Busters* smirking down on the masses from *his* balcony: "Holler, suckers; when I get through with you, you'll holler even louder." Vidor's distance from Rand is underscored by a moment in the novel. Dominique raves: "Is it an inspiring sight to see a man commit an heroic gesture, and then learn he goes to a vaudeville house for relaxation?" [11] That's *precisely* the daily heroism of *The Crowd*. But Vidor goes some of the way with Rand. A newspaper editor's office looks out onto a vast, *Crowd*-like open-plan office, but the battle now is among egoists only, walled off from the workers by a sheet of glass. "The system" has remained; the spontaneity of the people is dulled.

Expressionist styles often imbued film populism around 1930, disguising tensions for which *The Fountainhead* forges a new language, borrowing *film noir*'s angles and darkness, its paranoia, its focus on a beleaguered or tormented individual. In that sense, the *film noir* is anti-populist. Every man walks alone down dark, mean streets. In *The Fountainhead,* when the masses aren't hunched over their desks, they're out rioting, egged on by tycoons of media opinion. Without the tortured ego accessible to *noir* styles, you're "One of the Mob" (a projected title for *The Crowd*).

Ayn Rand's inspiration for Howard Roark was Frank Lloyd Wright, and Roark's mentor may recall Wright's "liebermeister," Louis Sullivan. But, however fond Wright was of bad puns like "them asses" for "the masses," or of labeling "the 'Democracy' of the man in the American street" "the Gospel of Mediocrity," [12] his idealism was as transcendental as Whitman's—or Vidor's. His equal and opposite overstatements are a *primitif* writer's way of asserting a dialectic. Rand's Roark, alas, is consistent to a fault (an unintentionally amusing one). For Rand's own screen adaptation was not merely explicit, but quite didactic. It asserted that (1) man's nature is brought to its pitch of moral perfection by an ego *über alles* selfishness, and (2) that progress throughout history comes from egoistic supermen who, in benefiting themselves, give their less dynamic fellows the benefit of a little by-product, spin-off, or (in Reagan-era lingo) trickle-down. When Roark agrees to design Keating's public-housing project, he insists that while the *result* may be humanitarian, the motive had better not be. It took an implacable egoism to tame fire, invent the wheel, and drag mediocre mankind from its caves into the atomic age. True egoism is sufficient unto itself and requires only its own approval. Today, alas, man's healthy egoism is the victim of mass society, which spreads its psychic plague of envy, jealousy, impotence, guilty altruism, socialistic liberalism, and communism. "The world is perishing in an

Figure 121. The Fountainhead *(1949). Four egoists: (a) Howard Roark (Gary Cooper); (b) Gail Wynand (Raymond Massey); (c) Ellsworth M. Toohey (Robert Douglas); and (d) Dominique Francon (Patricia Neal).*

orgy of self-sacrifice," Roark assures the jury. In modern America, the very captains of industry, who should be athletes of the spirit, are spiritually debilitated, petty profit seekers. Either they have been infected by hypocrisy or their visions have lost their grandeur, and they have come to pander to the mass instead of leading it.

Vidor treats *The Fountainhead* as a useful vehicle for some of his own beliefs and is less concerned with defining precisely where Rand's end and his own begin. "Both *War and Peace* and *The Fountainhead* were films that came to me through an agent, and I did not set out to do them as personal projects. The coincidence [with *The Fountainhead*] is that I had just gone through Jungian analysis a few years before and I was very conscious of this recognition of the 'self,' and of the power and divinity one has. I had been approaching this in my own way and not exactly through Jungian techniques. . . . It was almost as if the search I had been going through had been an absolute secret, then suddenly they come up to ask me to do these pictures right in line with my thinking."[13] Although it's true that the breadwinner-clown in *The Crowd* and the humble family in

Hallelujah would seem condemned to belong to the mediocrities of the mass, it's also true that most of Vidor's films *since* the mid thirties center on those who try to construct societies, who take the risk of egoism.

Vidor's film of *The Fountainhead* focuses its conflicts between Roark's true egoism and various counterfeits. Wynand the publisher (fig. 121b) is nerveless through infection rather than radically bad: his press campaigns—against, then for Roark—are fickle, like Dominique's affections. His failure lies in not becoming the strong leader Americans deserve, and to whom they respond at Roark's trial (a response anticipated during the debate over the co-op's constitution in *Our Daily Bread*). Similarly, Keating has argued for the negative path of giving "the public what it wants." But both men are exceptional enough to see their own failure, and to admit Roark's preeminence.

The one thoroughly rotten apple is a certain combination of the intellectual left with piss-elegant snobbism, here incarnated by a certain Ellsworth M. Toohey, architecture critic on Wynand's paper. This overdressed dilettante caresses a cigarette holder while exhaling devilishly (fig. 121c). He manages to unionize the staff and thus sneak his way to power by simultaneously collectivizing the paper and vilifying the rich, two thoroughly parasitical and mean-souled activities. For just as the critic creates nothing, merely cashing in on the artist's creativity, so the unionist creates no wealth, but merely negates and grabs, to build his paltry little empire of also-rans. Toohey's Europe-oriented and socialist realist aesthetic ("Artistic value is achieved collectively, by each member subordinating himself to the will of the majority") is a transparent mask over a scheme for the egoless masses to subordinate themselves to *his* will. In Vidor's film, Robert Douglas plays Toohey as if all concerned were utterly baffled by how to make a human being of Rand's cardboard caricature.

Otherwise, though, Rand's ultrapurist notions of selfishness as a new religion (the "Me Generation" before its time) are mellowed by Vidor's knowledge of frustration and suffering in the real world. After Roark's old teacher, dying and disappointed, recants his ideals, an ambulance takes him along Manhattan streets, and its red cross looms very large on the screen, as if to assert a cross of compassion (fig. 122). (Vidor remembered taking trouble, with process shots, for that cross [14]—though the interpretation is ours.) Maybe it's precisely Roark's un-Christian virtues that save him from having to follow the old man along, dare we say, the way of the cross. But his willingness to go through that sacrifice, if he must, makes Ayn Rand's "egoism" look more like what David Riesman called "autonomy" [15]—which accurately embodies what we find healthy and admirable about her ideas. Here Vidor diverges from Rand's hardnosed atheism. And on the attractiveness of Roark's egoism, he commented, "We've been thrown off by repentance, long suffering, and the

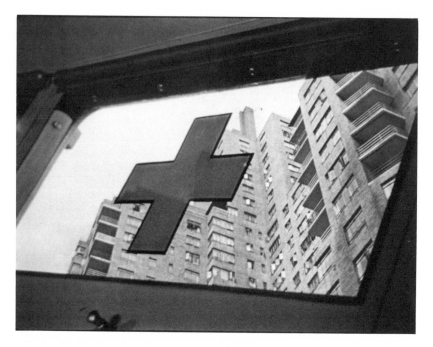

Figure 122.   The Fountainhead. *[Frame enlargement.]*

ideas of the church. . . . Where do you find God? in a church? a priest? a Pope? Truly it is a man's consciousness and his own self that represents God, that speaks for God in its own way. It really is a fine basic theme." [16]

In its concern with capitalism and society's reigning morality, *The Fountainhead* is a uniquely aggressive, right-wing contribution to a cycle of films that includes *The Best Years of Our Lives* (the bank-manager's dilemma), *The Man in the Gray Flannel Suit*, and *Executive Suite*. Thereafter the emphasis shifts slightly, but significantly, from principles of conscience to the mechanisms of social control (as in *Woman's World*, *Patterns*, and *The Big Knife*). Eventually any sort of approach to the nitty-gritty gets softened by comedy, musical or otherwise (*The Apartment*, *One Two Three*, *How to Succeed in Business without Really Trying*, *The Pajama Game*). We admire *The Fountainhead* for daring some radical criticisms of the system, alongside some unpopular films by Dmytryk, Wilder, and Fuller: *Give Us This Day*, *Ace in the Hole*, and *Shock Corridor*.

As it is, the scenario offers its very interesting four-cornered conflict of egoism—Roark, Wynand, Toohey, and Dominique (with Keating quickly turning apologetic and into—Rand's most damning phrase—"the totally selfless man"). It's surprising that the combined professionalism of Gary Cooper, Vidor, and Jack Warner could do so little to modify Ayn Rand's comic-strip dialogue. When Vidor asked her to write an adaptation, she volunteered to do it for free, providing no dialogue was changed without her consent. You have to give her philosophy its due: her Roarkian strategy achieved the best of both worlds: she got paid *and* retained that veto power. When she discovered Vidor shooting his cut version of Roark's courtroom summary, she ran to Jack Warner, who forced Vidor to abide by her contract terms. The extremist dialogue bolsters the film's air of urgency, and refreshingly avoids the usual Hollywood ambiguities, which would defeat its purpose. But it remains disconcerting that the villain intellectual should declare himself almost as boldly as in a Victorian melodrama: "Maybe I want to dishonor and discredit all greatness." And Roark is so constantly called a genius that it becomes a struggle for Gary Cooper to secure for us much identification with him, unlike his success with Capra's (modest, tuba-playing) Mr. Deeds. Ayn Rand's egoist tops even Aristotle's magnanimous man and Nietzsche's *Übermensch* by bearing the past, and even the present, no grudge. He always forgets insults, and is simply stating the truth when he tells Toohey that he never thinks of him at all, thus depriving him of the warped narcissism of being despised. When reduced to menial tasks, he doesn't compromise, complain, or ask for privilege or pity. He wields the pneumatic drill down in the granite quarry, preferring honest sweat to Keating's fear-induced compromise. Only Roark's *absence* allows certain Machiavellian compromises. "They're done all the time, but not talked about," Wynand comments when he offers Keating a commission on condition that he break his engagement to Dominique.

One might have expected Vidor to humanize this paragon, perhaps by brief gestures, indicating, at least, some spiritual conflicts behind the poker-faced pains. Instead, Vidor adopts another approach, easy for lovers of the mellower Vidor to misunderstand. Drawing from the out-of-context stereotype of Cooper's strong, silent gunslingers, Roark is a hero with complete trust in his disciplined reflexes. This tactic works well when the dramatic context gives help, as in that famous bravura passage, the double cadenza of slaps and kisses between two fine egoists. When Roark quits his quarry job and walks along a dirt road in a rumpled workshirt and shapeless hat, like Capra's John Doe, it looks like an infusion of Vidor's "average," yet spiritual, man, set on a long march toward "the people." But that image is a setup, its familiarity rudely shattered as

a   b

Figure 123.   The Fountainhead. *The woman with the whip.*

Dominique gallops up on her black horse to slash her riding crop across his unflinching, mocking face (fig. 123a–b). Coop can certainly set a thin mouth in a bleak face, and his edgy delivery is an intriguingly awkward style of aloofness.

Vidor would dearly have loved Bogart as Roark, perhaps because Bogart's countenance is more complex and intellectual, more hardbitten and insolent. Moreover, Bogart's city-street associations would assert Roark as a more powerful successor to Sam in *Street Scene*—the anti-gangster, who, having sought and found his wider horizons, returns, his violence undiminished, but disciplined by deeper thought. Roark is a "public enemy" planning not just to take over the city, but to transform it from the ground up.*

The script's one-dimensionality allows for rare directness in the Roark and Dominique love-hate story. Their struggle ends near enough a draw to constitute equality, the only basis on which egoists can come together. Their round of slaps and kisses is fittingly fierce, close to the set-to between Birkin and Gerald in *Women in Love* or that in Losey's *The Sleeping Tiger*, where Alexis Smith completes the implications of her wardrobe by following her blows at Dirk Bogarde with "I wish I was a man!" In a reversal of *Duel in the Sun*, the male in *The Fountainhead* is the more constructive figure. Dominique belongs to the line of postwar Vidor heroines, from Pearl to Sheba, whom some socio-spiritual frustration goads into destructively "male" outbursts. There's a long escalation, from Meli-

---

*Ironically, Roark's vision evokes two gangster-film slogans: "The World Is Yours" and "Top of the World, Ma!" The first comes from a neon sign shining down on the slumped Scarface, flushed out from the impregnable penthouse of his absolute egoism. The second comes from *White Heat*, where Cagney, Oedipally straddling an oil tank, achieves his self-destructive apotheosis. Both their fates contrast with Roark's wind-ruffled triumph atop the tycoon's memorial skyscraper.

sande's affectionate, but effective, slap, through Pearl's smashing of jellied bread impotently into Lewt's laughing face, to Dominique's socially haughty riding-crop, and, later, to Rosa Moline's and Ruby Gentry's tomboy rifles.

In Roark's moral, spiritual, and physical edge of superiority over Dominique, there's no doubt a traditional machismo, with the volatility found in "sex war" writers like Nietzsche, Strindberg, and D. H. Lawrence.* Conquering the Woman, indeed—a fantasy upon which the indomitable Ms. Rand imperiously insisted. Vidor doesn't really separate sex and work, or give the first a primacy of which the latter is its "sublimation." Rather they share a generalized energy. If anything his heroes are more likely to sacrifice their passions for their vocation than the other way around; and it's just this sense of separate energies colliding that makes Vidor's hate-into-love scenes so powerful. Here, Dominique's passionate plans for togetherness unmarred by Roark's quixotic vocation get stopped cold: "I wish I could say I was tempted."

When Roark finally condescends to test Dominique by asking her to help him blow up the imperfect housing project, it could seem a case of "he for God only, she for God through him." But the film's half-disguise of the hoary rape fantasy in Rand's Dominique, whether owing to Vidor's sexual politics or to Production Code restrictions, has the result of equalizing the struggle. (Rand was even blunter in her notes on the script, just in case Vidor didn't get it: "He raped her because he knew she wanted it.") What Rand's scenario gives to Roark in terms of steely control, Patricia Neal gives to Dominique. (Curiously, Neal bears a resemblance to Rand, in full face at least.) But while we can take the self-assurance in Gary Cooper's Roark on the faith of a persona, we watch the struggle for control in Neal's darting eyes and tightening jaw.

In Dominique's name is her self-image. But Vidor films her as only physically dominant in the remarkably sexualized scenes (blessedly free of Rand dialogue) where she paces like a caged leopard along a ridge above the lines of sweating, shirtless quarriers. The sleeping tiger in her is encaged in her sleek shirt and pants (fig. 124b). Roark gazes up at her, while—in all innocence, no doubt—thrusting his jackhammer into a tight hole in the granite (fig. 124a). While Vidor may have had difficulty departing from Rand's dialogue, his freedom came visually. Rand's film script calls Dominique "a fragile exquisite figure." Nothing fragile about the film's Dominique, dressed to meet Roark on terms of volatile, perverse equality. Roark and his fellow workers are poetic justice for her

---

*Although Lawrence and Vidor share some themes—the spirituality of the practical, the tactility and creativity of work, pantheism, community—the comparison sustains itself none too well. Vidor's dynamic pragmatism and acceptance of all relationships is completely at odds with the mixture of sensuous perfectionism and cosmic prophecy in Lawrence.

a   b

Figure 124.   The Fountainhead. *Gary Cooper and Patricia Neal. [Production stills.]*

hubris earlier, when, in black nightgown, she tosses a treasured statue of a nude male "god" out of her penthouse window (fig. 121d). "It's the things we admire and want that bring us into submission," she later informs Roark. That philosophy breaks down under these moments of sexual panic, which finally push her, bound tightly in furs against a cold that no one else seems to feel, into asking Wynand to take up her marriage offer. Still, on humbler, consumerist levels, there's much to be said for her notion—it goes far toward explaining the perversion of Wynand's own strength, when "the feeling" of "ownership" (of a newspaper and a new home) becomes the goal of his egoism. Indeed, from this angle, *The Fountainhead*'s rightist critique of where American capitalism went wrong leads into Marx's understanding of the fetishism of commodities and Lukács's concern about a "reified" world of disconnected social life.

But sexual reciprocity for Vidor isn't symmetry. Both as socialite and journalist, Dominique's role is that of mediator, of counsellor, of conscience, which is precisely what gives her role as genius's henchwoman its point. Roark finds in her an ideal antagonist, a mate, and a way back from his cold isolation. (Their union is yin to the yang of Dieterle's *Love Letters*, where Ayn Rand's script churns to a fever pitch the perfect spiritual unity, transcending all crimes, of a Vidorian couple—Jennifer Jones and Joseph Cotten.) Dominique plays her role of innocent bystander to the hilt at the dynamiting of the housing project—she slices through an artery with a piece of broken glass in a last flourish of rape-me masochism—and crosses the border into civil disobedience and antinomianism with Roark.* The couple's rare calm in her hospital room suggests her contribution to his shift from jailhouse vow of silence to condescending to defend himself before the jury. A temptation to martyrdom (through megalomania rather than through Mr. Deeds's despair) turns into a triumph.

One would have thought that Roark and Dominique broke the Production Code in conspiring to commit a crime that is richly rewarded. (Especially when a farsighted philanthropist returns to rebuild the demolished housing project Roark's way.) Vidor was under contractual constraint to follow the book, but in some interviews, he confessed his dislike of that explosive ending.[17] He could, of course, sympathize with Roark's position: "The slightest change by Thalberg or the studio would just wreck the whole thing if it was done in an insincere or careless manner."[18] But, having had to compromise his own control of projects so often, Vidor may have felt that Roark's perfectionism was more tetchy than principled, and that his sociophallic apotheosis at the top of the Wynand Building (fig. 121a) was too good to be true.

Rand's *Übermensch* theory leads straight to all the problems of leadership in democracy. Where Rand is grandly disdainful (and wildly unhistorical), Vidor likes to hypothesize a generous-souled reciprocity all around, like the inspirationalist switchovers of *Our Daily Bread* and *Northwest Passage*. Vidor's answer looks like a pragmatic put-down of a certain democratic dogma ("The people don't need leaders"), though only in a passionately democratic context. In *The Fountainhead* American democracy seems near breakdown, with Roark's strong leadership its last hope. At least the jury has the spirit left to respond and place the individualistic principle where it belongs—above the law. All of which made a pretty pernicious brew during the years of Senator Joe McCarthy, of whom Ayn Rand was a vociferous supporter. Profoundly treated, *An American Romance* might have brought up parallel points about whether big business, or labor, or some kind of individualism, or all three, or none, has the best moral right to be above the law, or to remake the law in its own interest.

---

*This tendency, particularly in America, is more strongly associated with transcendentalist movements (for example, the Anabaptists) than with puritan ones. But it fans out over the whole range of left/right options, relating particularly closely to the "nonconformist conscience" (with all its affinities to "autonomy" and "inner-direction") and to right-wing cults of the hero. There is also a range of commonsense antinomianisms, from patriotic Machiavellianism to the middle-of-the-road pragmatism whereby the law allows that the law may be a fool and adapts to its gradual disregard by the community.

Since Vidor disliked this ending, it's intriguing to speculate on other possibilities. Would his ideal Roark have had no alternative but to compromise, to resist the temptation to the most grandiose of tantrums, and yet remain undefeated within himself, holding the line against the spiritual littleness of big business? Since he earlier designs innovative country stores, farms, and gas stations—under the, astonishingly passive, egoist principle that "Any man who calls for me is my kind of man"—would he, after a spiritual crisis as grueling as John's in *The Crowd,* have contented himself with designing for hard-working "little men"? Vidor asserted that if Roark was right to demolish his compromised buildings, then he, as the film's director, should have destroyed its negative. When he put this point to Warner Brothers, who were insisting on the climactic sabotage, they are said to have replied, "Right, and we'll see if a jury exonerates you." Thus, ultimately, the *production's* relation to film's moral continuum is an ironic negation of its faith. One can sympathize with the United Artists executives who oversaw *Heaven's Gate,* doubly distraught in knowing that the film Michael Cimino had *really* wanted to remake for them was *The Fountainhead.*[19]

Although *The Fountainhead* has an affirmative script, its experience as filmed is bleaker and nobler. If you had to have this script and cast, it couldn't be more tightly and relentlessly done. Vidor sought Frank Lloyd Wright to execute Roark's designs, and Wright wryly agreed, for his standard 10 percent commission—of the film's entire budget. After that, Jack Warner, fearing a lawsuit, prevented Vidor from visiting Wright in Arizona. The substitute designs were uninspiringly "futurist." Vidor without Wright is almost *Hamlet* without the prince, though we can accept what we see as an abstract equivalent, like Hitchcock's "McGuffin." In theory at least, Wright's designs could have allowed Vidor to reach a harmony far past the script's contentiousness. After all, Wright's cherished Broadacres City project, as finally worked out in the fifties, outdid *Our Daily Bread* in its dream of Arcadian harmony, just as it topped Rand in elevating the architect to philosopher-king.* As the film was produced, Vidor's

---

*For Wright, as fully as for Thoreau, the dysfunctions of society were city-induced; and Broadacres would ultimately supersede existing cities by dispersing families onto small farms, each "not relatively, but absolutely self-sufficient" (thus, in theory, overcoming the problems of the *Our Daily Bread* community). Those whose occupations or inclinations put them outside of this Arcadia would live in towers scattered throughout the countryside. Wright's 1958 version of the Broadacres plan takes on the enthusiastic cadences of a nineteenth-century transcendentalist: "The citizen is now trained to see life as cliché whereas his architect should train his own mind, and thereby the citizen's, to see the nature of glass as Glass, the board as Board, a brick as Brick; see the nature of steel as Steel: see all in relation to each other as well as in relation to Time, Place, and Man. Be eager to be honest with himself and so not untrue to other men; . . . try to live in the richer sense because deep *in* nature; be native as the trees to the wood, as grass to the floor of the valley. Only then can the democratic spirit of man, individual, rise out of the confusion of commu-

sense of vast, unstably bold spaces makes an unusual conjunction with *film noir* lighting, and with International Style angularity at its most boring and inorganic. The film's vacuous interiors, heavily carpeted yet nastily hard-edged, have, as antithesis, two rare open-air scenes: one atop the skyscraper, the other in the quarry, where under a blazing sky (like a pocket of desert from *Duel in the Sun*) Roark batters at the stone, wresting something constructive out of Mother Earth, even at her most grudging-hearted. Meanwhile, New York's nightscape blazes like a collective vision of these Easter years of the American Dream.

Whatever one's disagreements with the bleak and bold answers here, Vidor's radicalism reached the core more effectively than most "liberal" films of his era. Looking back on *The Fountainhead* from the vantage of his—and the century's—eighties, Vidor had come to enjoy the hard power of its conclusion. How many olde worlde sewers, how many urban-renewal housing projects and socialist tower blocks remain, overripe for destruction?

Beyond the Forest

At the opening of Edward Albee's *Who's Afraid of Virginia Woolf?* George and Martha arrive home after a party. She looks around and imitates Bette Davis:

> "What a dump. Hey, what's that from? 'What a dump!'"
> "How would I know what . . ."
> "Aw, come on! What's it from? *You* know . . ."
> ". . . Martha . . ."
> "WHAT'S IT FROM, FOR CHRIST'S SAKE?"
> "What's what from?"
> "I just told you; I just did it. 'What a dump!' Hunh? What's that from?"
> "I haven't the faintest idea what . . ."
> "Dumbbell! It's from some goddamn Bette Davis picture . . . some goddamn Warner Brothers epic . . .
> "*I* can't remember all the pictures that . . ."
> "Nobody's asking you to remember every single goddamn Warner Brothers epic . . . just one! One single little epic! Bette Davis gets peritonitis in the end . . . she's got this big black fright wig she wears all through the picture and she gets peritonitis, and she's married to Joseph Cotten or something . . ."
> ". . . some*body* . . ."

---

nal life in the city to a creative civilization of the ground. We are calling that civilization of man and ground—really organic agronomy—democracy: intrinsically superior to the more static faiths of the past lying in ruins all about him" (Frank Lloyd Wright, *The Living City* [New York: Horizon Press, 1958], 25).

"Some*body* . . . and she wants to go to Chicago all the time, 'cause she's in love with that actor with the scar . . . But she gets sick, and she sits down in front of her dressing table . . ."

"What actor? What scar?"

"*I* can't remember his name, for God's sake. What's the name of the *picture?* I want to know what the name of the *picture* is. She sits down in front of her dressing table . . . and she's got this peritonitis . . . and she tries to put lipstick on, but she can't . . . and she gets it all over her face . . . but she decides to go to Chicago anyway and . . ."

"*Chicago!* It's called *Chicago.*"

"Hunh? What . . . what is?"

"The picture . . . it's called *Chicago* . . ."

"Good grief! Don't you know *anything? Chicago* was a 'thirties musical, starring little Miss Alice *Faye.* Don't you know *anything?*"

"Well, that was probably before my *time,* but . . ."

"Can it! Just cut that out! This picture . . . Bette Davis comes home from a hard day at the grocery store . . ."

"She works in a grocery store?"

"She's a housewife; she buys things . . . and she comes home with the groceries, and she walks into the modest living room of the modest cottage modest Joseph Cotten has set her up in . . ."

"Are they married?"

"Yes. They're married. To each other. Cluck! And she comes in, and she looks around, and she puts her groceries down, and she says, 'What a dump!'"

(*Pause*) "Oh."

(*Pause*) "She's discontent."

(*Pause*) "Oh."[20]

Martha captures the wild domesticity of *Beyond the Forest,* but possibly her plot summary could use a little sorting out:

Rosa Moline (Bette Davis) has long nursed her craving for city life and wealth, and loathes the small Wisconsin town where she lives with Dr. Lewis Moline (Joseph Cotten). No richer than his patients, he must haggle with the medical suppliers for badly needed blood plasma for the sick. Rosa is tormented by the insolence of her Indian maid, who, her work done, just strolls away to some rendezvous, as insolently free of soul as her mistress is trapped.

Rosa hopes that marriage will result from her affair with a Chicago millionaire, Neil Latimer (David Brian [not "that actor with the scar"— George Macready]). But her adulterous game is discovered by his game-warden, Moose, who threatens to reveal her pregnancy. She joins a hunting party to shoot him and brazens out the murder trial, but Neil puts off the marriage to avoid scandal. Through another "accident" she aborts herself and is brought home badly injured. Delirious, she attempts a final journey to her millionaire and stumbles as far as the train station, only to fall in the road a few feet from the level crossing across which the Chicago express rumbles, the lights from its cars fanning over her dead face.

This is Vidor's *film noir* re-vision of *Alice Adams* (the silent version of which he produced) and *Stella Dallas*—women trapped behind white picket fences while plotting rich catches. Disdained as ludicrous by liberal realists of its day, its exasperated melodrama wears a lot better after the resurgence of high melodrama in Albee and feminist murder à la Marguerite Duras, Chantal Ackerman, and Marleen Gorris. As Vidor himself said, "It looks better from a distance, like old wine." [21] Too mellow a metaphor. If Dr. Moline had been any match for Rosa in wit, they would have gone at it like George and Martha. As it stands, it's (dare we say?) a variant on *Duel in the Sun*—if the McCanles ranch had come with only one son and Jennifer Jones had given up on the codfish passions of Joseph Cotten. *This* Cotten character is appalled that Rosa went "crawling back" to her lover (as Jess McCanles might have been had he witnessed *Duel*'s happy end). Rosa "drags" herself to Neil "on hands and knees with no pride," and some of her pathos comes from not finding a Lewt willing to meet her on the mountaintop or a Roark to meet her on the rooftop. *Beyond the Forest* takes just a single, sad, lonely one of the wild egoists that fill *Duel* and *The Fountainhead* and smothers her within a world of good, gray responsibility.

Vidor astonishingly transforms Bette Davis into a sardonic caricature of Jennifer Jones, complete with peasant blouse, "black fright wig," hunting rifle, even frustrated writhing (fig. 125). Here all these emblems take on another meaning—desperate, ludicrous clinging to adolescence by a woman well into middle age. And so Rosa Moline loses the sophistication we know Bette Davis to have. Her *potential* self is degraded by the selfishness of this "Wisconsin Bovary" (as the source novel calls her). [22]

That *Madame Bovary* theme has lured many a moviemaker into its trap, which is the difficulty of sustaining the movie spectator's interest in a shallow woman in a shallow (or seemingly shallow) world. One has to work *against* the story, to stress what's positive in her yearnings, what's active in her passivity, and the richness she *doesn't* see in the life around her. In his 1933 film Jean Renoir sought to outflank these problems by a resolutely objective approach, wavering between a psychological center and local color with a French discursiveness alien to Hollywood.

Beyond the Forest slashes that Gordian knot with two brutal and decisive strokes. Its heroine, unlike Renoir's, is hyperactive. And, like Renoir, but unlike Flaubert, Vidor *appreciates* the life his Madame Bovary despises. The victim of "bourgeois mediocrity" becomes a "villain," but so distraught that our fascinated horror turns to pity, even sympathy. She personifies a devious, but oh how powerful, social mechanism: the small-

Figure 125.   Beyond the Forest *(1 ɔ49). Bette Davis (Rosa Moline) doing "Jennifer Jones." [Frame enlargement.]*

town girl so consumed with craving for the city that she becomes what looks like a camp caricature of herself. Rosa despises even her doctor-husband's responsibility. Yet she can't settle into its opposite either—the calm insolence of the Indian servant girl who so curiously resembles her. While the Wisconsin Bovary's romances are mundane magazine entice-ments (chicken à la King, venetian blinds) and ads mailed from Chicago ("Drudgery or Comfort—It's Up to You to Act Now"), the languors of her consciousness are crystallized into boldly dramatic attitudes. Melo-drama (the shooting accident) and sordid realism (the abortion accident) fuse together, just as her town's sawmill's shavings-furnace begins as documentary-style detail and ends as emblem of Rosa's nervous desire. The outrageous melodrama achieves the conviction of Grand Guignol. And so the film leads into two other studies in the pre- or post-menopausal paroxysms of American womanhood: *Sunset Boulevard* (1950) and *A Streetcar Named Desire* (1951). Its tendencies to simple moral ferocity are undermined by its sympathy for Rosa's life force, frustrated and de-ranged though it is. Her wild discontent is an equal and opposite sin to H. M. Pulham's dull deadness. But it makes for a grander show.

It was not merely a low budget that dictated the sparse presentation of Chicago—where Rosa flees in mid film to her temporarily distracted millionaire—by the song of that title and as a series of constricted spaces (a rear auto seat, a hotel room, dark porches, very brief and confined exteriors). This cramped minimalism evokes quick, restricted meetings, suffocated feelings, Rosa's narrow toehold in the cliff face of her dream world. The film's free space is in the town she disdains. The one large "Chicago" exterior duplicates an earlier shot of the small town, Rosa crossing two streets catercorner: sunny reflections are transmuted to rain-drenched *noir* pavements (fig. 126a–b); a wholesome wolf whistle becomes "Come on sister, I got a couple of bucks"; and her proud stride becomes a panicky run (fig. 126c–d). Chicago, with its heavy industry, is also alluded to by the steam locomotive, whose promise of a liberating journey is visually belied by its gigantic driving wheels, blocking the screen, while steam jets out. During shots of the wheels, Max Steiner heightens a string version of the "fun" pop song "Chicago" into a nightmarish Bernard Herrmann style. In contrast to the city's brutal industry, the film takes in its stride what is virtually a little documentary on small-town community, whose sawmills and rural industry set the slow, stolid, human pace to which

a

b

c

d

Figure 126.   The town and the city in Beyond the Forest.

Rosa's nervous intensity cannot adapt, and into whose neighborly concerns she cannot sink her spiritual roots.

While Vidor appreciates Doc Moline's responsible vocation, the doctor's help is secondary to an expectant mother's "will to live" through a tough delivery. Moline is vastly improved, beyond recognition indeed, from the novel's doctor, a weakling too flustered by Rosa's infidelities to notice the pregnant woman's ominous symptoms. In the film he has such saintly patience that we can't help but half sympathize with Rosa's exasperation, and admire the moment near the end when she summons a deathly strength of obsession to bat the last of her medicine out of her husband's hands and shout, "Well, you finally got the guts to hate me!" No such luck. He's off to get more medicine.*

It's assumed that Rosa is carrying his child, although she has known Neil for a year. Her long childless condition is notable in a town filled with baby boom children ("mass production," mutters Rosa). Within the limits of Production Code circumspection (and some Legion of Decency–imposed cuts), Rosa grumbles sexual dissatisfaction: "He doesn't do *anything* enough" and, sinking a pool ball, "*I'm* the shot in the family." When the doc says he's going to bed, Rosa shoots back, "That's big news. Where else could you go?" glossing their sexual relationship in an exchange that, with Davis's fine-tuned insolence, is worthy of Albee. Joseph Cotten gives a masterly passionless performance—enthusiasm overtaking awkwardness only once, at the dinner table (where Cotten's finest moments as an actor also come in *The Magnificent Ambersons* and *Shadow of a Doubt*), when he leans back with justified pride in the community's reliance on his GP skills.

If Vidor appreciates that community, it is not without qualification. The town is less than bucolic in the opening narrated prowl through vacant streets, overshadowed by the sawmill that "burns its way through closed eyelids, through sleep itself." The citizens, a mob of gossips, have packed the courthouse less for the verdict on Moose's death, we're told, than to learn what makes Rosa "different," a word so repeatedly applied to her that it becomes synonymous with evil. Perhaps to point out Vidor's qualifiers is to make too much of them. He isn't exposing some murderous underside of small-town "Loyalton," as, say, David Lynch does with "Lumberton" in *Blue Velvet*. Still, one feels a stab of *The Invasion of the Body Snatchers* when, before Neil's return, Rosa squats on a hillside, her hair bound tightly back, and passively accepts her husband's philosophy that it's "not so bad" to be indistinguishable from the rest (fig. 127).

*It was Vidor's insistence that Bette Davis retake this final confrontation to try for greater vehemence ("I could tell that she liked Joe") that led to her demand that he be replaced. See Charles Higham, *Bette: The Life of Bette Davis* (New York: Macmillan, 1981), 213–15.

Figure 127. Beyond the Forest. *Rosa and Dr. Moline (Bette Davis, Joseph Cotten). [Frame enlargement.]*

The plot can be read as puritanical: small sins leading to larger ones—discontent to adultery to murder, with abortion bringing self-destruction in its train. But it becomes depuritanized if one sees the murder as a Rubicon Rosa should not have crossed, and the self-destructive abortion as "poetic justice." (That is, as the irony of appropriate injustice: the lesser crime avenging the greater. Even if abortion can be considered murder, only the most paradoxical "pro-life" advocate could argue that it merits capital punishment.) In the film as Vidor cut it, Dr. Moline arrived in the nick of time to prevent Rosa's appointment with the abortionist. The release version is very confusing, because Warners' last-minute censorship required that abortion go unmentioned. Hence the abortionist's office is introduced by a poorly inserted shot of a *lawyer's* office sign. Thus, in the release cut, Rosa's final desperation looks like a first option—the *Gone with the Wind*–tested falling method, which is likewise the modus operandi of the heroine in John Stahl's *Leave Her to Heaven* (1945), a high-gloss, cold, deadpan variation on the same theme (murder and abortion in a cabin-and-lake setting; willful wife versus saintly husband). Perhaps such desperate methods carry a kind of poetic truth—just as in Losey's *The Prowler* the whole eerie sequence of clandestine childbirth in a windblown ghost town is a metaphor for the sadness of abortion, which that script would have featured had the Production Code allowed.

We never see Rosa's upper-class rival for Neil's affections, the society girl whose heart is like a book with uncut pages ("and nothing on 'em," Rosa snarls). When a perfectly groomed and mannered woman steps off the Chicago train, Rosa assumes from the evidence of monogrammed luggage that her fur coat is the spoils of a marriage to Neil. Actually she's Moose's long-lost daughter, who seems to have risen in the world by the simplest of methods: the straightforward sincerity Rosa despises as emptiness. That we also jump to Rosa's assumption (with the excuse of following melodrama's conventions) is one of the ways Vidor implicates us in her thinking, and gives us sympathy with her, while also criticizing her obsessional nature. Trapped in the "dump" of the nicest (middle-class) home in town, Rosa sees freedom on *both* economic sides. Her "redressings" give away her yearnings. In Chicago she wears a tailored suit, her homemade version of the high-class one in which Moose's daughter arrives (fig. 128a–b), and when she tries to flee town by bus unnoticed, she adopts her Indian maid's lower-class plaid workshirt and jeans, the very

a   b

c   d

Figure 128.   Beyond the Forest. *Rosa's borrowed styles.*

outfit that earlier provoked her outrage (fig. 128c–d). Unlike the male-imposed redressings we noted in connection with *Stella Dallas*, Rosa's pathos comes from how little self-identity she has once she leaves the town she despises, beyond that which she takes from the styles of women she hates.

Figure 129.   Vidor and Bette Davis on the set of Beyond the Forest.

Beyond the Forest is rooted—unusually for an American film, and still more for an American "woman's drama"—in the sense of a town's economics. To the doctor, Rosa's one unforgivable sin isn't adultery; it's collecting the debts owed him by the town (just as Ruby Gentry willfully alienates a town by calling in *her* husband's loans). Vidor's film belongs alongside other studies of regional cupidity and postwar greed, notably Wilder's *Ace in the Hole*. Where Wilder, with his more saturnine eye for America (and/or humanity), implies a very uneasy equilibrium between decency and callousness, Vidor tips the balance toward seeing Rosa as more her own victim than the community's. If the film does involve us in a certain horrified sympathy for, even identification with, the heroine, its dominant strategy, inherited from Jacobean drama, is a fascination with villainy—in which bad taste, like grotesqueness, plays its part. Its contrast with both glum, stiff-upper-lip martyrology à la Joan Crawford and the simple softness of Jane Wyman couldn't be more complete. While the film touches on a *film noir* expressionism, keyed by Bette Davis's paroxysmal despair, by the rain, by the steaming wheels, Vidor's transcendental, and in that sense blind, optimism leaves him short of explanations for a cynicism that would justify *noir* as the *predominant* tone. All the same, no clear line divides the vividly presented diagnosis from the in-depth analysis, and *Beyond the Forest* is a shout that "Attention must be paid to this woman!" Middlebrow critics of the era found an unsmart, unsophisticated Bette Davis most unwelcome, and the reviews were the worst of Vidor's career. He didn't, at the time, like the film himself. But Billy Wilder's enthusiasm for it strikes us as completely founded. It is one of the most deeply driven of the studies in the monstrosity of female folly that Hollywood filmmakers from Wilder to Aldrich, and American dramatists from Tennessee Williams to Edward Albee, have done with a mixture of moralistic wildness and mordant fascination that only *looks* like camp.

Lightning Strikes Twice

Out West to recover from New York City–induced nervous exhaustion, actress Shelley Carnes (Ruth Roman) finds herself ensnared in the aftermath of the inconclusive trials of Richard Trevelyan (Richard Todd) for the murder of his wife. Losing her way in a storm, she's sheltered in a barren, dark house by "Trev" and instinctively believes him innocent. Doubts begin with tales she hears from Liza (Mercedes McCambridge), a member of the second jury who runs a dude ranch with her crippled brother. Trev's wealthy step-parents, anxious over his whereabouts, insist that Shelley stay on at their ranch, where she's courted by a playboy (Zachary Scott) whose suavity turns sinister. Rebounding toward the lesser of two apparent evils, she marries Trev, but flees on her wedding night to Liza—who now reveals her own love for Trev, and attempts to strangle Shelley just as she strangled his first wife.

Vidor's fullest attempt at *film noir* "turned out terribly,"[23] owing in part to casting problems, but primarily to his own temperamental ones. Again, the despair and social entrapment inherent in *noir* presented Vidor with some revealing—and this time unsolvable—challenges.

The script looks all set to play on a contrast of genres. In the opening reels, Vidor is resourceful enough at creating a world of plotting, eaves-dropping, pushing, and prying, amidst the shifting of constricted spaces (from prison cell to bus to the hotel room where Shelley is awakened by a woman blithely displaying her passkey). The camera pans from a newspaper headlined "TREVELYAN INNOCENT" to one headed "TREVELYAN GUILTY," then pulls back to reveal an editor's office. This duplication of a shot from Fritz Lang's *You Only Live Once* (1937) suggests the moral quicksand Vidor was after. It's also an anachronism, one of several Warner Brothers films returning to a thirties tone. In the opening line, a warden hands over a pass to one of Warners' sententious Irish priests: "Here you are, father; the guards will take you to the deathhouse." If all of this plays quite without conviction, it's in part because it cuts right across Vidor's openness—a visual *and* philosophic preference.

The Texas setting suggests a Western. But the film is a deliberate hybrid, like those that put Cagney in Stetsons or Bogart against the Sierras. What it seeks is not a *noir*/West merger, but an unsettling effect, as in a weird hybrid like *Mystery Ranch* (1932): the landscape is *relief* from the Old Dark House intrigue. Alas, the scenic interest sags, for which Warners' tight budget must take some of the blame. (The "Trevelyan" ranch was Vidor's at Paso Robles.) The horse rides, working cattle ranches, and cac-tus flats slackly fail to offer up a fresh Western option against the world of *noir* suspicion. Sad, since Trev's explicit dilemma—whether he's seeking "a fresh start" or "running away"—encapsulates the Western and *noir* ways of labeling escape.

Where *film noir* does mesh with Vidor is in their common success in exploring sexual tension. The roundabout introduction to Shelley, the only woman on a desert bus ride, comes via a cowboy-hatted loudmouth who spouts his view of the recent murder for all within earshot: "Yeah, it *was* nice territory, 'till a foreigner like Trevelyan came in and dirtied it up a little." (The *High Noon* era looms again when Trev ventures for sup-plies into the gossipy small town.) Soon a jowly hair tonic salesman leers over at Shelley's legs, and (in a shot crowded with the cowboy's head pushing in) shoves up his hat with his thumb to give Shelley (still hiding behind a paperback) *his* measured opinion: "It's always the good lookers that get into trouble. Nobody ever bothers to kill the dogs" (fig. 130a). "Lookers" does catch the operative tension here. The bus scene follows

a

b

Figure 130.   Lightning Strikes Twice *(1951).*

hard from the office of the newspaper editor, who has an explanation for the hung jury that renders both headlines unusable: "Dames!"

Neatly enough, the sexual tensions staged in these early scenes turn into the film's theme. But the relative relaxation of the visual pairing between Shelley and Liza sets up cool sisterhood as a murderous hoax. Exhausted from being "strangled eight times a week" playing Desdemona, Shelley comes to believe she's found another blackamoor in Trev, but it's he who saves her from Liza's green-eyed clutches. Not that Mercedes McCambridge's lizardlike performance as the androgynous Liza doesn't telegraph its fair number of clues. With her butch haircut, high but throaty voice, cigarette fixings dangling from workshirt pocket, she's a darting bundle of sexual tensions all by herself (fig. 130b). Shelley, an Alice in Frontierland, first comes across Liza lovingly bottlefeeding what turns out to be a goat in a bassinet. Best stick to men!

Vidor's uncertainties here are familiar to us from *La Bohème.* Once again he seems to lose patience with surreptitious and pointless sacrifice. The whole plot machinery of *Lightning Strikes Twice* rests on Trev's assumption that his wife was murdered by his stepfather (her former lover). Thus Trev buries evidence and makes himself look thoroughly suspicious through two trials and beyond. The slightest infusion of "Vidorian" traits—enthusiasm, openness, vitality—would have brought the rickety structure tumbling down.

Return to Independence: *Japanese War Bride* (1952) and *Ruby Gentry* (1952)

In a bit of mutual aid, Vidor accepted producer Joseph Bernhard's *Japanese War Bride* quite late in its pre-production, after a preliminary script had been completed and major cast members set. Vidor's eye was on *Ruby Gentry*, which he initiated and Bernhard agreed to finance. Perhaps Vidor's frustration in not finding a producer for his latest farm script, *The Four Seasons*, again with his "average" couple, John and Mary Sims, allowed him to approach *Japanese War Bride* as a substitute variation on the veteran heading back to the land. Moreover, the working title at the time Vidor accepted it, *East Is East*, recalls the bright snatch of dialogue in *Bird of Paradise* that mocks Anglo/Asian sexual incompatibility (see p. 138). As yellow race and white trash variants on postwar prejudice, these two Bernhard co-productions are not unrelated. If America's melting pot had failed, there were implications enough for all races, ethnicities, and classes.

Japanese War Bride

Korean veteran Jim Sterling (Don Taylor) returns to his parents' California valley farm recovered from war wounds, and with his Japanese nurse, Tae (Shirley Yamaguchi), as bride. His extended family take to the marriage with acceptance, stoicism, or resentment. On the neighboring Hasagawa farm, second-generation Nisei provide models for the "real American" Tae hopes to become. But Jim's sister-in-law Fran finds ever more devious means to destroy her. When false rumors that Tae's new infant has been fathered by a Hasagawa threaten Jim's father's standing with the growers' association, Tae flees into Monterey's Japanese-American fishing community. After tracing her to the edge of the Pacific, Jim convinces her to give him, and America, another chance.

This film comes near the tag-end of the tolerance cycle, which worked its way from Jews in 1947 (*Crossfire, Gentleman's Agreement*), through blacks in 1949 (*Home of the Brave, Pinky*), and on to the unclaimed oppressed races. Vidor, with *Street Scene* and *Hallelujah*, had been in the advance guard for both earlier phases of this game, but *Japanese War Bride* hides any depth of commitment behind distanced B film setups and body language. Typical are the long-held two-shots of conflicting modes of threat or awkwardness—cheap from a production standpoint, but strikingly different from the whiplash physicality of the equally low-budget *Ruby Gentry* to come.

If the California valley-town racism against Mexican-Americans in Joseph Losey's *The Lawless* (1950) ages better, that's partly because of a continuing topicality. But it's more that Losey catches the interplay of media-bolstered frenzy with small-town insularity, a prophetic combination against which Vidor's family focus seems the most flaccid of fifties conventions. In *The Lawless*, a TV newswoman prepares an interview by casually unbuttoning the blouse of an "assaulted" teen, and the manipulation of racial/sexual assumptions grows into the community's paranoid-

Figure 131. Japanese War Bride *(1952).* Refusing reconciliation: Ed Sterling *(James Bell) and Hasagawa (William Yokota). [Frame enlargement.]*

noir violence. While *Japanese War Bride* also locates one source of racism in sexual fears, that's confined to the neurotic Fran, who has made over the brothers' boyhood room into her primping hall of mirrors.

Still, with its portrait of the Hasagawa family, one has to credit this film for having *its* social eye on the most concrete of American racist monuments, the World War II "relocation" camps for West Coast Japanese-Americans. Although the camps are key background in *Go for Broke* (1950), the Dore Schary–produced drama about Nisei troops in Italy, in that film a reasonable officer puts the camps in a context of wartime necessity—even as the troops pack up unsavory GI rations for the folks back home. Sharply enough, *Japanese War Bride* is set in Salinas, site of ferocious terrorist incidents against the few Japanese-Americans with the grit to return home in the early months of 1945. In the film, the Hasagawa Nisei, too, have come to "understand" the need for the camps, although "Old Man Hasagawa" stays bitter. When his children drive over with a gift for the newlyweds, he remains rigid in the cab of their produce truck ("sitting there like a cigar-store Indian," in Jim's mother's

Figure 132.   . . . and warily accepting it. From right: the Hasagawa Nisei (Lane Nakano, May Takasugi), the newlyweds (Don Taylor, Shirley Yamaguchi), and the Sterling family. [Frame enlargement.]

bright fusion of stereotypes) (fig. 131). Even the gift giving is staged with the wary formality so typical of the film, as the camera holds back to observe the present passed over a white picket fence (fig. 132). The senior Hasagawa is said to be still "sore because some people tried to buy his land while he was in the relocation center"—an emollient summary of Issei status under a complex of land laws that generally prevented their owning land at all in their own names. The oriental gong on the music track as Hasagawa stonily refuses an offer of iced tea underlines the film's scorn of such stubborn Old World resentment.

Hasagawa's long-held grudge parallels that of a gold star mother still black-garbed over her son's World War II death on the Bataan Death March (where much of the Salinas National Guard did die), still vengeful and neurotically clutching her purse between twitching hands. But her daughter, who as Jim's former girl has reason to turn sexual envy into racism, throws a welcome party for the newlyweds. The moral is clear: every race has its older generation stick-in-the-muds, but modern Americans can move on and let sleeping pasts lie. That's not, after all, such an unlikely moral from the maker of *Street Scene*. And it was not until John Korty's 1976 telefeature *Farewell to Manzanar* that the spectacle of Issei broken by their concentration-camp years gets more than perfunctory pity.

The visual style argues that *Japanese War Bride* remained an impersonal production for Vidor. Still, however rushed it was, he establishes the documentary texture of an agricultural community—the lettuce field-hands stooped beside a loader, the tour through the packing plant, Jim's search for Tae down Cannery Row.

As in *The Stranger's Return*, city/country conflicts are American film's model for every alien encounter. Racial suspicions are fused with city/country ones through the blond Fran, hometown girl turned sophisticate through her "secretarial" years in "Frisco." She moves in on Jim with innuendos of sexual experience well beyond that available down on the farm. To his country-boy refusal because "Certain things are right, certain things aren't," she lashes back, city girl *and* chauvinist, "Why don't you say what you've got to say straight—like an American." Her poison-pen letter about the parentage of Tae's infant almost turns the trick, but we last see her slapped down into the farm dirt by her husband, cringing beside his workboots—equilibrium restored in the Sterling (!) family. The heartland remains unscathed in the condemnation of racism, beyond an irrelevant town drunk. None of Vidor's *mutual* slapdowns here, and the violent restoration of male dominance isn't the most comfortable of finales. But this return to Vidor's rural moral standard wouldn't chafe so much if it weren't, this time, so demonstrably the reverse of historical truth: Japanese-Americans found in California's postwar cities nothing like the violence they faced in farming communities.

For a variety of reasons, the tolerance films had to work within a tight spectrum—from "psychological" explanations for racism at one end to resolvable crimes at the other. Thus Kazan's *Pinky* not only traces the psychological torment of "passing" but also lets us take Granny's bedrock assurance any way we like: she has black pride, *or* she knows her place, *or* she's too wise and archetypal to need to cause trouble. And, on the other side, even *The Lawless* does *The Ox-Bow Incident*'s sidestep whereby a victim's innocence of some public-rousing crime supersedes more complex questions (including the economic ones, pertinent to Vidor's film too, of agricultural competition from a minority group).

The tolerance cycle suspiciously parallels a loose "Korean War era" marked off by the opening of the HUAC Hollywood investigations in 1947 and the end of the Korean War (and, soon, of McCarthy's power) in 1953. Although it's easy to condescend to the admittedly passive reformism of the cycle, only the Western was a comparable liberal refuge—with *Broken Arrow* (1950) the genre's fullest connection to the cycle, and *Bad*

Day at Black Rock (1954) of note here as the racism-against-Japanese entry in contemporary Western form. Clearly, *Japanese War Bride* is of its time in finding the source of social tensions in individual neuroses. Moreover, like *Go for Broke* before it, *Japanese War Bride* is a mite insidious in the timing of its tolerance. With American warplanes based in ostensibly neutral Japan for daily bombing runs on Korea, it had to be evident even (or especially) to the right wing that time had come to give this race another look. *Japanese War Bride* opens on the life-or-death consequences, with a "Korea" title and the camera's *noir* prowl over American bodies. Jim's letter from Japan makes America's choice all the more stark: "I grew to hate the country—but then I was sent to Korea." Later in the year of its release, Issei were at last declared eligible for naturalized citizenship.

Ruby Gentry

Boake Tackman (Charlton Heston), the son of a decaying aristocratic line, dreams of reclaiming the swamplands, restoring the family name, and enriching his town. "A man and his work are one and the same," he believes. An implied condition for his financing is marriage to the town banker's socialite daughter. To this end he sacrifices his—is it love? is it sensual attraction?—for Ruby Corey (Jennifer Jones), a tomboy from "the wrong side of the tracks." On the rebound Ruby marries a businessman, Jim Gentry (Karl Malden), after the death of his invalid wife, Letitia. When Jim is killed in a yachting accident the townsfolk leap to the conclusion that Ruby murdered him, and ostracize her. She discovers that most of them owed money to Jim, and that she can ruin them all, Boake included. When he rejects her approach, she has his land flooded with salt water. He (apparently) rapes her. In an uneasy truce, as if their love for each other were freed by reciprocal devastation, they go hunting. Boake is shot by Ruby's brother, Jewel, a religious fanatic inflamed by their sins. Ruby shoots Jewel, cradles Boake's dying head, and seems set to end her days, expiating her past, on her trawler at sea.

Ruby Gentry is the *Kammerspiel*, the chamber play, that *Duel in the Sun* would have been if Vidor had had his way. It's the story of a woman against a southern town, yet we hardly see the town. The good ol' boys appear anonymously, collectively, almost like a chorus. The overdetermined social barriers of *Duel* are restated in more pertinent terms, as if some brooding, anxious fatality set the American themes—class, money, family, religion, ambition—all dancing around one another. Quickly, good motivations become equal and opposite overreactions, outrage matches counter-outrage, while cultivated and rational energy seems sapped at its source.

In the early drafts, Jennifer Jones's "Ruby" was again called "Pearl," prompting one of the many memo-outbursts to co-producer Joseph Bernhard from David O. Selznick:

> If he [Vidor] gets the character of Ruby in "Duel in the Swamps" all mixed up with the character of Pearl in DUEL IN THE SUN, you will have nothing. There could not conceivably be two characters more different than Ruby and Pearl—as to background, as to self-competence, as to innocence, as to anything else. I have heard Mr. Vidor talk about this picture in terms of DUEL IN THE SUN. Nothing could betray more confusion in his own mind about the character.[24]

But Selznick had no credited role on *Ruby Gentry* (though he helped secure Heston and Malden, as well as his wife). And so, much as Selznick might bluster, Vidor could treat this film as *his* revision of *Duel in the Sun*. Which must have been satisfying. Again Jennifer Jones is a passionate savage brought into a rich family and "trained for a life she can't have" (as it's put here). Again she finds a spiritually beautiful "foster-mother" who dies. Again she loves the scion of an unattainably superior family, who plays with her feelings and even repeats a few of Lewt's most annoying lines ("You're pretty when you lose your temper"). Again she's harassed by a demonic Bible-puncher. Again she falls back on betrothal to an older man who dies in ugly circumstances. Again love-hate escalates via rape to a brutal shootout. No less important is the physical atmosphere that links Jennifer Jones's two characters, and the recalcitrant egoism that Charlton Heston's Boake shares with Lewt.

If the cards are extensively reshuffled, and new ones played, *Ruby Gentry* is recognizably a variation on the theme, an alternative answer. In *Duel*, rugged individualism is tied to negative excesses that doom it to defeat. Here there's still hope. Boake is less perverse than Lewt. His vision—to drain the swamps that have come to cover his family plantation—is more than salvaging agricultural bottomland; it's a redemption of a family name that has been "slidin' down" since the Civil War. Ruby half-mocks her lover as "Boake Tackman, Empire Builder." But if his egoism were the only obstacle, then a *Fountainhead*-class erotic triumph could have emerged. He's also Boake Tackman, (literal) resurrecter of the Old South. And as such he's tied to social conventions that tame him into a good ol' boy hitched to the banker's daughter. In the final analysis, *Ruby Gentry* is not exactly "a woman against a town," any more than *Duel* was "a woman against a ranch." It's a woman against a passing way of life. But insofar as life in this North Carolina coastal port revolves around money and class, it's a way of life that *will* keep putting itself together, perversely.

To see Boake fresh, one has to filter out the post-Moses Charlton Heston and remember the sweaty desperation in his *Dark City*-era per-

Figure 133.   Ruby Gentry *(1952). Home is the hunter? Boake and his fiancée (Charlton Heston, Phyllis Avery); in the background, Jim Gentry (Karl Malden).*

sona. Boake might seem to incarnate a title from Vidor's 1924 *Wild Oranges:* "It's unjust to be condemned to die in a swamp, with all one's instincts in the sky." However, it's precisely that his "instincts," if not his aspirations, *are* close to the swamps that, for once, sexualizes Heston. Though Boake seems to sense that Ruby is his proper soul mate—and surely all spectators so assume—he rejects her for two reasons, a moral one and an immoral one, their paradoxical interplay being characteristic of modern melodrama. Ruby's fury at her jilting is justified insofar as she and Boake are meant for each other, as her love is intense, as he's misled her, and as his marriage has its cynical aspects. But it's unjustified insofar as it ignores her planned sexual entrapment of him, and as Ruby can't share his idealism but only complement his egoism.

Jim Gentry, like Gail Wynand, the publisher in *The Fountainhead,* seems to be the victim of spiritual indecision, and his mixture of weakness and strength creates another line of suspense. He's brave, and yet foolish enough to let his jealousy over Ruby goad him into a confrontation with Boake, and he gets a beating and a humiliation for his pains. Even his loans to the townsfolk can be seen as misplaced indulgence. He has coddled their lack of enterprise, and thus exposed them to the rapacities of his widow. Boake's swamp-draining scheme would, it is implied, have enlarged the whole town's economy in a more wholesome way. It's less Jim's reaction to Boake than the edgy immaturity in Karl Malden's style (prefiguring his role in *Baby Doll* [1956], another Southern of decay and jealousy) that suggests that he and Ruby won't make a complementary couple, but an ill-matched pair.

Jim loves his wife Letitia, but their marriage has been passionless for too long. In becoming infatuated with Ruby, he seems to admire an energy he has lost among all his profit-and-loss calculations and long devotion to a bedridden wife. And Letitia, with her southern gentility, had understood Ruby's soul, but nothing else. Later, Ruby, in her rough jeans, admires Letitia's opulent dresses, and holding one against her, dances with it, taking the male part to the ghost of Letitia's youth. A simple enough action creates a startling situation, for it contrasts Ruby's insensitivity and Letitia's bedridden pain—the latter sublimated into an unembittered nostalgia and a selfless pleasure in Ruby's vitality. And the contrast between Ruby's sudden bisexuality and Letitia's dress as her phantom is ominous. Jim's loser status is affirmed when, just as Letitia dies conveniently for him, he dies conveniently for Ruby. His "kindness" is the equal and opposite fault to Ruby's willfulness.

Ruby's father is as amiable as Jim, but his poor-white family creed also has its sharp teeth. He first urges his daughter to sexually entrap the

Figure 134.   The once and future Mrs. Gentry: Letitia (Josephine Hutchinson) and Ruby (Jennifer Jones).

town's big fish (he probably means Jim, but Ruby understands Boake) and then sets about avenging her blemished honor with a boathook in the back. Ruby's mother bends devotedly over the stove, but her only lines are negative, accusatory. While she is seen *only* at the stove, Letitia is seen only in bed—two "proper" realms for women in the town.

The running contrast in every character between weaknesses and excesses is nowhere more extreme than in Ruby's brother, Jewel. This fundamentalist preacher shoots his sister's lover in the back at the precise moment when reconciliation is possible and the town's prosperity might be revived. The similarity of Ruby's and Jewel's Christian names all but implies that they form a Jekyll-and-Hyde character—that is, Jewel incarnates Ruby's repressed class resentment, which explodes just as her ego assents to the end of her hatred of Boake.* Jewel is certainly his own Mr. Hyde, for he negates everything he preaches. As his ideals are the highest (in his sense of the spiritual) and his love the broadest (in his concern for the poor who are being thrown out of work by his sister's vengeance against the town), so his perversion of them is the narrowest and most destructive. Between these two extremes he lives, precariously balanced between vivacity and rage, love and melancholy, jocularly holding his guitar as if it were a rifle. And this mixture of country and Western sentiment, of hellfire fundamentalism and shotgun morality, enables him to incarnate the negative excesses of the rural puritanism Vidor's Populist films asserted against the abrasions of the city. Troubling, too, is his handsome virility, amidst which certain gestures, like an outcast consoling himself, fleetingly prefigure some James Dean of the deep South. And far from being totally loony, he's the only character to predict the actual course of events correctly, thanks to his Populist-socialist sense of class barriers.

It's as if Jewel is the extreme point, compounding Ruby's resentments, the town's stagnation, and Boake's egoism. He is made out of the negatives of the heroes, and bears the same relationship to them as many other celebrated eccentrics, notably Old Joshua in *Les Enfants du paradis* and

---

*The names of the siblings suggest an uneasy pattern, worth teasing out. For a girl, Ruby is a natural name (as is her original precious-stone name, Pearl, a shadow of which survives in Jewel's gunbarrel indictment of his "sinner" sister "bedecked with pearls"). But Jewel for a boy suggests doting parents, linking him with Vidor's recurrent theme of the potentially spoiled son (*The Big Parade, The Crowd, H. M. Pulham, Esq., Duel in the Sun, Lightning Strikes Twice*). The name Ruby is vulgar and lower-class, implying the materialistic ambitions only fulfilled when landed-class "Gentry" is attached. In this context, "Jewel" becomes an uneasily worldly name for another of Vidor's worldly preachers. Boake Tackman's name is of a piece with this pattern: beau + oak, but tacky like his family history of decline and decay. All this isn't to say that names are always symbolic—only that they sometimes are, and not in any absolute sense even then, but by relation to the general theme. Quite apart from any symbolism, they can carry information about background, which it is natural to read as part of a character's upbringing.

Figure 135.   Ruby Gentry. *Jewel (James Anderson).*

the working-class dwarf informer in *Le Crime de Monsieur Lange*. If he permeates the marsh and the mist like a malarial pestilence, it is because the whole town's spiritual climate has been deformed. The energy that should have been divine has become diabolical. A monstrous hatred speaks with the voice of the log-cabin pieties that reared Young Mr. Lincoln. He is everything Vidor most detests about the things he most loves, just as Ruby is Vidor's "magic" mother become demonic. But it's not her fault, in this cry of despair at the perversity, the complexity, of America's going wrong.

In the criticisms of Christianity and socialism in Jewel, in the unintentionally disastrous effects of Jim Gentry's "nice" capitalism, in Letitia's selflessness, which goes along with a weakened life force, and in the name Boake (like Roark), one can see a rub-off from Ayn Rand's objectivism. But the film's reiterated insistence on "wrong side of the tracks" prejudice "in this day and age" combines old fear-the-rich Populism with pessimism about the poor. Ruby turns moneyed despot and ruins the whole town. Often enough, this ambitious, competent woman resembles a Joan Crawford–type heroine, as featured in other postwar films titled by women's names (*Mildred Pierce, Harriet Craig*). But, age apart, Crawford's style would have been too cold for Vidor's taste. The logic of Ruby's behavior is so uncapitalist, *so* unlike what Buñuel delighted to call "the icy waters of bourgeois calculation," that the socialist accusations of her brother inculpate not capitalist principles but separable moral factors: sexual jealousy, inverted snobbery. Still, Jim's widow corresponds to the big rancher oppressing the small men in one Populist Western after another (including McCanles in *Duel in the Sun* and another woman, Jeanne Crain, in Vidor's next film, *Man without a Star*), or, in contemporary form, the capitalist despot required of "Dallas," "Falcon Crest," "Dynasty," and every afternoon soap opera.

It would be only too easy for a feminist to accuse the film as follows: Ruby is exiled to a life of empty loneliness at sea for (a) trying to rise in the world, (b) trying to be a businesswoman, and (c) being a gun-toting, phallic tomboy. However, Ruby's vitality is pointedly set against other women—the white-gloved arbiters of *town* power (Boake's wife, Letitia). With men the money-makers, the social circuit remains fully female, as it was back in *Stella Dallas*. So *Ruby Gentry* is also about *that* cultural network having become too complacent to accept Ruby's vigor, just as the town's male business community was too slow to finance Boake's project ("Boake, you got too much energy for a Carolina boy"). Far from being involved in a simple love-hate story, Boake and Ruby are "guilty" victims of the *community's* mediocrity (much as was Gary Cooper in *High Noon* the same year).

Vidor's film anticipates, by a few years, a little cycle of social-critical films, notably George Stevens' *Giant* and Elia Kazan's *Splendor in the Grass.** And many a *film noir* of the period was concerned with an ambient rich-poor resentment ("the wrong side of the tracks"). Left-liberal social problem films tended to stress snobbery, or rat-race greed; while the individual wasn't blameless, flaws in the social system were seen as the root of most evil. Right-of-center films found the corruptive agent in insufficient moral fiber, to which inspirationalist, not reformist, answers were the correct ones. (Radical films like *Salt of the Earth* [1954] were scarcely produced.) The tension between the two emphases is what made Theodore Dreiser's *An American Tragedy* so notoriously sensitive a subject, paraphrasing as it does the capitulation of the puritan ethic before social envy. Like *Ruby Gentry*, its revelatory moment is a boating "accident" where the drowning looks a lot like murder. That the accused is innocent this time doesn't make the film any less bitter.

If *The Fountainhead* suffered from Ayn Rand's determination to load

---

*These two films feature spoiled sons and chastened tycoons, and paraphrase Vidor's cherished projects (lyrical epics to steel and wheat) by their common theme, oil. Again in *Wild River* (1960), Kazan takes up themes not so far from Vidor's heart (the obstinate matriarch versus its Democratic hero). And Vidor's immigrant theme is approached—from a very different angle—in Kazan's *America, America* (1963).

every line of dialogue with her message, spelt out pamphlet-style, Vidor follows an opposite strategy here. The characters' vices and flaws look like animal reflexes. The moral hypotheses are established as baldly as in some tree-stump sermon by an in-the-future prologue, in which the doctor's voice directly addresses the audience, letting us in on Ruby's fate—a sort of Flying Dutchwoman, scapegoat for the town's sins. An epilogue moralizes again, and from time to time in between the doctor's reflexive voice returns. It's all as bald as Brecht, as effective and archaic. For the moral "forecloses" not the plot, but only the ending, leaving us to discover the overreactions and errors—which always surprise us and always retain enough justification to compel our sympathy, while provoking our vehement criticism. It's a fine demonstration of what Brecht so appallingly failed to understand: how "bourgeois drama," though based on "identification" with the protagonists, can also goad its spectators into relentless criticism of everything they think and do.

Here, Vidor's moralizing framework frees him to tell the story swiftly, physically, violently. Its brisk solution to Jamesian agonizing over point-of-view is a Chinese-box structure. At the opening: (1) the doctor moralizes over Ruby's present lonely seafaring life, and (2) takes us back a few years to when he and Jim Gentry visited Ruby's father's backwoods cabin, a time when Jim had narrated to him how (3) Ruby (at fifteen) had first come to live at his home and how (4) his wife Letitia had first met Ruby (a scene even Jim himself didn't witness). Thus this Southern is narrated by a Yankee-Jewish doctor several removes away (and, since he is too painfully shy to complete the sentence in which he begins to declare his own love for Ruby, our narrator is a protagonist by aspiration only and stands in awe of the passions he recounts).

Consider the more conventional ways this plotline could have unfolded. Chronologically: *The Rise and Exile of Ruby Gentry*. Or it lends itself easily to the *Lightning Strikes Twice* mode: a classic *film noir* murder mystery, beginning with the death of Jim. The townsfolk would be convinced that Ruby was guilty but, as the detective/doctor investigates, he discovers another story, incriminating the community's misogyny and malaise. The town dunnit! However, the Chinese-box method gets the exposition over early, leaving a clear field for whiplash bodily reflexes. Vidor puts social criticism into physical terms—that is, vitalist-transcendentalist terms.

The narrative style, rapid even for Vidor, is of a piece with the physical extremes. The dramaturgy is structured on bodily postures, pacings, and pivots as strongly as the ditch-digging climax of *Our Daily Bread*. Consider, for example, the film's first exchange between Ruby and Boake, newly returned from Brazil: her animal whistle and ambush in the dark with her flashlight, his turn-aside from the door, her pirouette through it, his casual tossing of the light she has hardly noticed she lost during their kiss, her jealous start up a short flight of steps until a reflex glance in the mirror revives her brittle confidence, her smart U-turn in her tracks, her slow, circling ambush round the table with the coffee-pot to get back to Boake, the little side-spurs of interaction with varied good ol' boys on the way, and a little climax in her deep "bobcat" scratches down Boake's face.

The physicality is worked through to the end. The stalkings and crawlings through the swamp evoke some collapse of humankind into creatures of mud and mist. Worthy of expressionism (that converse of transcendental confidence) is its "excremental vision." At the end, Ruby, having shot her brother, astonishingly kicks his body down a mudbank into the swampwater, and cradles Boake's dying head against her breast. The visibly studio-bound character of certain sets—including the swamp—nowise dilutes this pungent physicality, and the film belongs alongside certain triumphs of B feature expressionism, notably Frank Borzage's *Moonrise* (1948) and Charles Laughton's *The Night of the Hunter* (1955), towering over them thanks to its complex social drama.

In a masterly analysis, Michel Delahaye outlines the structure of the physical elements to which Vidor's work lends itself.[25] He uncovers its paradoxes in, of all films, *Northwest Passage:* the men are marched through the swamps and across the torrential river as if it were dry land, while the boats have to be carried over mountains (anticipating Herzog's *Fitzcarraldo*). Sometimes the enemy is an extreme, like the desert in *Duel in the Sun*, or the marsh in *Wild Oranges* and *Hallelujah*. It's always a community's task to *construct* a balance of the elements, epitomized by the irrigation ditch in *Our Daily Bread*. In *Ruby Gentry*, Boake seeks a union of land and water; and such unions recur—in Ruby's exile at sea, in Boake driving his car into the surf while its radio bawls a full-throated love song, in Jim's death by drowning as his wind-driven yacht cuts through sunlit waves (elemental antithesis of death in the stagnated marsh). The physical elements in Vidor's work all promise, but in the end disallow, easy patterns of association. For their essence is conflict (flooding), encounter (irrigation), and contrast (the idyllic forests, in *The Big Parade* and elsewhere, are venues for killing). The outcome of all these opposite excesses is a sense of equilibrium (Delahaye's word), although equilibrium can be taken too decorously, for it is equilibrium requiring a convulsive effort that makes a man or woman not so much nature's master as its resynthesis. Self-fulfillment requires a transcendental reconciliation of instincts with community and with the energies of nature.

The physical elements in Vidor's work can be glossed several ways. Perhaps the swamplands are where a man's will softens and decays; they're the primeval form of the overcivilized hot towels pampering Apperson's face, of the bubblebath to which H. M. Pulham returns from the wars. Perhaps they're the realm of underdifferentiation, of what Gilles Deleuze in his essay on Masoch calls the uterine-cloacal mother,[26] the "terrible mother" Ruby has become (and to whom Boake can oppose only the doubled desolation of a rape). Certainly Vidor's work would richly repay a phenomenological analysis, à la Gaston Bachelard perhaps, of how its physical substances carry psycho-spiritual overtones. And not the *natural* elements only. In *Beyond the Forest* (despite its title) Rosa dies just where the steel railroad tracks cross visually brutal asphalt. *The Fountainhead* (despite its title!) opposes skyscraper and quarry, riding crop and pneumatic drill. The deer shooting in *Ruby Gentry* is carefully ambiguous: justified as natural, earthy; yet Ruby and Boake's kiss is disconcertingly juxtaposed with their two knives digging into a warm body to settle a dispute over whose bullet hit nearest the heart. Isn't the swamp, that confusion of overgrowth and decay, the epitome of this film's spiritual ecology?

Disliked by most "serious" critics in the United States, *Ruby Gentry* won some respect from English critics, almost to their own surprise. Hollywoodwise, it was something of an anomaly, with major stars in such a low-budget, violently personal film. Perhaps American critics mistook the tragic for the morbid, the critical for the spiteful, and energy-

Figure 136.   Ruby Gentry. *Boake's death in the swamp.*

sense for simple-mindedness. In its anguished lyricism, *Ruby Gentry* marks the end of the line for the phase that began back with *Duel in the Sun*. The reasons for this sudden finale—Vidor's final three films show a much more subdued style—are no doubt a complex mix of the personal and professional. Vidor had every right to be satisfied with the responses he had been able to craft to that Selznick production, which had been troubling to him in so many professional and philosophic ways. Or perhaps he had finally passed out of some uneasy dark night of the soul. In any case, he would never again have such control over a studio production.

In *Ruby Gentry*, Vidor relies on the way in which our moral intuitions, just like our emotional ones, work faster than our conventional formulations, so that the counterpoint of excess leaves us in a state of exhilarated shock. As twist follows twist the moral tension is charged with the same suspense as the dramatic and physical tensions, and is absolutely inseparable from them. And that's one reason we would argue for *Ruby Gentry*'s status as a truly great American movie, the *film noir* imbued with new fervor, at once understanding and radically critical, "Hollywood" and personal.

Man without a Star (1955)

Aboard a northbound freight train, Dempsey (Kirk Douglas), a veteran cowpuncher, protects young Jeff (William Campbell) from a callous brakeman. They take a job at a ranch and he initiates Jeff into the realities of bunkhouse life, rather than the myths of violence. The ranch's new owner, Reed Bowman, is a beautiful woman (Jeanne Crain) who cares only for immediate profits and is quite prepared to overstock the common grazing land. The smaller ranchers want to protect some grass by enclosing it with barbed wire. Although Reed comes on to Dempsey, he detests her readiness to ruin the land even more than he hates, for some mysterious reason, the small ranchers' wire. In an effort to keep Dempsey near her, she captivates his friend. But Dempsey is disillusioned to find that what the youth most admires about him are his killer instincts. Reed imports gunmen who turn out to be Dempsey's old Texas enemies. Catching him defenseless, they humiliate him, and he stays to take the side of the small ranchers, eventually wrapping his enemies in barbed wire, which, years before, had been responsible for his brother's death. And he rides on, abandoning enclosure, and civilization, to follow his lonely star.

Both King Vidor and Kirk Douglas (this film's de facto producer as well as its star) expressed their discontent, for different reasons, with the result of their collaboration. One can only suggest which of the film's ideas they held in common, which ideas each was glad to accept from the other, which ideas each *un*willingly accepted from the other, which ideas each accepted in the hope of transforming them, and which ideas each was prevented from developing by the other.

Kirk Douglas's Dempsey, the ferocious loner, resembles earlier Vidor heroes. But *The Vikings* (produced by Kirk Douglas, directed by Richard Fleischer) is quite as ambivalent about an unbridled ferocity of life force as *Duel in the Sun*. Or consider the banjo with which Douglas affirms his insolent independence. It had already been linked to Zeke's lack of remorse in *Hallelujah;* and Lewt was reduced to strumming a guitar while Pearl briefly favored Jess; but, then again, Kirk Douglas could equally have brought it with him from Captain Nemo's submarine (in Walt Disney's, or rather Richard Fleischer's, *20,000 Leagues under the Sea*). Likewise, the cattle baroness's strength, if not her cool, recalls Vidor's earlier postwar heroines. Jeanne Crain's appearance, possessiveness, and harshness are closest to Ruby Gentry's. But the tough woman rancher is endemic to a fifties Western subgenre of managerial woman, notably in Anthony Mann's *The Furies,* Fritz Lang's *Rancho Notorious,* Nicholas Ray's *Johnny Guitar,* Allan Dwan's *Cattle Queen of Montana,* and Samuel Fuller's *Forty Guns.*

Another elaboration to the auteurist jumble comes from *Man without a Star*'s co-scriptwriter, Borden Chase, whose early entry in the manageress-rancher cycle, *Montana* (1950), also features the woman-as-crushing-monopolist doing battle with a collective of small ranchers. Indeed, Borden Chase could have brought Dempsey his banjo from Errol Flynn's mock-carefree guitar plucking. And the love/hate fraternity is so recurrent, so obsessive, a theme in Hollywood movies of the time that one can with equal ease trace its source here to Borden Chase (via *Red River* or *Winchester '73*) as to Kirk Douglas.

A final dimension is introduced by Hollywood's collective iconography—which is also an auteur. For instance, the barbed-wire theme could well have sprung from a strange detail in *Duel in the Sun.** There, Senator McCanles also hates the barbed-wire fences of the small ranchers, but isn't above stringing some himself against the railroads. It's the fair-minded Jess who, to avoid violence, offers to cut the first strand of his father's wire. But, as the wire cutting begins, loose strands curl around and clutch at a cutter's leg. The detail is emphasized although it has no narrative sense, and no clear meaning. But one might surmise the sense that the invasion of private empires isn't going to be won without a nasty little backlash from which the little men are going to suffer. However, at least as far back as Zane Grey's *Wild Horse Mesa,* a Jack Holt vehicle in 1925, barbed wire was at the symbolic center of both freedom's restraints *and* the ruthless plundering of nature.

---

*Neither barbed wire nor banjo comes from Dee Linford's novel *Man without a Star* (New York: Morrow, 1952), which served as only the loosest of inspirations.

Figure 137.   The saloon sequence in Man without a Star *(1955). William Campbell (Jeff), Jeanne Crain (Reed Bowman), and Kirk Douglas (Dempsey).*

However one chooses to sort such elements out, Douglas and Vidor, two incompatibles, seem to have collaborated brilliantly in concocting and choreographing Dempsey's snarling smile, his forked-lightning movements and his astonishing physico-spiritual vivacity. One must include the saloon sequence among the most dazzling sequences of each artist. Dempsey dances with a quick succession of passionate women (plunking away at his banjo behind their backs) and leaps from teasing them to taunting a brute who wants to pick a fight. (Borden Chase labeled the scene "pure King Vidor.")[27] More's the pity that there's no performance with which Douglas's can intermesh. Jeanne Crain's role allows her little scope to be more than stiffly imperious. Some business with a revolving office chair on casters creates brief excitement. All the dreary restraint of the Audie Murphy era overlays the playing of William Campbell as the youth whom Dempsey befriends and protects.

Whatever its source, the structure of sibling substitutes and the love/hate fraternity seems to interest Vidor much less than one would expect it to interest the producer of *The Vikings*, which possibly explains Douglas's complaint that Vidor didn't understand the story and kept setting up elaborate shots that had no place in it at all.[28] Some quite violent events are conspicuously distanced in the mid foreground of a valley sweeping up to a ridge, in such a way as to recall both the precious land and the *be-*

yond, into which Dempsey finally rides. We suspect that Vidor strove to
establish a wider theme, of land as a heritage deserving conservation, and
land as freedom—a wealth whose twofold aspects interact as paradoxically as sex and religion do in *Hallelujah*. Back in *The Sky Pilot*, with its
similar pattern of a youth taken under wing by the experienced cowhand
for workaday duties, Vidor's interest was also in the more realistic, everyday aspects of western life. Here it's the etiquette of ranch life (the foreman getting served first), or the care of one's horse and saddle (a personal
ecology).

The title *Man without a Star* at first seems to label Dempsey as a man
without a lawman's badge, and he is ill at ease in his temporary role as a
monopolist's enforcer. A Depression-era, wandering-laborer aura is established in the opening overhead shot of Kirk Douglas lying in the hay of
a freight car (fig. 138a)—like Spencer Tracy in Borzage's *Man's Castle*
(1933)—as a railroad goon clubs the boy out from under it. With Dempsey's saddle as his pillow, and his advice that a saddle is the only posses-
sion one should want, he's a literal saddletramp. His pulling of the unconscious boy's arm off the tracks (fig. 138b) prevents a reenactment of the
gruesome moment from another 1933 Depression-themed film, Wellman's *Wild Boys of the Road*.

Something of a puzzle is Dempsey's continued faith in a boy who
moves further from maturity with each savage act. But it's Dempsey's
faith, not the boy, that interests us, so his snarling admission that the boy
brings memories of his brother may be all the explanation we need. When
Dempsey rides off alone, he commends his toughness-obsessed friend to
the ministrations of a young woman who blends a fresh young femininity
with a tomboy gift for breaking broncos—which action will occur after
the end titles. The hasty production would account for the film's lack of
concern for the other cowhands, who, although established as people

a   b

Figure 138.   From the first sequence of Man without a Star.

rather than ciphers in Vidor's ranchhouse sequences, die anonymously in the stampede, filmed by a second unit.

Yet merely to rate *Man without a Star* as superior to nine Westerns out of ten fails to do it justice. It lifts its eyes above the horizon of violence, and attains an uneasy, intriguing middle ground between the gunfight obsession that dominates even the best movies of Mann and Boetticher in this period, and a reverent sense of property and ecology. Thus, like *Ruby Gentry*, it anticipates the conservationist concerns of the next generation.

Dempsey's ride off into the sunset is an archaic conclusion all the more bitter for refusing to indulge in the pathos of *Shane* (1953). Dempsey's dedication is not to a family ideal but to his freedom. And yet the beyond into which he rides seems an empty one. He will be driven on until, at last, his and everyone's individual freedom is as inward as H. M. Pulham's. That he "might just end up in Canada" sounds like dropping out of the American struggle. He concludes as a man without a star to follow; no ideal, no goal. The film indicates, without exploring, a transition between Vidor's critical trilogy of contemporary America and his more affirmative pair of costume epics. In the subsequent films, Vidor's interests seem to have moved on from America to an internationalized (that is to say, a generalized) philosophical concern—perhaps because, for him, America had become as constricted as the Old World had once been.

8

1956 to 1959

"Where the Technicolored End of Evening Smiles"

By the late fifties, Vidor found himself considering offers of big-budget costume spectaculars, a cycle that seems to have been entrusted only to veteran directors. Among the projects he declined were *The Big Fisherman* (eventually taken up by Frank Borzage) and several chances to return to a post–Louis B. Mayer MGM. (Vidor must be the only director to have turned down *both* the 1925 and 1959 versions of *Ben Hur*.) One might surmise that Vidor's recent failures—to turn *Man without a Star* in the direction he desired and to find producers for his more personal projects—engendered a certain defeatism, rendering him not unopposed to offers of costume epics, and yet also making the two he did accept so tactful about any divergence from the most popular moral interpretations that they must be counted among his potboilers, however efficient their execution.

More charitably, though, it looks as if real production problems flawed, or disguised, Vidor's real inspiration. In 1955 he accepted Dino De Laurentiis's offer of *War and Peace* (1956), even though the project was conditioned on beating to the screen the announced efforts of other independent producers (including David O. Selznick). By splitting Tolstoy's novel into segments and assigning them to a number of screenwriters, De Laurentiis was able to get a script draft out in a month, but with much of it in what Vidor knew was a "terrible translation" back from the Italian. He was still rewriting through the final day of Italian location shooting: "That's painful to have to do."[1] Determined that the spectacular scenes not lose the thread of his themes, he took over second-unit direction and left a few scenes with the major actors to Mario Soldati.

Solomon and Sheba (1959), for veteran producer Edward Small, was met by a director's ultimate nightmare. With six weeks of photography completed in Spain, star Tyrone Power died of a heart attack. Virtually everything had to be reshot, with Yul Brynner. And the original locations, picturesque in September, were unusable by December.

But the deepest problem plaguing both of Vidor's final productions arose from conflicts with the two lead actors. He had envisioned two troubled, hesitant spiritual searches, while both actors opted for stronger dramatic and moral consistency. "He is a damn good actor," Vidor said of Henry Fonda—who played Pierre in *War and Peace*—"but he just did not understand what I was trying to say." As Solomon, Yul Brynner was emotionally less vulnerable, less malleable, than Tyrone Power had been. Vidor spoke with fondness of the footage shot before Power's death and with rare public dislike for Brynner. "Cecil B. De Mille seemed to be his favorite director. . . . Tyrone Power had understood the dualistic problem of the anguished king. When Brynner took over . . . he fought the idea of a troubled monarch and wanted to dominate each situation without conflict. It was an attitude that affected . . . the integrity of the film." The first half of Vidor's Hollywood career had broken off with his deep disappointment over *An American Romance;* the second half, too, ended traumatically.

Figure 139.   Vidor with Tyrone Power on the set of Solomon and Sheba . . .

Figure 140.   . . . and with his replacement, Yul Brynner.

War and Peace (1956)

It's ironic, no doubt, that the director of *Northwest Passage* and *An American Romance* should have rediscovered so many of his favorite themes in a novel by a Russian anarchist who came to preach pacifism and to denounce private property.* But Tolstoy's thought connects with several Vidorian themes: of individualism and its transcendence, of belonging to a family and a nation, of pastoral egalitarianism versus a corruptive system, of the organic rural community, and of a nation in moral travail. As Vidor commented, "The strange thing about it is that the character of Pierre was the same character I had been trying to put on the screen through many of my own films"—from the first spiritual searcher of *The Turn in the Road.*[2]

The epic sprawl of Tolstoy's novel and its contrast between the man of war (Napoleon) and the man of peace (Pierre) lend themselves only too easily to a mixture of sentimentality and superficial realism as tedious as the 1967 Soviet adaptation. Tolstoy's novel had its toughest bite, no doubt, when the European world was gearing itself, industrially and spiritually, to the militaristic horrors of 1914–18. By 1955 the moral antithe-

---

*We'll admit defeat over a plot summary, and fall back on Woody Allen's boast about speed-reading *War and Peace* in a day: "It's about Russia."

sis implicit in the title could lead to pious banalities—a hazard emphasized, not overcome, by the piecemeal script construction. But: "My
favorite theme is the search for truth. It's also the essence of Tolstoy's
book. It's Pierre who strives to discover it. He goes to observe the battle
so as to observe what lies in the heart of man." [3] Vidor's theme is less
Pierre's external excursions than the inner journey that brings him back
to where he might have started, had he been a wiser man. And the search
for moral truth needs stressing, because Tolstoy's morality draws on what
he conceived as everyman's commonplace wisdom. And the resultant
moral affirmations are disguised by the script's superficiality, which does
little to keep the usual dramatic polarities of success/failure and safety/
danger from taking precedence in the spectator's mind. Pierre's long, devious pilgrim's progress, with its mixtures of anarchism and pacifism,
negativity and responsibility, indecision and firmness, is a most complex
spiritual course—too complex, perhaps, to be felt through Henry Fonda's
performance, which is consistently mature, steady, noble, honorable, but
sadly lacking in the ferocious precision of his youthful roles for Ford.
Peter Ustinov, Vidor's initial choice, would have excelled at "everyman-
ish" hesitations and uncertainties, and made the storyline, about suc-

Figure 141. War and Peace *(1956). Audrey Hepburn (Natasha) and Henry
Fonda (Pierre).*

cessive *decisions*, clear. In the silent era, John Gilbert had regularly brought Vidor's heroes something impressionable, excitable. Pierre's journey should come somewhere between Apperson's in *The Big Parade* (the privileged son discovering reality) and the cartographer's in *Northwest Passage* (the man of knowledge learning the discipline of the long march). Both Pierre's confusion and his freedom stem from his marginal position in a rigid society. The dying count is honest enough to pay his dues to nature and legitimate the illegitimate Pierre (Vidor maintains his usual diffidence toward established religion—he is careful to show the Orthodox priests filing out in disapproval).

The film *is* structured around polarities but not exclusively war/peace (battles break in three times). Rather, the film traces Pierre's thesis-antithesis of idealism and embitterment—in which his nature seems initially set to coarsen and disintegrate—through a series of reactions, each of which, until the end, is excessive, and must be checked by events. Following a suicidal, drunken windowledge stunt, his return to social values at his father's deathbed overreaches itself when it betrays him into fascination with, and marriage to, the coldly beautiful Princess Helene (Anita Ekberg). He even fights a duel over her infidelity—for Napoleon's is not the only form of militarism at large. The other structuring polarity is the familiar city/country one. Thus Pierre's first escape from nihilism results in his overenthusiastic schemes to improve the land and the lot of the serfs (like *Anna Karenina*'s Levin). Pierre's wide-eyed agrarian dreams recall *Our Daily Bread*'s John, just as Helene, who stirs herself from recumbent torpor in her bed only at the thought of a bright season in Moscow, recalls Sally, that film's bed-lolling city gal. Pierre's diastolic (or dialectic) progress continues when he contradicts his own pacifism by helping to load cannonballs during the battle. And he remains behind in Moscow to assassinate Napoleon. But he is unable to fulfill his purpose, overwhelmed partly by the (inspiring? debilitating?) atmosphere of the church from which he takes aim, partly by Napoleon's greatness, partly by his own scruples. The last seems the most spiritually positive.

Vidor is, if anything, less concerned than Tolstoy with vindicating Pierre's as the most human odyssey, and more concerned with according it a place of honor among an array of attitudes, none of which he wants primarily to denounce. Prince Andrei (Mel Ferrer) takes up his social responsibility honorably, even if he remains a little priggish, and is, until his deathbed reversal, rigidly unable to forgive his fiancée, Natasha (Audrey Hepburn), for her youthful folly. Pierre, taken prisoner, finds a traveling companion on the long winter march in Platon (John Mills), a peasant philosopher. His creed of joyful resignation has its beauties, but fosters a spiritual weakness that allows him to die contentedly in the snow, while the physically sheltered Pierre can keep struggling—even if the mechanical way in which Pierre counts his steps, to keep on moving, prevents him awhile from seeing the older man's fatal fall. And Napoleon (Herbert Lom) has but minimal humanity. Bathed in royal red lighting shading over to indulgent pinks, he adores his son—as future emperor of Rome. Napoleon acknowledges a tactical error when his infantry is scattered by shellfire but, without compassion, orders, "Send in the cavalry." His imperturbable obsession creates militaristic-totalitarian unity.

The film's special concern is reserved for the most devious forms of heroism, and not only Pierre's. General Kutuzov (Oscar Homolka) beats a continuous retreat, refusing even the least daring chances of counterattack, and finally "beheads" Mother Russia by abandoning its capital city to the enemy. Natasha must relinquish, in her sheltered existence, the successive objects of her infatuation: the young Pierre, Prince Andrei, and the dissolute Anatole (Vittorio Gassman). Finally she is reunited in the ruined shell of her family's Moscow home with Pierre, a lovely image whose romanticism should be placed in its context—at the end of two people's long, difficult moral maturation. Pierre, achieving understanding without cynicism, has become another man.

Indeed, Vidor draws a distinction here close to his heart. No doubt Natasha's privileged upbringing has imbued her with a Bovaryism that corresponds to Pierre's weaker side. (John, in *The Crowd*, takes a long time to live down the false conviction of superiority derived from his sheltered youth.) Yet weakness and strength are not so easily distinguished. (A weaker John might have learned his lesson more quickly.) And perhaps the film's most beautiful scene is all but an act of worship of the young Natasha, leaning over the bowed balcony against the night sky, and dreaming of a love so perfect it's like "flying off to the moon." Although the film has Natasha dreaming of Andrei (a notion Tolstoy did toy with, but abandoned in an early draft), she moves beyond his image to a wider expectation that is, in its way, an expression of life's plentitude, a testimony to her vulnerable élan vital and to her status as the film's reigning "anima" (to adopt Vidor's characterization).[4]

The absurdity of Natasha's untempered sensibility is tenderly exposed during her first ball. Vidor's bright, lavish spaces gently ironize over her fragile innocence (her success in achieving a disdainful expression that frightens off everybody except one old man, who gallantly rescues her from her isolation, but then becomes a threat when he promises to return again—the twists comprise a succession of surprises). Meanwhile Andrei decides, "If she looks back at me and smiles on the next turn, she'll be my wife." One hardly need refer to Vidor's repeated insistence on the normality of love at first sight for Natasha and Andrei's separation to seem tragic.

Their society's feudalism must also bear its blame for Andrei's harshness to Natasha, and for her personal defenselessness. Where family happiness is concerned, the plot allows Vidor and Tolstoy a modus vivendi (rather than agreement), and its uneasiness is briefly crystallized by the sequestration of Natasha, to keep her from Anatole. The case of family despotism against Natasha comes uneasily close to Old Europe's destruction of the romantic Manya in *The Wedding Night*. Distinct as casuistry and art may be, seldom are they more intertwined than in Tolstoy's *War and Peace,* where (reversing Tolstoy's earlier views) unwavering historicist principles rule men's actions. Vidor's insistence on the importance of the moral message in his movies is only one reason to distinguish the family tyranny of *War and Peace* from that of *The Wedding Night*. The jagged, snaky Anatole, like a deranged version of Dempsey in *Man without a Star,* carrying out seduction-kidnappings like Gritzko in *His Hour,* lacks any spiritual affinity with the writer of *The Wedding Night.*

The story line of *War and Peace* inevitably involves the issue of individual freedom versus the state. The peasants' instinctive resistance to Napoleon is complemented by czarist conscription and scorched earth—which one might have expected Vidor to view as, at best, a tragic necessity. One is invited, by Vidor and Tolstoy alike, to prefer czarism to Napoleon's militaristic totalitarianism, as presumably the lesser of two evils. Vidor's admiration in *Our Daily Bread* and *Northwest Passage* of *both* strong leadership *and* enthusiastic response might lead to an acceptance of conscription as no more than a passing phase between these two poles of communal goodwill. Equally, Napoleon's intervention might be a blessing for some, a curse for others, depending on the life force in them. Platon (too unworldly, too docile) and Andrei (too encased in social correctness) are doomed. The socially marginal, the uncertain, the resilient survive: Pierre and Natasha.

If the film *can* seem the most docile transliteration of Tolstoy's novel, it's owing in some measure to the production factors we've mentioned. The dialogue was finally credited to six writers (including Vidor) and sounds no better than what it is—a translation by committee. Beyond Vidor's conflict with Fonda, there were additional difficulties with a multilingual cast: as a representative of worldliness, Anita Ekberg is vastly less interesting than Hedy Lamarr in *H. M. Pulham, Esq.* Vestigial characters and relationships (notably Nicholai Rostov with Sonya and Princess Maria) look like more evidence of the hasty scriptwriting. And given its three-and-a-half-hour sprawl, the film lacks those "echo" settings and symbols that might recall specific issues in earlier scenes at the moment of their negation and clarify the moral structure. But it would be difficult for even a film of this length to carry the psycho-moral commentary that is an ordinary idiom of the novel. And if Lukács is right about the essence of Tolstoy's novel—that it replaces the fetishism of objects with a Homeric

a

b

Figure 142.   War and Peace.

unity between character and the dreck of his world—then it could be argued that the ontology of film itself might doom *any* version.[5] But it's thus fitting that the most affecting scenes in Vidor's film are of the Rostovs tossing out furniture and the debris of their social lives to make room in their carts for the broken, glazed-eyed soldiers (fig. 142a). For once, a symbolic reflection, a moral marker, of the family's humanity can later be found in the discarded plunder in the snow as the French army makes its dying retreat (fig. 142b).

"I was in accord with, you might say, what Tolstoy was trying to do . . . a search for truth on the part of Pierre. . . . but even though it is, for me, the greatest novel, nevertheless it is not something that came out of my own insides."[6] Vidor's *distanced* respect is apparent in the (Vista-Vision) film style itself—extended tracking shots, infrequent close-ups, strong cuts. Perhaps Vidor's respect for Tolstoy led him to adopt the usual cautions for "big" historical topics. The stylistic distance extends even to a gestural heaviness, rare in Vidor, as characters recoil from the touches of others. However, by hemming Natasha into such a world of deliberation, Vidor short-circuits Audrey Hepburn's tendency to bone-china gentility and makes her vitality's anima. Peter John Dyer suggests that the film lacks the novel's sense of compassion.[7] Vidor's concern with moral success and his crisper American tone seem to have conflicted with Tolstoy's Russian sense of endurance.

Vidor certainly challenges the American audience's longing for violence. He keeps Pierre in the foreground of a battle, a flower in his hand—like a flower child before his time. Yet Vidor quietly insists that Pierre's contemplation be taken seriously and identified with, like his later flinching at the assassination attempt. Not that we should enlist Vidor among the pacifists: *Solomon and Sheba* is as unrepentant about the slaughter of the aggressors as *Northwest Passage.* Nonetheless, he is prepared to respect a quasi-pacifist position, just as Wyler did, about this time, in *The Big Country* and *Ben Hur.* There's insolence there. One need only recall

Howard Hawks's declared fury over the fact that Gary Cooper asks for help in *High Noon*, and his decision to make *Rio Bravo* as proof that your real red-blooded American sheriff is always ready to go it alone. In its respect for an unrepentant pacifism, *War and Peace* is something of a retort to *Sergeant York*. Meanwhile, Vidor is as careful to respect opposite moral attitudes as he is to emphasize no moral points that would banish Tolstoy's. The film seems impersonal also in its moral struggle and growth, a painless flow of the givens that ethics *begins* from.

The Soviet version of Tolstoy's *Resurrection* (1960/61), with its empty gigantism, reveals much that is simplistic in Tolstoy's morality, as salutary as its emphasis on responsibility and expiation may be. Tolstoy and Jean Renoir can be seen, from certain angles, as moral opposites;[8] and Vidor is, we think, of their stature, although less obviously so, precisely because he occupies a middle position. Vidor's sense of instinct is linked with will rather than with Renoir's fraternity; and his sense of spontaneous energy contrasts with Renoir's accommodation of layers (civilization, theater . . .). But both have individual liberty, and cooperatives, at heart. *Boudu Saved from Drowning* and *Man without a Star* are approximate pairs, like *Our Daily Bread* and *The Crime of Monsieur Lange,* or *Beyond the Forest* and *Madame Bovary*. And just as Renoir, at one stage, declared himself more American than French (he said that the Americans corresponded to the French of 1910, in that they were still free in their exuberance), so Vidor observed after *War and Peace* that he had outgrown his narrower Americanism. A passing mood perhaps, but one that corresponds to what the abandoned projects and independent shorts of the next twenty years reveal of a personal evolution.

Solomon and Sheba (1959)

As King David lies dying, war between Israel and Egypt rages. On the battlefield, impatient Adonijah (George Sanders) pronounces himself king of Israel to the queen of Sheba (Gina Lollobrigida). But David names as successor his other son, the peaceloving "poet" Solomon (Yul Brynner). Sheba promotes herself to the pharaoh as mightier than his armies against Solomon, and enters Jerusalem for a campaign of studied seduction. He is drawn to her, despite a steely struggle to remain true to Abishag (Marisa Pavan), to his national mission to unify the twelve tribes, and to his God.

It appears that only the bargains a vengeful Lord strikes with Abishag and then with Sheba prevent the total destruction of Solomon and his race. Sheba, now a true believer, bargains her future for Solomon's life, as he faces certain defeat on the battlefield by the combined forces of the pharaoh and Adonijah. Solomon, a public victor only, watches Sheba, carrying his child, exit Jerusalem forever.

Vidor's careful exclusions of orthodox religious sects from the more positive acts right from *The Turn in the Road* through *War and Peace*, and the destructive role of lay preachers in *Duel in the Sun* and *Ruby Gentry*, suggest a consistent distrust of Christianity, whether established or inspired. But just as Vidor's respect for the force bound up in romantic love inspires his fascination with its corruptions, so true religion as something deeply infused inspires a criticism of its narrow, paraded forms. Transcendentalism can hardly condemn national faith lock, stock, and barrel, especially given certain parallels between Israel as the promised land and America as God's Country. The Old Testament was a focus for Vidor's ambivalence—all the more, given the problems it poses for Christian morality: "an eye for an eye" versus loving thy neighbor, chosen people–ism versus universalism, and splits between cosmic energy and spiritual intention (for example, the death of Uzzah, who touched the Ark of the Covenant).

Solomon and Sheba is the Old Testament according to Emerson, while retaining something of *Hallelujah*'s conjunction of passions religious, communal, erotic, and revengeful. If the film's sense of moral struggle and growth is as low-profile as that of *War and Peace*, it is for similar reasons. Vidor had as much respect for the Bible as for Tolstoy's novel. He wouldn't be the first—or the last—filmmaker to produce a quietly personal film almost hidden within the film his public prefers to see.

Any personal meaning in *Solomon and Sheba* is further camouflaged by its being a late entry in a long biblical cycle that began at the end of the forties with *Samson and Delilah* and ran through the fifties. Vidor had thought of entering the cycle earlier, with a 1954 version of Clare Boothe Luce's *Pilate's Wife*, which, however, was abandoned after the script stage. It's tempting to relate the biblical cycle to a Hollywood *crise de sujet*, arising partly from a McCarthyite discouragement of the honest discussion of social issues, and secondarily from suburban America's attitudes to continuing social tensions. For all its qualities, the forties *film noir* can be seen as part of a gradual exclusion from Hollywood's consciousness of all the social and environmental factors thirties Hollywood was at least prepared to debate. *On the Waterfront, The Blackboard Jungle,* and *Rebel without a Cause* are among the films that brought the mid-fifties *film noir* back to social urgency.

The biblical films represent an alternative option. In suburban areas, church affiliations were replacing ethnic ties, or, at least, religious language was looming tactfully larger and ethnic language tactfully smaller. Because the melting pot hadn't done its work as well as was expected, "Americanism" fell back on two useful totems: the flag, for its patriotic-militaristic aspect, and (instead of the cross, which excluded the Jewish population) the Old Testament, which involved WASPs, Catholics, and Jews in less controversy. (Even when the New Testament was involved, the tendency, as Thorold Dickinson observed, was to make the Romans largely responsible for the crucifixion, reducing the Jewish crowd to a little ashamed rabble who were obviously just lumpen in the pay of the high priest—who, by analogy with American political bosses, wouldn't be the Jewish people as a whole at all.)[9] Christianity had taken on a second topical meaning as idealistic, spiritualistic, and individualistic, and therefore opposite to atheistic communism. As guarantors of the free world, the Americans were, more than ever, God's chosen people.

The biblical cycle also provided a shock of surprise. Simplistic as these films might seem in themselves, their very choice of theme forced a challenge between (a) Christian idealism and (b) the scientific rationality that played just as large a part in the general cultural amalgam. The audience was startled, not by "miscarriages of justice" but by "miscarriages of science," as the films affirmed miracles, visions, and vocations as moral imperatives devoid of rational support. A traditional American ideology (Christian rationalism) was re-endowed with emotional presence at precisely its weakest point (biblical miracles). And this constituted the audacity of their challenge-cum-affirmation. Clearly, many Americans must have swiftly transposed the genre's supernatural assertions into terms of superior moral fiber or of manifest destiny (vis-à-vis communism, or evil, or anything anti-Christian or un-American).

Nonetheless, it's doubtful whether the cycle would have caught on if it hadn't touched on tougher, more cynical elements. As several commentators noted, and with surprise, these biblical films, unlike their twenties progenitors, made very little use of their generous opportunities for flaunting sexual temptations (a notable exception, *David and Bathsheba*, transposes fairly easily into contemporary terms of a tycoon's love life). In *Solomon and Sheba*, the orgy in celebration of Sheba's god of love, cut short by God's thunderbolts, is so stylized in body gestures and angular sets as to be closer to *West Side Story* than to even Vidor's half-hearted von Stroheimian debauch in *His Hour*. By and large, the genre involved sex very much less than violence, and in this respect the contrast between Vidor's two orgies, and between the twenties and fifties versions of *Ben Hur*, is reinforced by the emphases in Fleischer's *Barabbas*, Huston's *The Bible*, and Aldrich's *Sodom and Gomorrah*. The God of the fifties was the God of the atom. And the Bomb, not Hiroshima, was Son Amour. This is made quite clear by the grueling fates dealt out to a variety of impious communities. Although Wyler, Fleischer, and Vidor maintain something of themselves against (or within) the dreary and bloody conventions of the Old Testament according to Cecil B. De Mille, it is Aldrich and Huston who, amazingly, sink with scarcely a trace of dissent or doubt. Throughout *Sodom and Gomorrah,* Aldrich honors the fundamentalist-Populist equation of the rustic, God-fearing Hebrews with the American pioneers, and of Sodom and Gomorrah with the effete vices of the big cities.* *The Bible* deserves no better title than *How the World Was Won;* its climactic sacrifice celebrates obedience to arbitrary authority; the Tower of Babel sequence is very congenial to Bible Belt xenophobia; and even the ecological undertones of Noah's Ark come over weakly in contrast with Huston's own *The Roots of Heaven,* or Vidor's *Man without a Star.* Perhaps Huston enjoyed surprising himself rather than repeating himself.

We have already sketched a rough division within the genre—between a crude survivalist moralism à la De Mille and the repudiations of worldly violence in the Wyler and the Fleischer. A third, less memorable group is constituted by the cautious revival by veteran directors of personal and romantic themes in biblical dress, such as Raoul Walsh's *Esther and the King,* Henry King's *David and Bathsheba,* and Borzage's *The Big Fisherman.* The genre's fifties cycle is opened and closed by cross formations between the personal-romantic and the survivalist-apocalyptic themes. De Mille's *Samson and Delilah* works its way from *film noir* misogyny to a heroic and morally redemptive destruction.

Solomon and Sheba also interweaves individual passion with wholesale slaughter. But Vidor's interest isn't primarily in smiting the heathen hip and thigh. Tragedy and corruption begin nearer home. Solomon's deadliest enemy is not some alien totalitarianism (pharaoh, Rome) but his meaner-souled brother, his failed, envious rival in power and love alike. Solomon's responsibility is to his community, and what might have been the Old Testament According to Ayn Rand involves a broader responsibility. Nor is there any repudiation of egalitarianism. If Solomon might correspond to Rogers in *Northwest Passage,* Sheba is an only slightly softer version of Napoleon in *War and Peace.* Or: Solomon is another Boake, at once sacrifice and king, and Sheba is another Ruby Gentry, whose royalty is power displayed for its own vengeful uses, without service. (Indeed, the first script for *Solomon and Sheba,* in 1957, was by *Ruby Gentry*'s writer, Sylvia Richards, who was not given screen credit.) Perhaps Sheba's tyrant streak arises because her multiple gods are not the God of a *people.* As with others in the cycle, the film's theology splices an Old Testament God (who speaks softly but carries a big lightning bolt and is open to a harsh bargain) onto a democratic God ("who teaches that all men are equal and none are slaves"). Its version of the United

---

**Duel in the Sun has fun with this equation in one of the "sin-killer's" rants: "Why, El Paso and Amarillo ain't no different from Sodom and Gomorrah. On a smaller scale, of course."

Figure 143.   Solomon and Sheba *(1959). King David and his sons. Top right: Ty-rone Power as Solomon, in the first version. [Production still.] Bottom right: Yul Brynner as Solomon. [Frame enlargement—widescreen "Super Technirama".]*

States flag is "the tablet of unity"—with a precious stone for each tribe, like a star for each state—smashed by the prophets when Solomon forgets his national duty.

Solomon's responsibility to God and his people is also the source of his tragedy. His fiancée Abishag dies in a disaster that is partly self-sacrifice, partly Solomon's fault, partly destructive miracle. Whereas *Samson and*

Delilah concludes with a destruction so massive, so joyous, and so whole-heartedly accepted by the lovers themselves that it's really a happy ending (and less complicatedly so than in *Duel in the Sun*), *Solomon and Sheba* concludes with a tragic parting. God's yoke isn't easy and his burden is heavy indeed. Vidor presents both George Sanders and Marisa Pavan as pallid-faced, using the same visual iconography as Jean Renoir in *French Can-Can* to suggest their relative lack of spiritual vitality. By such weakness, the mediocre blackmail the *Übermensch*. But if the *Übermensch* has it in him to resist such blackmail, how can he avoid the opposite pitfall of irresponsibility (a king cannot be a Roark) or tyranny (like Sheba)? Whatever its origins, a tragic situation is one from which there is no escape without amputation of large tracts of one's soul.

La Lolla's authentically Vidorian attack isn't accompanied by any

Figure 144. Solomon and Sheba. *Gina Lollobrigida (Sheba) and George Sanders (Adonijah). [Frame enlargements.]*

warmth. Thus Lollobrigida's encounter with Brynner looks more like that of a godly, reserved egoist with a proud, childlike one, which eclipses the more transcendental theme—the helplessness of Sheba's worldliness (wealth, power, beauty, Ayn Randian will) before a wisdom that is neither Machiavellian nor Clausewitzian, but the *reconciliatory* strength needed for a chosen people, or a Christian democracy. George Sanders plays as coolly as a lounge lizard done up in fancy dress, and with a moral simplicity befitting De Mille, thus depriving the film of another source of complexity. Likewise, Vidor's complaints about Brynner's refusal to display vulnerability are borne out on film. Without these weaknesses, the film (finally credited to three very old-fashioned Hollywood writers) might well have challenged, more clearly, the Sunday School fundamentalism that can hardly bring itself to criticize the Old Testament view of God—might even have subverted it in the style of *Ruby Gentry*.

Individual sequences come over with characteristic impact—notably Sheba wielding her chariot whip to chip lumps of flesh out of the face of Adonijah, who betrays his weakness by his paralysis before her beauty and mastery (fig. 144). In the climax, Solomon's small force dooms the larger army by burnishing its shields until the sun's dazzle lures the charging cavalry into a canyon. The genre's de rigueur miracle thus comes down to human ingenuity and effort. Solomon's cleverly orchestrated idea remains as ambiguous a miracle as is Doctor Manson's revival of the "dead" infant in *The Citadel*. Insofar as transcendentalism accommodates other moral systems as developments toward itself, Vidor ends his Hollywood career by acknowledging the liberating aspects of *preliminary* ethical codes.

9

Envoi

*I accept the clangor and jangle of
contrary tendencies.*
Ralph Waldo Emerson, "Experience"

Solomon and Sheba has the reputation of being the disaster that killed King Vidor's career. Certainly it was a bad-luck film, but the situation was more complex. Although Vidor was unhappy with the artistic results, the film more than earned back its costs, which had ballooned from four million to six because of reshooting after Tyrone Power's death, and he continued to be offered spectaculars. But, at sixty-five, he could hardly help having been wearied by the production chaos of the previous two epics. In retrospect anyway, his next proposals seem to have barely tried to be commercial. Evidently Vidor was intent on returning to projects closer to his own spirit, or to take on nothing at all.

In 1960 he put into pre-production his fifteen-year-old *The Turn in the Road* remake, a.k.a. "The Milly Story," now retitled *Conquest*. The cost of a ferry crash and river rescue sequence led to cancellation by minuscule-budget Allied Artists. Nonetheless, the script revisions are revealing. The film would have begun in Hollywood, with a director wearied by "handshakes that come with switchblades" (fig. 145a). From his father he inherits a gas station in "Arcadia, Colorado," and opts to work it for a time (fig. 145b). "Thinking about what? Quitting?" asks his assistant director. "Not quitting. Looking," he responds, and muses, glossing with bare disguise some of the titles of Vidor's silent successes, "I suppose it's a dissatisfaction with myself. I feel I'm marching in a parade down the wrong street. I know there's another parade. Somewhere. Marching down the right one, but a crowd seems to be blocking the way." Even in Arcadia he finds only a *Ruby Gentry/Stranger's Return* world of small-town gossip and rural envy, and within himself only "the

a

b

Figure 145.   Storyboards from The Turn in the Road *remake.*

same discontent as I had in Hollywood." At this point the film would have taken a strange turn, introducing a gas-pumping saint (not so far from the one in Godard's *Hail Mary,* a film that also seeks the spiritual within the everyday). Vidor described more of the project in a late interview: Stepping off the bus one day comes a teenage girl,

> a character that looked the furthest thing from a saint as possible, dressed in blue jeans and checked shirt. . . . There would never be a full explanation as to who she was and where she came from. . . . This story grows out of my psyche, the feminine idea, the feminine archetype. It's called the soul figure in Jungian philosophy. This was an image of integration that the

male character lacked. . . . She comes to town, works at the gas station, and gradually becomes the answer to everyone's problems, . . . and then got on the bus and continued on her way. . . . I could always tell the story, but when people read the script I wrote, they never quite got the idea. . . . It was a deeply felt thing; otherwise I would have given it up instead of sticking with it for ten years. When I was actually working on the production of the picture at Allied Artists, I was interviewing girls and I had a terrible time.[1]

Small wonder, as Vidor was literally casting a dream girl. He finally accepted the film's impossibility, except as self-reflection, when he corresponded with Fellini after reading an interview about the Italian director's attempts to make a film along similar Jungian lines. "That's why I enjoyed 8½ [in which Claudia Cardinale plays the stand-in film director's anima figure] so much," he said. Fellini "was smart enough to make a picture about his problems. I never made the picture. His whole picture is based on something he was trying to do but had to *not* do."[2]

In Vidor's script, the director returns to Hollywood, to put what he's learned and felt onto film. Real-life Hollywood was less taken with Vidor's unfashionable projects. Among those that found no backers were his biopic of Mary Baker Eddy, *Bright Answer* (see p. 17), his version of Hawthorne's *The Marble Faun* (see p. 17), and his several updatings of *The Crowd* (see p. 86). Another script, by Vidor and Herbert Dalmas from Bruno Frank's *A Man Called Cervantes,* was contracted in 1965 by the Salkinds; but Vidor, frustrated with script alterations, withdrew from direction and removed his name from the version filmed by Vincent Sherman in 1967. Vidor's research for a script based on the "silencing" of the 1922 William Desmond Taylor murder led to his solution of it, as fascinatingly recounted by Sidney D. Kirkpatrick in *A Cast of Killers.*[3]

Concurrent with these commercial frustrations, Vidor turned to 16mm projects which he could control completely. The most finished is *Truth and Illusion: An Introduction to Metaphysics* (1964), in which he set himself the task of finding images to counterpoint his abstract narration. To judge from the printed page, it's nearer Whitman than Emerson: "Nature gets the credit which in truth should be reserved to ourselves, the rose for its scent, the nightingale for its song, the sun for its radiance. The poets are entirely mistaken; they should address their lyrics to themselves and should turn them into odes of self-congratulation." Another, *Metaphor,* which he never finished to his satisfaction, arose from a fan letter from Andrew Wyeth: "For years I have wanted to write and tell you that I consider your war film *The Big Parade* the only truly great film ever produced."[4] *Metaphor* apparently explores Wyeth's imagery, particularly the influence of *The Big Parade,* which, in the course of the film, he tells Vidor he's seen "180 times, and that's no exaggeration."

Figure 146. *Vidor filming* Truth and Illusion *in 1964.*

Figure 147. *Vidor, in pajama costume, on the set of* Love and Money *with director James Toback (1980).*

After having taught film production courses at Los Angeles universities, he published an anecdotal guidebook, *On Film Making*, in 1972. At eighty-five, curious about changed Hollywood production methods, he accepted his first acting role that was more than a cameo, playing the hero's amusingly senile grandfather in James Toback's *Love and Money* (released, barely, in 1982), in which he spouts such lines as "If it's worth doing, it's worth overdoing."

Not a bad epitaph, that. King Vidor died, of a heart attack, on November 1, 1982. The previous weekend he and his longtime friend Colleen Moore had driven up to San Simeon to watch home movies made when they had been Hearst's guests there, sixty years before.

Even if Vidor had had the opportunity to produce the one film that would have constituted some sort of total statement (as Renoir's *The Rules of the Game* is sometimes thought to be), it would, we suspect, be as full of contradictory answers as his episodes. *Our Daily Bread*, perhaps because it's often revived or because it was an independent production, is often mistaken for this total statement. But, as we have intimated, even that film occupies a fascinating, shifting position, somewhere between a collective farm story, anarcho-syndicalist Populism, "vertical" corporationism as favored by certain right-wing thinkers, and New Deal eclecticism. In the postwar years, without rejecting social preoccupations, Vidor refrained from most of Hollywood's subdued social pieties.

In letters protesting the "unwarranted and unsanctioned" use of his name by the Willkie presidential campaign in 1940, Vidor declared himself a "rabid Roosevelt supporter." But he may have trod a path parallel to that of another Hollywood Roosevelt-booster, Ronald Reagan, if *Positif* is correct in including Vidor among Barry Goldwater's 1964 supporters.[5] In 1944, Vidor had been among the founders of the rightist Motion Picture Alliance for the Preservation of American Ideals, later so rabid in its blacklisting efforts. By McCarthy's era, he seems to have dropped his membership; and 1944 was not, perhaps, such a poor time to question Roosevelt's lack of paranoia toward Stalin. In reviewing *War and Peace*, a *Positif*ist raises the issue of Vidor's incipient fascism, a charge heard when *New Theatre* attacked *Our Daily Bread* and again in connection with *The Fountainhead*.[6] Rather than dismissing the charge out of hand as unthinkable, it's worth remembering just how many artists have at some time or another moved so far toward the ultra-right as to count among its fellow travellers and sometimes guiding lights: Carlyle (not without influence on Emerson), Shaw, Yeats, Pound, Eliot, Lawrence. But if only indefinite boundaries exist between later Populism, McCarthyism, Goldwaterism, and Reaganism, the boundaries are virtually nonexistent between the ultra-right and ultra-left: the party as vanguard of the proletariat, the party secretary as dictator. Even democracy may be a tyranny to its minorities, which was the point of agreement between Federalist and anti-Federalist founding fathers in the 1780s.

Far from remaining within one political quadrant, most people's political opinions form a kind of amorphous mass, moving in different directions simultaneously across several of the usual boundaries, sending out pseudopods and then withdrawing them, seeing no farther than a few particular issues or crises. While Vidor is conventionally thought of as on the right rather than the left, the line between right- and left-wing individualism is no clearer than that between socialism and National Socialism, or between Labour and Liberal center in Britain, or between neo-liberal and conservative in the United States. A speech Vidor made in Los Angeles in January 1966 shouldn't be too surprising, even with its quite early call for U.S. troop withdrawal from Vietnam, "not tomorrow, but today," and its long view of male dominance as the real obstacle to peace: "Men Like War" was his speech's title, and its refrain.

Initially surprising, too, is Forsyth Hardy's talk of affinity between the impulsive anarchy of *Our Daily Bread* and the documentaries of John Grierson, with their sober, establishmentarian emphasis on frameworks.[7] Yet in Grierson the Scots puritan, one can see parallels to the dedicated energy of *Our Daily Bread* and to the emphasis on pragmatic (rather than scrupulously democratic) leadership that appears so often in Vidor. The anti-Populist aloofness of *The Fountainhead* also demands an accounting. And yet: there's a time for fraternity, a time for withdrawal . . . Indeed, Populism itself is quite prone to paranoia, while some partly Populist despotisms (Prohibition) have coexisted with sympathy toward some civil rights issues. Just such difficulties crystalize in Stevens' *Giant* when tycoon Rock Hudson rolls up his sleeves to dispute, man to man, the diner owner's spiritual right to deny a Mexican-American her civil right to be his customer. No doubt some highly suspicious people would interpret Vidor's long-standing antiracism as racism inverted, but racism still. To which all we can say is that paranoia must have its limits, even though no one can know where they are. Hence transcendentalism's leap of faith.

Vidor's overall movement was one of withdrawal from the world rather than advance into the fray. He observed that over the years his hopes had shifted from individuals in the crowd to those who "deserve more."[8] He concludes in withdrawal because, if he despaired of the crowd, his love of freedom remained. And if (to borrow Frank Lloyd Wright's contrast) genius must repudiate overmuch concern for the "mobocracy," it also resigns control over anything but its own works. It's a wise faith that accepts its own limitations—failure or only modest success.

Vidor's last three commercial films—*Man without a Star, War and*

Peace, and *Solomon and Sheba*—celebrate heroes who, although deeply tainted by their societies, achieve a *private* integrity. The cowboy rides out beyond the barbed wire, the ethical thinker ricochets through every temptation and mistake to achieve a mature romanticism, and the king, identifying himself with his people, quietly sacrifices his happiness to their destiny. Each man becomes distant, silent—and perhaps that's Vidor's personal contribution, the "flaw," that conspires with production problems to render those last epics so anonymous.

As Vidor, like *Man without a Star*'s Dempsey, rides away from America in these late fifties films, there dawns the era of "liberal conservatism" à la George Stevens, to be rapidly succeeded by the tormented liberalism of Elia Kazan, until he too cedes to the mêlées of Don Siegel, Arthur Penn, Sam Peckinpah, and Stanley Kubrick. How one regrets the cut-and-thrust a freer Hollywood might have allowed between Vidor and Kazan, a less grand Stevens, a more topical Wyler, and (particularly where the formation of character by society is concerned) Losey.

History is so complex that arrière-gardes unpredictably become avant-gardes (and vice versa), and grandfathers like Vidor, Renoir, and Buñuel have strange affinities with radical visions. Vidor's thought chimes strangely with the anarcho-collective aspirations that arose around the time his career was ending and grew through the next generation. *Man without a Star* contains seeds of ecological consciousness, as if Vidor, at least, never forgot the dangers of the dustbowl. Even *The Fountainhead,* in its backward-facing way, protests against big business, intellectual trendiness, media control, and an apathetic populace. There, and in *The Citadel,* Vidor celebrates, not quite terrorism, but "direct action" with dynamite. A sense of violence as systemic—for strength as for tragedy—flows through Vidor's work, in *Wild Oranges* as in *War and Peace.*

Vidor's concern with both community and individualist options becomes relevant once more in an era when radicalism requires increasing self-reliance. The corporation (Eisenhower's "military-industrial complex") now dominates democracy, with the result that Christopher Lasch's observation of twenty years ago looks truer than ever: "The United States is a society in which capitalism itself, by solving the problem of capital accumulation, has created the material conditions for a humane and democratic socialism, but in which the consciousness of alternatives to capitalism, once so pervasive, has almost faded from memory." [9] And yet another American spirit remains, which is populist and enthusiastic, pragmatic and religious, open to visions and impulses of change. Vidor's work remains its classic expression.

Precisely because of his curiously *central* position alluded to in the conclusions to our discussions of *The Big Parade* and *War and Peace,* Vidor often strives after a synthesis, and so makes alternatives clear. If he has earned those two reputations as wild emotionalist *and* intellectual, it's because of his fidelity to his instincts *and* his principles, a fidelity that places him outside the liberal-conservative consensus, in a kind of anarcho-pragmatism with which all political factions must come to terms. Godard's *One Plus One* and *Our Daily Bread* would make an odd, but instructive, double bill—as the negative and positive poles of radicalism. For one can often learn more, faster, from one's spiritual antagonists than from allies who agree a little too quickly. What better counterinfluence to the left's brooding intellectuality than Vidor's acceptance of instinct and emotion? to the left's self-imposed alienation than his sense of emancipation as a tragic ending? to its denunciation of the patriarchal family than his joy in maternal bonds? to its brutal "abolition of the subject" than his delight in work and action? to its obsession with factional purity than his transcendental tolerance of contradiction?

We've suggested that an Emersonian transcendentalism, the puritan ethic, and an optimistic dynamism are three centers around which Vidor's thought, constantly turning, never came to rest. Often Vidor evokes a latter-day Whitman whose faith in nature, man, progress, and America can, with increasing difficulty, sustain unhappier and more complex

Figure 148.   King Vidor, in costume for his cameo in Our Daily Bread.

terms—which is to say that Vidor completed the project that broke Hart Crane. Ours isn't the first commentary on Vidor's works; the first was written half a century before he was born: Emerson's *Essays*.* Vidor's work returns the compliment, by antithesis—partly because a carnivorous pragmatism asserts itself more nakedly in it than in Emerson's smoothly idyllic prose, but largely because one can see Vidor's attempt to adapt Emersonian principles to a markedly changing America. If Vidor is the humbler artist, it's because he had to reconcile the equivocations that underlie transcendentalism with those that underlie two other, equally different, consensuses: his audience's, and Hollywood's. But when an artist *means* his films, the very discrepancies can bring out the contradictions that turn entertainment, or conformist art, into something subversive. Thus *Northwest Passage* leaves one with a worse conscience than *Drums along the Mohawk*. *Duel in the Sun* leaves one uneasy about America where *Gilda* reduces its potential criticism of capitalism to a thing about a gang of crooks. *Ruby Gentry* lashes out while *Giant* is as drowsily complacent as a banquet, brandy, and cigars.

Our exploration of Vidor's films hasn't, we hope, been merely nostalgic, or a disentanglement and thus an eradication of their wild flair. The restless verve that lies as deep within his movies as their politics allows them, as a body, to be central without being flaccid, ambivalent without being disengaged. King Vidor's evolution from a personal vitality through

---

*We've chosen from an infinite supply: *The Crowd:* "Our strength grows out of our weakness. . . . A great man is always willing to be little" ("Compensation," 298); *Hallelujah:* "The essence of genius, of virtue, and of life, . . . we call Spontaneity or Instinct. . . . To his involuntary perceptions a perfect faith is due. . . . But perception is not whimsical, but fatal" ("Self-Reliance," 269); *The Stranger's Return/Our Daily Bread/The Wedding Night:* "Whatever events in progress shall go to disgust men with cities, and infuse into them the passion for country life, and country pleasures, will render a service to the whole face of this continent" ("The Young American," 216); *Stella Dallas:* "Grief too will make us idealists" ("Experience," 473); *H. M. Pulham, Esq.:* "Another sort of false prayers are our regrets. Discontent is the want of self-reliance: it is infirmity of will" ("Self-Reliance," 276); *An American Romance:* "It seems so easy for America to inspire and express the most expansive and humane spirit; new-born, free, healthful, strong, the land of the laborer, of the democrat, of the philanthropist, of the believer, of the saint, she should speak for the human race. It is the country of the Future" ("The Young American," 217); *The Fountainhead:* "The populace think that your rejection of popular standards is a rejection of all standard, and mere antinomianism. . . . I have my own stern claims and perfect circle. It denies the name of duty to many offices that are called duties. But if I can discharge its debts, it enables me to dispense with the popular code. . . . And truly it deserves something godlike in him who has cast off the common motives of humanity" ("Self-Reliance," 274); *Ruby Gentry:* "Human life is made up of two elements, power and form, and the proportion must be invariably kept, if we would have it sweet and sound. Each of these elements in excess makes a mischief as hurtful as its defect. Everything runs to excess: every good quality is noxious, if unmixed, and to carry the danger to the edge of ruin, nature causes each man's peculiarity to superabound" ("Experience," 481–82). Ralph Waldo Emerson, *Essays and Lectures, 1832–1860* (New York: Library of America, 1983).

social optimism to a withdrawn and reflective metaphysics made a long and winding road. And our concern is not to pigeonhole him on the left or the right, nor yet to praise his critical-radical side while shrugging off everything generous and bracing in his Americanism. He sought to ally what is ferocious with what is generous in the American ethos. It's that dialectic that interests, moves, convinces us.

Notes

When not otherwise identified, factual information and quotations are drawn from King Vidor's papers—scripts, correspondence, and unpublished writings—generously made available by the Vidor family, and intelligently organized by Sidney D. Kirkpatrick and Ned Comstock. This material is now on deposit at the University of Southern California, Department of Special Collections. A smaller group of papers, from which we also draw, was donated during Vidor's lifetime to the University of California, Los Angeles.

Preface

1. Raymond Durgnat, "King Vidor" [Part 1], *Film Comment* 9, no. 4 (July/August 1973): 10–49; Raymond Durgnat, "King Vidor" [Part 2], *Film Comment* 9, no. 5 (September/October 1973): 16–51.
2. Raymond Durgnat, *Films and Feelings* (Cambridge, MA: MIT Press, 1967).
3. Raymond Durgnat and Scott Simmon, "Six Creeds That Won the Western," *Film Comment* 16, no. 5 (September/October 1980): 61–70; and Scott Simmon [assisted by Raymond Durgnat], "Wayne Wanes, Reagan Reigns," serialized, 5 parts, *Films,* August 1983–March 1984.

1. Introduction: Vidor times Four

1. King Vidor, *On Film Making* (New York: David McKay, 1973), 73.
2. "White Elephant Art vs. Termite Art" [1962], in Manny Farber, *Negative Space* (New York: Praeger, 1971), 134–44.

2. Hollywood versus America

1. Clive Denton, "King Vidor," in *The Hollywood Professionals,* vol. 5 (London: Tantivy, 1976), 7. The other study is John Baxter, *King Vidor* (New York: Monarch, 1976).

2. Etienne Chaumeton, "King Vidor—Le Dernier des romantiques," *Cinema 56* 2, no. 11 (May 1956): 53.

3. Among the useful reviews are Edward Buscombe's "The Idea of Authorship," *Screen* 14, no. 3 (Autumn 1972), and Janet Staiger's "The Politics of Film Canons," *Cinema Journal* 24, no. 3 (Spring 1985).

4. King Vidor, *A Tree Is a Tree* (New York: Harcourt, Brace, 1953).

5. King Vidor, "From a Vidor Notebook," *New York Times,* 10 March 1935.

6. A *continuous* rightward bias is documented in Larry Ceplair and Steven Englund, *The Inquisition in Hollywood: Politics in the Film Community, 1930–1960* (Berkeley and Los Angeles: University of California Press, 1983).

7. Peter Biskind, *Seeing Is Believing: How Hollywood Taught Us to Stop Worrying and Love the Fifties* (New York: Pantheon, 1983).

8. F. Scott Fitzgerald, "Crazy Sunday," in *Taps at Reveille* (New York: Scribner, 1935), 201–22.

9. David Thomson, *America in the Dark: The Impact of Hollywood Films on American Culture* (New York: Morrow, 1977), 205.

10. Leslie A. Fiedler, *Love and Death in the American Novel* (New York: Dell, 1966), esp., "The Revenge on Women: From Lucy to Lolita," 288–335.

11. *Variety,* 24 November 1982, p. 22.

12. "Paradoxical" is the final judgment on Christian Science tenets by Sidney E. Ahlstrom, *A Religious History of the American People* (New Haven: Yale University Press, 1972), 1024.

13. *Bright Answer* was co-written with Herbert Dalmas, but this addition is penciled in Vidor's hand.

14. Ahlstrom, *Religious History,* 1024.

3. 1913 to 1925: "Into the Vale of Soul Making"

1. Except as otherwise cited, information in this and the subsequent biographical introductory sections is from the King Vidor Papers; Vidor's autobiography, *A Tree Is a Tree* (hereafter cited as *Tree*); King Vidor, *On Film Making;* a draft version of Edward Schilling, ed., "A Directors Guild of America Oral History: King Vidor," conducted by Nancy Dowd and David Shepard (1980; unpublished, forthcoming from the Directors Guild of America; hereafter cited as DGA); and two conversations with King Vidor in 1981 and 1982.

2. He was probably christened *Charles* King Wallis Vidor but never used that name, even in the family. In later years he fudged his birth year ahead to 1895.

3. *Moving Picture World* (hereafter cited as *MPW*), 19 January 1918.

4. *Motion Picture News* (hereafter cited as *MPN*), 21 June 1919.

5. If it ever existed, a script has not been located. The storyline is pieced together from reviews, the copyright description, and Vidor's unpublished short story.

6. *MPN*, 23 August 1919.

7. King Vidor, "My Life in Metaphysics" (unpublished).

8. *Tree*, 79.

9. *MPN*, 8 May 1920.

10. See, for instance, Vlada Petric, "David Wark Griffith," in *Cinema: A Critical Dictionary*, ed. Richard Roud (New York: Viking, 1980), 449–61.

11. *MPW*, 14 August 1920.

12. *Tree*, 85.

13. J. Hartley Manners, *Peg o' My Heart* (New York: Samuel French, 1918), 61.

14. DGA.

15. *MPN*, 22 September 1922.

16. In conversation with Scott Simmon.

17. Richard Hofstadter, *The Age of Reform: From Bryan to F.D.R.* (New York: Random House, Vintage Books, 1955), 73.

18. Eric Bentley, *The Life of the Drama* (New York: Atheneum, 1964), 205.

19. Leslie A. Fiedler, "Come Back to the Raft Ag'in, Huck Honey!" [1948] in *The Collected Essays of Leslie Fiedler* (New York: Stein & Day, 1977), 1: 142–51.

20. Peter Brooks, *The Melodramatic Imagination: Balzac, Henry James, Melodrama, and the Mode of Excess* (New Haven: Yale University Press, 1976), 4.

21. See esp. Richard Chase, *The American Novel and Its Traditions* (Garden City, NY: Doubleday, 1957).

22. Brooks, *Melodramatic Imagination*, 5.

23. Charles Affron, *Cinema and Sentiment* (Chicago: University of Chicago Press, 1982), 16.

24. Bentley, *Life of the Drama*, 216.

25. See, for instance, Richard Schickel [interviewer], *The Men Who Made the Movies* (New York: Atheneum, 1975), 159: "I don't think I've ever had a villain in my films. I can't remember one real villain, you know. It's the straw man we set up to knock down. . . . We don't need to symbolize or construct one. . . . Life is enough of a battle in itself."

26. *Literary Digest* 74 (22 July 1922): 28.

27. Charles Higham and Joel Greenberg [interviewers], *The Celluloid Muse: Hollywood Directors Speak* (Chicago: Henry Regnery, 1969), 227.

28. Elinor Glyn, *His Hour* (New York: D. Appleton, 1912), 253.

29. DGA.

4. 1925 to 1928: "Silent and Amazed"

1. Lillian Gish, with Ann Pinchot, *The Movies, Mr. Griffith, and Me* (New York: Avon, 1970), 278.

2. Higham and Greenberg, *Celluloid Muse*, 229.

3. The full story and its long consequences are recounted in *Dark Star* (New York: St. Martin's Press, 1985), by John Gilbert's daughter, Leatrice Gilbert Fountain.

4. *Tree*, 112.

5. Schickel, *Men Who Made the Movies*, 140.

6. Ado Kyrou, *Amour-érotisme et cinéma* (Paris: E. Losfeld, 1967).

7. *Tree*, 116.

8. Charles Affron, *Star Acting: Gish, Garbo, Davis* (New York: Dutton, 1977), 66–78.

9. See Alexis de Tocqueville, *Democracy in America* [1835], trans. Henry Reeve (London: Longman, Green, Longman & Roberts, 1862), 2:190–94 [vol. 2, bk. 2, chap. 20].

5. 1929 to 1935: "Looking Forth on Pavement and Land"

1. Schickel, *Men Who Made the Movies*, 148.

2. Higham and Greenberg, *Celluloid Muse*, 234.

3. Bernard Cohn [interviewer], "Propos de King Vidor," *Positif*, no. 79 (October 1966).

4. *Tree*, 175.

5. Henri Agel, *Romance américaine* (Paris: Editions du Cerf, 1963), 103–10. See also Agel, *Les Grands Cinéastes que je propose* (Paris: Editions du Cerf, 1967), and *Le Cinéma a-t-il une âme?* (Paris: Editions du Cerf, 1952).

6. Charles Barr, "King Vidor," *Brighton Film Review*, no. 21 (June 1970).

7. Alexander Walker, *The Shattered Silents: How the Talkies Came to Stay* (New York: Morrow, 1979), 189.

8. James Agate, "Prancing Niggers," in *The Tatler*, 1930, repr. in *Around Cinemas*, 2d ser. (London: Home & Van Thal, 1948), 29.

9. Agel, *Romance américaine*, 105.

10. Baxter, *King Vidor*, 43.

11. Kyrou, *Amour-érotisme*, 213.

12. Norman Mailer, *The White Negro* (San Francisco: City Lights, 1957).

13. Luc Moullet and Michel Delahaye, "Entretien avec King Vidor," *Cahiers du Cinéma*, no. 136 (October 1962): 18.

14. Emerson Hough, "Billy the Kid: The True Story of a Western 'Bad Man,'" *Everybody's Magazine* 5 (1901): 309; quoted in Stephen Tatum, *Inventing Billy the Kid: Visions of the Outlaw in America, 1881–1981* (Albuquerque: University of New Mexico Press, 1982), 57.

15. See Scott Simmon, "The Kid Hangs Tough," *Films* 4, no. 3 (March 1984): 30–33.

16. Higham and Greenberg, *Celluloid Muse*, 233.

17. Elmer L. Rice, *Street Scene*, in *Plays of Elmer Rice* (London: Gollancz, 1933), 166.

18. Ibid., 137.

19. Geoffrey Gorer, *The American People: A Study in National Character* (New York: Norton, 1948), esp. "Europe and the Rejected Father," 23–49.

20. Higham and Greenberg, *Celluloid Muse*, 234.

21. Baxter, *King Vidor*, 5.

22. See Jackie Cooper, with Dick Kleiner, *Please Don't Shoot My Dog* (New York: Morrow, 1981), 54–56.

23. *Tree*, 193.

24. Higham and Greenberg, *Celluloid Muse*, 234.

25. Schickel, *Men Who Made the Movies*, 149.

26. "Up the Coulee," in Hamlin Garland, *Main-Travelled Roads* [1891] (New York: Signet, 1962), 54–97.

27. Robert Stebbins, "Ungrateful for Gift Horses," *New Theatre* 1, no. 10 (November 1934): 22.

28. B. G. Braver-Mann, "Vidor and Evasion," *Experimental Cinema* 1, no. 3 (February 1931): 27.

29. T. W. Adorno et al., *The Authoritarian Personality* (New York: Harper & Bros., 1950), esp. "Pseudoconservatism," 675–85.

30. *Tree*, 220.

31. Alexander Legge, as told to Neil M. Clark, "Back to the Land?" *Reader's Digest* 22 (November 1932): 45; see also Malcolm McDermott, "An Agricultural Army," *Reader's Digest* 21 (June 1932): 95–97.

32. The National Industrial Recovery Act of 1933 included a Subsistence Homestead Division. For an overview of the political climate in relation to Vidor's film, see James Tice Moore, "Depression Images: Subsistence Homesteads, 'Production-for-Use,' and King Vidor's *Our Daily Bread*," *Midwest Quarterly* 26, no. 1 (1984): 24–34.

33. For a summary of the idea in Franklin and Whitman, see "Utilitarian and Expressive Individualism" in Robert N. Bellah et al., *Habits of the Heart: Individualism and Commitment in American Life* (Berkeley and Los Angeles: University of California Press, 1985), 32–35.

34. *Tree*, 226.

35. Barr, "King Vidor."

36. Edmund Wilson, *Apologies to the Iroquois* (New York: Farrar, Straus & Cudahy, 1960).

37. George Seaton, "Getting Out on a Limb," *Films and Filming* 7, no. 7 (April 1961): 9.

6. 1935 to 1944: "Through Dim Lulls of Unapparent Growth"

1. W. J. Cash, *The Mind of the South* [1941] (New York: Random House, Vintage Books, 1969), esp. "Of an Ideal and Conflict," 61–102.

2. *Tree*, 189.

3. Nick Roddick, *A New Deal in Entertainment: Warner Brothers in the 1930s* (London: British Film Institute, 1983), 104–9.

4. Durgnat and Simmon, "Six Creeds That Won the Western."

5. *Tree*, 191.

6. Joel Greenberg [interviewer], "War, Wheat and Steel," *Sight and Sound* 37, no. 4 (Autumn 1968): 195.

7. Maurice Bardèche and Robert Brasillach, *Histoire du film* (Paris: André Martel, 1948).

8. See Linda Williams, "'Something Else besides a Mother': *Stella Dallas* and the Maternal Melodrama," *Cinema Journal* 24, no. 1 (Fall 1984): 24 n. 10, for a list of treatments.

9. Repr in Pauline Kael, *I Lost It at the Movies* (New York: Bantam Books, 1966), 27–39.

10. Affron, *Cinema and Sentiment*, 5.

11. We are not unaware that feminists can see the scene differently. A character in Marilyn French's novel *The Women's Room* ends her memory of it by exclaiming, "How they got us to consent to our own eradication!" ([New York: Summit Books, 1977], 227). Linda Williams quotes this passage in her essay on the film cited above, which concludes that Vidor's *Stella Dallas* produces "a divided female spectator"—identifying with and yet criticizing Stella's victimization. It's our view that the moral division of the spectator is a perfectly routine condition, like being able to see two sides to a question. Williams's reading is at least a sophisticated response to E. Ann Kaplan's argument that the film moves the viewer away from Stella's point of view into an upper-class one ("The Case of the Missing Mother: Maternal Issues in Vidor's *Stella Dallas*," *Heresies* 16 [1983]: 81–85). Vidor's restaging of the conclusion also argues against Kaplan.

12. Along such lines we concur with the principles of Charles Eckert's seminal discussion of how melodrama treats class conflict in "The Anatomy of a Proletarian Film: Warner's *Marked Woman*," *Film Quarterly* 27, no. 3 (Spring 1974): the film "attenuate[s] conflicts at the level of real conditions to amplify and resolve them at the level of melodrama."

13. Marshall McLuhan, *The Mechanical Bride: The Folklore of Industrial Man* (New York: Vanguard, 1951), esp. "Woman in a Mirror," 80–81, and "Husband's Choice," 82–84.

14. Roud, *Cinema*, 550.

15. *New York Times*, 13 November 1938.

16. J. P. Marquand, *H. M. Pulham, Esquire* (Garden City, NY: Sun Dial Press, 1940), 45.

17. Sinclair Lewis, *Babbitt* (New York: Harcourt, Brace & World, 1922); William H. Whyte, *The Organization Man* (New York: Simon & Schuster, 1956).

18. *Tree*, 258.

19. See Louis Adamic, *My America* (New York: Harper & Bros., 1938); *From Many Lands* (New York: Harper & Bros., 1940); *Plymouth Rock and Ellis Island* (New York: Common Council for American Unity, 1940).

20. King Vidor, "The Actor and How to Cast Him," in *On Film Making*, 43–65.

21. Fiedler, *Love and Death*, 150–51.

22. Joseph Schumpeter, *Capitalism, Socialism and Democracy* (London: Allen & Unwin, 1943), 375.

23. Peter F. Drucker, *The Future of Industrial Man: A Conservative Approach* (New York: John Day, 1942), 297.

24. *Tree*, 256.

25. *New York Times*, 24 November 1944.

7. 1945 to 1955: "Sing the Body Electric"

1. Ronald Haver, *David O. Selznick's Hollywood* (New York: Knopf, 1980), 352–68.

2. *Variety*, 6 January 1949.

3. Haver, *Selznick*, 355.

4. Schickel, *Men Who Made the Movies*, 154.

5. *Tree*, 266.

6. Kyrou, *Amour-érotisme*, 93.

7. Curtis Harrington, "The Later Years: King Vidor's Hollywood Progress," *Sight and Sound* 22 (April–June 1953): 179–82, 203–4.

8. See esp. Sergei Eisenstein, "A Dialectic Approach to Film Form" [1929] in *"Film Form" and "The Film Sense,"* ed. Jay Leyda (New York: Meridian, 1957), 45–63.

9. Moullet and Delahaye, "Entretien avec King Vidor," 5.

10. Ayn Rand, *The Fountainhead* [1943] (New York: Signet, 1971), 64.

11. Ibid., 144.

12. Robert C. Twombly, *Frank Lloyd Wright: An Interpretive Biography* (New York: Harper & Row, 1973), 216.

13. DGA.

14. Greenberg, "War, Wheat and Steel," 197.

15. David Riesman, *The Lonely Crowd: A Study of the Changing American Character* (New Haven: Yale University Press, 1950), esp. "Autonomy," 285–306. See also Bellah et al., *Habits of the Heart*, 49.

16. DGA.

17. E.g., Donald Lyons and Glenn O'Brien, "King Vidor," *Andy Warhol's Interview*, October 1972, 15; Higham and Greenberg, *Celluloid Muse*, 240.

18. DGA.

19. Steven Bach, *Final Cut: Dreams and Disaster in the Making of "Heaven's Gate"* (New York: New American Library, 1985), 91–94.

20. Edward Albee, *Who's Afraid of Virginia Woolf?* (New York: Atheneum, 1962), 3–6.

21. Lyons and O'Brien, "King Vidor," 14.

22. Stuart Engstrand, *Beyond the Forest* (New York: Creative Age, 1948), 45.

23. Higham and Greenberg, *Celluloid Muse*, 241.

24. Memo, David O. Selznick to Joseph Bernhard, 2 June 1952 (unpublished: King Vidor Papers, USC).

25. Michel Delahaye, "La Sagesse de Vidor," *Cahiers du Cinéma*, no. 136 (October 1962).

26. Gilles Deleuze, *Masochism* (London: Faber & Faber, 1971), chap. 5.

27. Quoted in DGA.

28. Michel Ciment and Bertrand Tavernier, "Propos de Kirk Douglas," *Positif*, no. 112 (January 1970): 15–16.

8. 1956 to 1959: "Where the Technicolored End of Evening Smiles"

1. Schickel, *Men Who Made the Movies*, 157.

2. DGA.

3. Moullet and Delahaye, "Entretien avec King Vidor," 20.

4. King Vidor, "Transforming Tolstoy," *New York Times*, 12 August 1956.

5. "Tolstoy and the Development of Realism" [1936], in György Lukács, *Studies in European Realism* (London: Hillway, 1950), 126–205.

6. Schickel, *Men Who Made the Movies*, 157.

7. Peter John Dyer, *"War and Peace" Monthly Film Bulletin* 24, no. 276 (January 1957), 4.

8. As discussed in Raymond Durgnat, *Jean Renoir* (Berkeley and Los Angeles: University of California Press, 1974), 404–5.

9. In conversation with Raymond Durgnat; in reference to *Ben Hur* (1959).

9. Envoi

1. DGA.

2. Lyons and O'Brien, "King Vidor," 15.

3. Sidney D. Kirkpatrick, *A Cast of Killers* (New York: Dutton, 1986).

4. Andrew Wyeth to King Vidor, 6 January 1970 [Vidor Papers, USC].

5. *Positif,* no. 66 (January, 1966): 107.

6. Louis Seguin, "Les Malheurs de la paix," *Positif,* no. 21 (February 1957).

7. In conversation with Raymond Durgnat.

8. Or to those who "are worth more"—the hazards of translation back! Cohn, "Propos de King Vidor."

9. Christopher Lasch, *The Agony of the American Left* (New York: Knopf, 1969), 212.

Filmography

This filmography is incomplete through 1917. All Vidor's films prior to 1920 are presumed lost, except for *The Intrigue* and reel 1 of *Bud's Recruit*. Descriptive titles in square brackets have been supplied for early films whose titles are unknown. Films not discussed in the text are annotated here.

1913

[Galveston hurricane]
Producers/photographers: King Vidor and Ray Clough.
(Theatrical release only in Texas.)

1914

[Army troop parade in Houston]
Mutual Weekly
Producers: King Vidor and John Boggs.
Director/photographer: King Vidor.

In Tow
Producers: King Vidor and John Boggs.
Director/writer: King Vidor.
Photography: John Boggs.
2 reels; completed August 1914.
(Theatrical release only in Texas.)
Cast: King Vidor (Carson); Pansy Buchanan (Helen); D. Y. Cole (Abie).

Beautiful Love

Hotex

Director: Edward Sedgwick.

Writers: Edward Sedgwick and King Vidor.

1 reel(?); completed September 1914.

Cast: Josie Sedgwick; King Vidor; Eileen Sedgwick; D. Y. Cole.

The Heroes

Hotex

Director: Edward Sedgwick.

Writers: Edward Sedgwick and King Vidor.

1 reel(?); completed September 1914.

Cast: Edward Sedgwick; Eileen Sedgwick; D. Y. Cole; Josie Sedgwick.

Other Hotex films, the titles of which are lost, were made by the same production team.

1915

[Houston sugar refining documentary] (1915?)

Directors/writers: King Vidor and John Boggs.

With: Florence Vidor.

[A car theft in Fort Worth]

Directors: King Vidor and Clifford Vick.

(No commercial release)

[Simulated documentary.]

[Newsreel footage]

Ford Weekly

Photographers: King Vidor and Clifford Vick.

[Shot during trip from Houston to San Francisco.]

1916

When It Rains, It Pours

Vitagraph

Producer/director: William Wolbert.

Writer: King Vidor.

1 reel; released July 1916.

Cast: Mary Anderson (Sue Monroe); Reggie Morris (Bobby); Otto Lederer (Mr. Monroe); Anne Schaefer (Aunt Susan).

The Intrigue

Paramount/Pallas

Director: Frank Lloyd.

5 reels; released September 1916.

Cast: Lenore Ulrich (the countess); Cecil Van Auker (the hero); Howard Davies (the villain); Florence Vidor (the countess's maid); Paul Weigel; King Vidor (a chauffeur).

1917

What'll We Do with Uncle?
Universal/Victor
Director: William Beaudine.
Writer: King Vidor.
1 reel; released October 1917.
Cast: Henry Murdock (Henry); Mildred Davis (Flossie); Milt Uhl (the dealer).
[Comedy: Henry, an artist, attempts various forms of suicide, after mistaking Flossie's theatrical rehearsal for infidelity.]

A Bad Little Good Man
Universal/Nestor
Director: William Beaudine.
Writer: King Vidor.
1 reel; released October 1917.
Cast: Mattie Comont (Idaho Ida); Henry Murdock (Texas Tommy); Edwin Baker (Montana Joe).
[A Western: Idaho Ida, a dancehall girl who wears a six-gun, protects Texas Tommy. He reciprocates, saving her from Montana Joe.]

Dan's Daring Drama; or, Harem-Scare Em (1917?)
Universal/Nestor
Director: Al Santell.
Writer: King Vidor.
2 reels.
Cast: Dave Morris (the Sultan); Harry Mann (Harmon Naigs); Gladys Tennyson (Lily White).
[Apparently released under another title. Listed here under Vidor's original title.]

Just My Sister (1917?)
Universal/Nestor
Director: Al Santell.
Writer: King Vidor.
2 reels.
[Apparently released under another title. Listed here under Vidor's original title.]

1918: The Judge Brown Series

Boy City Film Corp. (released by General Film Corp.). All directed by King Vidor; produced and written by Judge Willis Brown. 2 reels each. Other titles in the Judge Brown series were announced in 1918, but never filmed by Vidor. The series resumed without him in 1919.

Bud's Recruit
Released January 1918.
Wallis Brennan (Bud); Robert Gordon (Reggie); Ruth Hampton (Reggie's fiancée).

The Chocolate of the Gang
Released January 1918.
Thomas Bellamy (Chocolate); Judge Willis Brown.

The Lost Lie
Released 2 March 1918.
William Vaughn, Mike O'Rourke (two boys); Ruth Hampton (Mike's sister); Judge Willis Brown.
[Originally announced as *Two Boys and Two Lies*.]

Tad's Swimming Hole
Released 16 March 1918.
Ernest Butterworth (Tad); Ruth Hampton (rescued girl); Judge Willis Brown.

Marrying Off Dad
Released 16 March 1918.
Wallis Brennan, Ernest Thompson (two brothers); Sadie Clayton (housekeeper/wife); Ruth Hampton (girl next door); Judge Willis Brown.

The Preacher's Son
Released 30 March 1918.
Guy Hayman (Charles); Wharton Jones (his father); Ernest Thompson; William DuVaull; Charles Force; Judge Willis Brown.

Thief or Angel
Released 30 March 1918.
Ruth Hampton (Antonetta/Tony); Charles Richards (doctor); W. T. Horn (judge); Helen Muir; Ernest Thompson; Grace Marvin; Judge Willis Brown.

The Accusing Toe
Released 27 April 1918.
Dale Faith (Steve, the boy); Wharton Jones (the miller); Judge Willis Brown.

The Rebellion
Released 27 April 1918.
Doug Lansing, Robert Planett, Martin Pendleton (three boys); William White; Wharton Jones; J. G. Underhill; Sadie Clayton; Hugh Saxon; Judge Willis Brown.

I'm a Man
Released May 1918.
Martin Pendleton (Frank Eisel, the boy); Wharton Jones (Jules de Courcey); Ruth Hampton (Ruth Eisel); Lloyd Hughes (David Smith); William Davenport (Simon Eisel); Judge Willis Brown.

1919

The Turn in the Road
Brentwood/Robertson-Cole (released by Exhibitors Mutual)
Director/writer: King Vidor.

5 reels; released March 1919.

Cast: Helen Jerome Eddy (June Barker); Lloyd Hughes (Paul Perry); George Nichols (Hamilton Perry); Ben Alexander (Bob); Winter Hall (Rev. Matthew Barker); Pauline Curley (Evelyn Barker).

Better Times

Brentwood/Robertson-Cole (released by Exhibitors Mutual)

Director/writer: King Vidor.

Photographer: William Thornley.

5 reels; released June 1919.

Cast: ZaSu Pitts (Nancy Scroogs); David Butler (Peter); Jack MacDonald (Ezra Scroogs); William DuVaull (S. Whittaker); Hugh Fay (Jack Ransom); George Hackathorne (Tony).

The Other Half

Brentwood/Robertson-Cole (released by Exhibitors Mutual)

Director/writer: King Vidor.

5 reels; released August 1919.

Cast: Florence Vidor (Katherine Boone); Charles Meredith (Donald Trent); ZaSu Pitts (the Jazz Kid); David Butler (Corporal Jimmy); Thomas Jefferson (Caleb Fairman); Alfred Allen (J. Martin Trent); Frances Raymond (Mrs. Boone); Hugh Saxon (James Bradley); Arthur Redden (reporter).

Poor Relations

Brentwood/Robertson-Cole (released by Exhibitors Mutual)

Director/writer: King Vidor.

5 reels; released October 1919.

Cast: Florence Vidor (Dorothy Perkins); William DuVaull (Pa Perkins); ZaSu Pitts (Daisy Perkins); Charles Meredith (Monte Rhodes); Lillian Leighton (Ma Perkins); Roscoe Karns (country yokel).

[Country girl Dorothy Perkins succeeds as an architect in the city, but then is scorned by her old-moneyed in-laws. Reviews were poor: "The slender, fragile story has just about all it can do to make its way through the new-mown hay atmosphere" (*Exhibitors' Trade Review*, 25 October 1919).]

1920

The Family Honor

King W. Vidor Productions (released by First National)

Producer/director: King Vidor.

Script: William Parker; from a story by John Booth Harrower.

Photographer: Ira H. Morgan.

5 reels; released May 1920.

Cast: Florence Vidor (Beverly Tucker); Roscoe Karns (Dal Tucker); Ben Alexander (Little Ben Tucker); Charles Meredith (Merle Curran); George Nichols (Mayor Curran); John P. Lockney (Felix); Willis Marks (Dobbs); Harold Goodwin (grocery boy).

[Lost film.]

The Jack-Knife Man

King W. Vidor Productions (released by First National)
Producer/director: King Vidor.
Script: King Vidor; from the novel *The Jack-Knife Man* (1913) by Ellis Parker
    Butler.
5 reels; released August 1920.
Cast: Fred Turner (Peter Lane); Harry Todd (Booge); Bobby Kelso (Buddy);
    Claire McDowell (Liz Merdin); Willis Marks (Rev. Briggles); Lillian Leighton
    (Mrs. Potter); Florence Vidor (Mrs. Montgomery); James Corrigan (George
    Rapp); Charles Arling (the doctor).
[Vidor's first surviving feature.]

1921

The Sky Pilot

Cathrine Curtis Corp. (released by First National)
Producer: Cathrine Curtis.
Director: King Vidor.
Script: John McDermott; adaptation: Faith Green; from the novel *The Sky Pilot*
    (1899) by Ralph Connor [pseud. Charles William Gordon].
Photographer: Gus Peterson.
7 reels; released April 1921.
Cast: John Bowers (the sky pilot); Colleen Moore (Gwen); David Butler (Bill
    Hendricks); Harry Todd (the old timer); James Corrigan (Ashley); Donald
    MacDonald (the duke); Kathleen Kirkham (Lady Charlotte).

Love Never Dies

King W. Vidor/Thomas Ince Productions (released by Associated Exhibitors)
Producer: Thomas Ince.
Director: King Vidor.
Script: King Vidor; from the novel *The Cottage of Delight* (1919) by Will N.
    Harben.
Photographer: Max Dupont.
7 reels; released November 1921.
Cast: Lloyd Hughes (John Trott); Madge Bellamy (Tilly Whaley); Joe Bennett
    (Joel Eperson); Lillian Leighton (Mrs. Cavanaugh); Fred Gambold (Sam
    Cavanaugh); Julia Brown (Dora Boyles); Frank Brownlee (Ezekiel Whaley);
    Winifred Greenwood (Jane Holder); Claire McDowell (Liz Trott).

1922

The Real Adventure

Florence Vidor/Cameo (released by Associated Exhibitors)
Producer: Arthur S. Kane.
Director: King Vidor.
Script: Mildred Considine; from the novel *The Real Adventure* (1915) by Henry
    Kitchell Webster.
Photographer: George Barnes.

5 reels; released July 1922.

Florence Vidor (Rose Stanton); Clyde Fillmore (Rodney Aldrich); Nellie Peck Saunders (Mrs. Stanton); Lilyan McCarthy (Portia); Philip Ryder (John Walbraith).

[Lost film. A well-received drama about a woman who, bored by purely physical companionship with her lawyer husband, joins him in mastering law. But she gets only condescension, and leaves, at first finding work as a chorus girl. After she has risen to be a celebrated Broadway costume designer, her husband sees the error of his ways.]

Dusk to Dawn

Florence Vidor Productions (released by Associated Exhibitors)

Director: King Vidor.

Script: Frank Howard Clark; from the novel *The Shuttle Soul* by Katherine Hill.

Photographer: George Barnes.

6 reels; released September 1922.

Cast: Florence Vidor (Marjorie Latham/Aziza); Jack Mulhall (Philip Randall); Truman Van Dyke (Ralph Latham); James Neill (John Latham); Lydia Knott (Mrs. Latham); Herbert Fortier (Mark Randall); Norris Johnson (Babette); Nellie Anderson (Marua); Sidney Franklin (Nadar Gungi); Peter Burke (Rajah Nyhal Singh).

[Lost film.]

Conquering the Woman

King W. Vidor Productions (released by Associated Exhibitors)

Producer/director: King Vidor.

Script: Frank Howard Clark; from the story "Kidnapping Coline" (1913) by Henry C. Rowland.

Photographer: George Barnes.

6 reels; released 10 December 1922.

Cast: Florence Vidor (Judith Stafford); Bert Sprotte (Tobias Stafford); Mathilde Brundage (Aunt Sophia); David Butler (Larry Saunders); Roscoe Karns (Shorty Thompson); Peter Burke (Count Henri); Harry Todd (Sandy MacTavish).

[A society girl (Florence Vidor) is sent off on a merchant ship by her father to cure her of affected European manners—Americans to her are "crude barbarians." Stranded with her on a desert island, a cowboy (David Butler) enacts the action of the title. "The picture, while directed by King Vidor, who when given a chance can show something in the way of imaginative ideas, does not leave its orthodox groove" (*MPN*, 30 December 1922).]

Peg o' My Heart

Metro

Supervisor: J. Hartley Manners.

Director: King Vidor.

Script: Mary O'Hara; from the play *Peg o' My Heart* (1912) by J. Hartley Manners.

Photographer: George Barnes.

8 reels; released 18 December 1922.

Cast: Laurette Taylor (Margaret O'Connell [Peg]); Mahlon Hamilton (Sir Gerald Adair); Russell Simpson (Jim O'Connell); Ethel Grey Terry (Ethel Chichester); Nigel Barrie (Christian Brent); Lionel Belmore (Hawks); Vera Lewis (Mrs. Chichester); Sidna Beth Ivins (Mrs. Jim O'Connell); D. R. O. Hatswell (Alaric Chichester); Aileen O'Malley (Peg as a child); Fred Huntly (butler).

1923

The Woman of Bronze

Samuel Zierler Photoplay Corp. (released by Metro)
Producer: Harry Garson.
Director: King Vidor.
Script: Hope Loring and Louis Duryea Lighton; from the play *Woman of Bronze* (U.S. premiere, 1920) by Henry Kistemaeckers.
Photographer: William O'Connell.
Art director: Joseph Wright.
6 reels; released February 1923.
Cast: Clara Kimball Young (Vivian Hunt); John Bowers (Paddy Miles); Kathryn McGuire (Sylvia Morton); Edwin Stevens (Reggie Morton); Lloyd Whitlock (Leonard Hunt); Edward Kimball (Papa Bonelli).
[Lost film. A "heavy emotional drama" (*MPW*, 14 April 1923) centering on the long-suffering wife (Clara Kimball Young) of a temperamental artist. He recovers from infatuation with a young model when he recognizes his wife's "soul." For Vidor, "It was out of my line."]

Souls for Sale

Goldwyn
Producer/director/writer: Rupert Hughes.
8 reels; released March 1923.
[King and Florence Vidor play two of the real-life celebrities encountered by a smalltown girl (Eleanor Boardman) when she seeks a job in Hollywood.]

Alice Adams

Encore Pictures (released by Associated Exhibitors)
Producer: King Vidor.
Director: Rowland V. Lee.
Script: Rowland V. Lee; from the novel *Alice Adams* (1921) by Booth Tarkington.
Photographer: George Barnes.
6 reels; released April 1923.
Cast: Florence Vidor (Alice Adams); Claude Gillingwater; Harold Goodwin.
[Lost film? Vidor commented, "I had a few conferences with Rowland before the film started, and perhaps put more time in on the script than in supervising direction."]

Three Wise Fools

Goldwyn
Director: King Vidor.

Script: King Vidor and June Mathis; adaptation: John McDermott and James O'Hanlon; from the play *Three Wise Fools* (1919) by Austin Strong and Winchell Smith.
Photographer: Charles Van Enger.
7 reels; released July 1923.
Cast: Claude Gillingwater (Theodore Findley); Eleanor Boardman (Rena Fairchild/Sidney Fairchild); William H. Crane (Hon. James Trumbull); Alec B. Francis (Dr. Richard Gaunt); John Sainpolis (John Crawshay); Brinsley Shaw (Benny); Fred Esmelton (Gray); William Haines (Gordon Schuyler); Lucien Littlefield (Douglas); ZaSu Pitts (Mickey); Martha Mattox (Saunders); Fred J. Butler (Poole); Charles Hickman (Clancy); Craig Biddle Jr. (Findley as a boy); Creighton Hale (Trumbull as a boy); Raymond Hatton (Gaunt as a boy).
[Three sedentary bachelors are surprised by a visit from the daughter (Eleanor Boardman) of the woman all three have loved. She appears to be involved in a robbery scheme until she catches the real crook. "King Vidor has reproduced the atmosphere, comedy and romance [of the stageplay] with great success, and elaborated considerably on the suspense angle" (*MPW*, 14 July 1923).]

1924

Wild Oranges
Goldwyn
Director: King Vidor.
Script: King Vidor; from the novel *Wild Oranges* (1919) by Joseph Hergesheimer.
Photographer: John W. Boyle.
7 reels; released January 1924.
Cast: Virginia Valli (Nellie Stope); Frank Mayo [and, in some exteriors, James Kirkwood] (John Woolfolk); Ford Sterling (Paul Halvard); Nigel De Brulier (Lichfield Stope); Charles A. Post (Iscah Nicholas).

Happiness
Metro
Producer/director: King Vidor.
Script: J. Hartley Manners; from his one-act play *Happiness* (U.S. premiere, 1914).
Photographer: Chester A. Lyons.
8 reels; released March 1924.
Cast: Laurette Taylor (Jenny Wreay); Pat O'Malley (Fermoy MacDonough); Hedda Hopper (Mrs. Crystal Pole); Cyril Chadwick (Philip Chandos); Edith Yorke (Mrs. Wreay); Patterson Dial (Sallie Perkins); Joan Standing (other Jenny); Lawrence Grant (Mr. Rosselstein); Charlotte Mineau (head saleslady).

Wine of Youth
MGM
Producer/director: King Vidor; assistant director: David Howard.
Script: Carey Wilson; from the play *Mary the Third* (1923) by Rachel Crothers.
Photographer: John Mescall.

Art director: Charles L. Cadwallader.

7 reels; released August 1924.

Episode of 1870: Eleanor Boardman (Mary); James Morrison (Clinton); Johnnie Walker (William). Episode of 1897: Eleanor Boardman (Mary); Niles Welch (John ["Robert" in credits]); Creighton Hale (Richard). The Modern Story: Eleanor Boardman (Mary); Ben Lyon (Lynn); William Haines (Hal); William Collier, Jr. (Max); Pauline Garon (Tish); Eulalie Jenson (mother); E. J. Ratcliffe (father); Gertrude Claire (Granny); Robert Agnew (Bobbie); Lucille Hutton (Anne); Virginia Lee Corbin, Gloria Heller (flappers); Sidney De Grey (doctor).

His Hour

MGM

Supervisor: Elinor Glyn.

Director: King Vidor; assistant director: David Howard.

Script: Elinor Glyn; from her novel *His Hour* (1910); titles: King Vidor and Maude Fulton.

Photographer: John Mescall.

Art director: Cedric Gibbons; gowns: Sophie Wachner.

7 reels; released September 1924.

Cast: Aileen Pringle (Tamara Loraine); John Gilbert (Gritzko); Emily Fitzroy (Princess Ardacheff); Lawrence Grant (Stephen Strong); Dale Fuller (Olga Gleboff); Mario Carillo (Count Valonne); Jacquelin Gadsdon (Tatiane Shebanoff); George Waggoner (Sasha Basmanoff); Carrie Clark Ward (Princess Murieska); Bertram Grassby (Boris Varishkine); Jill Reties; Wilfred Gough; Frederick Vroom; Mathilde Comont; E. Eliazaroff; David Mir; Bert Sprotte.

Wife of the Centaur

MGM

Director: King Vidor; assistant director: David Howard.

Script: Douglas Z. Doty; from the novel *Wife of the Centaur* (1923) by Cyril Hume.

Photographer: John Arnold.

Editor: Hugh Wynn.

Art director: Cedric Gibbons; costumes: Sophie Wachner.

7 reels; released December 1924.

Cast: Eleanor Boardman (Joan Converse); John Gilbert (Jeffrey Dwyer); Aileen Pringle (Inez Martin); Kate Lester (Mrs. Converse); William Haines (Edward Converse); Kate Price (Mattie); Jacquelin Gadsdon (Hope Larrimore); Bruce Covington (Mr. Larrimore); Lincoln Stedman (Chuck); William Orlamond (Uncle Roger).

[Lost film. A novelist (John Gilbert) is unable to choose between a "jazz girl" (Aileen Pringle) and a more stable woman (Eleanor Boardman). He marries the latter but keeps returning to the former. Although the cast and situation unpromisingly combine elements of *Wine of Youth* and *His Hour*, perhaps Vidor was learning to use Gilbert's strengths. As much is suggested by a review that found Gilbert's performance "masterly" but "neurotic," and likely to arouse "disgust" in audiences (*MPN*, 17 January 1925).]

1925

Proud Flesh

MGM

Director: King Vidor; assistant director: David Howard.

Script: Harry Behn and Agnes Christine Johnston; from the novel *Proud Flesh* (1924) by Lawrence Rising.

Photographer: John Arnold.

Art director: Cedric Gibbons.

7 reels; released April 1925.

Cast: Eleanor Boardman (Fernanda); Pat O'Malley (Pat O'Malley); Harrison Ford (Don Jamie); Trixie Friganza (Mrs. McKee); William J. Kelly (Mr. McKee); Rosita Marstini (Vicente); Sojin (Wong); Evelyn Sherman (Spanish aunt); George Nichols (Spanish uncle); Margaret Seddon (Mrs. O'Malley); Lillian Elliott (Mrs. Casey); Priscilla Bonner (San Francisco girl); Joan Crawford (girl at party).

The Big Parade

MGM

Director: King Vidor; assistant directors: David Howard and George W. Hill.

Script: Harry Behn; from a story by Laurence Stallings; titles: Joseph W. Farnham.

Photographer: John Arnold.

Editor: Hugh Wynn.

Art directors: Cedric Gibbons and James Basevi; wardrobe: Ethel P. Chaffin.

Musical score: William Axt and David Mendoza.

12 reels; released November 1925.

Cast: John Gilbert (James Apperson); Renée Adorée (Melisande); Hobart Bosworth (Mr. Apperson); Claire McDowell (Mrs. Apperson); Karl Dane (Slim); Tom O'Brien (Bull); Claire Adams (Justyn Reed); Robert Ober (Harry); Rosita Marstini (Melisande's mother).

1926

La Bohème

MGM

Director: King Vidor.

Script: Ray Doyle, Harry Behn, and Fred De Grasse; from the novel *Scènes de la vie de Bohème* (1851) by Henri Murger; titles: William Conselman and Ruth Cummings.

Photographer: Hendrik Sartov.

Editor: Hugh Wynn.

Art directors: Cedric Gibbons and Arnold Gillespie.

Musical score: William Axt.

9 reels; released February 1926.

Cast: Lillian Gish (Mimi); John Gilbert (Rodolphe); Renée Adorée (Musette); George Hassell (Schaunard); Roy D'Arcy (Vicomte Paul); Edward Everett

Horton (Colline); Karl Dane (Benoit); Frank Currier (theater manager); Mathilde Comont (Madame Benoit); Gino Corrado (Marcel); Gene Pouyet (Bernard); David Mir (Alexis); Catherine Vidor [King Vidor's sister] (Louise); Valentina Zimina (Phemie); Blanche Payson (factory supervisor).

Bardelys the Magnificent

MGM

Director: King Vidor.

Script: Dorothy Farnum; from the novel *Bardelys the Magnificent* (1905) by Rafael Sabatini.

Photographer: William Daniels.

Art directors: Cedric Gibbons, James Basevi, and Richard Day; wardrobe: Andriani and Lucia Coulter.

9 reels; released September 1926.

Cast: John Gilbert (Bardelys); Eleanor Boardman (Roxalanne de Lavedan); Roy D'Arcy (Chatellerault); Lionel Belmore (vicomte de Lavedan); Emily Fitzroy (vicomtesse de Lavedan); George K. Arthur (St. Eustache); Arthur Lubin (King Louis XIII); Theodore von Eltz (Lesperon); Karl Dane (Rodenard); Edward Connelly (Cardinal Richelieu); Fred Malatesta (Castelroux); John T. Murray (Lafosse); Joseph Marba (innkeeper); Daniel G. Tomlinson (sergeant of dragoons); Emile Chautaud (Anatol); Max Barwyn (Cozelatt).

[Lost film? Bardelys, a courier of Louis XIII's, wagers that he can win Roxalanne. To do so he disguises himself as a revolutionary, but he is arrested and sentenced to death. The king saves him, and Roxalanne forgives him. "Not intended to be taken seriously but it should provide genuine pleasure for all who go to the movies looking solely for entertainment" (*MPW*, 13 November 1926).]

1928

The Crowd

MGM

Director: King Vidor.

Script: King Vidor, John V. A. Weaver and Harry Behn; from a story by King Vidor; titles: Joseph W. Farnum.

Photographer: Henry Sharp.

Editor: Hugh Wynn.

Art directors: Cedric Gibbons and Arnold Gillespie.

9 reels; released February 1928.

Cast: James Murray (John Sims); Eleanor Boardman (Mary); Bert Roach (Bert); Estelle Clark (Jane); Daniel G. Tomlinson (Jim); Dell Henderson (Dick); Lucy Beaumont (Mary's mother); Freddie Burke Frederick (son); Alice Mildred Puter (daughter).

The Patsy

MGM

Director: King Vidor.

Script: Agnes Christine Johnson; from the play *The Patsy* (1925) by Barry
   Conners; titles: Ralph Spence.
Photographer: John Seitz.
Editor: Hugh Wynn.
Art director: Cedric Gibbons; wardrobe: Gilbert Clark.
8 reels; released March 1928.
[British title: *The Politic Flapper.*]
Cast: Marion Davies (Patricia Harrington); Marie Dressler (Mrs. Harrington);
   Dell Henderson (Mr. Harrington); Orville Caldwell (Tony Anderson); Law-
   rence Grey (Billy); Jane Winton (Grace Harrington).

Show People
MGM
Director: King Vidor.
Writers: Agnes Christine Johnson, Wanda Tuchock, and Laurence Stallings;
   titles: Ralph Spence.
Photographer: John Arnold.
Editor: Hugh Wynn.
Art director: Cedric Gibbons; wardrobe: Henrietta Fraser.
Music (synchronized): William Axt and David Mendoza.
9 reels; released October 1928.
Cast: Marion Davies (Peggy Pepper); William Haines (Billy Boone); Dell Hender-
   son (Colonel Pepper); Paul Ralli (Andre); Tenen Holtz (casting director);
   Harry Gribbon (comedy director); Polly Moran (maid); Albert Conti (pro-
   ducer); John Gilbert, Mae Murray, Charles Chaplin, Douglas Fairbanks,
   Elinor Glyn, William S. Hart, Lew Cody, Karl Dane, George K. Arthur, Renée
   Adorée, Leatrice Joy, Rod La Rocque, Louella Parsons, Aileen Pringle, Dorothy
   Sebastian, Norma Talmadge, Estelle Taylor, Claire Windsor, King Vidor
   (themselves).

1929

Hallelujah
MGM
Producer/director: King Vidor; assistant director: Robert A. Golden [and Lionel
   Barrymore and Harold Garrison, uncredited].
Scenario: Wanda Tuchock; treatment: Richard Schayer; dialogue: Ransom Ride-
   out; from a story by King Vidor.
Photographer: Gordon Avil.
Editors: Hugh Wynn and Anson Stevenson.
Art director: Cedric Gibbons; costumes: Henrietta Fraser.
Music: traditional, and Irving Berlin's "Waiting at the End of the Road" and
   "Swanee Shuffle."
Sound: Douglas Shearer.
108 minutes; released August 1929.
[Silent version, 7 reels; titles: Marian Ainslee]
Cast: Daniel L. Haynes (Zeke); Nina Mae McKinney (Chick); William E. Foun-

taine (Hot Shot); Harry Gray (parson [Pappy]); Fannie Belle DeKnight (Mammy); Everett McGarrity (Spunk); Victoria Spivey (Missy Rose); Milton Dickerson, Robert Couch, Walter Tait (Johnson children); Dixie Jubilee Singers.

1930

Not So Dumb

MGM

Producers: Marion Davies and King Vidor.

Director: King Vidor.

Continuity: Wanda Tuchock; dialogue: Edwin Justus Mayer; from the play *Dulcy* (1921) by George S. Kaufman and Marc Connelly.

Photographer: Oliver Marsh.

Editor: Blanche Sewell.

Art director: Cedric Gibbons; gowns: Adrian.

Sound: Douglas Shearer, Fred R. Morgan, and Paul Neal.

75 minutes; released January 1930.

[Silent version; 7 reels(?); titles: Lucille Newmark]

Cast: Marion Davies (Dulcy); Elliott Nugent (Gordon); Raymond Hackett (Bill); Franklin Pangborn (Leach); Julia Faye (Mrs. Forbes); William Holden (Mr. Forbes); Donald Ogden Stewart (Van Dyke); Sally Starr (Angela); George Davis (Perkins).

Billy the Kid

MGM

Producer/director: King Vidor.

Continuity: Wanda Tuchock; dialogue: Laurence Stallings; additional dialogue: Charles MacArthur; from the book *The Saga of Billy the Kid* (1926) by Walter Noble Burns.

Photographer: Gordon Avil.

Editor: Hugh Wynn.

Art director: Cedric Gibbons; wardrobe: David Cox.

Sound: Douglas Shearer and Paul Neal.

95 minutes; released October 1930, in standard aperture and widescreen "Realife Grandeur."

Cast: Johnny Mack Brown (Billy); Wallace Beery (Garrett); Kay Johnson (Claire); Karl Dane (Swenson); Wyndham Standing (Tunston); Russell Simpson (McSween); Blanche Frederici (Mrs. McSween); Roscoe Ates (Old Stuff); Warner P. Richmond (Ballinger); James Marcus (Donovan); Nelson McDowell (Hatfield); Jack Carlyle (Brewer); John Beck (Butterworth); Chris Martin (Santiago); Marguerita Padula (Nicky Whoosiz); Aggie Herring (Mrs. Hatfield); King Vidor (man at bar).

1931

Street Scene

Goldwyn (released by United Artists)

Producer: Samuel Goldwyn.
Director: King Vidor; assistant director: H. B. Humberstone.
Script: Elmer Rice; from his play *Street Scene* (1929).
Photographer: George Barnes.
Editor: Hugh Bennett.
Art director: Richard Day.
Music: Alfred Newman.
80 minutes; released August 1931.
Cast: Sylvia Sidney (Rose Maurrant); William Collier, Jr. (Sam Kaplan); Max
    Montor (Abe Kaplan); David Landau (Maurrant); Estelle Taylor (Mrs. Maur-
    rant); Russell Hopton (Sankey); Louis Natheaux (Easter); Greta Granstedt
    (Mae Jones); Beulah Bondi (Emma Jones); T. H. Manning (George Jones);
    Matthew McHugh (Vincent Jones); Adele Watson (Olga Olsen); John Qualen
    (Karl Olsen); Anna Konstant (Shirley Kaplan); Nora Cecil (Alice Simpson);
    Lambert Rogers (Willie Maurrant); Allan Fox (Dick McGann); George Hum-
    bert (Filippo Fiorentino); Eleanor Wesselhoeft (Greta Fiorentino); Virginia
    Davis (Mary Hildebrand); Helen Lovett (Laura Hildebrand); Kenneth Seiling
    (Charlie Hildebrand); Conway Wasburne (Buchanan); Howard Russell (Dr.
    Wilson); Richard Powell (Officer Harry Murphy); Walter James (Marshall
    James Henry); Harry Wallace (Fred Cullen).

The Champ
MGM
Producer/director: King Vidor; assistant director: Robert A. Golden.
Script: Leonard Praskins; additional dialogue: Wanda Tuchock; from a story by
    Frances Marion.
Photographer: Gordon Avil.
Editor: Hugh Wynn.
Art director: Cedric Gibbons.
Sound: Douglas Shearer.
86 minutes; released November 1931.
Cast: Wallace Beery (Champ); Jackie Cooper (Dink); Irene Rich (Linda); Roscoe
    Ates (Sponge); Edward Brophy (Tim); Hale Hamilton (Tony); Jesse Scott
    (Jonah); Marcia Mae Jones (Mary Lou).

1932

Bird of Paradise
RKO
Producer: David O. Selznick.
Director: King Vidor; assistant directors: H. B. Humberstone and Fred Fleck.
Script: Wells Root; additional dialogue: Wanda Tuchock and Leonard Praskins;
    suggested by the play *Bird of Paradise* (1911) by Richard Walton Tully.
Photographer: Clyde De Vinna.
Art director: Carroll Clark.

Music: Max Steiner.

Sound: Clem Portman.

80 minutes; released August 1932.

Cast: Dolores Del Rio (Luana); Joel McCrea (Johnny); John Halliday (Mac); Creighton Hale (Thornton); Richard "Skeets" Gallagher (Chester); Bert Roach (Hector); Pukai (the king); Agostino Borgato (medicine man); Sophie Ortego (old native woman).

Cynara

Goldwyn (released by United Artists)

Producer: Samuel Goldwyn.

Director: King Vidor.

Script: Frances Marion and Lynn Starling; from the play *Cynara* (1930) by H. M. Harwood and Robert Gore-Brown and the novel *An Imperfect Lover* by Robert Gore-Brown.

Photographer: Ray June.

Editor: Hugh Bennett.

Art director: Richard Day.

Music: Alfred Newman.

78 minutes; released December 1932.

[Re-released as *I Was Faithful*, 1945]

Cast: Ronald Colman (Jim Warlock); Kay Francis (Clemency Warlock); Phyllis Barry (Doris Lea); Henry Stephenson (Sir John Tring); Viva Tattersall (Milly Miles); Florine McKinney (Gorla); Clarissa Selwyne; George Kirby; Paul Porcasi; Donald Stuart; Wilson Benge; C. Montague Shaw.

1933

The Stranger's Return

MGM

Producer: King Vidor; associate producer: Lucien Hubbard.

Director: King Vidor.

Script: Brown Holmes and Phil Stong; from the novel *The Stranger's Return* (1933) by Phil Stong.

Photographer: William Daniels.

Editor: Dick Fantl.

Art director: Frederic Hope; interior decoration: Edwin B. Willis; gowns: Adrian.

Sound: Douglas Shearer.

88 minutes; released July 1933.

Cast: Lionel Barrymore (Grandpa Storr); Miriam Hopkins (Louise Storr); Franchot Tone (Guy Crane); Stuart Erwin (Simon); Irene Hervey (Nettie); Beulah Bondi (Beatrice); Grant Mitchell (Allen); Tad Alexander (Widdie); Aileen Carlyle (Thelma).

1934

Our Daily Bread

Viking (released by United Artists)

Producer/director: King Vidor; assistant directors: Ralph Slosser, Mortimer
   Offner, and Lloyd Brierly.
Writers: King Vidor and Elizabeth Hill; additional dialogue: Joseph Mankiewicz.
Photographer: Robert Planck; assistant: Reggie Lanning.
Editor: Lloyd Nosler.
Music: Alfred Newman.
Sound: Russell Hanson and Vinton Vernon.
74 minutes; released October 1934.
[Re-released as *Hell's Crossroads*, 1940, Astor Pictures]
Cast: Karen Morley (Mary Sims); Tom Keene (John Sims); John Qualen (Chris
   Larsen); Barbara Pepper (Sally); Addison Richards (Louie); Harry Holman
   (Uncle Anthony); Alma Ferns (Mrs. Larsen); Lionel Baccus (barber); Harris
   Gorden (cigar salesman); Frank Minor (plumber); Henry Hall (carpenter);
   Frank Hammond (undertaker); Henry Burroughs (politician); Alex Schumberg
   (violinist); Bud Rae (stonemason); Harold Berquist; Marion Ballow; Bill
   Engel; Madame Boneita; Lloyd Ingraham; Sidney Bracey; Lynton Brant;
   Harry Brown; Harry Bradley; Captain Anderson; Harrison Greene; Si Clogg;
   Ray Spiker; Eddy Baker; Harry Barnard; Doris Kemter; Florence Enright;
   Harry Samuels; Sidney Miller; Nelly Nichols; Bob Reeves; Ed Biel; Jack
   Baldwin; King Vidor.

1935

The Wedding Night
Goldwyn (released by United Artists)
Producer: Samuel Goldwyn.
Director: King Vidor; assistant director: Walter Mayo.
Script: Edith Fitzgerald; from "Broken Soil" by Paul Green and Edwin Knopf.
Photographer: Gregg Toland.
Editor: Stuart Heisler.
Art director: Richard Day; costumes: Omar Kiam.
Music: Alfred Newman.
81 minutes; released March 1935.
Cast: Gary Cooper (Tony Barrett); Anna Sten (Manya Nowak); Ralph Bellamy
   (Frederik Sobieski); Helen Vinson (Dora Barrett); Sig Rumann (Nowak); Otto
   Yamaoka (Taka); Walter Brennan (Bill Jenkins); Esther Dale (Mrs. Nowak);
   Leonid Snegoff (Mr. Sobieski); Eleanor Wesselhoeft (Mrs. Sobieski); Milla
   Davenport (Grandmother); Agnes Anderson (Helena); Hilda Vaughn (Hezzie
   Jones); Douglas Wood (Heywood); George Meeker; Hedi Shope; Violet
   Axelle; Ed Eberle; Robert Bolder.

So Red the Rose
Paramount
Producer: Douglas MacLean.
Director: King Vidor; [assistant director: Elizabeth Hill, uncredited].
Script: Laurence Stallings, Maxwell Anderson, and Edwin Justus Mayer; from
   the novel *So Red the Rose* (1934) by Stark Young.

Photographer: Victor Milner.
Editor: Eva Warren.
Art directors: Hans Drier and Ernst Fegte; costumes: Travis Banton.
Music: W. Franke Harling.
82 minutes; released November 1935.
Cast: Margaret Sullavan (Vallette Bedford); Randolph Scott (Duncan Bedford);
    Walter Connolly (Malcolm Bedford); Janet Beecher (Sally Bedford); Elizabeth
    Patterson (Mary Cherry); Dickie Moore (Middleton Bedford); Clarence Muse
    (Cato); Harry Ellerbe (Edward Bedford); Robert Cummings (George Pendle-
    ton); Charles Starrett (George McGehee); James Burke (Maj. Rushton); Johnny
    Downs (Yankee boy); Warner Richmond (Confederate sergeant); Daniel
    Haynes (William Veal); Alfred Delcambre (Charles Tolliver).

1936

The Texas Rangers
Paramount
Producer/director: King Vidor.
Script: Louis Stevens; story: King Vidor and Elizabeth Hill; from the book *The
    Texas Rangers: A Century of Frontier Defense* (1934) by Walter Prescott
    Webb.
Photographer: Edward Cronjager.
Art directors: Hans Drier and Bernard Herzbrun.
Music: Sam Coslow.
95 minutes; released August 1936.
Cast: Fred MacMurray (Jim Hawkins); Jack Oakie (Wahoo); Lloyd Nolan (Sam
    McGee); Jean Parker (Amanda); Edward Ellis (Major Bailey); Bennie Bartlett
    (David); Elena Martinez (Maria); Frank Shannon (Captain Stafford).

1937

Stella Dallas
Goldwyn (released by United Artists)
Producer: Samuel Goldwyn; associate producer: Merritt Hulburd.
Director: King Vidor; assistant director: Walter Mayo.
Script: Victor Heerman and Sarah Y. Mason [and Elizabeth Hill, uncredited];
    from the play *Stella Dallas* (1924) by Harry Wagstaff Gribble and Gertrude
    Purcell, and the novel *Stella Dallas* (1923) by Olive Higgins Prouty.
Photographer: Rudolph Maté.
Editor: Sherman Todd.
Art director: Richard Day; set decorator: Julia Heron; costumes: Omar Kiam.
Music: Alfred Newman.
106 minutes; released July 1937.

Cast: Barbara Stanwyck (Stella Martin/Stella Dallas); John Boles (Stephen Dallas); Anne Shirley (Laurel Dallas); Barbara O'Neil (Helen); Alan Hale (Ed Munn); Marjorie Main (Mrs. Martin); Edmund Elton (Mr. Martin); George Walcott (Charlie Martin); Gertrude Short (Carrie Jenkins); Tim Holt (Richard); Nella Walker (Mrs. Grosvenor); Bruce Satterlee (Con); Jimmy Butler (grown-up Con); Jack Egger (Lee); Dickie Jones (John); Anne Shoemaker (Miss Phillibrown); Al Shean.

1938

The Citadel
MGM
Producer: Victor Saville.
Director: King Vidor; assistant director: Pen Tennyson.
Script: Ian Dalrymple, Frank Wead, and Elizabeth Hill [and John Van Druten, uncredited]; additional dialogue: Emlyn Williams; from the novel *The Citadel* (1937) by A. J. Cronin.
Photographer: Harry Stradling.
Editor: Charles Frend.
Art directors: Lazare Meerson and Alfred Junge.
Music: Louis Levy.
Sound: A. W. Watkins and C. C. Stevens.
110 minutes; released October 1938.
Cast: Robert Donat (Andrew Manson); Rosalind Russell (Christine); Ralph Richardson (Denny); Rex Harrison (Dr. Lawford); Emlyn Williams (Owen); Penelope Dudley Ward (Toppy LeRoy); Francis Sullivan (Ben Chenkin); Mary Clare (Mrs. Orlando); Cecil Parker (Charles Every); Nora Swinburne (Mrs. Thornton); Edward Chapman (Joe Morgan); Athene Seyler (Lady Raebank); Felix Aylmer (Mr. Boon); Joyce Bland (Nurse Sharp); Percy Parsons (Mr. Stillman); Dilys Davis (Mrs. Page); Basil Gill (Dr. Page); Joss Ambler (Dr. Llewellan).

1939

The Wizard of Oz
MGM
Director: Victor Fleming [and King Vidor, uncredited].
Released August 1939.
[Vidor directed the final three weeks of principal photography.]

1940

Northwest Passage (Book I: Rogers' Rangers)
MGM
Producer: Hunt Stromberg.
Director: King Vidor [and Jack Conway, uncredited].

Script: Laurence Stallings and Talbot Jennings [and Robert E. Sherwood, Jules Furthman, Sidney Howard, Richard Schayer, and Frances Marion, uncredited]; from the novel *Northwest Passage* (1937) by Kenneth Roberts.

Photographers: Sidney Wagner and William V. Skall; Technicolor supervisor: Natalie Kalmus.

Editor: Conrad A. Nervig.

Art directors: Cedric Gibbons and Malcolm Brown; sets: Edwin B. Willis; makeup: Jack Dawn.

Music: Herbert Stothart.

Sound: Douglas Shearer.

125 minutes, Technicolor; released February 1940.

Cast: Spencer Tracy (Major Robert Rogers); Robert Young (Langdon Towne); Walter Brennan ("Hunk" Marriner); Ruth Hussey (Elizabeth Browne); Nat Pendleton ("Cap" Huff); Louis Hector (Reverend Browne); Robert Barrat (Humphrey Towne); Lumsden Hare (Lord Amherst); Donald McBride (Sergeant McNott); Isabel Jewell (Jennie Coit); Douglas Walton (Lieutenant Avery); Addison Richards (Lieutenant Crofton); Hugh Sothern (Jesse Beacham); Regis Toomey (Webster); Montague Love (Wiseman Clagett); Lester Matthews (Sam Livermore); Truman Bradley (Captain Ogden).

Comrade X

MGM

Producer: Gottfried Reinhardt.

Director: King Vidor.

Script: Ben Hecht and Charles Lederer; from a story by Walter Reisch.

Photographer: Joseph Ruttenberg; special effects: Arnold Gillespie.

Editor: Harold F. Kress.

Art directors: Cedric Gibbons and Malcolm Brown; sets: Edwin B. Willis; gowns: Adrian; men's costumes: Giles Steele; makeup: Jack Dawn.

Music: Bronislau Kaper.

Sound: Douglas Shearer.

90 minutes; released December 1940.

Cast: Clark Gable (McKinley B. Thomson); Hedy Lamarr (Theodore); Oscar Homolka (Vasiliev); Felix Bressart (Vanya); Eve Arden (Jane Wilson); Sig Rumann (Emil von Hofer); Natasha Lytess (Olga); Vladimir Sokoloff (Michael Bastakoff); Edgar Barrier (Rubick); George Renevant (Laszlo); Mikhail Rasumny (Russian officer).

[MGM looked for another *Ninotchka* from this film—an unfortunate, unavoidable comparison. Here Westerners venture into Russia, not vice versa, but the comedy rests on the same male amazement over a coldly logical Russian beauty (Hedy Lamarr for Garbo), and on jokes about shortages by the same stock company of loony foreigners (Sig Rumann, Felix Bressart). The story is by Walter Reisch (who, with Billy Wilder and Charles Brackett, scripted *Ninotchka*), with the new twist from Ben Hecht's patented figure of a cynical newspaperman. Here, the Soviets have taken to treating the world press as "enemies of the state" in frustration over "Comrade X" (a.k.a. McKinley B. Thomson [Clark Gable]), who's sending accurate dispatches. His hottest story, of an assassination attempt, gets sidetracked when a hotel valet (Bressart) bumblingly blackmails him, through knowledge of his true identity, into seeing that his daughter (Lamarr) gets out of the country.

Vidor dismissed the film as "an insignificant light comedy, [which] represented a change of pace." Politically, the tone is absolutely anomalous for Vidor. It's like *Room Service* with Groucho as Stalin and the thirties purge trials a belly laugh. Even in Lubitsch terms, it's less a second *Ninotchka* than an anticipation of *To Be or Not To Be*. Black comedy punctuates a funeral (gunfire from a coffin in a passing cortege) and the execution of Lamarr's friends (Thomson asks for a translation of their song: "The same thing they always sing in prison—'We Are Free!'"). Set in the USSR, this film can be openly a class-struggle farce, instead of just a comedy of manners. Until the escape to America. There, "the problem of taking the masses from boogie-woogie" remains "a difficult one."

Comrade X's politics made sense only within the briefest of eras: *after* the Russo-German nonaggression pact of August 1939, but *before* Germany's attack on Russia in June 1941 (although the film makes prescient jokes about such an attack). Six months after its first release, MGM hastily tacked on a disclaimer to the effect that the film was just good fun among friendly allies.]

1941

H. M. Pulham, Esq.
MGM
Producer/director: King Vidor.
Script: Elizabeth Hill and King Vidor; from the novel *H. M. Pulham, Esquire* (1941) by J. P. Marquand.
Photographer: Ray June.
Editor: Harold F. Kress.
Art directors: Cedric Gibbons and Malcolm Brown; sets: Edwin B. Willis; gowns: Kalloch; men's costumes: Giles Steele; makeup: Jack Dawn.
Music: Bronislau Kaper; musical director: Lennie Hayton.
Sound: Douglas Shearer.
120 minutes; released November 1941.
Cast: Robert Young (Harry Pulham); Hedy Lamarr (Marvin Myles); Ruth Hussey (Kay Motford Pulham); Charles Coburn (Mr. Pulham, Sr.); Van Heflin (Bill King); Fay Holden (Mrs. Pulham); Bonita Granville (Mary Pulham); Douglas Wood (Mr. Bullard); Charles Halton (Walter Kaufman); Leif Erickson (Rodney "Bo-Jo" Brown); Phil Brown (Joe Bingham); David Clyde (Hugh); Sara Haden (Miss Rollo).

1944

An American Romance
MGM

Producer/director: King Vidor.

Script: Herbert Dalmas and William Ludwig; from a story by King Vidor [for uncredited writers, see p. 223 above].

Photographer: Harold Rosson; Technicolor supervisors: Natalie Kalmus and Henri Jaffa; special effects: Arnold Gillespie.

Editor: Conrad A. Nervig.

Art directors: Cedric Gibbons and Urie McCleary; sets: Edwin B. Willis and Richard Pefferle; costumes: Irene; makeup: Jack Dawn.

Music: Louis Gruenberg.

Sound: Douglas Shearer.

Released at 151 minutes, October 1944; cut to 122 minutes later in the same month; Technicolor.

Cast: Brian Donlevy (Steve Dangos/Stefan Dangosbiblichek); Ann Richards (Anna O'Roarke Dangos); Walter Abel (Howard Clinton); John Qualen (Anton Dubechek); Horace McNally (Theodore Roosevelt Dangos); Robert Lowell (George Washington Dangos); Mary McLeod (Tina Dangos); Ray Teal; Jackie "Butch" Jenkins.

1946

Duel in the Sun

Vanguard Productions/Selznick Releasing Organization

Producer: David O. Selznick.

Director: King Vidor [and William Dieterle, Josef von Sternberg, William Cameron Menzies, Hal Kern, and Chester Franklin, uncredited]; second unit: Otto Brower and Reeves Eason.

Script: David O. Selznick; from Oliver H. P. Garrett's adaptation of the novel *Duel in the Sun* (1944) by Niven Busch.

Photographers: Lee Garmes, Harold Rosson, and Ray Rennahan [and Charles Boyle, Rex Wimpy, and W. Howard Greene, uncredited]; special effects: Clarence Slifer and Jack Cosgrove; Technicolor supervisor: Natalie Kalmus.

Editors: Hal Kern, William H. Ziegler, and John Faure.

Production designer: J. McMillan Johnson; art directors: James Basevi and John Ewing; costumes: Walter Plunkett.

Music: Dimitri Tiomkin.

Released at 135 minutes, December 1946; cut to 126 minutes for wide release, May 1947; Technicolor.

Cast: Jennifer Jones (Pearl Chavez); Gregory Peck (Lewt McCanles); Joseph Cotten (Jess McCanles); Lionel Barrymore (Senator McCanles); Lillian Gish (Laura Belle McCanles); Charles Bickford (Sam Pierce); Butterfly McQueen (Vashti); Walter Huston (the sin-killer); Herbert Marshall (Scott Chavez); Tilly Losch (Mrs. Chavez); Harry Carey; Joan Tetzel; Otto Kruger; Sidney Blackmer; Scott McKay; Francis McDonald; Victor Kilian; Griff Barnett; Steve Dunhill; Lane Chandler; Lloyd Shaw; Thomas Dillon; [Orson Welles (narrator), uncredited].

1948

A Miracle Can Happen
Miracle Productions (released by United Artists)
Producers: Benedict Bogeaus and Burgess Meredith.
Directors: King Vidor and Leslie Fenton [and John Huston and George Stevens, uncredited].
Script: Laurence Stallings and Lou Breslow; from a story by Arch Oboler; Fonda/Stewart episode by John O'Hara.
Photographers: Edward Cronjager, Joseph Biroc, Gordon Avil, and John Seitz.
Editor: James Smith.
Art directors: Ernst Fegte and Duncan Cramer; sets: Robert Priestley and Eugene Redd; women's wardrobe: Greta; men's wardrobe: Jerry Bos; makeup: Otis Malcolm.
Music: Heinz Roemheld; musical directors: David Chudnow and Skitch Henderson; "Baby Made a Change in Me" by Skitch Henderson and Donald Kahn; "Queen of Hollywood Islands" by Frank Loesser.
Sound: William Lynch.
106 minutes; released June 1948.
Cast: Burgess Meredith (Oliver Pease); Paulette Goddard (Martha Pease); Fred MacMurray (Al); James Stewart (Slim); Henry Fonda (Lank); Dorothy Lamour (Gloria Manners); Victor Moore (Ashton Carrington); William Demarest (Floyd); Hugh Herbert (Elisha Hobbs); Eileen Janssen (Peggy Thorndyke); Dorothy Ford (Lola); Charles D. Brown (editor); Betty Caldwell (Cynthia); David Whorf (Sniffles Dugan); Frank Moran (a bookie); Tom Fadden (deputy sheriff); Paul Hurst (second deputy); Harry James (himself); Eduardo Ciannelli; Carl Switzer.
[Little of Vidor's work remains here, notwithstanding his name above co-director Leslie Fenton's. The episodic narrative is held together by a newlywed (Burgess Meredith), who bluffs his way into a job as a newspaper's roving question-man by coming up with a question that touches on the essence of his baby-boom era: "What great influence has a little child had upon your life?" In the first episode (directed without credit by John Huston and George Stevens), jazz-men Henry Fonda and James Stewart recount to him how a swinging older "babe" came to take over their band. The two Fenton-directed sequences are comedies of the manipulative power of children. A fourth episode, directed by Vidor, was cut after failing with a preview audience. Intended as a relatively dramatic interlude, it featured Charles Laughton as a minister loosely rein-terpreting the Bible. Of his contributions to the film, Vidor had good words only for this sequence: "I felt the Laughton episode was most effective and thought it absolutely ridiculous that it wasn't included in the film." In another effort to stress its comedy, the picture was retitled *On Our Merry Way* two months after initial release.

Vidor's framing sequences, with Meredith and his (on- and off-screen) wife, Paulette Goddard, come across with a desperate domesticity. Vidor might well have been in sympathy with the wife's complaint that the public is tired of entertainment divorced from "the way people really live," but his functional style here never engages that idea. The gag treatment of this frighteningly chipper, penniless go-getter bounding through city streets is like nothing so much as a parody of *The Crowd*. From fortress home, the managerial wife pushes him into the world ("I love him, but today's the day"), and (after a disconcertingly savage beating from a collection agent) welcomes him back with glamor, champagne, and understanding. As a demonstration that nothing is so important as his success, she slashes out one of her abstract paintings; her announcement of pregnancy is the final ecstatic touch—in honor of which the repossessers leave them a bed.]

1949

The Fountainhead
Warner Brothers
Producer: Henry Blanke.
Director: King Vidor; assistant director: Dick Mayberry.
Script: Ayn Rand; from her novel *The Fountainhead* (1943).
Photographer: Robert Burks; special effects: William McGann, Edwin DuPar, H. F. Koenekamp, and John Holden.
Editor: David Weisbart.
Art director: Edward Carrere; sets: William Kuehl; wardrobe: Milo Anderson; makeup: Perc Westmore.
Music: Max Steiner; orchestrations: Murray Cutter.
Sound: Oliver S. Garetson; dialogue director: Jack Daniels.
114 minutes; released June 1949.
Cast: Gary Cooper (Howard Roark); Patricia Neal (Dominique Francon); Raymond Massey (Gail Wynand); Kent Smith (Peter Keating); Robert Douglas (Ellsworth M. Toohey); Henry Hull (Henry Cameron); Ray Collins (Enright); Moroni Olson (Chairman); Jerome Cowan (Alvah Scarret); Paul Harvey (a businessman); Harry Woods (the superintendent); Paul Stanton (the dean); Bob Alden; Tristram Coffin; Roy Gorden; Isabel Withers; Almira Sessions; Tito Vuolo; William Haade; Gale Bonney; Thurston Hall; Dorothy Christy; Frank Wilcox; John Doucette; Fred Kelsey; Creighton Hale.

It's a Great Feeling
Warner Brothers
Director: David Butler.
Released August 1949.
[King Vidor plays himself as one of the directors who refuse to work with Jack Carson.]

Beyond the Forest
Warner Brothers
Producer: Henry Blanke.
Director: King Vidor; assistant director: Al Alleborn.
Script: Lenore Coffee; from the novel *Beyond the Forest* (1948) by Stuart Engstrand.

Photographer: Robert Burks; special effects: William McGann and Edwin DuPar.
Editor: Rudi Fehr.
Art director: Robert Haas; set decorator: William Kuehl; Bette Davis's wardrobe: Edith Head; makeup: Perc Westmore.
Music: Max Steiner; orchestrations: Murray Cutter.
Sound: Charles Lang.
96 minutes; released October 1949.
Cast: Bette Davis (Rosa Moline); Joseph Cotten (Dr. Lewis Moline); David Brian (Neil Latimer); Ruth Roman (Carol); Minor Watson (Moose); Dona Drake (Jenny); Regis Toomey (Sorren); Sarah Selby (Mildred); Mary Servoss (Mrs. Wetch); Frances Charles (Miss Elliott); Creighton Hale; Harry Tyler; Robert Littlefield; Joel Allen; Ann Doran.

1951

Lightning Strikes Twice
Warner Brothers
Producer: Henry Blanke.
Director: King Vidor; assistant director: Frank Mattison.
Script: Lenore Coffee; from the novel *A Man without Friends* (1940) by Margaret Echard.
Photographer: Sid Hickox.
Editor: Thomas Reilly.
Art director: Douglas Bacon; set decorator: William Wallace; wardrobe: Leah Rhodes.
Music: Max Steiner; orchestrations: Murray Cutter.
Sound: Charles Lang; dialogue director: Felix Jacoves.
91 minutes; released March 1951.
Cast: Ruth Roman (Shelley Carnes); Richard Todd (Richard Trevelyan); Mercedes McCambridge (Liza McStringer); Zachary Scott (Harvey Turner); Frank Conroy (J. D. Nolan); Kathryn Givney (Myra Nolan); Rhys Williams (Father Paul); Darryl Hickman (String); Nacho Galindo (Pedro).

1952

Japanese War Bride
Bernhard Productions (released by Twentieth Century–Fox)
Producers: Joseph Bernhard and Anson Bond.
Director: King Vidor; assistant director: Wilber McGaugh.
Script: Catherine Turney; from a story by Anson Bond.
Photographer: Lionel Lindon.
Editor: Terry Morse.
Art director: Danny Hall; set decorator: Murray Waite; wardrobe: Izzy Berne and Adele Parmenter; makeup: Gene Hibbs.
Music: Emil Newman and Arthur Lange.
Sound: Vic Appel and Ed Borschell.

91 minutes; released January 1952.

Cast: Shirley Yamaguchi (Tae Shimizu); Don Taylor (Jim Sterling); Cameron Mitchell (Art Sterling); Marie Windsor (Fran Sterling); James Bell (Ed Sterling); Louise Lorimer (Harriet Sterling); Philip Ahn (Eitaro Shimizu); Sybil Merritt (Emily Shafer); Lane Nakano (Shiro Hasagawa); Kathleen Mulqueen (Milly Shafer); Orley Lindgren (Ted Sterling); George Wallace (Woody Blacker); May Takasugi (Emma Hasagawa); William Yokota (Mr. Hasagawa); Susie Matsumoto (Tae's mother); Weaver Levy (Kioto); Jerry Fujikawa; Cheiko Sato; Tetsu Komai; Hisa Chiba; David March.

Ruby Gentry

Bernhard-Vidor Productions (released by Twentieth Century–Fox)

Producers: Joseph Bernhard and King Vidor.

Director: King Vidor; assistant director: Milton Carter.

Script: Sylvia Richards; from a story by Arthur Fitz-Richard.

Photographer: Russell Harlan.

Editor: Terry Morse.

Art director: Dan Hall; set decorator: Ed Boyle; wardrobe: Marie Hermann and William Edwards; makeup: Del Armstrong.

Music: Heinz Roemheld; music supervisor: David Chudnow.

Sound: Jean L. Speak.

82 minutes; released October 1952.

Cast: Jennifer Jones (Ruby Corey/Ruby Gentry); Charlton Heston (Boake Tackman); Karl Malden (Jim Gentry); Tom Tully (Jud Corey); Bernard Phillips (Dr. Saul Manfred); James Anderson (Jewel Corey); Josephine Hutchinson (Letitia Gentry); Phyllis Avery (Tracy McAuliffe); Herbert Heyes (Judge Tackman); Myra Marsh (Ma Corey); Charles Cane (Cullen McAuliffe); Sam Flint (Neil Fallgren); Frank Wilcox (Clyde Pratt).

1954

"Light's Diamond Jubilee"

[Produced for television by David O. Selznick; broadcast simultaneously on CBS, NBC, ABC, and the DuMont networks, 8:00–10:00 P.M., 24 October 1954. Celebrating seventy-five years of Edison's electric light, the show mixed live and filmed segments, two of which Vidor directed: "A Kiss for the Lieutenant" (story by Arthur Gordon, script by Ben Hecht), a tiny slice of passion in which Kim Novak, settled sultrily into her sports car, obliges a lieutenant with a kiss on which he's wagered with fellow officers; and "Leader of the People" (story by John Steinbeck, script by Ben Hecht), a little rural drama with Walter Brennan as an elderly former wagonmaster who increasingly irritates his son (Harry Morgan) by repeating the same tales of the old West. After the son explodes at breakfast, the wounded old man finds a new audience among the next generation, in his grandson (Brandon De Wilde). "It was a job for men, but only little boys want to hear about it."]

1955

Man without a Star
Universal-International
Producer: Aaron Rosenberg.
Director: King Vidor; assistant directors: Frank Shaw and George Lollier.
Script: Borden Chase and D. D. Beauchamp; from the novel *Man without a Star* (1952) by Dee Linford.
Photographer: Russell Metty; Technicolor consultant: William Fritzsche.
Editor: Virgil Vogel.
Art directors: Alexander Golitzen and Richard H. Riedel; set decorators: Russell A. Gausman and John Austin; costumes: Rosemary Odell; makeup: Bud Westmore.
Music: Joseph Gershenson; "Man without a Star," lyrics by Frederick Herbert, music by Arnold Hughes, sung by Frankie Laine; "And the Moon Grew Brighter and Brighter," by Jimmy Kennedy and Lou Singer, sung by Kirk Douglas.
Sound: Leslie I. Carey and Joe Lapis; dialogue director: William Bailey.
89 minutes, Technicolor; released April 1955.
Cast: Kirk Douglas (Dempsey Rae); Jeanne Crain (Reed Bowman); Claire Trevor (Idonee); William Campbell (Jeff Jimson); Richard Boone (Steve Miles); Mara Corday (Moccasin Mary); Myrna Hansen (Tess Cassidy); Jay C. Flippen (Strap Davis); Eddy C. Waller (Bill Cassidy); Frank Chase (Little Waco); Roy Barcroft (Sheriff Olson); Millicent Patrick (Boxcar Alice); Casey MacGregor (Hammer); Jack Ingram (Jessup); Ewing Mitchell (Johnson); Sheb Wooley; George Wallace; Paul Birch; Bill Phillips; William Challee; James Haywood.

1956

War and Peace
Ponti–De Laurentiis Productions (released by Paramount)
Producer: Dino De Laurentiis.
Director: King Vidor [and Mario Soldati, uncredited]; assistant directors: Piero Mussett and Guidarino Guidi.
Script: Bridget Boland, Robert Westerby, King Vidor, Mario Camerini, Ennio DeConcini, and Ivo Perilli; from the novel *War and Peace* (1869) by Leo Tolstoy.
Photographer: Jack Cardiff; second unit: Aldo Tonti.
Editors: Stuart Gilmore and Leo Catosso.
Art directors: Mario Chiari, Franz Bachelin, and Gianni Polidori; set decoration: Piero Gherardi; costumes: Maria De Matteis; makeup: Alberto De Rossi.
Music: Nino Rota; musical director: Franco Ferrara.
Sound: Charles Knott; sound editor: Leslie Hodgson; dialogue coach: Guy Thomajan.
208 minutes, Technicolor, VistaVision; released November 1956.
Cast: Audrey Hepburn (Natasha); Henry Fonda (Pierre); Mel Ferrer (Andrei); Vittorio Gassman (Anatole); Anita Ekberg (Helene); Oscar Homolka (Gen-

eral Kutuzov); Herbert Lom (Napoleon); John Mills (Platon); Helmut Dantine (Dolokhov); Milly Vitale (Lise); Barry Jones (Count Rostov); Wilfred Lawson (Prince Bolkonsky); Lea Seidl (Countess Rostov); Sean Barrett (Petya Rostov); Anna Maria Ferrero (Mary Bolkonsky); May Britt (Sonya); Tullio Carminati (Kuragine); Patrick Crean (Denisov); Gertrude Flynn (Peronskava); Jeremy Brett.

1959

Solomon and Sheba
Theme Pictures (released by United Artists)
Producers: Edward Small and Ted Richmond.
Director: King Vidor; assistant directors: Piero Mussett, Joseph Kenny, and Jose Mario Ochoa; second unit: Noel Howard.
Script: Anthony Veiller, Paul Dudley, and George Bruce [and Sylvia Richards, uncredited]; from a story by Crane Wilber.
Photographer: Freddie Young; special effects: Alex Weldon.
Editor: Otto Ludwig.
Art directors: Richard Day, Alfred Sweeney, and Luis Perez Espinoza; sets: Dario Simoni; costumes: Ralph Jester.
Music: Mario Nascimbene; musical director: Franco Ferrara.
Choreographers: Jeroslav Berger and Jean Pierre Genet.
Sound: David Hildyard.
139 minutes, Technicolor, Super Technirama [70mm]; released December 1959.
Cast: Yul Brynner (Solomon); Gina Lollobrigida (Sheba); George Sanders (Adonijah); David Farrar (Pharaoh); Marisa Pavan (Abishag); John Crawford (Joab); Lawrence Naismith (Hezrai); Jose Nieto (Ahab); Alejandro Rey (Sittar); Harry Andrews (Baltor); Julio Pena (Zadok); Finlay Currie (King David); William Devlin; Jean Anderson; Jack Gwillim.

1964

Truth and Illusion: An Introduction to Metaphysics
Producer/director/writer: King Vidor.
Assistant director: Michael Neary.
Editor: Fred Y. Smith.
25 minutes; 16mm.
(No commercial release in the United States)

1980

Metaphor (ca. 1980)
Producer/director/writer: King Vidor.
With: Andrew Wyeth and King Vidor.
ca. 40 minutes; 16mm.
(No commercial release)

1982

Love and Money
Lorimar (released by Paramount)
Producer/director/writer: James Toback.
90 minutes; released January 1982.
Cast: Ray Sharkey (Byron Levin); Ornella Muti (Catherine Stockheinz); Klaus
  Kinski (Frederick Stockheinz); Armand Assante (Lorenzo Prado); King Vidor
  (Walter Klein).

Select Bibliography

Affron, Charles. *Cinema and Sentiment*. Chicago: University of Chicago Press, 1982.

———. *Star Acting: Gish, Garbo, Davis*. New York: Dutton, 1977.

Agel, Henri. *Romance américaine*. Paris: Editions du Cerf, 1963.

Amengual, Barthélemy. "Entre l'horizon d'un seul et l'horizon de tous" [on *The Big Parade* and *The Crowd*]. *Positif*, no. 161 (September 1974): 32–43.

———. "La Crise et son miroir" [on *Show People*]. *Positif*, no. 163 (November 1974): 25–27.

Barr, Charles. "King Vidor." *Brighton Film Review*, no. 21 (June 1970): 22–25.

Baxter, John. *King Vidor*. New York: Monarch Press, 1976.

Braver-Mann, B. G. "Vidor and Evasion." *Experimental Cinema* 1, no. 3 (February 1931): 26–29.

Brownlow, Kevin. "King Vidor." *Film*, no. 34 (Winter 1962): 19–28.

———. *The Parade's Gone By . . . .* New York: Knopf, 1968.

———. *The War, the West, and the Wilderness*. New York: Knopf, 1979.

Chaumeton, Etienne. "King Vidor—le dernier des romantiques." *Cinema 56* 2, no. 11 (May 1956): 53–64.

Ciment, Michel. "Le New Deal et le mythe de la frontière" [on *Our Daily Bread*]. *Positif*, no. 163 (November 1974): 30–36.

Cohn, Bernard [interviewer]. "Propos de King Vidor." *Positif*, no. 79 (October 1966): 105–10.

———. "Entretien avec King Vidor." *Positif*, no. 161 (September 1974): 13–22.

Cohn, Bernard. "Sur quelques films muet méconnus de Vidor." *Positif*, no. 161 (September 1974): 25–30.

Combs, Richard. "King Vidor." In *Cinema: A Critical Dictionary*, ed. Richard Roud, 1026–35. New York: Viking, 1980.

Cripps, Thomas. *Slow Fade to Black: The Negro in American Film, 1900–1942*. London: Oxford University Press, 1977.

Davies, Marion. *The Times We Had*. Indianapolis: Bobbs-Merrill, 1975.

Delahaye, Michel. "La Sagesse de Vidor." *Cahiers du Cinéma*, no. 136 (October 1962): 22–25.

Demonsablon, Philippe. "La Conjuration" [on *Ruby Gentry*]. *Cahiers du Cinéma*, no. 33 (March 1954): 54–57.

Denton, Clive. "King Vidor." In *The Hollywood Professionals*, vol. 5, 7–55. London: Tantivy Press, 1976.

Durgnat, Raymond. "King Vidor." *Film Comment* 9, no. 4 (July/August 1973): 10–49, and no. 5 (September/October 1973): 16–51.

Dyer, Peter John. "*War and Peace*." *Monthly Film Bulletin* 24, no. 276 (January 1957): 4.

Everson, William K. *American Silent Film*. London: Oxford University Press, 1978.

Fountain, Leatrice Gilbert. *Dark Star*. New York: St. Martin's Press, 1985.

Gish, Lillian, with Ann Pinchot. *The Movies, Mr. Griffith, and Me*. New York: Avon, 1970.

Greenberg, Joel [interviewer]. "War, Wheat and Steel." *Sight and Sound* 37 (Autumn 1968): 193–97.

Harrington, Curtis. "The Later Years: King Vidor's Hollywood Progress." *Sight and Sound* 22 (April–June 1953): 179–82, 203–4.

Haver, Ronald. *David O. Selznick's Hollywood*. New York: Knopf, 1980.

Henry, Michael. "Le Blé, l'acier et la dynamite." *Positif*, no. 163 (November 1974): 41–48.

Higham, Charles. "King Vidor." *Film Heritage* 1, no. 4 (Summer 1966): 15–25.

Higham, Charles, and Joel Greenberg [interviewers]. "King Vidor." In *The Celluloid Muse: Hollywood Directors Speak*, 223–43. Chicago: Henry Regnery, 1969.

Intérim, Louella. "Le King à Paris" and "Scénario de King Vidor" [extract from unproduced *The Actor*]. *Libération*, 19 October 1981.

Isenberg, Michael T. "*The Big Parade* (1925)." In *American History/American Film: Interpreting the Hollywood Image*, ed. John E. O'Connor and Martin A. Jackson, 17–37. New York: Ungar, 1979.

Jacobs, Lewis. *The Rise of the American Film: A Critical History*. New York: Harcourt, Brace, 1939.

Kaplan, E. Ann. "The Case of the Missing Mother: Maternal Issues in Vidor's *Stella Dallas*." *Heresies* 16 (1983): 81–85.

Kirkpatrick, Sidney D. *A Cast of Killers*. New York: Dutton, 1986.

Kyrou, Ado. *Amour-érotisme et cinéma*. Paris: E. Losfeld, 1967.

Leguebe, Eric [interviewer]. "King Vidor." In *Le Cinéma américain par ses auteurs*, 271–77. Paris: Editions Guy Autier, 1977.

Lorentz, Pare. *Lorentz on Film*. New York: Hopkinson & Blake, 1975.

Luft, Herbert G. "King Vidor." *Films in Review* 33 (December 1982): 587–611.

———. "King Vidor: A Career That Spans Half a Century." *Film Journal* 1, no. 2 (Summer 1971): 27–44.

Lyons, Donald, and Glenn O'Brien [interviewers]. "King Vidor." *Andy Warhol's Interview*, October 1972, 12–15, 51.

Marcorelles, Louis. "L'Homme au fouet." *Cahiers du Cinéma*, no. 104 (February 1960): 13–21.

Moore, James Tice. "Depression Images: Subsistence Homesteads, 'Production-for-Use,' and King Vidor's *Our Daily Bread.*" *Midwest Quarterly* 26, no. 1 (1984): 24–34.

Moullet, Luc, and Michel Delahaye. "Entretien avec King Vidor." *Cahiers du Cinéma*, no. 136 (October 1962): 1–21.

Mulvey, Laura. "Afterthoughts on 'Visual Pleasure and Narrative Cinema' Inspired by *Duel in the Sun* (King Vidor, 1946)." *Framework* 15/16/17 (Summer 1981): 12–15.

Pratt, George C. *Spellbound in Darkness: A History of the Silent Film*. Greenwich, Conn.: New York Graphic Society, 1973.

Roffman, Peter, and Jim Purdy. *The Hollywood Social Problem Film: Madness, Despair, and Politics from the Depression to the Fifties*. Bloomington: Indiana University Press, 1981.

St. Johns, Adela Rogers. "A Young Crusader." *Photoplay* 17, no. 1 (December 1919): 64–66.

Schickel, Richard [interviewer]. "King Vidor." In *The Men Who Made the Movies*, 131–60. New York: Atheneum, 1975.

Schilling, Edward, ed.; Nancy Dowd and David Shepard, interviewers [1980]. "A Directors Guild of America Oral History: King Vidor." Directors Guild of America, forthcoming.

Segond, Jacques. "The Bad and the Beautiful" [on *Stella Dallas* and *The Wedding Night*]. *Positif*, no. 163 (November 1974): 37–40.

Seguin, Louis. "Les Malheurs de la paix" [on *War and Peace*]. *Positif*, no. 21 (February 1957): 31–32.

Sherman, Eric. "King Vidor." In *American Directors*, ed. Jean-Pierre Coursodon, vol. 1, 347–50. New York: McGraw-Hill, 1983.

Shivas, Mark, and V. F. Perkins. "Interview with King Vidor." *Movie*, no. 11 (July/August 1963): 7–10.

Stebbins, Robert. "Ungrateful for Gift Horses" [review of *Our Daily Bread*]. *New Theatre* 1, no. 10 (November 1934): 22–23.

Vidor, King. "Director's Notebook: Why Teach Cinema?" *Cinema Progress* 4, no. 1 (June–July 1939).

———. "From a Vidor Notebook." *New York Times*, 10 March 1935.

———. "The Giant in Rompers." *Motion Picture Director*, July 1926, 35.

———. "Me . . . and My Spectacle." *Films and Filming* 6, no. 1 (October 1959): 6.

———. *On Film Making*. New York: David McKay, 1973.

———. "Rubber Stamp Movies." *New Theatre* 2, no. 9 (September 1934): 11–12. Repr. in *Hollywood Directors, 1914–1940*, ed. Richard Koszarski, 278–82. London: Oxford University Press, 1976.

———. "Transforming Tolstoy." *New York Times*, 12 August 1956.

———. *A Tree Is a Tree*. New York: Harcourt, Brace, 1953.

Vidor, Suzanne. "Memoirs of a Movie Childhood." *Western's World* September–October 1980.

Walker, Alexander. *The Shattered Silents: How the Talkies Came to Stay.* New York: Morrow, 1979.

Williams, Linda. "'Something Else besides a Mother': *Stella Dallas* and the Maternal Melodrama." *Cinema Journal* 24, no. 1 (Fall 1984): 2–27.

Index

the Sun, 239–41, 246; as director of:
All That Money Can Buy, 167 n; Dr.
Ehrlich's Magic Bullet, 122, 208; The
Garden of Allah, 239; Love Letters,
266–67; Portrait of Jennie, 240, 241;
The Story of Louis Pasteur, 122, 208
Dietrich, Marlene, 239
Directors Guild of America, 16, 172. See
also Screen Directors Guild
Disney, Walt, 160, 230, 296
Dmytryk, Edward, 159, 160, 262
Dr. Ehrlich's Magic Bullet (1940), 122,
208
Dog's Life, A (1918), 120–21
Donat, Robert, 206, **210**, 211, **212**
Donlevy, Brian, 221, **222**, 223, **225**, 226,
226, 228, 229
Donovan's Reef (1963), 14
Dostoyevski, Feodor, 77
Double Indemnity (1944), 204
Double Suicide (1969), 255
Douglas, Kirk, 295–98, **297, 298**
Douglas, Robert, **260**, 261
Downstairs (1932), 72
Dreiser, Theodore, 224, 291
Dressler, Marie, **88**, 89, 93
Drucker, Peter, 227
Drums along the Mohawk (1939), 190,
198, 323
Duel in the Sun (Busch), 238, 247
Duel in the Sun (1946): discussed, 235,
237–56; and The Fountainhead, 264–
65, 269; and melodrama, 2, 13, 47, 48;
and Ruby Gentry, 285–86, 291, 293,
295; the "sin-killer" in, 38, 309, 311 n;
and The Stranger's Return, 143, 146;
mentioned, vii, 7, 8, 10, 11, 15, 17, 34,
44, 75, 105, 131, 138, 186, 187, 190,
236, 271, 289 n, 296, 313, 323, 354
Dulcy (Kaufman & Connelly), 93
Dumas, Alexandre, 241
Dumbrille, Douglass, 126
Dusk to Dawn (1922), 26, 38, 339
Dwan, Allan, 82, 187, 296
Dyer, Peter John, 307

Early, Stephen, 152
Earp, Wyatt, 162
Eddy, Helen Jerome, **29**
Eddy, Mary Baker, 16–17, 28, 50, 317.
See also Christian Science
Edwards, Jonathan, 112–13, 123. See also
Puritanism
8½ (1963), 317
Eisenhower, Dwight D., 321
Eisenstein, Sergei, 64–65, 72, 77, 157,

249; as director of: Alexander Nevsky,
196; The General Line, 159–60
Ekberg, Anita, 304, 306
Eliot, George, 48
Eliot, T. S., 319
Emerson, Ralph Waldo, 16–17, 113, 152,
170, 214, 215, 219, 256, 309, 315, 317,
319, 322–23. See also Transcenden-
talism
End of Ideology, The (Bell), 184 n
Endfield, Cy, 160–61
Enfants du paradis, Les (1944), 298
Environmentalism, 11–12, 131–32
Erwin, Stu, 143, **144**
Escape from Ft. Bravo (1953), 175
Esther and the King (1960), 311
Executive Suite (1954), 262
Experiment in Criticism, An (Lewis), 253 n
Experimental Cinema (periodical), 149
Expressionism in film, 74, 78–79, 82–83,
85, 101–2, 211, 259, 293

Falwell, Jerry, 108
Family Honor, The (1920), 25, 30, 337
"Fantasies of the Art-House Audience"
(Kael), 200
Farber, Manny, 2
Farewell to Arms, A (Hemingway), 65
Farewell to Manzanar (1976), 284
Fassbinder, Rainer Werner, 47
Father of the Bride (1950), 218
Fejos, Paul, 78
Fellini, Federico, 317
Female of the Species, The (1912), 32
Feminism, viii, 15–16, 291
Fenton, Leslie, 355
Ferrer, José, 169
Ferrer, Mel, 304
Fetchit, Stepin, 243 n
Fiedler, Leslie A., 16, 44, 46, 224
Fièvre (1921), 52
File on Thelma Jordon, The (1949), 204
Film Comment (periodical), vii
Films and Feelings (Durgnat), vii, 252 n
Finch, Flora, 80
Fitzcarraldo (1982), 293
Fitzgerald, Edith, 165
Fitzgerald, F. Scott, 15–16, 55–56, 61,
165, 173
Flaherty, Robert, 136
Flaubert, Gustave, 271–72
Fleischer, Dave and Max, 93
Fleischer, Richard, 296, 310–11
Fleming, Victor, 173, 236; as director of:
Code of the Sea, 50; Gone with the
Wind, 172, 173, 176, 179, 193 n, 239,

Compositor: G & S Typesetters
Text: 10/12 Sabon
Display: Helvetica Bold
Printer: The Murray Printing Co.
Binder: The Murray Printing Co.